CHOOSING
THE RIGHT
BUSINESS ENTITY

CHOOSING THE RIGHT BUSINESS ENTITY
Tax Practitioner's Guide

1999 Edition

William R. Bischoff, M.B.A., CPA

HARCOURT BRACE PROFESSIONAL PUBLISHING

A Division of
Harcourt Brace & Company
SAN DIEGO   NEW YORK   CHICAGO   LONDON

Printed in the United States of America

ISBN: 0-15-606863-X

99 00 01 02 03 MY 5 4 3 2 1

PREFACE

Why Do You Need This Guide?

The options for the business owner continue to grow. Over the past year alone, changes in the tax rules have led to the following changes in this edition of the book and the software:

- Full coverage of single-member LLCs

- Complete updates for the 1998 IRS Restructuring and Reform Act

- Full coverage of new favorable AMT changes

- More on minimizing payroll taxes via S corporations

- More on tax-advantaged fringe benefits

- More on benefits available under qualified Subchapter S subsidiaries (QSSSs)

Add these changes to those in recent years and the result is a virtual overhaul of this entire area of law. Here is what we have seen:

1. The Revenue Reconciliation Act of 1993 (RRA '93), which raised individual income tax rates significantly above corporate rates;

2. Passage of LLC acts in all states, which makes LLCs a highly attractive entity choice for closely held businesses;

3. The emergence of LLPs, which are attractive for many professional service businesses;

4. The enactment of significant tax breaks for qualified small business corporations (QSBCs);

5. The release of the "check-the-box" regulations, which enable taxpayers to know with certainty how their entities will be treated for federal income tax purposes and which grant favorable treatment to single-member LLCs; and

6. Effects of the Small Business Job Protection Act of 1996 on S corporations, including QSSSs.

Choosing the Right Business Entity helps you advise your clients on the advantages and disadvantages—tax and otherwise—of the major forms of business organization available today. It provides extensive Examples to clarify specific situations and Observations to spotlight critical details. Text and practice aids alike contribute to thorough and consistent advice for clients. This Guide—and especially its accompanying software—will dramatically improve the quality of your service to clients and the investment of your time in routine aspects of the engagement.

Why Was This Guide Written?

Choosing the Right Business Entity was created to help you serve your clients faster and better than ever before as they consider selecting the optimal legal form of organization for business start-ups and business reorganizations. The Guide covers sole proprietorships, limited liability companies (LLCs), limited liability partnerships (LLPs), "traditional" limited and general partnerships, family limited partnerships (FLPs), and C and S corporations.

While recent events have clearly added complexity to the choice-of-entity decision process, they also have created greater opportunities for business owners and investors to meet both their tax-planning and their financial objectives.

Who Can Benefit from This Guide?

This publication and the related software are intended primarily for practitioners who provide tax and accounting services to clients. Other financial and legal professionals involved with business formation and acquisition transactions will also find this product helpful. It will be of particular interest to:

1. Tax and financial accounting practitioners—CPAs, Enrolled Agents, and others—who render tax planning and structuring advice.

2. Attorneys engaged in business formation and acquisition deals, regardless of the level of tax and business law expertise they possess. In particular, attorneys may find the software "Interview" feature helpful in rendering advice in a systematic fashion.

3. Financial officers in industry, because the choice-of-entity considerations associated with business formations and acquisitions are the same for the financial professionals employed by the affected businesses or owners as they are for the CPAs and attorneys who advise them.

How Is This Product Different?

This Guide and the companion software were not stitched together by updating tax and business law information that was written years before the six developments listed above. On the contrary, this product was designed from the ground up to convey the most current and practical guidance on the choice-of-entity issue. Current software technology has been put to work to provide additional value and ease of use. (See page xii for a description of the software's unique features.)

Using this book, the software, and the accompanying practice aids ensures an efficient, systematic, and state-of-the-art approach to choice-of-entity decisions.

Acknowledgments

The author is grateful for the comments and suggestions of the following practitioners: James T. Ashe, CPA, Marcum & Kliegman, CPAs; Cris M. Branden, CPA, Machen, Powers, Disque & Boyle, Chartered CPAs; Steven J. Brown, Rubin, Brown, Gornstein & Co., CPAs; Jerry W. Dickson, CPA, Dickson Brooks, LLP; James R. Hamill, CPA, The Robert O. Anderson School and Graduate School of Management, University of New Mexico; Robert W. Jamison, CPA, Indiana University; William H. Lester, Attorney at Law, Cox & Smith, Inc.; John C. Morgan, Esquire, Comptroller of the Currency, Kansas City, Missouri; James W. Sansone, CPA, Berg, DeMarco, Lewis, Sawatski & Co.; Henry J. Schwartz, CPA, Clumeck, Stern, Phillips & Schwartz, CPAs; Albert M. Shifberg-Mencher, E.A., Shifberg-Mencher Associates; James C. Thomas III, Esquire, Law Offices of Burnstein, Beck & Thomas; and Robert T. Thul, CPA.

Many users of the software from the first edition were also helpful with their tips and suggestions for improving the program: Mark R. Campbell, CPA, Haberbush & Campbell; Deanna Eastwood, CPA; Lynn Viscioni, CFS Services/Viscioni & Rosenberg; George Benneh, Aligeb Tax & Accounting Consultants; Robert T. Thul, CPA; and E. Jordan Mills, E. Jordan Mills PC.

The author welcomes suggestions for additional coverage and improvements. Please send comments to Business Entity Editor, Harcourt Brace Professional Publishing, 525 B Street, Suite 1900, San Diego, California 92101.

ABOUT THE AUTHOR

William R. Bischoff, M.B.A., CPA, is the president of Practical Knowledge, Inc., and a licensed CPA with 18 years of practice experience. He has an extensive background in writing for tax professionals and regularly presents tax training seminars. Bischoff also writes the monthly tax column for *Smart Money* magazine (a joint venture between *The Wall Street Journal* and Hearst Corporation) and contributes regularly to a monthly newsletter published by the National Taxpayers Union. Bischoff formerly served as a tax consultant with Arthur Andersen and Kenneth Leventhal & Co. in Dallas and is a past voting member of the AICPA's Partnership Taxation Committee and Tax Communications Committee. Bischoff received his B.A. from UCLA and his M.B.A. from Santa Clara University.

ABOUT THE SOFTWARE

The companion Windows™ software to *Choosing the Right Business Entity* features our unique *Entity Wizard* online interview and resulting detailed report—a logical, systematic approach to choice-of-entity recommendations. The disk also contains all appropriate in-text practice aids: "cradle-to-grave" calculation templates, engagement workprograms, client letters, checklists, and more. Customize them or use them as is to provide your clients with a high-quality work product, and to provide yourself with well-documented workpapers.

Our software includes valuable practice and client management tools as well. For example, when you complete the online interview, *Entity Wizard* creates a directory that lists all practice aids appropriate to that client's entity choice. The "cradle-to-grave" calculation templates let you show your client the projected after-tax value of the business upon sale or dissolution for up to a ten-year period.

Improvements in the new version of the software include:

- Improved formatting of the printed interview for a higher-quality work product.

- More options within the interview, so experienced users can bypass the author observations, which are called Wizards.

- Server installation now possible (call Software Support at 888-551-7127 for instructions and to purchase network licenses) for use in larger firms.

For a complete list of practice aids, please see Chapter 10. The *Entity Wizard* interview, its corresponding detailed report, and all relevant text practice aids are available in Word®, WordPerfect®, and Rich Text Format (RTF) versions and are compatible with any Windows-based word processor capable of translating Microsoft Word or WordPerfect files. More detail on the software features appears in Chapter 1.

The Software User's Guide that accompanies the software is reproduced on the following pages as well as on the disk itself.

CONTENTS

SOFTWARE USER'S GUIDE

Introduction

This section provides an overview of the software system and instructions for using this product both with and without the Interview feature. Click on a topic to view it.

- Software Overview
- Using This Product *with* the Software Interview
- Using This Product *without* the Software Interview

Software Overview

Choosing the Right Business Entity has been created to help you identify, analyze, and document critical decision factors so that you can effectively produce choice-of-entity recommendations for your clients. It provides all of the technical guidance, working documentation, and other tools necessary to complete choice-of-entity engagements.

This software system is designed to accompany the practitioner's guide book *Choosing the Right Business Entity*. It consists of an interactive question-and-answer interview and a series of on-line practice aids. In the interview, you answer yes or no to each of the questions until you reach the end of the path, which is a recommendation of the optimal choice-of-entity. Along the path to the recommendation, the interview dialog provides various observations and more information dialogs to assist you in answering specific questions about a client's needs. The interview is followed by a series of practice aids in the form of word processing documents and calculating spreadsheets that you can customize as needed. You can use these practice aids in conjunction with the interview to support the interview recommendation, or you can use them independently.

The interactive interview and on-line practice aids truly automate the process, determining the appropriate choice-of-entity and documenting all phases of the engagement. With these timesaving tools, you should be able to complete any choice-of-entity engagement more effectively and make each one more profitable.

Software Installation and Setup

The following instructions show you how run the *Choosing the Right Business Entity* Setup program. Setup will install this software on your hard disk and configure it so that it runs properly on your system. Before running Setup, make sure that you have installed either Microsoft Word for Windows (version 6.0 or better), WordPerfect for Windows (version 6.0

or better), or any other word processor that will load/convert these file formats. If your Windows word processor does not support these file formats, select the Other (Rich Text Format files) option described in step 6 below. Also, before running Setup, close all other applications to ensure that they do not interfere with Setup.

1. Place the program disk in floppy drive A. (If running Setup from floppy drive B, substitute B for A in the following command.) If you are running from Windows 3.x, from the Program Manager, select Run from the File menu. From Windows, run the file A:\SETUP.EXE. This will start the Setup program and you will see the Welcome dialog box. Click on OK to continue or on Cancel to abort the installation. If you are running on Win95 or NT, choose control panels from the start menu. Select Settings and Control Panel. Then, double-click on the "Add/Remove Programs" icon. Click on the Install button and then follow the instructions on your screen.

2. If this is the first time you have run Setup, you will see the Setup-Registration dialog box. Enter the user name and the company name and then click on OK. You will then see the Registration Verification dialog box. Make sure that the registration information is correct, because you cannot change it later. If the information is correct, click on Yes; otherwise, click on No to change it.

   If Setup has already been run once, you will receive a notification stating that if you are not the registered user you must select Cancel or you will be in violation of the software license agreement. If you receive this notice, select Cancel if you are not the registered user or select OK if you are authorized to proceed.

3. Setup will then search for prior installations. If it does not find a prior installation, Setup will take you directly to the Select Destination Directory dialog box.

   If it does find a prior installation, Setup will display the location of the current version of the program in the Prior Installation Found dialog box. Click on OK to proceed to the Select Destination Directory dialog box.

4. From the Select Destination Directory dialog box, you can choose the directory where you want to install the program files. If Setup does not find any prior installations, the default directory will be C:\ENTITY. If Setup does find a prior installation, the default directory will be the same one that contains the current version of the program. To change the destination directory, either edit the Destination Directory field or use the Browse list to navigate to the desired directory. Once the Destination Directory field contains the desired drive and directory, click on OK to proceed.

5. After choosing the Destination Directory, you will see the Make Backups dialog box, which gives you the option to make backup copies of all files replaced during the installation. If you select Yes, you will see the Select Backup Directory dialog box. Either accept the default directory or use

the Browse window to change the backup directory and then click on OK. Setup will put the prior version of all replaced files in this backup directory. If you select No to bypass the backup, you will go directly to the Select Document Format dialog box.

6. In the Select Document Format dialog box, you have the option to install the practice aid documents with one of the three available document formats: Microsoft Word for Windows (6.0), WordPerfect for Windows (6.0), or Other (Rich Text Format files). Click on the desired document format and then click on OK.

   If you select either the MS Word format or the WordPerfect format, Setup will search for the word processor's executable file (i.e., WINWORD.EXE or WP.EXE, respectively). If it finds the correct executable file, Setup will go directly to the Installing dialog and install all program files to the appropriate directories.

   If you select MS Word or WordPerfect and Setup does not find the correct executable file, Setup will notify you with the Can't Find Word Processor dialog box. At this point, click on OK to activate the Enter Word Processor Path dialog box.

   If you select MS Word or WordPerfect and Setup cannot find the respective executable file, or if you select Other (Rich Text Format files) from the Select Document Format dialog box, Setup will activate the Enter Word Processor Path dialog box. In the input field, enter the complete path to your word processor's executable file. Use the example in this dialog box as a guide. Once you enter the complete path, click on OK and Setup will verify if this path is correct or not. If the path is correct, Setup will go to the Installing dialog box and install all program files to the appropriate directories. If the path is not correct, Setup will notify you with the Invalid Path dialog box. Click on OK to re-enter the path.

7. While Setup is copying the files to your hard disk, you will see the Installing dialog box. This dialog displays the file currently being copied and a progress meter that measures the overall copy progress. After Setup copies all files, it will display the Install Icons dialog box. Click on Yes to add icons to your desktop or click on No to complete the installation without adding icons. If you click on Yes, Setup will activate the Select Program Manager Group dialog box. The default group name is Choice of Entity. If you want to change the group name, either select an existing name from the list or enter a new name. After selecting (or entering) the desired program group, click on OK. Setup will place the program icon and the uninstall icon into this program group, and you will see the Setup Complete dialog box.

8. From the Setup Complete dialog box, click on Yes to run the program or click on No to exit Setup. Now that Setup has installed Choosing the Right Business Entity on your system, you can load it directly from the program manager by double-clicking on the program icon or by running the file ENTITY.EXE. To uninstall this software, double-click on the Uninstall Choice of Entity icon.

Using This Product *with* the Software Interview Feature

Take the following steps if you choose to take advantage of the Interview feature of the software (strongly recommended).

1. Read the Executive Summary in section 1.02 of Chapter 1.

2. Review General Practice Aid 10 and quickly familiarize yourself with the other practice aids available in this chapter. You are now "up to speed" on the general issues.

3. Consider drafting an engagement letter. See General Practice Aid 1. (An electronic version of this document can be accessed by activating the Practice Aid Documents.)

4. Use the Interview feature in the software program to generate a choice-of-entity recommendation. At the end of the interview process, save the interview and then print the Interview Q&A Report.

5. Before exiting the software program, carefully review the printout and note any answers that you want to reconsider. If you decide you want to answer certain questions differently, go to Step 6 below. If you are satisfied with your answers, skip Step 6 and go directly to Step 7.

6. If you decide that the answers to certain questions were inappropriate or could "go either way," rerun the software with the new answers and see if different choice-of-entity recommendations result.

7. If you wind up with two or more different recommendations, review the chapters on the recommended types of entities. Then, make a final decision on the best entity choice. Now skip Step 7 and go directly to Step 8.

8. If you are satisfied with your answers to the interview questions, review the chapter on the recommended type of entity to validate the software's recommendation. It may also be prudent to review the chapter on what you consider to be the second-best entity choice, just to make sure you are completely satisfied with your conclusion.

9. In the software, go to the Practice Aid Documents. View the General Practice Aids and the Entity-Specific Practice Aids for the recommended type of entity. Then simply edit, save, and print out the appropriate practice aids for transmittal to the client or inclusion in your workpaper file.

10. You have now completed the choice-of-entity recommendation engagement in a logical, systematic, and efficient manner.

Using This Product *without* the Software Interview Feature

Take the following steps if you choose not to take advantage of the Interview feature of the software. Using the Interview feature is strongly recommended—even if you are highly competent in this area. The Interview process "forces" you to focus consistently on the most critical issues affecting the choice-of-entity decision.

Note: Even if you forego using the Interview feature of the software, make sure you take advantage of the available electronic practice aids. To review these, follow the instructions to go directly to the Practice Aids dialog box.

Initial Steps

1. Read the Executive Summary in section 1.02 of Chapter 1.

2. Review General Practice Aid 10 and quickly familiarize yourself with the other practice aids available in this chapter. You are now "up to speed" on the general issues.

3. Consider drafting an engagement letter. See General Practice Aid 1. (You can access an electronic version of this document by activating the Practice Aid Documents.)

4. Determine if the business or investment activity in question will have more than one owner. (See section 5.04 of Chapter 5 regarding "creating" more than one owner even in situations where there is effectively only a single owner.)

Secondary Steps If Only a Single Owner

1. Your choices are narrowed down to sole proprietorships, single-member LLCs, C corporations, qualified small business corporations (QSBCs), and S corporations. After reviewing Chapter 9, you should quickly be able to either select or reject the sole proprietorship as the best choice of entity. If you reject sole proprietorship status, go to Step 2 below.
   If the sole proprietorship is the best choice, you are finished.

   CAUTION: Advising that a business be operated as a sole proprietorship might be viewed as a "risky" recommendation—because of the issue of unlimited personal liability of the owner.

2. In most cases involving single-owner businesses, the single-member LLC turns out to be the best choice, because double taxation is avoided without having to meet the S corporation qualification rules. However, read section 6.02 of Chapter 6 for guidance on when C corporations make sense even in light of double taxation. Also read Chapter 7 to determine if your client could form a corporation that would meet the definition of a QSBC.

   OBSERVATION: Despite the double taxation disadvantage, C corporations make sense for capital intensive and growth businesses, such as manufacturing and high tech ventures. Such businesses typically need to retain all earnings to finance capital expenditures and growing receivable and inventory levels. Operating as a C corporation maximizes cash flow by minimizing current outlays for federal income taxes. If the corporation is a QSBC, the combined corporate-level and owner-

level tax rates on corporate income may be comparable to or lower than the tax rate on income earned by a pass-through entity. (See Chapter 7.) C corporations also make sense when corporate income can be "zeroed out" with deductible payments to or for the benefit of the owners. (See section 6.02 of Chapter 6.)

3. Review General Practice Aids 4, 5, and 7 in Chapter 10. Consider completing the blank calculation templates shown in General Practice Aids 6 and 8 to quantify the difference in taxes from using an S corporation versus a C corporation or QSBC. (Go to the Practice Aid Spreadsheets to access and fill out the electronic versions of these templates.)

4. Review Chapters 6 and 7 (on C corporations and QSBCs) and Chapter 8 (on S corporations) and select the best type of corporation given the facts in your client's situation.

   CAUTION: In evaluating S corporations, make sure you consider the impact of the eligibility rules both now and in the reasonably foreseeable future (see section 8.02 of Chapter 8).

5. In the software, go to the Practice Aid Documents. View the General Practice Aids and the Entity-Specific Practice Aids for the recommended type of corporation. Then simply edit, save, and print out the appropriate practice aids for transmittal to the client or inclusion in your workpaper file.

6. You have now completed the choice-of-entity recommendation engagement in a logical, systematic, and efficient manner.

Secondary Steps If More Than One Owner

1. The full range of entity choices (other than sole proprietorships) is available. Your first task is to determine if the C corporation or the qualified small business corporation (QSBC) represents the best choice or if these alternatives can be eliminated.

2. Read section 6.02 of Chapter 6 for guidance on when C corporations make sense even in light of double taxation. Also read Chapter 7 to determine if your client(s) could form a corporation that would meet the definition of a QSBC.

   OBSERVATION: Despite the double taxation disadvantage, C corporations make sense for capital intensive and growth businesses, such as manufacturing and high tech ventures. Such businesses typically need to retain all earnings to finance capital expenditures and growing receivable and inventory levels. Operating as a C corporation maximizes cash flow by minimizing current outlays for federal income taxes. If the corporation is a QSBC, the combined corporate-level and owner-level tax rates on corporate income may be comparable to or lower than the tax rate on income earned by a pass-through entity. (See Chapter 7.) C corporations also make sense when corporate income can be "zeroed out" with deductible payments to or for the benefit of the owners. (See section 6.02 of Chapter 6.)

3. Review General Practice Aids 4, 5, and 7 in Chapter 10. Consider completing the blank calculation templates shown in General Practice Aids 6 and 8 to quantify the difference in taxes from using a pass-through entity versus a C corporation or a QSBC. (Electronic versions of these templates can be accessed and filled out by going to the Practice Aid Spreadsheets.)

4. If the C corporation or QSBC is the best choice, go directly to Step 10 below. If these alternatives are rejected, go to Step 5 to consider pass-through entities.

5. In the author's opinion the LLC, when available, is the best pass-through entity choice. Review Chapter 3 and the description of partnership taxation in section 5.08 of Chapter 5. Conclude whether LLC status should be recommended to your client(s). If "Yes," go directly to Step 10 below. If "No," continue to Step 6.

6. In the author's opinion, the limited partnership is the next best pass-through entity choice. Review Chapter 5 and the description of partnership taxation in section 5.08 of Chapter 5. Conclude whether limited partnership status should be recommended to your client(s). If "Yes," go directly to Step 10 below. If "No," continue to Step 7.

7. At this point, you have rejected LLCs and limited partnerships. In the author's opinion, the S corporation generally is the third-best pass-through entity choice. However, you must be able to conclude that the S corporation eligibility rules can be met without insurmountable difficulty both now and in the foreseeable future. (Review Chapter 8, especially section 8.02.) If the S corporation is the best choice, go directly to Step 10 below. If S corporation status is unavailable or unacceptable, the remaining choices are limited liability partnerships (LLPs) and general partnerships.

> *CAUTION: In evaluating S corporations, make sure you consider the impact of the eligibility rules both now and in the reasonably foreseeable future (see section 8.02 of Chapter 8).*

8. If the business in question is a professional practice, consider whether a limited liability partnership (LLP) might be a better choice than an S corporation. Review Chapter 4 and see section 5.08 of Chapter 5 regarding the advantages of partnership taxation over S corporation taxation. If the LLP is the better choice, go directly to Step 10 below. If not, continue to Step 9.

9. You have eliminated all entity choices except general partnerships. Therefore, the general partnership has been selected by default.

> *CAUTION: Advising that a business be operated as a general partnership might be viewed as a "risky" recommendation—because of the issue of unlimited personal liability of the partners. (See Chapter 5.)*

10. In the software, go to the Practice Aid Documents. View the General Practice Aids and the Entity Specific Practice Aids for the recom-

mended type of entity. Then simply edit, save, and print out the appropriate practice aids for transmittal to the client or inclusion in your workpaper file.

11. You have now completed the choice-of-entity recommendation engagement in a logical, systematic, and efficient manner.

Getting Started

The following help topics describe the first steps that you need to complete after loading the program. Click on a topic to view it.

- Create New / Open Existing Client

- Engagement Management Information

Create New / Open Existing Client

Once you have loaded the program from Windows, select New from the File menu to create a new client file or select Open from the File menu to open an existing client file.

If you select File | Open, you will see the following dialog box:

All existing client files appear in the selection window. To open a client file, either click on a client name and then on OK, or simply double-click on a client name. To delete a client file, click on the client name and then click on Delete. Click on the Cancel button to close this dialog box.

Engagement Management Information

After creating a new client file or opening an existing one, you will see the Engagement Management Information dialog box:

```
Engagement Management Information                                      ☒

        Client Name:  Jones Construction Co.|        Date   6/30/99

        Billing Code: JON 3-1700

               User:  MAS

   User Billing Rate: $100/hr


   ┌──────────────────┐   ┌──────────────────┐   ┌──────────────────┐
   │  Start Interview │   │ Go to Practice Aids│  │      Cancel      │
   └──────────────────┘   └──────────────────┘   └──────────────────┘
```

In the Engagement Management Information dialog box, you must enter at least one character in the Client Name field or the program will not let you proceed. Entering data in any of the other fields is optional. The program uses a variation of the client name to create a client subdirectory on your hard drive. All files related to a specific client are stored in this client subdirectory.

If you look at the names of the subdirectories (i.e., those located off the main program directory), it should be readily apparent which subdirectory belongs to which client. Therefore, in order to back up all of the individual files related to a specific client, simply back up all of the files contained in that client's subdirectory.

After completing the inputs in the Engagement Management Information dialog, click on either the Start Interview button to start the interview process, or click on the Go to Practice Aids button to bypass the interview and go directly to the Practice Aids. Click on Cancel to close this dialog box.

Conducting the Interview

The following help topics describe how to conduct the interview. Click on a topic to view it.

- Interview Questions
- More Information Items
- Interview Wizards
- Interview Recommendation
- Engagement Report Options

Interview Questions

From the Engagement Management Information dialog box, click on the Start Interview button to open the Interview dialog box:

```
Jones Construction Co. - Question QB13                    [X]

  Is it of paramount importance for employee/owners to have the
  ability to borrow against their qualified retirement plan accounts?
  This is generally allowed only if the plan is set up to benefit
  employees (including employee/shareholders) of C corporations.
  Note: A "yes" answer to this question will result in selection of the C
  corporation as the entity of choice.




  ○ Yes
                [ More Info ]   [ <Back ]   [ Next> ]   [ Cancel ]
  ⦿ No
```

Read each question and answer "Yes" or "No" by clicking on either the Yes or No "radio" buttons. After you select Yes or No, the program will proceed to the next question along the logical path.

For certain questions, the More Info button becomes activated. Click on this button to open a dialog box that displays additional information which may help you answer the current question.

Click on the Back button to go to the previous question, where you can review or change your answers. When you are at the very first interview question, the Back button will be dimmed because you cannot go back any further. Click on the Next button to go to the next question. Please note that the Next button will be dimmed unless the next question is already answered. The Next and Back buttons are most useful after you have completed an interview and you want to "step" through it in either direction to review the questions and your answers.

More Information Items

From the Interview dialog box, click on the More Info button (if it is not dimmed) to activate the More Info dialog.

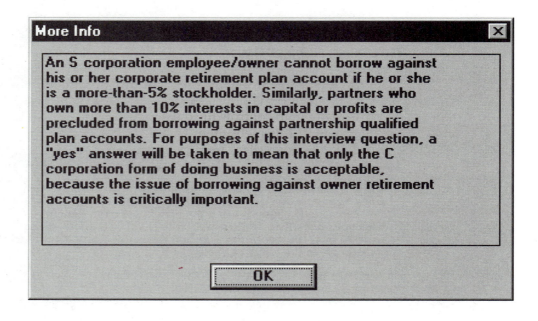

You will notice that for some questions, the More Info button is dimmed and for other questions it is activated. For a given interview question, if the More Info button is active, click on it to open the More Info dialog box. If it is dimmed, there is no more information related to that question.

The More Info dialog displays more detailed information related to a specific interview question. This information is provided to help you answer the current interview question. Please note that before you print the Interview Q&A Report, you have the option to include or exclude the More Info text for each interview question along the selected path.

When you are finished reviewing the More Info text, click on OK to close the dialog box.

Interview Wizards

During the course of the interview, you will notice various Wizard dialogs that appear between certain interview questions.

These Wizard screens provide critical obervations from the author of *Choosing the Right Business Entity* about prior answers, and they may offer you some insight that would cause you to reconsider a prior answer. In some Wizards, you will have to use the vertical scroll bar to view all of the text. Please note that the Wizard text can be included or excluded when you print the Interview Q&A Report.

In addition, advanced users may want to prevent the Wizards from appearing during the course of the interview. To do this, select Options from the menu and then select the Show Wizards menu item. The Show Wizards menu item controls the disabling and enabling of Wizards during the interview. If this menu item has a check mark next to it, Wizards are enabled. If there is no check mark, Wizards are disabled. When the Wizards are enabled, click on Show Wizards and you will receive a confirmation message to disable the Wizards. From the confirmation dialog box, click on Yes to hide the Wizards. Please note that if you disable Wizards, they will be disabled for all client interviews, not just the current interview.

After considering a Wizard, click on the Back button to go back to the prior interview question and change your answer, or click on the Next button to proceed to the next interview question (or recommendation). You can use the Next and Back buttons to "step" through interview questions that have already been answered. If you arrive at an unanswered interview question, the Next button will be dimmed because you must select either Yes or No to proceed to the next interview question.

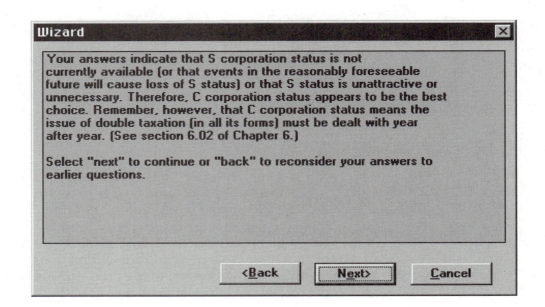

Interview Recommendation

The last screen in the interview is the Recommendation, which appears in a Wizard dialog box. The following example shows one of the possible recommendations:

```
┌─────────────────────────────────────────────────────────────┐
│ Wizard                                                    [×] │
├─────────────────────────────────────────────────────────────┤
│ ┌─────────────────────────────────────────────────────┐ [▲] │
│ │ Your answers indicate that the C corporation may be  │     │
│ │ the best choice. Remember, however, that C           │     │
│ │ corporation status means the potential issue of      │     │
│ │ double taxation (in all its forms) must be dealt     │     │
│ │ with year after year. (See section 6.02 of Chapter   │     │
│ │ 6.)                                                  │     │
│ │                                                      │     │
│ │ Warning #1: The use of a corporation will generally  │     │
│ │ not protect an owner's personal assets from exposure │     │
│ │ to liabilities from his or her own practice of a     │     │
│ │ profession. If there is exposure to such             │     │
│ │ professional malpractice or negligence claims, the   │     │
│ │ owner should consult an attorney on how the choice   │     │
│ │ of entity decision is impacted.                      │     │
│ │                                                      │     │
│ │ Warning #2: The favorable C corporation graduated    │     │
│ │ tax rate structure does not apply to C corporations  │     │
│ │ that are personal service corporations (PSCs). PSCs  │     │
│ │ must pay tax on all income at a flat 35%             │     │
│ │ rate. Several other unfavorable tax rules apply to   │ [▼] │
│ │ PSCs. (See                                           │     │
│ └─────────────────────────────────────────────────────┘     │
│                                                              │
│              [ <Back ]   [ Next> ]   [ Cancel ]              │
└─────────────────────────────────────────────────────────────┘
```

This Recommendation is based on your answers to all of the interview questions. In some Recommendations, you will have to use the vertical scroll bar to view all of the text. Please note that the Recommendation text is always included in the Interview Q&A report.

When you have finished reviewing the Recommendation, click on the Next button; if you have made any changes to the interview, you will be prompted to save it. Click on Yes to save the interview or No to proceed without saving the interview.

If you select Yes, to save the interview, first the questions and answers will be saved and then the Save As dialog box will appear. The Save As dialog allows you to save the interview report to a Rich Text Format (RTF) file that can be modified and printed from virtually any Windows word processing program. Either accept the default file name, INTERVIEW.RTF, or enter a unique file name (with an .RTF extension) and then click on the OK button to save the file. You can then open this file with any Windows word processor and make modifications as needed. When opening an RTF file with your Windows word processor, be sure to specify RTF or All Files in the Type of Files field of your word processor's Open dialog box.

After saving (or not saving) the interview and the associated RTF report file, the program activates the Engagement Report Options dialog. The Engagement Report Options dialog allows you to return to the Interview, print the Interview Report, go to the Practice Aids, or return to the Engagement Management Information dialog.

Engagement Report Options

At the end of the interview (i.e., the interview Recommendation), click on the Next button to activate the Engagement Report Options dialog box:

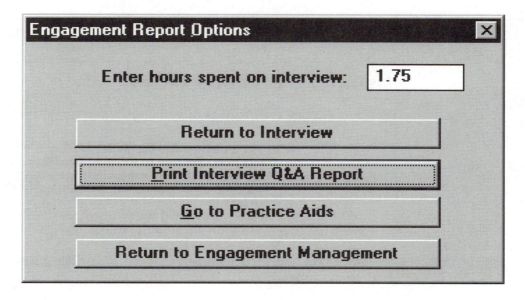

In the field provided, enter the number of hours spent in the interview. This item is optional and is used for reference purposes only.

Click on the Return to Interview button to return to the interview.

Click on the Print Interview Q&A Report button to activate the What to Print dialog box:

In the What to Print dialog, click the check boxes to turn the individual items on and off. If an item is on, it will be included in the report printout. If an item is off, it will not be included. After selecting the items you want to print, click on OK to open the Print dialog box (this is the standard Windows Print dialog).

From the Print dialog, click on OK to print the Interview Q&A Report. You can change the various options in the Print dialog and access the Print Setup dialog by clicking on the Setup button.

Click on the Return to Engagement Management to return to the Engagement Management Information dialog box.

Using the Practice Aids

You can activate the Practice Aids dialog box in two ways:

1. From the Engagement Management Information dialog box (which appears after you open or create a new file), click on the Go to Practice Aids button. This will bypass the interview and take you directly to the Practice Aids dialog box.
2. From the Engagement Report Options dialog box (which appears after completing the interview) click on the Go to Practice Aids button.

Once you have activated the Practice Aids dialog box, you can access both of the following:

- Practice Aid Documents
- Practice Aid Spreadsheets

Practice Aid Documents

The names of the Practice Aid Documents and the associated exhibit numbers (which refer to exhibits in the book) are displayed in the Practice Aids dialog box. Use the vertical scroll bars to review the available documents.

This dialog box will display different documents depending upon whether or not you have completed the interview. If you have completed the interview, the program will display only the general practice aid documents and the documents related to type of entity specified in the interview recommendation. If you have not completed the interview, the program will display all of the available practice aid documents. Therefore, if you want to see all of the documents, create a new client and go directly to the practice aids without completing the interview.

To open one of the documents, first click on the document name. The Make Document button will become active. Then click on the Make Document button. At this point, the program will start the word processor (i.e., the one you selected when you installed this program) and load the selected document. Use your word processor to edit the document as needed.

After making changes to a document, use your word processor to save the document with a unique file name. To do this in Microsoft Word, for example, you would select Save As from the File menu, edit the File Name field, and click on the OK button. For more detailed instructions, refer to the documentation provided with your word processor.

Practice Aid Spreadsheets

From the Practice Aids dialog box, click on the Spreadsheets button to activate the Spreadsheet Practice Aids dialog box. This dialog controls the three practice aid spreadsheets. Each of these three spreadsheets measures the tax savings of a PSE when compared to a C corporation, but each is based upon a separate set of assumptions. In addition, there is a Common Data Input spreadsheet. You enter data into it once and the program transfers this shared data into the other three spreadsheets. Click on one of the following topics to view it.

- Common Data Input Spreadsheet

- C Corp vs. PSE, Liquidation

- C Corp vs. PSE, Sale of Ownership Interest

Please note that, in all of the spreadsheets, before you enter data you must enter the number of years you want to include. The default is five years, but you can enter from 1 to 10 by editing the Number of Years field in the top right corner of this dialog box. If you change the number of years after entering data, this data will not be lost; the spreadsheet formulas will adjust to accommodate the new number of years.

Click on the "radio" buttons in the top left corner of this dialog to activate the desired spreadsheet. Remember to save the current spreadsheet before activating a different one. If you make changes to the current spreadsheet and do not save your changes, then attempt to activate a different spreadsheet, the program will prompt you to save your changes. When prompted, click on Yes to save. If you click on No, any unsaved changes will be lost.

You will notice that some spreadsheet cells are locked and others are unlocked. You can enter data only in the unlocked cells. In the numeric input area of the spreadsheet, unlocked cells have a white background and locked cells have a cyan (aqua) background. The items in the gray heading area of the spreadsheet are unlocked. You can edit all of the items in the heading area of the spreadsheet as needed.

To enter data into any unlocked cell, click on the cell to highlight it, type the desired number or text, and either press the [Enter] key or click on another cell. If you start typing and then decide you want to restore the prior contents of the cell, simply press the [Esc] key before entering the data (i.e., before pressing [Enter] or clicking on another cell).

When entering dollar values or text, just type the whole dollar value (no cents) or type the text and then press [Enter] or click on another cell. However, when you enter tax rates as percentages, you must enter the decimal equivalent. For example, to enter 34.0% you would type ".34" and press [Enter] or click on another cell.

Always complete the Common Data Input spreadsheet first. This spreadsheet stores data that is shared by the other three spreadsheets. It is designed so that you enter shared data in a common area and the program controls the transfer of this data to the appropriate locations in the other three spreadsheets.

Once you have entered the data required in the Common Data Input spreadsheet, you are ready to complete the other three calculating spreadsheets. Each of these calculating spreadsheets requires unique inputs. Click on the Help topics above for an explanation of the unique inputs related to each of the calculating spreadsheets.

From the Spreadsheet Practice Aids dialog box, you can print the active spreadsheet and/or export it for further manipulation with your external spreadsheet program. Click on the Help topic above for a detailed explanation of these functions. Please note that all spreadsheet files are stored in the client subdirectory. The file names and corresponding spreadsheet titles are as follows:

COESS1.VTS = C Corp vs. PSE, Liquidation

COESS2.VTS = C Corp vs. PSE, Sale of Ownership Interest

COESS3.VTS = Common Data Input Spreadsheet

Common Data Input Spreadsheet

When you activate the Spreadsheet Practice Aids dialog box, the program always loads the Common Data Input spreadsheet by default. This spreadsheet stores data that is shared by the three calculating spreadsheets. You enter the shared data once in this spreadsheet and the program transfers it to each of the other spreadsheets as you open them. The program will display from 1 to 10 years, depending on upon the number of years you enter in the top right corner of the Spreadsheet Practice Aids dialog box.

Enter the Assumed Tax Rates for each of the three line items and for each year. The program will transfer these rates to the appropriate location in the other three calculating spreadsheets. Enter all tax rates as decimal numbers.

Enter the Assumed Taxable Income & Cash Distributions for each of the four line items and for each year. The program will also transfer these dollar values to the appropriate location in the other three calculating spreadsheets.

Remember, if you make changes to the data in this spreadsheet, the program does not update the other three spreadsheets until you open them.

Click on Save to save any changes, Print to print the spreadsheet, and Export to export the spreadsheet. See the section titled Saving, Printing, and Exporting Spreadsheets, below, for a detailed explanation of these functions. Click on Cancel to return to the Practice Aids dialog box.

C Corp vs. PSE, Liquidation

From the Spreadsheet Practice Aids dialog box, click on the "radio" button labeled C Corp vs. PSE, Liquidation to activate this spreadsheet. The program will display from 1 to 10 years, depending on the number of years you enter in the top right corner of the Spreadsheet Practice Aids dialog box.

This calculator is one way to estimate the annual and cumulative tax savings from operating as a pass-through entity (PSE) rather than as a C corporation. The assumption is that the owner will make the same initial investment to acquire his or her ownership interest in the PSE or C corporation and that subsequent taxable income of the business each year is the same whether the business is operated as a PSE or as a C corporation.

If operated as a PSE, the business is assumed to distribute enough cash to its owner to pay the annual tax on the passed-through income. If operated as a C corporation, each year the business pays tax on its income at the corporate rates. In addition, you can input amounts for annual cash distributions to the owner.

It is assumed that there is an annual increase in the value and tax basis of the business assets equal to the taxable income for the year less taxes paid (for the C corporation) and distributions. In the case of the PSE, it is further assumed that the tax basis of the ownership interest increases each year by an amount equal to the taxable income less the distributions for that year.

In addition, on line 7 for the final year of the projection period, you can enter the amount of assumed gain on sale of all business assets due to appreciation in the value of those assets. (The same gain amount should be input in both the PSE column and the C corporation column.) Note that this gain increases the basis of the PSE ownership interest.

The PSE and the C corporation are then assumed to be liquidated at the end of the final year, with the owners exchanging their ownership interests for the liquidating distributions shown on line 11.

Please note that you must enter tax rates on lines D, E, and F. These rates are used for various final year calculations.

Lines 15 through 19 have been provided as user-defined practitioner adjustments. Use these open line items to make positive or negative adjustment. Any positive number that you enter is added to the column and row totals. Any negative number that you enter is deducted from the column and row totals.

The differences between the PSE and C corporation after-tax cash to owner amounts (annual and cumulative) are due solely to the tax savings achieved by operating as a PSE rather than as a C corporation. The tax savings amounts are shown on the last line, Tax Savings from PSE Status.

See General Practice Aid 7 for a filled-in version of this form.

Click on Save to save any changes, on Print to print the spreadsheet, and on Export to export the spreadsheet. See the section titled Saving, Printing and Exporting Spreadsheets, below, for a detailed explanation of these functions. Click on Cancel to return to the Practice Aids dialog box.

C Corp vs. PSE, Sale of Ownership Interest

From the Spreadsheet Practice Aids dialog box, click on the "radio" button labeled C Corp vs. PSE, Sale of Ownership Interest to activate this spread-

Print button, you will see the Page Setup dialog box. In the Page Setup dialog, you can control the following items:

- **Header/Footer:** Enter text to be printed as a header or footer on each page.

- **Margins:** Set the top, bottom, left, and right page margins (in inches).

- **Page Order:** This item controls the print order when the spreadsheet spans more than one page. Since print scale is turned on, you can disregard this item.

- **Center:** Set the page to be centered horizontally and/or vertically.

- **Print Options:** Turn Grid Lines on to print all column and row gridlines. Turn Black & White off to attempt to print in color (black and white printers will print color in grayscale). Turn on Row Heading to print the row numbers. Turn on Column Heading to print the column letters.

- **Scale:** The Fit To Pages option is turned on by default and is set to print 1 page high by 1 page wide. This way each spreadsheet will print on one page, regardless of the number of years (columns) contained in the spreadsheet. If the text on a spreadsheet prints too small with these settings, try setting the scale to 2 pages wide.

After setting any options in the Page Setup dialog, click on the OK button and you will see the Print dialog box. From the Print dialog, click on OK to print the spreadsheet. Please note that the spreadsheets are set to print with a "landscape" orientation. If you want to print them "portrait," click on the Setup button and change the orientation in Print Setup dialog box.

Exporting a Spreadsheet

You can export the active spreadsheet at any time by clicking on the Export button in the Spreadsheet Practice Aids dialog box. After you click on the Export button, you will see the Export Spreadsheet Practice Aids dialog box. This dialog allows you to export the active spreadsheet as either an Excel 4.0 Worksheet (XLS) or a Tab-Delimited Text (TXT) file for further manipulation in an external spreadsheet program.

The default export format is Excel 4.0 Worksheet (XLS). This format is preferable because all spreadsheet formulas and cell formatting are retained after you export. If your spreadsheet program cannot read Excel 4.0 files, select Tab-Delimited Text (TXT) from Save File As Type list. Almost all spreadsheet programs can convert tab-delimited text files. However, spreadsheet formulas and cell formatting are not retained in tab-delimited text files. Consult your spreadsheet documentation to determine the appropriate file export format.

After selecting a file format, enter a file name in the File Name field. By default, Excel 4.0 Worksheet files have XLS extensions and Tab-Delimited Text files have TXT extensions. In order to keep all files in the client subdirectory, you should not change the Directories field or the Drives selection. Click on OK to export the file. You can then open and edit the exported file with your spreadsheet program.

Contacting Technical Support

If you require assistance with the operation of this program or have any questions about it use, please do not hesitate to call technical support at (888) 551-7127. Free technical support is available to all registered users of *Choosing the Right Business Entity*.

CHAPTER 1 • HOW TO USE THIS PRODUCT IN ENGAGEMENTS; AN EXECUTIVE SUMMARY OF ENTITY ALTERNATIVES

CONTENTS

1.01 INTRODUCTION

When a new business or investment activity is contemplated, one of the first considerations is to choose the type of legal entity that will be formed to conduct the activity. The choice-of-entity landscape has been altered dramatically by six recent developments:

1. The Revenue Reconciliation Act of 1993 (RRA '93), which raised individual income tax rates significantly above the corporate rates;

2. The passage of limited liability company (LLC) acts in all states (LLCs are probably now the *preferred* entity choice for closely held businesses);

3. The emergence of limited liability partnerships (LLPs), which can be attractive for professional service businesses;

4. The enactment of two significant tax breaks for qualified small business corporations (QSBCs); and

5. The so-called "check-the-box" income tax regulations, which allow taxpayers to be certain of how entities will be classified for federal income tax purposes.

6. Liberalizations to the S corporation qualification rules included in the Small Business Job Protection Act of 1996.

The current environment offers greater opportunities than ever before for clients to achieve their tax-planning and financial objectives by making the right choice. Your clients will look to you for advice and recommendations on this critical decision.

Why Should You Keep This Product?

Unlike many competing products, this publication and the companion software were *not* created simply by updating and stitching together old information written long before the major developments listed above. Instead, they were designed from the ground up to supply the most *current* and *practical* guidance on the issue of entity choice.

A number of *practice aids* are included (see the listing below), and if you make use of the corresponding software, all appropriate practice aids in the book are also available in an *electronic format* that can be edited, saved to your hard drive, and printed out for mailing to clients or including in client workpaper files.

Using this book, the software, and the practice aids ensures that you will approach choice-of-entity advisory engagements in a state-of-the-art, systematic, and efficient manner. This maximizes your ability to deliver high-quality consulting services to your clients. We believe no other publication can deliver these results.

Practice Aids Included in Book and Software

General Practice Aids

- Sample Choice-of-Entity Engagement Letter
- Engagement Workprogram *with* Use of Entity Selection Interview Software
- Engagement Workprogram *without* Use of Entity Selection Interview Software
- Effective Tax Rates on C Corporation and QSBC Income
- Blank "Cradle to Grave" Tax Calculator Comparing Results for Pass-Through Entity and C Corporation (Assuming Eventual Sale of Ownership Interests)
- Blank "Cradle to Grave" Tax Calculator Comparing Results for Pass-Through Entity and C Corporation (Assuming Eventual Sale of Assets and Liquidation of Entity)
- Sample Client Letter Summarizing Choice-of-Entity Alternatives
- Side-by-Side Summary of Entity Attributes
- Summaries of When Entity Choices Are Attractive

LLC-Specific Practice Aids

- Sample Client Letter When Multi-Member LLC Appears to Be Best Entity Choice
- Sample Client Letter When Single-Member LLC Appears to Be Best Entity Choice
- Sample "Generic" Client or Contact Letter Regarding Which Types of Businesses and Activities Are Suited for LLCs
- Checklist for LLC Articles of Organization
- Sample LLC Articles of Organization
- LLC Operating Agreement Checklist
- Sample LLC Operating Agreement

LLP-Specific Practice Aids

- Sample Client Letter When LLP Appears to Be Best Entity Choice

Partnership-Specific Practice Aids

- Sample Client Letter When General Partnership Appears to Be Best Entity Choice
- Sample Client Letter When Limited Partnership Appears to Be Best Entity Choice
- Partnership Agreement Checklist

C Corporation-Specific Practice Aids

- Analysis of Effective Tax Rates on C Corporation Income
- Sample Client Letter When C Corporation Appears to Be Best Entity Choice

QSBC-Specific Practice Aids

- Analysis of Effective Tax Rates on QSBC Income
- Sample Client Letter When QSBC Appears to Be Best Entity Choice

S Corporation-Specific Practice Aids

- Sample Client Letter When S Corporation Appears to Be Best Entity Choice

Underlying Assumptions

The book and software assume that:

- A new business or investment activity is being started up, *or*
- The assets of an existing activity have been acquired by new ownership in a taxable transaction.

In either of these cases, the owner(s) of the venture must select a legal form of doing business.

The software does *not* provide guidance on switching the legal or federal income tax form of an existing business. Examples of such switches include changing from corporate to partnership status (a change in legal status) or changing from C corporation to S corporation status (a change in federal income tax status). However, within the book there is coverage of such "midstream" entity switches.

Neither the book nor the software deals with foreign entities, foreign taxes, or state and local taxes. Nor does the book or the software deal with such "special" entities as real estate investment trusts (REITs), other types of trusts, and registered investment companies (RICs). Instead, the focus is on the types of business entities that typically make sense for small to medium-sized closely held businesses.

Within the above framework, available entity options include:

- Limited liability companies (LLCs), including single-member LLCs;
- Limited liability partnerships (LLPs);

- General partnerships;
- Limited partnerships;
- C corporations;
- Qualified small business corporations (QSBCs, which are simply C corporations that meet certain tax law standards);
- S corporations; and
- Sole proprietorships (which actually are *not* separate legal entities apart from their owners).

All of the above are considered in the software program and fully discussed in the book.

Instructions on how to use this book—with or without the software interview feature—are included in the Software User's Guide preceding this chapter.

1.02 EXECUTIVE SUMMARY OF ENTITY ALTERNATIVES

This section summarizes the major issues to be considered in selecting the type of entity under which to operate a business or an investment activity. Read the following to quickly "get up to speed" on the topic. However, this discussion is not a substitute for reviewing the more detailed information in Chapters 2 through 10.

Limited Liability Companies (LLCs)

LLCs are increasing in popularity because they combine the best legal and tax characteristics of corporations and partnerships while avoiding many of their disadvantages. Specifically, an LLC can offer limited liability protection to all its owners (referred to as "members") while being treated as a partnership for federal income tax purposes. Almost all states also allow single-member LLCs, which are entities with only one owner. Single-member LLCs owned by individuals are ignored for federal income tax purposes. In other words, all of the entity's activity is simply reflected on the owner's Form 1040. Throughout this chapter, the term *LLC* will mean an LLC with more than one member. LLCs with only a single member will be referred to as *single-member LLCs*.

LLCs are covered in detail in Chapter 3.

Legal Considerations

Even though LLCs are *unincorporated,* the fundamental intent of LLC statutes in the various states is to allow the formation of entities that legally are more similar to corporations than to partnerships.

Nevertheless, LLCs can be taxed as partnerships. The critical point is that, legally, LLCs are *not* corporations; nor are they partnerships.

While the personal assets of LLC members and managers are protected from "general" LLC debts and obligations (often referred to as "contract liabilities"), these persons generally remain *exposed* to LLC liabilities resulting from their own tortious acts and their own professional errors and omissions. (*Tortious acts* are defined as wrongful acts leading to civil actions, other than those involving breach of contract.)

The issue of members' and managers' exposure to liabilities related to tortious acts and professional errors and omissions is a matter of state law. Consult an attorney regarding specific questions.

Like corporate shareholders, LLC members may be required on occasion to personally guarantee certain of the entity's debts as a condition of obtaining financing or for other reasons. Members are personally obligated with respect to LLC debts that are specifically guaranteed.

Single-member LLCs are also unincorporated entities that legally are more similar to solely owned corporations than to sole proprietorships. The liability protection aspects of single-member LLCs are generally the same as for multi-member LLCs.

Tax Treatment of LLCs

The key *tax* attribute of LLCs is that they can be treated as partnerships for federal income tax purposes. The tax advantages of partnership status are covered later in this summary (see the discussion of general partnerships). The existence of single-member LLCs is ignored for federal income tax purposes. Therefore, when a single-member LLC is owned by an individual and is used to conduct a trade or business activity, the tax information will be reported on Schedule C of the individual's Form 1040. If the LLC is used to operate a rental real estate operation, the tax information will be reported on Schedule E. If the single-member LLC is owned by another legal entity, such as a corporation, a partnership, or another LLC, the tax information will be reported in the same fashion as for an unincorporated branch or division of the parent entity.

Conclusions on LLCs

Because LLC laws are new, there inevitably are legal uncertainties associated with choosing to operate as an LLC rather than as a partnership or a C or S corporation. There are also some unanswered questions regarding how certain federal tax law provisions apply to multi-member LLCs. These uncertainties are the major disadvantage of LLCs.

However, only multi-member LLCs are able to offer both the legal advantage of limited liability for all owners and the tax advantage of partnership taxation—combining pass-through treatment with maximum flexibility. Somewhat similarly, single-member LLCs offer liability protection with maximum simplicity from a federal tax perspective. This unique combination of legal and tax benefits is the driving force behind the growing use of LLCs.

When Should an LLC Be Used?

Multi-member LLCs are suitable for many business and investment activities, including, but not limited to, the following:

- Corporate joint ventures (where the corporate co-owners desire both pass-through taxation and limited liability);
- Real estate investment and development activities (because the partnership taxation rules allow investors to obtain basis from entity-level debt and because special tax allocations can be made to benefit investors);
- Oil and gas exploration (where the partnership rules can be used to make special allocations of intangible drilling cost deductions to benefit investors);
- Venture capital investments (where the partnership rules allow pass-through taxation and the creation of "customized" ownership interests with varying rights to cash flow, liquidating distributions, and tax items);
- Business start-ups expected to have tax losses in the initial years (which can be passed through to investors);
- Professional practices—if allowed under state law and applicable professional standards (where pass-through taxation can be combined with specially tailored ownership interests that reflect each member's contributions to the practice); and
- Estate-planning vehicles (where the older generation can gift LLC ownership interests to younger family members while retaining control by functioning as the managers, and where all taxable income is passed through to the members).

Under some state laws and/or applicable professional standards (such as state bar association rules), LLCs may be prohibited from operating certain professional practices. Some states do not permit the use of LLCs in certain lines of business, such as banking, insurance, and farming.

When permitted, however, LLCs are an excellent choice. In some states, professional LLCs offer better liability protection than limited liability partnerships (LLPs), and the ability to create differing types of LLC ownership interests (for example, to reflect the activity levels of the members) can often be attractive to professional groups.

According to a survey published in the December 1995 issue of *Journal of Accountancy*, the top 10 types of businesses actually operated as LLCs are:

- Engineering and management support services (26%),
- Real estate services (19%),
- Construction and general contracting (12%),
- Investment companies (9%),

- Retailers (8%),
- Health services (7%),
- Agriculture (7%),
- Oil and gas extraction (2%),
- Restaurants (2%), and
- Leasing companies (2%).

Generally, the single-member LLC is the preferred choice when pass-through taxation is desired for a single-owner business. However, as this book went to press, not all states permitted single-member LLCs. The only other pass-through alternative for a single-owner business is the S corporation, which has strict qualification rules.

Recommendation

Most advisors agree that the multi-member LLC is the best entity alternative if there is more than one owner and pass-through taxation is desired (such as with a service business where there is no need to retain significant amounts of earnings within the business entity).

As would be expected, empirical evidence shows that LLCs are seldom formed to operate capital-intensive and high-growth businesses, such as manufacturing and high tech ventures. Because such businesses typically need to retain all earnings to finance capital expenditures and growing receivable and inventory levels, they are most often operated as C corporations in order to maximize cash flow by minimizing current outlays for federal income taxes.

Because LLCs allow all members to participate fully in management without risk of losing limited liability protection (which can happen with a limited partnership), they are ideally suited for closely held entrepreneurial businesses.

In summary, multi-member LLCs may be the best choice for business and investment ventures if:

- There will be more than one owner; and
- Limited liability protection for the co-owners is an important consideration; and
- Pass-through taxation is desired; and
- The advantages of partnership taxation are significant compared to the alternative of S corporation taxation, or the entity cannot qualify for S corporation status; and
- The business (or investment) activity can be operated as an LLC under state law; and
- The co-owners can tolerate the uncertainties of LLC status.

CAUTION: *Although LLC statutes place no limits on the number of members, there is a tax problem if ownership interests are so widely held that they are* *"publicly traded" within the meaning of IRC §7704. If an LLC's ownership interests are publicly traded, the LLC will be treated as a C corporation for federal income tax purposes.*

Limited Liability Partnerships (LLPs)

LLPs are a relatively new type of entity that can be particularly useful for the operation of professional practices. LLPs are formed and operated pursuant to state LLP statutes. Chapter 4 covers LLPs in detail.

Liability of LLP Partners

In some states (such as Texas), the partners of an LLP remain personally liable for the general debts and obligations—the "contract liabilities"—of the LLP, for example, bank loans, lease obligations, and vendor accounts payable. In other states (such as California and New York), LLP partners are not personally liable for the LLP's contract liabilities unless the liabilities are expressly guaranteed by the partners. In other words, these states offer "LLC-like" liability protection to LLP partners.

In addition, LLP partners remain personally liable for their own tortious acts and their own professional errors and omissions. However, LLP partners generally are *not* liable for the professional errors, and omissions of other LLP partners or employees.

LLP Advantages and Disadvantages

LLPs are partnerships (both for state law and for federal income tax purposes), and they therefore are subject to the legal and tax implications that generally apply to partnerships.

The major advantage of LLPs is their ability to benefit from pass-through taxation without being affected by the restrictions that apply to S corporations (such as the one-class-of-stock rule and other limitations discussed later in this summary). In addition, LLPs enjoy the other tax advantages that partnerships have over S corporations (covered in the discussion of general partnerships below).

In states where LLP partners are not protected against contract liabilities, the principal disadvantage is this lack of "complete" liability protection.

However, under some state laws and certain professional standards, the use of LLCs may be prohibited. If such is the case, LLPs offer better liability protection than general partnerships and are not burdened with the double taxation problems of C corporations.

Recommendation

LLPs are probably the best entity choice for professional service ventures if:

- Pass-through taxation is desired; and
- LLC status is unavailable, or LLPs offer LLC-like liability protection; and
- LLP status is permitted under the statute and applicable professional standards; and
- Qualifying as an S corporation would be inconvenient, difficult, or impossible, *or* when the entity could qualify as an S corporation but the benefits of the partnership taxation rules are significant compared to the S corporation taxation rules; and
- The co-owners can live with their exposure to the entity's contract liabilities (in states not offering LLC-like liability protection).

In many cases, professional practices can be operated as C corporations and avoid the double taxation problem by "zeroing out" corporate income with deductible payments to or for the benefit of the owners. When this is possible, the author believes C corporations are superior to LLPs in states that do not offer LLC-like liability protection to LLP partners.

General Partnerships

The partners of a general partnership are personally liable (without limitation) for all debts and obligations of the partnership. The liability of general partners is "joint and several" in nature, which means any one of the general partners can be forced to make good on all partnership liabilities. That partner may be able to seek reimbursement from the partnership for payments in excess of his or her share of liabilities, but this depends on the ability of the other partners to contribute funds to allow the partnership to make such reimbursement.

Note that general partners are also jointly and severally liable for partnership liabilities related to the tortious acts and professional errors and omissions of the other general partners and the partnership's employees. In addition, general partners are personally liable for their own tortious acts and professional errors and omissions.

Finally, each general partner usually has the power to act as an agent of the partnership and enter into contracts that are legally binding on the partnership (and ultimately on the other partners). For example, a partner can enter into a lease arrangement that is legally binding on the partnership. For this reason, it is critical that the partners have a high degree of trust in each other. If that is *not* the case, a general partnership is inadvisable.

General partnerships are covered in detail in Chapter 5.

Advantages of Pass-Through Taxation

The major advantage of general partnerships is the ability to benefit from pass-through taxation without being affected by the various restrictions that apply to S corporations.

The major features of pass-through taxation are as follows:

- Partnerships are not tax-paying entities. Instead, the partnerships's items of income, gain, deduction, loss, and credit are passed through to the partners, who then take those items into account in their own tax returns.

- Adjustments to basis in ownership interests. When the partnership's income and losses are passed through to a partner, that partner's basis in his or her partnership interest is adjusted accordingly. Specifically, the partner's basis is increased by his or her passed-through share of income and gains and decreased by his or her share of losses and deductions. This procedure ensures that income is subject to only a single level of taxation, at the partner level.

- Cash distributions. Distributions reduce the partner's basis in his or her interest. Only distributions in excess of basis trigger taxable gain to the partner.

Multi-Year Impact of Pass-Through Taxation

Being able to avoid double taxation of entity income makes a big (and favorable) difference when an entity earns substantial amounts of taxable income over a period of several years.

However, it must be remembered that the C corporation tax rates on the first $75,000 of annual income are considerably lower than the individual tax rates that apply if the same income is passed through by a partnership (or an S corporation). Even at higher income levels, the C corporation rates are still lower than the individual rates. (See Chapter 6.) If all income is expected to be retained in the business indefinitely (for example, to finance growing receivable and inventory levels), the more favorable C corporation rates can partially or wholly offset the negative effects of double taxation. In such cases, operating as a C corporation may be preferable to pass-through entity status.

Differences between Partnership and S Corporation Taxation

The above discussion of pass-through taxation applies to partnerships and S corporations equally. (Simply substitute *corporation* and *shareholder* for *partnership* and *partner*, respectively.) However, there are also significant *differences* between partnership taxation and S corporation taxation, mostly in favor of partnerships. They include the following:

- Partners can receive additional tax basis (for loss deduction purposes) from entity-level liabilities, while S corporation shareholders can receive additional tax basis only from loans made by them to the corporation. (Shareholder guarantees of corporate debt have no effect on shareholder basis.)

- Partners who purchase a partnership interest from another partner can step up the tax basis of their shares of partnership assets.

- Partners and partnerships have much greater flexibility to make tax-free transfers of appreciated property than do S corporations and their shareholders.
- Partnerships can make disproportionate allocations of tax losses and other tax items among the partners. In contrast, all S corporation pass-through items must be allocated among the shareholders strictly in proportion to stock ownership.

There are also several disadvantageous tax rules that apply to partnerships but not to S corporations. (See Chapter 5.) However, most tax advisors believe that partnership taxation is considerably more favorable, overall, than S corporation taxation.

Activities Suitable for General Partnerships

Business and investment activities where general partnerships make sense include, but are not limited to, the following:

- Corporate joint ventures (where the corporate co-owners desire pass-through taxation);
- Real estate investment and development activities (where the partnership taxation rules allow partners to receive preferred returns, special allocations of tax losses, and additional basis from partnership-level debt);
- Oil and gas exploration (where the partnership taxation rules allow preferred returns and special allocations of deductions from intangible drilling costs);
- Venture capital investments (where the partnership rules allow pass-through taxation and the creation of ownership interests with varying rights to cash flow, liquidating distributions, and tax items);
- Business start-ups expected to have tax losses in the initial years (which can be passed through to the partners); and
- Professional practices (where pass-through taxation can be combined with specially tailored ownership interests that reflect each member's contributions to the practice).

Recommendation

General partnerships are probably the best entity choice if:

- There are at least two co-owners, each of whom has a high degree of trust in the other(s); and
- Pass-through taxation is desired; and
- LLC and LLP status are unavailable; and
- Liability concerns can be managed with insurance; and

- Qualifying as an S corporation would be inconvenient, difficult, or impossible, *or* the entity could qualify as an S corporation but the benefits of the partnership taxation rules are significant compared to the S corporation taxation rules; and

- The co-owners can live with the fact that the general partnership will not have an unlimited legal life or free transferability of ownership interests.

In most cases, the desire to limit owner liability is so significant that only a limited partnership, as opposed to a general partnership, will make sense to clients.

In the case of professional practices, operating as an LLC, an LLP, or a C corporation should be explored. Most advisors agree that general partnerships and sole proprietorships are by far the least attractive entity options.

> *CAUTION: Advising that a business be operated as a general partnership might be viewed as a "risky" recommendation—because of the issue of unlimited personal liability of the partners.*

Limited Partnerships

A limited partnership is a separate legal entity (apart from its limited partners) that owns its assets and is liable for its debts. Therefore, the personal assets of the limited partners generally are beyond the reach of partnership creditors. This is the nontax selling point of limited partnerships.

Limited partners are, however, still personally responsible for partnership liabilities resulting from their own tortious acts.

The key negative factor associated with limited partnerships is that they must have at least one general partner with unlimited personal exposure to partnership liabilities. Usually this problem can be addressed by forming a corporate general partner—often an S corporation jointly owned by the persons who would otherwise function as individual general partners. Under this strategy, the amount the general partners can lose is effectively limited to the value of the assets held by the corporation.

Another potentially significant negative factor is that limited partners can lose their limited liability protection if they become too actively involved in managing the limited partnership. As a result, limited partnerships are not suitable for activities where all partners are heavily involved in the business (for example, professional practices). Again, this problem may be addressed by using a corporate general partner, with the corporation owned by the limited partners in proportion to their limited partnership ownership percentages.

The key tax advantage of limited partnerships is that they can be treated as partnerships for federal income tax purposes. (See the earlier discussion under the General Partnership heading.)

Limited partnerships are covered in detail in Chapter 5.

Activities Suitable for Limited Partnerships

Business and investment activities where limited partnerships make sense include, but are not limited to, the following:

- Real estate investment and development activities (where the partnership taxation rules allow investors to receive preferred returns, special allocations of tax losses, and additional basis from partnership-level debt),

- Oil and gas exploration (where the partnership taxation rules allow preferred returns and special allocations of deductions from intangible drilling costs),

- Venture capital investments (where the partnership rules allow pass-through taxation and the creation of ownership interests with varying rights to cash flow, liquidating distributions, and tax items)

- Business start-ups expected to have tax losses in the initial years (which can be passed through to the partners), and

- Estate-planning vehicles (where the older generation can gift limited partnership interests to younger family members while retaining control by functioning as the general partners, and where all taxable income is passed through to the partners).

Recommendation

Limited partnerships can be attractive if:

- There are at least two co-owners (but not so many co-owners that the ownership interests would be considered publicly traded under IRC §7704); and

- Pass-through taxation is desired; and

- LLC status is unavailable; and

- Qualifying as an S corporation would be inconvenient, difficult, or impossible, *or* the entity could qualify as an S corporation but the benefits of the partnership taxation rules are significant compared to the S corporation taxation rules; and

- The co-owners who will be limited partners can live with the fact that they cannot become too actively involved in management of the venture without losing their limited liability protection; and

- The co-owners can live with the fact that the limited partnership will not have an unlimited legal life or free transferability of all ownership interests.

> **OBSERVATION:** *Most advisors agree that LLCs, when available, are superior to limited partnerships. However, when pass-through taxation is desired, limited partnerships are usually considered the second best choice.*

S Corporations

Legally, S corporations and C corporations are identical. Corporations offer the greatest certainty in terms of protecting the personal assets of owners from the risks of the business. A corporation is treated as a distinct legal entity separate and apart from its shareholders. Therefore, the corporation owns its own assets and is liable for its own debts. As a result, the personal assets of shareholders (including shareholder-employees) generally are beyond the reach of corporate creditors.

Shareholders generally remain *exposed* to corporate liabilities resulting from their own tortious acts and their own professional errors and omissions.

Shareholders may be required on occasion to personally guarantee certain of the corporation's debts as a condition of obtaining financing or for other reasons. Shareholders are personally obligated with respect to corporate debts that are specifically guaranteed.

S corporations are covered in detail in Chapter 8.

Federal Income Tax Treatment of S Corporations

See the earlier discussions of pass-through taxation and the differences between partnership and S corporation taxation under the General Partnerships heading. (See Chapter 8 for a detailed description of the S corporation taxation rules.)

Election of S Status

The election of S corporation status is made by filing Form 2553 (Election by a Small Business Corporation). The form can be filed during the preceding tax year for an election to become effective for the following tax year. For an S election to be effective for the current tax year, it must be filed by the fifteenth day of the third month of that year.

Newly formed corporations generally intend for the election of S status to be effective for the initial tax year. The election must be filed by the fifteenth day of the third month after the "activation date" of the corporation, which is the earliest date the corporation has shareholders, acquires assets, or begins conducting business.

Special Restrictions on S Corporations

To qualify for the benefits of pass-through taxation, S corporations must meet a number of strict eligibility rules. Unfortunately, these rules greatly restrict stock ownership and capital structure possibilities and can therefore make operating as an S corporation much less attractive than it first appears.

If the eligibility rules are not met at any time during the tax year, the S status of the corporation is immediately terminated and the corporation falls under the C corporation taxation rules.

To qualify for S status, a corporation must:

- Be a domestic corporation;
- Have no more than 75 shareholders;
- Have no shareholders other than individuals who are U.S. citizens or resident aliens, estates, or certain types of trusts; and
- Have only one class of stock (issuing voting and nonvoting shares is permitted, but there can be no preferred stock or common stock classes with differing economic characteristics).

These restrictions can hamper attempts to raise capital, and they may frustrate plans to transfer stock for income tax planning, estate planning, and business succession reasons.

Ineligible Corporations

The following types of corporations are by definition ineligible for S status:

- Financial institutions allowed to deduct bad debts,
- Domestic international sales corporations (DISCs) or former DISCs,
- Insurance companies other than certain casualty companies, and
- Certain corporations electing to take the possessions tax credit.

Recommendation

In general, S corporations may be preferred to C corporations, LLCs, LLPs, partnerships, and sole proprietorships if:

- Limiting owner liability is a critical concern; *and*
- Pass-through taxation is desired; *and*
- The S corporation eligibility rules can be met without undue hardship; *and*
- The restrictions on eligible S shareholders do not cause undue hardship with regard to the owners' future plans to transfer ownership interests to others for estate planning, family tax planning, or business succession planning purposes; *and*
- There will be only one owner (making partnership taxation by definition unavailable), and single-member LLCs are not allowed by state law; *or*
- The activity cannot be operated as an LLC under state law and/or applicable professional standards; *or*
- The business cannot be operated as an LLC, because the owners cannot live with the legal uncertainties associated with LLC status; *and*
- The activity cannot be operated as a limited partnership, because the owners who would be limited partners and cannot live with the fact

that they must avoid management involvement to maintain their limited liability protection; *and*

- Either the business cannot be operated as an LLP, or the liability protections offered by LLP status are considered inadequate; *or*
- The benefits of partnership taxation compared to S corporation taxation are not considered significant enough to warrant setting up a partnership, LLC, or LLP.

> **OBSERVATION:** *Assessing the attractiveness of S corporation status involves balancing the advantages of pass-through taxation and superior liability protection for owners against the restrictive eligibility rules. Most tax advisors agree that LLCs, LLPs, and limited partnerships are superior to S corporations from a tax standpoint. However, when there is only a single owner and double taxation must be avoided, the S corporation is the only alternative to sole proprietorship status in states that do not allow single-member LLCs.*

Regular Corporations ("C Corporations")

The principal advantage of C corporations is their ability to protect owners from liabilities related to the business. As discussed earlier, the liability-limiting attributes of C and S corporations are identical.

C corporations are covered in detail in Chapter 6.

Federal Income Tax Treatment of C Corporations

The key disadvantage of C corporations is that they are subject to double taxation. The double taxation issue appears in several different ways, described briefly below.

- Dividend distributions—If the corporation has accumulated earnings and profits, nonliquidating distributions to shareholders are treated as dividends. These are taxed as ordinary income to the recipient shareholders, but the corporation cannot deduct the payments. In some situations, the corporation may be forced to make dividend distributions to avoid being hit with corporate-level penalty taxes on "excessive" retained earnings.

- Double taxation on sale of stock—When a C corporation earns taxable income, the tax basis of the shareholders' stock is not adjusted upward. The retained income increases the value of the stock, which creates a bigger capital gain when shares are eventually sold. As a result, the retained income is, in effect, taxed again when shares are sold.

- Double taxation on liquidation—If the corporation holds appreciated property and eventually liquidates, the property to be distributed in liquidation is treated as sold by the corporation for its fair market value (FMV). The corporation must pay the resulting taxes. When the corporate assets (net of corporate-level taxes) are distributed to shareholders in liquidation, shareholders also must recognize taxable gain to the extent the FMV of the liquidating distributions exceeds the tax basis of their shares.

- Double taxation of appreciating assets—If the corporation holds appreciating assets, the resulting gains will be subject to double taxation if they are sold by the corporation, if the corporation is liquidated, or if the corporate stock is sold.

  CAUTION: The author strongly recommends that, when possible, assets expected to appreciate significantly (such as real estate, patents, and copyrights) be owned by a pass-through entity (in turn owned by the C corporation's shareholders), which can then lease the assets to the C corporation. With this arrangement, the C corporation can reduce its taxable income by making deductible rental payments that benefit its shareholders. Any gains upon the eventual sale of the appreciated assets owned by the pass-through entity will not be subject to double taxation.

Other negative aspects of C corporation taxation apply in the following circumstances:

- When the corporation has significant tax losses, and
- When the corporation has significant long-term capital gains, capital losses, or tax-exempt income.

There are also situations, however, where the C corporation tax provisions are *more* favorable than the rules applying to pass-through entities. See Chapter 6 for a detailed discussion of the C corporation taxation rules.

When Are the Corporate Tax Rules Harmless or Even Favorable?

Corporations can often solve the double taxation problem by "zeroing out" corporate income with deductible payments to or for the benefit of shareholder-employees. Such payments can be for salary, fringe benefits, interest on shareholder loans, and rent for property owned by shareholders. When corporate income can be zeroed out, the issue of double taxation is not applicable.

Even when zeroing out income is not possible, the favorable graduated corporate tax rates can make C corporations attractive compared to pass-through entities. This is the case when businesses earn relatively small amounts and intend to retain all earnings indefinitely in order to finance their growth internally. A pass-through entity might have to distribute up to 39.6% of the taxable income earned by the business to enable the owners to pay their personal taxes, whereas the average tax rate on the first $75,000 of corporate income is only 18.33%.

Even at taxable income levels above $75,000, the C corporation tax rates are significantly lower than those for individuals. As a result, the use of a C corporation can maximize the current cash flow of the business. It must be remembered, however, that the cost of this current benefit is the double taxation that may apply in later years. (See Appendix 6A.)

CAUTION: Personal service corporations (PSCs) are ineligible for the favorable corporate graduated tax rates. Instead, all PSC income is taxed at a flat 35% rate. Other unfavorable tax rules may also apply to PSCs. (See Chapter 6.)

Recommendation

C corporations may be preferred to LLCs, LLPs, general and limited partnerships, and sole proprietorships if:

- Limiting owner liability is a critical concern; *and*

- There will be only one owner (making partnership taxation by definition unavailable) and single-member LLCs are not permitted under state law, and the S corporation restrictions make operating as an S corporation difficult or impossible; *or*

- The activity cannot be operated as a limited partnership, because the owners who would be limited partners cannot live with the fact that they must avoid management involvement to maintain their limited liability protection; *and*

- The activity cannot be operated as an LLC under state law and/or applicable professional standards; *or*

- The business cannot be operated as an LLC, because the owners cannot live with the legal uncertainties associated with LLC status; *or*

- The benefits of pass-through taxation are not required (because the graduated corporate rates counteract the ill effects of double taxation, or because the venture's income can be drained with deductible payments to or for the benefit of the owners); *or*

- The ability of the owners to borrow against their qualified retirement plan accounts is a critical issue.

Because of the issue of double taxation, C corporations are "underrated." However, the differences between corporate tax rates and individual tax rates mean that pass-through taxation often results in higher current outlays for federal income taxes.

Recent empirical evidence shows that C corporations are still being formed to operate capital-intensive and growth businesses, such as manufacturing and high tech ventures, which typically need to retain all earnings to finance capital expenditures and growing receivable and inventory levels. Operating as a C corporation maximizes cash flow by minimizing current outlays for federal income taxes. And for very successful businesses, the C corporation format lays the best groundwork for going public.

In contrast, businesses that distribute essentially all of their income to owners generally should be operated via one of the pass-through entities to avoid double taxation.

Qualified Small Business Corporations (QSBCs)

If a C corporation meets the definition of a QSBC, shareholders (other than C corporations) are potentially eligible to exclude from taxation up to 50% of their gains on sale of the corporation's stock. Of perhaps more significance, QSBC shareholders can also sell their stock and roll the resulting gain over tax-free into replacement shares of a new QSBC investment.

A number of rules must be met for a corporation to qualify for QSBC status, and shareholders must own their stock for more than five years to benefit from the gain exclusion provision.

QSBCs are covered in detail in Chapter 7. Also, see Appendix 7A for a table showing how the ill effects of double taxation may be largely offset by the gain exclusion.

QSBCs present a real alternative to pass-though entities in cases where corporations will qualify for QSBC status.

Note that QSBCs are treated the same as "regular" C corporations for all other tax and legal purposes.

Recommendation

C corporations that meet the definition of a QSBC may be preferred to LLCs, partnerships, and sole proprietorships if:

- Limiting owner liability is a critical concern; *and*
- The entity will qualify for QSBC status; *or*
- There will be only one owner (making partnership taxation by definition unavailable) and single-member LLCs are not permitted under state law, and the S corporation restrictions make operating as an S corporation difficult or impossible; *or*
- The activity cannot be operated as a limited partnership, because the owners who would be limited partners cannot live with the fact that they must avoid management involvement to maintain their limited liability protection; *and*
- The activity cannot be operated as an LLC under state law; *or*
- The business cannot be operated as an LLC, because the owners cannot live with the legal uncertainties associated with LLC status; *or*
- The benefits of pass-through taxation are not required (because the graduated corporate rates and QSBC gain exclusion counteract the ill effects of double taxation, or because the venture's income can be drained off with deductible payments to or for the benefit of the owners); *or*
- The ability of the owners to borrow against their qualified retirement plan accounts is a critical issue.

See the earlier comments regarding C corporations. The same comments apply to QSBCs, except that QSBCs are more attractive than "regular" C corporations because of the 50% gain exclusion tax break.

Sole Proprietorships

As discussed in Chapter 9, the major attraction of sole proprietorships is their administrative simplicity. However, as soon as a business begins to generate significant income and wealth for the owner, the use of a liability-limiting entity is highly advisable.

Generally, the S corporation or single-member LLC (if permitted by state law) will prove to be the best choice for a single-owner business, because double taxation is avoided. However, in businesses where it is critical to retain the maximum amount of capital to finance growth, the lower graduated tax rates of the C corporation can make the C corporation the better choice—particularly if the corporation can meet the definition of a QSBC.

Recommendation

The sole proprietorship may be the preferred form of doing business if:

- There is only a single owner and single-member LLCs are not permitted by state law; and
- Adequate liability insurance is available at an acceptable cost; *or*
- The major liability exposures are from the owner's practice of a profession (a problem that generally is not "cured" by a liability-limiting entity); and
- The business is in the early stages, and minimizing administrative expenses and paperwork is a major objective; and
- The owner does not currently wish to deal with the issue of how future transfers of ownership interests (for estate planning, succession planning, or other reasons) will be accomplished; and
- The owner does not currently wish to deal with the issue of how additional equity capital might be raised in the future; and
- At present, the business is small enough that operating as a sole proprietorship is still a rational choice in light of *all* the above considerations.

    CAUTION: *Advising that a business be operated as a sole proprietorship might be viewed as a "risky" recommendation—because of the issue of unlimited personal liability of the owner.*

State Tax Considerations

No choice of entity decision is complete without assessing the state tax implications. For example, Texas LLPs do not offer LLC-like liability protection to LLP partners. Therefore, Texas professional service firms would be expected to operate as LLCs. However, most are actually run as LLPs. Why? Because the state imposes its corporate franchise tax (which is actually similar to an income tax) on LLCs, while LLPs are exempt. Most Texas professionals have concluded that the state tax advantage of LLP status is more valuable than the additional liability protection offered by LLC status.

CHAPTER 2 • LIMITING OWNER LIABILITY— A CRITICAL GOAL

CONTENTS

2.01 INTRODUCTION

In almost all cases involving significant business or investment activities, the owners will have a *very* strong interest in structuring deals so as to limit their personal exposure to liabilities related to the activity. Most owners understand that their investment in the activity will always be "at risk," but they cannot accept having their personal assets put at risk because of their involvement.

Given the litigious environment of business today, limiting owner liability should be the most critical issue in selecting the appropriate entity to use in conducting business or investment activities. That is the focus of this chapter.

> *CAUTION: Obviously, the issue of owner exposure to liabilities is a legal question, as is the issue of taking steps to minimize such exposure. In general, liability exposure is a matter of state law, and state laws can vary considerably. The discussion in this chapter is by necessity very general in nature, and it may be inconsistent with the laws of certain states. In dealing with specific client circumstances and questions, competent legal counsel should be sought.*

2.02 SOURCES OF LIABILITY EXPOSURE

The nature of a proposed business or investment activity is the key factor in assessing the owners' potential exposure to liabilities resulting from that activity. Generalizations are difficult to make. However, if the following conditions exist, exposure to liabilities is indicated, and steps that will limit exposure should be carefully considered:

1. The activity will have employees (employees inevitably create exposure to liabilities in any number of ways—for example, one employee may harass another, employees can be injured on the job or premises, discriminatory hiring or firing practices can be alleged, embezzlement and theft can occur, unauthorized borrowing or spending transactions can occur);

2. The activity itself is by nature hazardous (for example, potentially dangerous tools are used, heavy equipment is used, toxic chemicals

are handled, employees must work at heights or in the middle of vehicular traffic);

3. The formation and operation of the activity will result in significant debts to financial institutions, lessors, vendors, etc.;

4. The activity will involve the delivery of professional services, with the resulting risk of malpractice claims;

5. The activity will involve employees whose foreseeable actions can create liabilities (for example, employees are expected to regularly use their cars in the activity);

6. The potential for product liability claims exists (for example, the products demand specialized training to operate, are inherently dangerous, or can be mishandled, with resulting injuries or property damage); and

7. The activity is potentially exposed to environmental liabilities (as is the case with almost any manufacturing or processing business and perhaps almost any activity that involves the ownership of real estate that may be contaminated or polluted or have asbestos problems, lead pipes, or lead paint).

> **OBSERVATION:** *The above list is by no means all-inclusive. Practitioners can no doubt add "liability indicators" based on their own experiences and those of clients. It's a very rare business or investment activity that does* not *expose its owners to potentially substantial liability risks.*

The most foolproof way to attempt to limit the exposure of the owners' personal assets to liabilities is with a "liability-limiting entity," such as a corporation or limited liability company. Such entities are what much of this book and the related software are all about.

2.03 THE BENEFITS OF USING LIABILITY-LIMITING ENTITIES

Corporations

Arguably, the *surest* way to minimize owner exposure to liabilities is to incorporate. The legal relationships between corporations, their shareholders, and corporate creditors are well established under existing law, as discussed in Chapter 6.

For a client whose overriding objective is protecting personal assets "to the max," the use of a corporation is probably advisable. In such cases, the choice-of-entity decision boils down to comparing C corporations to S corporations.

If the various qualification rules can be met (see Chapter 8), the S corporation is generally the better choice, because S corporations are not subject to double taxation.

As far as offering liability protection to owners, however, S corporations are no different than C corporations; an S corporation is simply a corporation created under state law that also qualifies for special federal income tax treatment.

> **OBSERVATION:** *If the business or investment activity will have only one owner, the only viable liability-limiting entity choices are C and S corporations unless state law permits single-member LLCs. See Chapter 5 for some thoughts on how to arrange to have more than one owner, and see Chapter 3 regarding single-member LLCs.*

See Chapters 6, 7, and 8 for coverage of C corporations, qualified small business corporations (a special type of C corporation that offers a potential tax benefit), and S corporations, respectively.

"Piercing the Corporate Veil"

Procedural details (such as holding directors' meetings, establishing separate bank accounts, keeping separate financial records, holding title to property) must be respected in order to establish that a corporation and its owners are actually separate entities for legal and tax purposes.

Otherwise, the existence of the corporation may be ignored, a situation referred to as "piercing the corporate veil," and the corporation's technical existence will not protect the owners from being personally responsible for the entity's debts and obligations. (The issue of piercing the corporate veil is a matter of state law.)

> **OBSERVATION:** *Some commentators feel that extensive case law effectively paints a road map on how to pierce the corporate veil, thus making corporations less effective than newer liability limiting entities such as LLCs and LLPs. Buttressing this position is the fact that LLC and LLP statutes may not require corporate-type formalities such as conducting annual meetings, keeping minutes, etc. Thus, LLCs and LLPs may afford owners fewer opportunities to trip up and thereby lose hoped-for liability protection benefits. Balancing this consideration is the fact that well-established corporate case law also paints a road map on how* not *to lose corporate liability protection advantages. In other words, if the corporate rules are scrupulously followed, there is great certainty that the existence of the corporation will in fact succeed in shielding the personal assets of its owners.*

Tortious Acts, Professional Malpractice, and Personal Guarantees

Under state law, the existence of a corporation generally will not protect a person from personal liability for his or her own tortious acts. *Tortious acts* are defined as wrongful acts leading to civil actions other than those involving breach of contract. An example of a tortious act is careless driving of a vehicle (whether or not on business) that results in injuries or property damage.

In addition, the use of a corporation generally will not protect a professional practitioner (such as a doctor, lawyer, accountant, architect) from liabilities resulting from his or her own professional errors, omissions, and acts of professional negligence or from those of other persons (such as employees) under his or her direct supervision.

Often the creditors of closely held corporations will require the owners to personally guarantee the corporation's debts. In such cases, the existence of the corporation does not change the fact that the owners are ultimately liable for the guaranteed debts.

However, the corporation generally *will* protect owners from the other liabilities that can arise in the activity, such those arising from product liabilities or the acts of employees.

Limited Partnerships

As discussed in Chapter 5, a limited partnership can be an effective way to limit the liability of owners. There are, however, two significant problems with limited partnerships:

1. At least one partner must be a general partner. General partners are exposed to unlimited personal liability for all of the limited partnership's debts and obligations. (Often, this shortcoming can be sidestepped by setting up a corporation as the general partner, but that creates additional administrative and tax compliance burdens.)

2. Limited partners cannot be actively involved in managing the limited partnership without losing their liability protection. In other words, if they become too active, they are considered general partners, despite their purported limited partner status. This precludes the use of limited partnerships in professional practices, for example, where virtually all owners are by definition active in management. (Again, this problem may be addressed by using a corporate general partner, with the corporation owned by the limited partners in proportion to their limited partnership ownership percentages. However, the existence of an additional legal entity creates administrative and tax filing burdens.)

These two factors, along with the potential complexities of partnership taxation (which "scare away" some clients), can make S corporations, C corporations, and limited liability companies seem more attractive.

> **OBSERVATION:** *If there is to be only a single owner, the use of a limited partnership is impossible, because by definition a partnership requires more than one owner. Thus, if a single-owner entity wants to limit liability, there is no viable alternative to incorporation in states that do not allow single-member LLCs. See Chapter 5 for some thoughts on how to arrange to have more than one owner, and see Chapter 3 regarding single-member LLCs.*

As is the case with a corporation, a limited partnership will afford a limited partner no protection against liabilities caused by his own actions, such as professional malpractice or tortious conduct.

Limited Liability Companies (LLCs)

Limited liability companies (LLCs)—now available in all states—combine the best attributes of S corporations and partnerships by offering:

- Liability protection to all owners (like S corporations);
- The ability to create flexible ownership and capital structures (like partnerships); and
- The ability to avoid double taxation (like both S corporations and partnerships).

Unlike the individuals in limited partnerships, all LLC owners (referred to as "members") can participate fully in the management of the entity, with no threat of losing their limited liability protection.

The negative aspects of LLCs are as follows:

- Depending on state law, certain businesses (such as professional practices and banks) may not be able to operate as LLCs; and
- They are so new that legal uncertainties remain (such as the true degree of liability protection offered in various circumstances).

The liability-limiting advantages of LLCs are discussed at length in Chapter 3.

> **OBSERVATION:** *At this time, C and S corporations still offer somewhat more assurance than LLCs that the expected benefits of limited liability for owners will be actually be realized.*

Like corporations, LLCs generally will not protect their owners from personal liability for their own tortious acts; their own professional errors, omissions, and negligence; or personally guaranteed LLC debts.

Almost all states now allow single-member LLCs, which have only one owner but provide the same liability protection advantages as multi-member LLCs. The tax treatment of single-member LLCs is favorable. Specifically, the existence of single-member LLCs is ignored for federal income tax purposes. Therefore, when a single-member LLC is owned by an individual and used to conduct a trade or business activity, the tax information will be reported on Schedule C of the individual's Form 1040. If the LLC is used to operate a rental real estate operation, the tax information will be reported on Schedule E. If the single-member LLC is owned by another legal entity, such as a corporation, a partnership, or another LLC, the tax information will be reported in the same fashion as for an unincorporated branch or division of the parent entity.

Limited Liability Partnerships (LLPs)

Limited liability partnerships (LLPs) can be an effective way for professionals to limit their exposure to liabilities related to the tortious acts, errors, omissions, and negligence of others (such as fellow partners and firm employees).

However, the significant negative feature of LLPs is that, in some states (such as Texas), the partners are jointly and severally liable (in the same fashion as general partners) for all contract liabilities of the LLP. Contract liabilities include all of the commercial debts that arise in the course of business operations, such as amounts owed to financial institutions, lessors, and vendors. From a liability-limiting perspective, in these states LLPs are clearly inferior to corporations and LLCs. However, as discussed in Chapter 4, there are still circumstances where LLPs can be the best entity choice.

In other states (such as California and New York), LLP partners are *not* personally liable for the LLP's contract liabilities unless the liabilities are expressly guaranteed by the partners. In these states, LLPs are the equal of LLCs in terms of offering the "complete package" of liability protection benefits.

Like corporations and LLCs, LLPs generally will not protect their owners from personal liability for their *own* tortious acts or their *own* professional errors, omissions, and negligence.

CHAPTER 3 • LIMITED LIABILITY COMPANIES—THE NEW GAME IN TOWN

CONTENTS

3.01 INTRODUCTION

Limited liability companies (LLCs) are increasingly popular because they can combine the best legal and tax characteristics of corporations and partnerships while avoiding many of the disadvantages associated with these more traditional ways of doing business. Specifically, an LLC can offer liability protection to all its owners (referred to as "members"), along with the advantages of being treated as a partnership for federal income tax purposes.

Although most practitioners are familiar with their advantages, until recently LLCs may have been of only theoretical interest. This was because a relatively large number of states had not enacted LLC statutes (the set of laws governing the formation and operation of LLCs). Now, however, all 50 states and the District of Columbia have laws permitting the formation and operation of LLCs within their borders.

With the growing popularity of LLCs comes recognition of the fact that it is now important for well-rounded practitioners to understand the advantages and disadvantages of the LLC format. The purpose of this chapter is to facilitate such understanding and help practitioners identify situations when LLCs should be recommended to clients.

> *CAUTION: Because there is considerable variation in state LLC statutes, the discussion of LLCs in this chapter is by necessity general and may be inconsistent with the provisions of certain LLC statutes. While this chapter conveys useful general information, practitioners should address specific client issues only after a detailed examination of the applicable LLC statute.*

Note: All states permit LLCs with more than one member (multi-member LLCs), and all but a few states now also permit LLCs with just one owner (single-member LLCs). Unless otherwise indicated, the term *LLC* will be used in this chapter to mean a multi-member LLC. Section 3.11 is devoted to the topic of single-member LLCs.

3.02 WHAT IS AN LLC?

LLCs are unincorporated legal entities created under state law. Even though LLCs are unincorporated vehicles, the fundamental intent of state LLC statutes is to allow the formation of entities that are legally more similar to corporations than to partnerships. Nevertheless, LLCs usually can be treated as partnerships for federal income tax purposes (as discussed in section 3.08 of this chapter). The critical point to remember is that, legally, LLCs are *not* corporations; nor are they partnerships.

As mentioned earlier, LLC owners are referred to as "members" rather than shareholders or partners. This is indicative of the fact that LLCs are completely distinct legal creatures that are permitted and governed by state LLC statutes.

It is probably best to address the most significant shortcomings of LLCs up front, before moving on to a more detailed analysis. From a business entity selection viewpoint, if these "threshold" negative factors are considered decisive, there is little use in spending additional time considering how LLCs work and assessing the various other pluses and minuses.

Negative Factor of Legal Uncertainty

Because LLC laws are new, inevitably there are legal uncertainties associated with making the choice to operate as an LLC rather than as a partnership or a C or S corporation.

For example, when an LLC operates in several states that all have LLC statutes, it is not always clear which LLC statute has precedence—the one in the state of formation or the one in the state where operations are conducted. Most LLC statutes provide that the LLC laws in the state of formation apply, but this may be limited to the types of businesses permitted to operate as LLCs in the state where the operations are conducted.

If an LLC will operate in several states, it is important to research the issue of which LLC statute will control (and any limitations on a general conclusion that the laws in the state of formation will control).

Even when an LLC operates only in the state of formation, the novelty of LLC statutes means there are inevitably some legal uncertainties that do not exist with more established types of entities. The LLC statutes provide legal frameworks, but these can never anticipate all the questions and issues that arise from real-life events and transactions.

In summary, LLCs have a very short legal track record. There is essentially no LLC case law. As a result, the rights and obligations of LLC members, creditors, and other third parties contracting with LLCs are not as well understood as would they would be if operations were conducted via limited or general partnerships or corporations.

For example, the legal doctrine of "piercing the corporate veil" may apply when a corporation and its shareholders conduct themselves as if they were a single entity. In other words, the corporate veil may be pierced if the corporation is thinly capitalized and/or if there is a failure to observe the formalities (such as holding meetings of the corporation's board of directors) that would establish that the corporation is indeed a separate and distinct "person" under the law. In such cases, the shareholders' personal assets may become exposed to corporate liabilities because the limited liability protection theoretically offered by the corporation is "pierced." Whether this same concept will eventually be applied to LLC members remains to be seen (however, the prudent assumption is that it will).

As LLC statutes evolve and as a base of LLC common law is established by litigation over the years, many legal uncertainties will be resolved. For now, however, it must be recognized that LLCs *do* expose their members to at least some legal risks that may be avoided with the more traditional business entities. As a result, LLCs may be unattractive to business owners who have low risk tolerances.

An alternative view espoused by some commentators is that well-established case law effectively provides a recipe for piercing the corporate veil, thus making corporations less reliable than LLCs in terms of liability protection. Supporting this outlook is the fact that some LLC statutes may explicitly obviate the need for complying with corporate-type formalities such as conducting annual meetings, keeping minutes, and so forth. Failure to observe these corporate formalities can cause shareholders to lose hoped-for liability protection benefits. Balancing this consideration is the fact that corporate case law also provides clear guidance on how *not* to lose liability protection benefits. If the corporate rules are scrupulously followed, there is great certainty that the corporation will deliver the anticipated liability protection benefits. The same may not necessarily be true for LLCs, with their virtually nonexistent legal track record.

> **RECOMMENDATION:** *The issue of legal uncertainty should be discussed explicitly with business owners considering LLCs. Too often, the advantages of LLCs are "hyped" and the disadvantages are given little or no attention. When this happens, the choice of entity decision is, for all intents and purposes, taken out of the hands of the business owners, who are the parties who should be making this decision.*

Negative Factor of LLC Statute Variations

Another negative factor is that while there is now a Uniform Limited Liability Company Act (similar to the Uniform Partnership Act (UPA) and the Revised Uniform Limited Partnership Act (RULPA), both of which have been adopted by almost all states, it has not yet been adopted by all the states. The result is considerable diversity among the states' LLC laws. Most statutes are a mixed bag of provisions derived from state business corporation acts and partnership acts.

Differences in state laws cause confusion when operations will be conducted in several states.

Negative Factor of State Tax Rules in Certain States

In a few states, LLCs are subject to entity-level state income taxes, while partnerships are not, putting LLCs comparatively at a disadvantage. (See the discussion in section 3.09 of this chapter.)

Advantages of LLC Status

LLC status has considerable advantages.

An LLC is a separate legal entity (apart from its members) that owns its assets and is liable for its debts. Therefore, the personal assets of LLC members generally are beyond the reach of LLC creditors. By the same token, the assets of the LLC generally are beyond the reach of members' creditors.

In contrast, a general partnership can be viewed as an aggregation of partners who share ownership in partnership assets and who are jointly and severally liable for all partnership debts. Even a limited partnership must have at least one general partner who is held liable for all partnership debts.

The limited liability of *all* LLC members is the fundamental *nontax* advantage of LLC status.

The key *tax* advantage of LLCs is that they can be treated as partnerships for federal income tax purposes.

Only LLCs are able to offer both the legal advantage of limited liability for all owners and the tax advantage of partnership taxation—combining pass-through treatment with maximum flexibility. This unique combination of legal and tax benefits is the driving force behind the increasing popularity of LLCs.

For summary comparisons of LLCs to other entity choices, see sections 3.13 and 3.14 of this chapter.

3.03 BUSINESSES ELIGIBLE (AND SUITABLE) TO OPERATE AS LLCs

Generally, state LLC statutes permit LLCs to conduct any lawful business or investment activity except those prohibited by the statutes themselves or those prohibited under the particular LLC's articles of organization.

Under some state laws and/or applicable professional standards (such as state bar association rules), LLCs may be prohibited from operating certain professional practices. However, when permitted, LLCs are an excellent choice. In some states, professional LLCs offer better liability protection than limited liability partnerships (LLPs), as discussed in Chapter 4. And the ability to create differing types of LLC ownership interests (for example, to reflect the activity levels of the members) can often be attractive to professional groups.

Some states do not permit the use of LLCs in certain lines of business, such as banking, insurance, and farming.

Business and investment activities where LLCs make sense include, but are not limited to the following:

- Corporate joint ventures (where the corporate co-owners desire both pass-through taxation and limited liability);

- Real estate investment and development activities (where the partnership taxation rules allow investors to receive special allocations of tax losses and obtain basis from entity-level debt);

- Oil and gas exploration (where the partnership taxation rules allow special allocations of deductions for intangible drilling costs);

- Venture capital investments (where the partnership rules allow pass-through taxation and the creation of ownership interests with varying rights to cash flow, liquidating distributions, and tax items);

- Business start-ups expected to have tax losses in the initial years (which can be passed through to investors); and

- Professional practices—if allowed under state law and applicable professional standards (where pass-through taxation can be combined with specially tailored ownership interests that reflect each member's contributions to the practice); and

- Estate-planning vehicles (where the older generation can gift LLC ownership interests to younger family members while retaining control by functioning as the managers and where all taxable income is passed through to the members).

CAUTION: Although LLC statutes place no limits on the number of members, there is a tax problem if ownership interests are so widely held that they are "publicly traded" within the meaning of IRC §7704. If an LLC's ownership interests are publicly traded, the LLC will be treated as a C corporation for federal income tax purposes.

Because LLCs allow all members to participate fully in management without risk of losing limited liability protection (which can happen with a limited partnership; see section 3.06 of this chapter), they are ideal for many closely held entrepreneurial businesses.

According to a survey published in the December 1995 issue of *Journal of Accountancy*, the top 10 types of businesses actually operated as LLCs are:

- Engineering and management support services (26%),
- Real estate services (19%),
- Construction and general contracting (12%),
- Investment companies (9%),
- Retailers (8%),
- Health services (7%),
- Agriculture (7%),
- Oil and gas extraction (2%),
- Restaurants (2%), and
- Leasing companies (2%).

Most advisors agree that the LLC is the best entity alternative if pass-through taxation is desired (such as with a service business where there is no need to retain significant amounts of earnings within the business entity). As would be expected, empirical evidence shows that LLCs are seldom formed to operate capital-intensive and high-growth businesses, such as manufacturing and high tech ventures. Such businesses typically need to retain all earnings to finance capital expenditures and growing receivable and inventory levels. These businesses are most often operated as C corporations in order to maximize cash flow by minimizing current outlays for federal income taxes.

In summary, LLCs may be the best choice for business and investment ventures in the following circumstances:

- There will be more than one owner;
- Limited liability protection for the co-owners is an important consideration;
- Pass-through taxation is desired;
- The advantages of partnership taxation are significant compared to the alternative of S corporation taxation, or the entity cannot qualify for S corporation status (see section 3.09 of this chapter);
- The business or investment activity can be operated as an LLC under state law and applicable professional standards; and
- The co-owners can tolerate the uncertainties of LLC status and the fact that the LLC may not have an unlimited legal life or free transferability of ownership interests.

3.04 NAME OF THE LLC

State LLC statutes require the use of specific words in the names of entities operating as LLCs. For example, the statute may require that the name of every LLC include "limited liability company" or "LLC." This puts creditors and other third parties on notice that the entity they are dealing with has limits on the liability exposure of its owners. LLCs may also be required to comply with statutes dealing with assumed or fictitious names.

If the LLC fails to use its exact name in its business dealings, the result may be joint and several liability exposure for the members—similar to that of general partners.

3.05 FUNDAMENTAL FORMATION AND OPERATING ISSUES

Articles of Organization

LLCs are formed under the laws of a particular state by filing "articles of organization" with a state official, usually the Secretary of State.

The articles of organization of an LLC are similar to the articles of incorporation of a corporation. The document will include, at a minimum, the LLC's name, registered agent, registered office, and such other information as may be required under the statute.

Generally, the LLC's registered agent must reside in the state of organization and have a street address. In many cases, law firms and commercial services with offices in each state are employed as the registered agents of LLCs.

Other required information in the articles of organization may include the identities and addresses of the initial organizers, the LLC's purpose (for example, "to engage in any lawful business permitted under the LLC statute" or "to engage in real estate acquisition, investment, and development"), and whether the LLC will be managed by all members or by designated managers.

See Appendix 3D for a checklist of items appropriately included in an LLC's articles of organization, and see Appendix 3E for a sample organization document.

Operating Agreement

In addition to drafting articles of organization, the LLC usually will draft an "operating agreement." The operating agreement is a separate contractual arrangement among the members and in some states may be called "regulations" or "limited liability company agreements." An LLC operating agreement is similar to the partnership agreement of a limited or general partnership or the bylaws of a corporation.

Taken together, the LLC's articles of organization and operating agreement are often referred to as the "governing documents."

A thoughtfully drafted operating agreement will include provisions regarding issues such as how votes are conducted, the members' required contributions of cash and/or property, sharing ratios for operating profits and losses and nonrecurring gains and losses, sharing ratios for current and liquidating distributions, allocations of tax items, rights of members to transfer their ownership interests, rights of members when they withdraw from the LLC, and events causing dissolution or winding up of the LLC.

LLC statutes generally provide for the possibility that an operating agreement will *not* exist in written or oral form. In such case, the statutes supply so-called "default" language specifying the contractual relationships between the members. The default rules cover basic issues such as how the LLC is managed, rights of members to profits and distributions, restrictions on transfers of ownership interests, and events causing dissolution of the LLC.

> **CAUTION:** *Unless an operating agreement exists to override statutory default provisions, they will apply. Because these default provisions are necessarily general in nature, they will be inadequate to deal satisfactorily with many of the "real life" situations and problems that inevitably arise. For example, it is unrealistic to expect statutory default language to deal satisfactorily with an LLC operating primarily as an investment vehicle (similar in function to a limited*

*partnership) and an LLC formed by three entrepreneurs to operate a manufactur-
ing business (that would probably be operated as an S corporation if LLCs did not
exist). A written operating agreement that contemplates the unique aspects of the
business at hand and the specific needs of the various members is highly advisable.*

State LLC statutes include certain mandatory provisions that cannot be modified by agreement among the members. For example, the statute may be inflexible regarding the member consents required for transfers of LLC ownership interests. LLC statutes also include certain provisions to protect creditors. For example, members generally are required to make all agreed-upon contributions to LLCs, and LLCs generally are prohibited from making distributions that would cause insolvency.

Some statutes include mandatory provisions that were originally intended to ensure that LLCs would be treated as partnerships for federal income tax purposes. (See discussion of these so-called "bulletproof" statutes in section 3.08 of this chapter.)

Notwithstanding the existence of such mandatory statutory provisions, members usually can customize their operating agreements to meet most objectives. However, it is still necessary to adequately understand what is permitted and what is prohibited by the applicable LLC statute in order to draft an operating agreement that complies with the law. (Provisions that do not comply will be unenforceable.)

See Appendix 3G for a sample operating agreement.

Picking the State of Organization

As stated earlier, LLC statutes vary significantly among the states. When all activities will be conducted in a single state, it is easy enough to pick the state of organization. However, the same is not true when there will be multi-state operations.

Before filing the LLC's articles of organization, differences in laws among the state of organization and state(s) of operation should be considered. Specifically, variations in the following areas should be carefully studied:

- Management and voting provisions;

- Rights of members upon withdrawal from the LLC (generally, it is desirable for the LLC to be able to limit withdrawals and avoid requirements to immediately pay withdrawing members for their ownership interests); and

- Whether the statute includes "bulletproof" provisions originally intended to ensure partnership tax treatment for federal income tax purposes.

OBSERVATION: *The check-the-box federal income tax entity classification
regulations now ensure partnership tax treatment for **all** multi-member LLCs. As
a result, some provisions in "bulletproof" statutes may be viewed as unfavorable,*

because they place what are now unnecessary limits on LLCs and their members. For example, a bulletproof statute will place significant restrictions on the ability of members to transfer LLC ownership interests.

Member Contributions in Exchange for Ownership Interests

Most state LLC statutes allow the contribution of virtually anything of value in exchange for an LLC ownership interest. Theoretically, a contribution could be as amorphous as a promise to provide future services to the LLC or the granting of the right for the LLC to use (but not own) property. However, several states limit contributions to cash or property, and several prohibit the receipt of ownership interests in exchange for promissory notes or promises to provide future services.

Contributions in exchange for LLC ownership interests are often referred to as "capital contributions," and they may or may not be evidenced by the issuance of certificates of ownership interest (similar to shares of stock). Generally, LLCs can issue such certificates, but this is not required. In any case, contributions should be documented by maintaining member capital accounts as part of the LLC's books and records.

Members generally are liable to the LLC (and in effect to the LLC's creditors) for any capital contribution requirements that were agreed to but that remain unsatisfied.

Other Steps in the LLC Formation Phase

Beyond filing the articles of organization and drafting the operating agreement (in a manner to ensure treatment as a partnership for federal income tax purposes), the other steps needed to establish an LLC are similar to those for setting up a corporation or a partnership. These steps generally include:

- Opening a bank account in the LLC's name;
- Transferring title to any contributed assets to be owned by the newly formed LLC;
- Obtaining liability, property, business interruption, and worker's compensation insurance coverage;
- Obtaining federal and state employer ID numbers (also used for income tax purposes);
- Establishing accounting and payroll tax withholding and payment procedures;
- Registering with states and localities for collection of sales taxes, and obtaining all required business licenses and permits; and
- Registering to do business as an LLC in foreign states (those other than the state of organization), as discussed later in this section.

Ownership of Property

Under the LLC statutes, property is owned by the LLC rather than by its members. It is this legal fact that makes LLC assets unavailable to satisfy any legal claims against LLC members. This is similar to the circumstances surrounding ownership of property by a corporation or a limited partnership.

However, as discussed later in this section (under the subheading "LLC Ownership Interests"), a member's creditors may become entitled to certain rights with respect to that member's ownership interest.

Management of the LLC

Members generally can choose to manage the LLC themselves or appoint one or more "managers." If the members reserve all management powers for themselves, the LLC is run more or less like a general partnership. Such LLCs are often described as "member-managed."

Most LLC statutes provide default language calling for member management unless managers are stipulated in the articles of organization or operating agreement. If the members appoint managers who are also members, the arrangement resembles a limited partnership run by its general partners.

Managers generally can be nonmembers as well, except that some LLC statutes require the managers of professional LLCs to be members. LLCs run by managers are often described as "manager-managed."

Manager-Managed LLCs

When the LLC is manager-managed, the nonmanager LLC members generally have very limited management rights, similar to those of corporate shareholders. In other words, their management rights usually are limited to voting for or against the existing or proposed managers and voting on certain major decisions, such as whether to sell substantially all the LLC's assets.

Although managers generally can be removed at will and without cause, this is difficult as a practical matter unless formalized election and removal procedures are set forth in the operating agreement.

Most statutes provide for election of managers based on a majority vote of the members or on a majority-of-interest vote. However, different voting rules than these usually can be established in the operating agreement.

> **RECOMMENDATION:** *To the extent allowed by statute, the operating agreement of a manager-managed LLC should be drafted thoughtfully with regard to the ability of the members to elect, authorize the actions of, and remove managers. Members may wish to specifically reserve the right to vote on certain issues, such a decisions to sell substantially all the assets of the LLC, liquidate the LLC, or amend the operating agreement.*

Member-Managed LLCs

With member-managed LLCs, perhaps the most critical management concerns relate to voting. The state LLC statute and the operating agreement together determine which matters must come to a vote, what degree of voting approval (majority, supermajority, or unanimous) is required to take certain actions, and how votes are counted (one vote per member, or based on members' relative ownership interest percentages).

For example, the basic voting rule may be as follows: A unanimous vote is required to amend the operating agreement or authorize an action prohibited under the terms of the operating agreement, but only a majority of interest vote (based on relative ownership percentages) is needed to conclude on other business matters.

Generally, the statutes provide voting rules. But these usually can be overridden by providing different rules in the operating agreement.

Authority of Members and Managers to Legally Bind the LLC

Under most LLC statutes, any member of a member-managed LLC has authority to legally bind the LLC in ordinary business transactions with third parties (for example, a property lease). However, the LLC generally is not bound if the member has no actual authority to engage in the transaction and the third party knows this. This is similar to the authority of a general partner to bind a partnership.

Generally, the rules described in the preceding paragraph apply to managers of a manager-managed LLC as well. The members of a manager-managed LLC may include certain restrictions in the operating agreement in an attempt to restrain the managers' ability to legally bind the LLC. However, such restrictions may be ineffective with regard to third parties who have no knowledge of the restrictions and who contract with an LLC manager in transactions that are apparently in the ordinary course of business.

Generally, the nonmanager members of a manager-managed LLC do not have authority to bind the LLC.

LLC Ownership Interests

As stated earlier, the owners of the LLC are called "members." They are analogous to partners of a partnership or shareholders of a corporation.

LLC ownership interests (sometimes referred to as "membership interests") comprise financial interests in capital, profits, contributions, distributions, and pass-through allocations of tax items. In addition, LLC ownership interests have a nonfinancial component in the form of rights to participate in management or vote on certain management issues.

Ability to Transfer Ownership Interests

Generally, LLC members can treat their financial interests in the LLC as personal property and can assign these interests to others, unless the operating agreement states otherwise.

The members will likely have significant restrictions on their ability to transfer management or voting rights to nonmembers without obtaining the consents specified in the statute and/or operating agreement. Some LLC statutes require that transfers be approved unanimously by the nontransferring members unless the operating agreement provides different rules. Other states require less than unanimous consent for such transfers. Statutory consent requirements usually can be modified by the LLC's governing documents.

Until proper member consent is obtained (in compliance with the statute and/or operating agreement), the transferee generally does not become a full-fledged member entitled to all rights of membership (including the right to vote, the right to withdraw from the LLC, and the right to be paid for one's ownership interest).

In other words, until full membership is attained through the consent of the other members, the transferee is entitled to step into the financial shoes of the transferor member only with regard to his or her share of capital, profits, etc.

Evidence of Ownership

Ownership interests may or may not be evidenced by the issuance of LLC ownership interest certificates. State laws generally permit but do not require it. While the issuance of certificates may be desirable from a recordkeeping standpoint, it may increase the likelihood that the interests will be considered securities (see discussion below).

> *RECOMMENDATION: If LLC ownership interest certificates are issued, they should include legends (similar to those used with restricted stock) stating that ownership cannot be transferred without the consents specified in the LLC's governing documents.*

Creditors' Rights

Generally, LLC members can assign or pledge (use as security for borrowings) their LLC ownership interests. Upon foreclosure, a creditor will acquire only the financial interest component of the ownership interest, unless the creditor is voted in as a full LLC member.

Under state law, an unsecured creditor of an LLC member may be able to obtain a charging order against the LLC ownership interest. A charging order generally gives the creditor the same financial rights (such as the right to receive distributions) as the member. But it does not convey full membership in the LLC (which includes the right to vote, etc.).

Are LLC Ownership Interests Securities?

If LLC ownership interests are deemed securities under federal or state law, there are a number of negative implications. Securities generally must be registered before they can be sold, sellers of securities are subject to laws and regulations covering securities dealers, state "blue sky" laws may have to be complied with, etc.

The question of whether LLC ownership interests can be securities is unclear. However, it is fair to say the ownership interests of some manager-managed LLCs with relatively large numbers of members probably meet the definition. Ownership interests of relatively small, closely held, member-managed LLCs are very unlikely to be considered securities.

However, the issue of whether the ownership interests of a particular LLC are securities should be analyzed by competent legal counsel.

Qualifying to Do Business Outside the LLC's State of Formation

Foreign LLCs (those organized in a state other than the state(s) in which operations are conducted) generally are required to register (or "qualify to do business") in each state. This process includes naming a registered agent in each state.

The definition of "doing business" varies from state to state. The foreign LLC registration requirements also vary and are specified in the various LLC statutes.

Of course, failure to register has consequences that vary by state. For example, an unregistered LLC may be subject to penalties and fines, may (if discovered) lose the right to do further business in that state, and may lose the right to file lawsuits (which can effectively void contracts formed in that state).

Generally, however, failure of a foreign LLC to register to do business will *not* result in loss of limited liability protection for the members of the LLC.

3.06 LIABILITY OF LLC MEMBERS AND MANAGERS

As stated earlier, LLCs offer the advantageous corporate characteristic of limiting the exposure of members and managers to entity-level liabilities. This is a fundamental reason for considering the LLC as a form of doing business.

Specifically, status as an LLC member or manager does not in and of itself expose the member or manager to any risk of personal financial loss beyond the value of the LLC ownership interest, plus any unfulfilled capital contribution obligations. (Nonmember managers are not exposed even to that risk.) However, members generally are liable for distributions made to them that cause the LLC to become insolvent. These rules are analogous to laws covering corporate shareholders and limited partners.

If the LLC's articles of organization are not properly filed with state authorities, the persons purportedly conducting activities as an LLC may be exposed to third-party liabilities.

> **RECOMMENDATION:** *As stated earlier, LLC statutes provide that members and managers are not liable for LLC debts and obligations just because they are members and/or managers. Nevertheless, it is advisable for members and managers to follow certain guidelines when conducting the LLC's business. Specifically, when LLC members or managers sign contracts on behalf of the LLC, the LLC should be clearly identified as the contracting party, and the exact name of the LLC should be used (see section 3.04 of this chapter). The person signing the contract should be clearly designated as a member or manager signing on behalf of the LLC and not personally.*

Liability Exposure of LLC Members Compared to Limited Partners

With regard to the issue of liability, LLCs possess two significant advantages over limited partnerships.

First, a limited partnership must have at least one general partner with unlimited exposure to partnership liabilities. This problem can be addressed by forming a corporate general partner (usually an S corporation owned by the limited partners), which effectively "stops the bleeding" because the amount the general partner can lose is limited to the value of the assets held by the corporation. But, setting up and maintaining another entity for this purpose creates an administrative burden. (See the discussion of limited partnerships in Chapter 5.)

In an LLC, however, *no* member need be exposed to *any* LLC liabilities.

Second, a limited partner can lose his or her limited liability protection by becoming too actively involved in managing the limited partnership. As a result, limited partnerships are not suitable for certain activities, such as the practice of a profession where all partners are virtually by definition heavily involved in the business. Again, this issue can be addressed by using a corporate general partner, with the corporation owned by the limited partners in proportion to their limited partnership ownership percentages. Again, however, the existence of an additional legal entity creates administrative and tax filing headaches. State limited partnership laws based on the Revised Uniform Limited Partnership Act also give some relief by specifying a number of actions that limited partners can take *without* being deemed to participate in management. Nevertheless, the issue is always lurking in the background for limited partnerships and their partners.

For the LLC, this issue is simply not a concern. Members can have any degree of management involvement without risking loss of their limited liability protection.

Liability for Tortious Acts, Errors, Omissions, and Negligence

The liability-limiting advantages of LLCs are critically important, but they should not be overstated. While the personal assets of LLC members and managers are protected from "general" LLC debts and obligations (often referred to as "contract liabilities"), these persons generally remain *exposed* to LLC liabilities resulting from their own tortious acts and their own professional errors and omissions.

Tortious acts are defined as wrongful acts leading to civil actions, other than those involving breach of contract. (Examples of tortious acts include professional malpractice and negligent driving of an auto resulting in injuries and property damage.)

In addition, under state law an LLC member or manager may be personally liable for the professional negligence of another person who is supervised (or should have been supervised) by the member or manager.

In short, LLCs generally do *not* offer liability protection to members and managers beyond what corporations are able to offer to their shareholders.

> *RECOMMENDATION: The issue of members' and managers' exposure to these types of liabilities is a matter of state law. The practitioner should research it carefully before answering specific client questions.*

> *CAUTION: The assets of the LLC are always fully exposed to liabilities and claims resulting from the LLC's business activities. Thus, members are always exposed to the risk that their shares of LLC capital may be lost as a result of a catastrophic event or a judgment against the LLC.*

Example 3.06(1): Professional Malpractice and Negligence Assume an LLC is used to operate a professional practice. The LLC itself generally is primarily liable for professional malpractice and negligence on the part of its members, managers, and employees.

However, the members and managers generally are *also* personally liable for damages caused by their own professional malpractice or negligence and for their own negligence in directly supervising other professionals (who may be members, managers, or employees).

A claimant generally can move first against the assets of the LLC. If those assets are insufficient to satisfy the judgment, the claimant can then move against the personal assets of the "guilty" member or manager.

The key point is that the assets of the LLC (and the capital of the "innocent" members) can be wiped out by a liability resulting from the tortious acts, errors, omissions, or negligence of any one of the LLC's members, managers, or employees.

Example 3.06(2): Tortious Act by a Member An LLC member uses his car on LLC business and becomes involved in a serious accident that causes injuries and property damage. The LLC may be secondarily liable for the damages, but the member will also be personally liable for this tortious act.

The injured parties generally can attempt to recover first from the "guilty" member's personal assets. The claimants can then pursue the LLC's assets.

Guarantees of LLC Debts

Like corporate shareholders, LLC members may be required on occasion to personally guarantee certain of the entity's debts as a condition of obtaining financing or for other reasons. Members are personally obligated with respect to LLC debts that are specifically guaranteed.

Summary

LLC members and managers are in the favorable position of generally being insulated from exposure to entity-level debts (unless they have personally guaranteed those debts) and liabilities resulting from tortious acts, omissions, and negligence of other LLC members, managers, or employees.

However, with regard to the issue of liability for tortious acts, omissions, and negligence the preceding statement is a generalization. State laws and regulations should be researched, especially if the business will be the conduct of a professional practice.

3.07 WITHDRAWAL OF LLC MEMBERS AND DISSOLUTION OF LLCs

Withdrawal and Disassociation of LLC Members

LLC members generally have the right to voluntarily withdraw (which may be referred to as "resignation" or "retirement") from the LLC and receive some form of payment for their ownership interests. Members' voluntary withdrawal rights are controlled by the terms of the operating agreement and/or the state LLC statute. The amount and timing of payments owed to withdrawing members can vary considerably.

Under the various statutes, voluntary withdrawal may be conditioned upon a member giving proper notice or the occurrence of certain events. The operating agreement may impose limitations on the ability of members to voluntarily withdraw. From financial and management standpoints, such limitations may be desirable if the LLC does not hold sufficient liquid assets to pay withdrawing members for their ownership interests.

Disassociation of an LLC member can occur for reasons beyond voluntary withdrawal—for example, as a result of a member's death, insanity, bankruptcy, expulsion, or other events specified in the operating agreement. Like voluntary withdrawals, these other forms of disassociation ("dissolution events") will also generally terminate the legal existence of the LLC unless the remaining members vote to continue. Under the state statutes, disassociating members generally are entitled to some form of payment for their ownership interests.

For federal income tax purposes, LLCs are deemed to continue in existence after dissolution events unless they result in a change in ownership of 50% or more of the capital and profits interests within a 12-month period. [See IRC §708(b)(1)(B).] See section 3.09 of this chapter for additional discussion of IRC §708 "technical terminations."

> **RECOMMENDATION:** *The operating agreement should specify the methodology that will be used to value the ownership interests of withdrawing or disassociating members. In addition, the operating agreement can specify payment terms (to the extent they do not contradict the statute), such as installment payments or payment with noncash property distributions. In other words, payment terms should be structured to ensure that required payments to withdrawing or disassociating members will not cripple the LLC's ability to continue operations.*

> **CAUTION:** *After the withdrawal or disassociation of one or more members, at least two members generally must remain for the LLC to continue to be treated as a partnership for federal income tax purposes.*

Dissolution of the LLC

As discussed above, LLCs are considered to legally dissolve upon the occurrence of certain events, such as the retirement, resignation, expulsion, death (or legal dissolution), or bankruptcy of a member. However, the remaining members generally can vote to continue the existence of the LLC after such dissolution events.

Also as discussed above, for federal income tax purposes, LLCs are deemed to continue to exist after dissolution events unless they result in a "technical termination" resulting from a change in ownership of 50% or more of the capital and profits interests within a 12-month period.

Most LLC statutes also allow dissolution upon the unanimous written consent of the members.

In addition, the LLC's articles of organization or operating agreement may call for dissolution as of a fixed date, after a designated number of years of existence, or after the attainment of a stated business goal (such as the development, leasing, and sale of a real estate project).

In other words, LLCs have limited legal life spans that end upon the occurrence of specified events, many of which are in the nature of events affecting the LLC members rather than the LLC itself. This is not the case for corporations, whose legal lives continue indefinitely regardless of the fates of their shareholders.

If the decision is made to dissolve (or "liquidate") the LLC (because the members fail to vote to continue or because the business of the LLC is to be wound up), certain formalities must be observed. The LLC generally must file papers with the Secretary of State of the state in which the LLC was organized. In addition, state law may require the LLC to give public notice so that its creditors and other third parties are aware of the impending dissolution.

After dissolution, the LLC continues to exist long enough to wind up its affairs. Assets are sold, the LLC's creditors are paid off, and any remaining assets are distributed to the members in liquidation of their ownership interests.

> **RECOMMENDATION:** *The operating agreement should provide for the possibility that the LLC may hold illiquid assets (such as real estate or nonpublicly traded securities) that will be distributed to members upon dissolution. The composition of the LLC's assets may be such that some members will receive only liquid assets, some will receive only illiquid assets, and some may receive a mixture. The critical issue in such cases is how to value the illiquid assets, so that all members will receive distributed property with the proper value. The operating agreement can specify valuation methods to prevent disputes upon dissolution.*

3.08 CLASSIFICATION AS A PARTNERSHIP FOR TAX PURPOSES

The attractiveness of multi-member LLCs is critically dependent on their classification as partnerships for federal income tax purposes. However, partnership classification was not automatic under the former entity classification regulations (former Regs. §301.7701-1 through -3). Under the former rules, an unincorporated entity—such as an LLC—could *not* be classified as a partnership if it possessed more than two of the following four corporate attributes:

1. Limited liability,
2. Centralized management,
3. Continuity of life, and
4. Free transferability of ownership interests.

If more than two of these attributes *were* present, the entity was treated as an association taxable as a corporation for federal income tax purposes, regardless of its status under state law. Under the former regulations, limited partnerships also had to meet the specific requirements of Revenue Procedure 89-12 (1989-1 CB 319) to be assured of partnership tax status and LLCs had to meet the specific requirements of Revenue Procedure 95-10 (1995-1 CB 501). Meeting these rules was more of an art than a science, and as a result, there was often at least some uncertainty that partnership status would be sustained in the event of IRS scrutiny.

Fortunately, this situation was rectified with the release of final "check-the-box" entity classification regulations (current Regs. §301.7701-1 through -3) in December 1996. The check-the-box regulations became effective on January 1, 1997, and superseded the former entity classification regulations on that date.

Summary of the Check-the-Box Regulations

Under the check-the-box rules, unincorporated entities with more than one owner (such as LLCs, LLPs, and limited partnerships) generally are classified as partnerships by default. The default tax treatment of single-owner unincorporated entities (such as single-member LLCs) is that generally they are ignored for federal income tax purposes. For example, a single-member LLC engaged in a trade or business and owned by an individual would be treated as a sole proprietorship.

The check-the-box regulations apply only to "business entities." These are entities that are recognized for federal tax purposes and are not properly classified as a trust or are not subject to other special classification rules under the Internal Revenue Code.

Determining Whether a Separate Tax Entity Exists

As was the case under the former regulations, the first step in the entity classification process is to decide if there is a separate entity for tax purposes. This is a matter of federal income tax law rather than state law, and the preexisting tax rules in this area were *not* affected by the check-the-box provisions.

To illustrate this issue, consider corporate joint ventures and real estate cotenancies. In some cases, these arrangements may not be considered separate entities apart from their owners under state law. However, they *may* be treated as separate entities for federal income tax purposes. Regulations §301.7701-4 covers entities classified as trusts.

Per Se Corporations

Some entities are automatically treated as corporations under the regulations and are therefore ineligible for check-the-box treatment, which applies only to *un*incorporated entities. Per se corporations are treated as C corporations unless they qualify for S status and make the S election (see Chapter 8). Per se corporations include the following:

1. Business entities organized as corporations under a federal or state statute or under a statute of a federally recognized Indian tribe;
2. Business entities that are joint stock companies or joint stock associations organized under a state statute;
3. Business entities taxable as insurance companies under Subchapter L, Chapter 1, of the Internal Revenue Code;

4. State chartered business entities conducting banking activities, if any deposits are insured under the Federal Deposit Insurance Act, as amended, or a similar federal statute;

5. Business entities wholly owned by a state or any political subdivision thereof;

6. Business entities formed in foreign jurisdictions or certain U.S. possessions, territories, or commonwealths and specifically listed in the regulations (subject to the special transition rule explained below for existing entities that claimed noncorporate status on May 8, 1996); and

7. Business entities taxable as corporations under a provision of the Internal Revenue Code *other* than §7701(a)(3) (the association taxable as a corporation rule).

Foreign entities treated as per se corporations include the Australian Public Limited Company, Canadian Corporation, German Aktiengesellschaft, Japanese Kabushiki Kaisha, and Mexican Sociedad Anonima. Regulations §301.7701-2(b) sets forth the complete list.

Entities treated as per se corporations under Internal Revenue Code sections other than §7701(a)(3) include publicly traded partnerships (§7704), taxable mortgage pools [§7701(i)], and REITs [§856(c)]. Tax-exempt entities generally are classified as corporations or trusts under §501(c) or §401(a). Entities covered by these other Internal Revenue Code provisions are *unaffected* by the check-the-box regulations.

Entities Eligible for Check-the-Box Rules

Unincorporated entities that are omitted from the per se corporation list, such as LLCs, *are* eligible for check-the-box treatment and are referred to in the regulations as "eligible entities." Eligible entities can be treated as:

1. Partnerships if they have more than one owner (this is the default treatment);

2. Not existing for tax purposes if they have only a single owner (default treatment), as in the case of single-member LLCs (see section 3.11);

3. Associations taxable as C corporations if they so elect (usually undesirable because of the double taxation issue explained in Chapter 6); or

4. Associations taxable as S corporations if the entity elects to be treated as a corporation, meets the requirements for making the S election [see Regs. §1.1361-1(c)], and makes an S election (the S corporation qualification requirements are covered in Chapter 8).

Eligible Entities with More than One Owner

Under the check-the-box regulations, a domestic organization (formed under U.S. laws) with at least two owners that is *not* treated as a per se corporation is a partnership by default. In other words, such eligible entities will be treated as partnerships unless:

1. They *elect* to be classified as associations taxable as corporations, or
2. They *"elect out"* of Subchapter K pursuant to Regs. §1.761-2 (which is unaffected by the check-the-box rules).

This regulatory scheme provides the greatest benefits to LLCs and limited partnerships. Both could sometimes wind up being classified as associations taxable as corporations under the former entity classification regulations.

Foreign Eligible Entities

Foreign entities *not* treated as per se corporations are also eligible for favorable tax classification rules.

If any member of a foreign eligible entity with two or more members has personal liability for some or all of the organization's debts, the default classification is as a partnership. If the entity has only one member, the default result is that the organization is disregarded as a separate entity.

If there are at least two members and all members have limited liability, the default classification will be as an association taxable as a corporation. However, these entities can still elect to be treated as partnerships by making an affirmative election of partnership status.

If there is only a single owner with limited liability, the default classification is as an association taxable as a corporation. However, these organizations can elect to be disregarded for tax purposes by making an affirmative election to that effect.

Note that the above treatment applies only to eligible foreign entities. Foreign entities treated as per se corporations are ineligible for the check-the-box rules *unless* they are existing entities eligible to be treated as partnerships under the special transition rule explained below.

Transition Rules for Existing Domestic Entities

Domestic eligible entities in existence as of January 1, 1997, generally can retain their existing noncorporate tax status by default. A special transition rule applies to existing eligible single-owner entities that claimed partnership status under the former entity classification regulations. These entities are classified by default as entities that are disregarded for tax purposes, rather than as partnerships.

In the regulations, the IRS states that generally it will *not* challenge an existing domestic eligible entity's claimed tax status for periods prior to January 1, 1997, *if*:

1. There was a reasonable basis (within the meaning of §6662) for the claimed noncorporate classification;

2. The entity and all its members properly recognized any federal tax consequences resulting from any change in claimed tax classification within 60 months prior to January 1, 1997 (such as the deemed liquidation treatment that applies when an entity classified as a corporation converts to LLC status); and

3. Neither the entity nor any member had been notified in writing on or before May 8, 1996, that the issue of classification of the entity was under examination by the IRS (in which case the tax classification issue will be resolved as part of the audit process).

Existing eligible entities can also *change* their classification, by making an affirmative check-the-box election in the manner explained below.

Transition Rules for Existing Foreign Entities

There is a special transition rule for *foreign* entities in existence as of January 1, 1997, that now are classified as per se corporations under the check-the-box regulations. The foreign entity can retain its existing noncorporate classification *if*:

1. It was in existence and claimed to be a partnership, sole proprietorship, or unincorporated branch or division on May 8, 1996;

2. As of May 8, 1996, the entity's existing classification was relevant in determining the federal income tax liabilities of any person (such as one of the owners);

3. No person treated the entity as a corporation for the taxable year that includes May 8, 1996;

4. No changes in the classification of the entity occurred within the 60-month period preceding May 8, 1996, except in response to changes in the entity's governing documents (with any federal tax consequences of such changes properly recognized);

5. As of May 8, 1996, the entity had a reasonable basis (within the meaning of §6662) for claiming noncorporate status; and

6. Neither the entity nor any member had been notified in writing on or before May 8, 1996, that the issue of classification of the entity was under examination by the IRS (in which case the tax classification issue will be resolved as part of the audit).

Foreign single-owner entities that qualify for the above transition rule and that previously claimed partnership status are classified by default as entities that are disregarded for tax purposes, rather than as partnerships.

Apparently, existing foreign entities that qualify for the above transition rule are covered for pre-1997 periods by the same rules that apply to existing domestic eligible entities. In other words, such entities could retain their noncorporate tax status for pre-1997 and post-1996 periods even though they now appear on the per se corporation list.

How to Make Affirmative Check-the-box Elections

If a domestic or foreign eligible entity's default classification is acceptable, nothing need be done. The default classification automatically applies, and no affirmative election is necessary.

An eligible entity wishing to elect a classification *different* from its default classification or wishing to *change* its current classification must make an affirmative check-the-box election to do so.

An affirmative election is made by filing Form 8832 (Entity Classification Election) with the designated IRS Service Center and with the entity's tax return for the year the election is made.

Generally, the effective date of the election will be the date specified on Form 8832. However, the effective date cannot be more than 75 days prior to the election filing date or more than 12 months after the election filing date. If Form 8832 does not specify a date, the effective date is the election filing date.

Form 8832 must be signed by each owner of the entity—or by an authorized officer, manager, or member if this is permitted under local law. A second check-the-box election cannot be made within 60 months after the first election. However, the waiting period is waived for existing entities that change their classification effective January 1, 1997. Existing entities can retain their current employer identification numbers.

Check-the-Box Pitfalls and Planning Opportunities

The preamble to the check-the-box regulations makes it clear that the new entity classification rules do *not* alter existing rules regarding the tax outcomes of changes in classification. For example, many corporations would find the tax results of changing to LLC or partnership status extremely unfavorable. Such entity switches are treated as taxable corporate liquidations. The effects of corporate entity switches are covered at length in Chapters 3, 4, and 5.

Tax advisors should also be aware that some states may fail to accept the check-the-box classification scheme for state tax purposes. Thus, the analysis of the four corporate characteristics may remain relevant in certain states. This raises the unpleasant possibility that an LLC could be treated as a partnership for federal income tax purposes and as a corporation for state tax purposes because it possesses more than two of the corporate attributes.

Finally, although theoretically there are no limits on the number of partners in a partnership or members in an LLC, there is a big tax problem if the entity's ownership interests are so widely held that they are "publicly traded" within the meaning of §7704. If ownership interests *are* publicly traded, the entity will be treated as a C corporation for federal income tax purposes. The publicly traded partnership issue is rarely a problem for LLCs, but it can be an issue for large limited partnerships. (See §7704, Regs. §1.7704-1, and Chapter 5.) The check-the-box regulations have no impact on the potential application of §7704.

On the plus side of the ledger, before the check-the-box regulations came into being, many LLC operating agreements and limited partnership agreements included restrictive provisions solely to ensure partnership tax status. If the owners wish (and to the extent allowed under state law), these can now be removed without undermining the partnership status of the entity.

Examples of restrictive provisions that may now be viewed as undesirable include language causing legal termination of the entity upon the death, insanity, etc., of a member or general partner (previously necessary to avoid the corporate attribute of continuity of life), limits on the transferability of ownership interests (previously necessary to avoid the corporate attribute of free transferability), and corporate general partner net worth requirements (previously necessary for limited partnerships to avoid the corporate attribute of limited liability for all members).

"Bulletproof" State LLC Statutes

All state LLC statutes clearly intend for LLCs to be eligible for partnership tax classification. Unfortunately, drafting LLC articles of organization and operating agreements in conformity with some statutes did not *ensure* partnership classification under former Regs. §301.7701-1 through -3.

However, there *are* several state LLC statutes that, if followed, automatically resulted in partnership classification. These laws, often referred to "bulletproof" statutes, generally are worded such that LLCs cannot possess the corporate attributes of continuity of life or free transferability of ownership interests. LLCs formed under these statutes are "bulletproof." They would by definition qualify as partnerships under the former regulations, because they could not possess more than two of the four corporate attributes.

State-Law Conformity with Check-the-Box Rules

Most states have formally or informally indicated they will follow the federal check-the-box entity classification rules for state tax law classification purposes. However, this should not be taken for granted. In classifying LLCs with more than one member, some states may eventually decide to retain the four-factor analysis embodied in former Regs. §301.7701-1 through -3. And some states could decide to tax single-member LLCs as corporations.

If there will be a discrepancy between the classification of the LLC for federal and state tax law purposes, this should be evaluated as part of the choice of entity decision process.

In addition, while it's likely that only a few states will impose any entity-level taxes on single-member LLCs, they may still be subject to separate state tax return or form filing requirements, even though no separate federal returns are required.

3.09 TAXATION OF LLCs IN GENERAL

Introduction

The tax advantage of operating as a multi-member LLC is that the entity can be treated as a partnership for federal income tax purposes.

The following discussion assumes that the LLC is classified as a partnership for federal income tax purposes.

The partnership tax provisions are found in Internal Revenue Code Subchapter K, which encompasses IRC §§701–777. The tax rules for partnerships are considered much more favorable than those for C corporations, because partnerships are subject to only a single level of federal income tax under the principles of pass-through taxation.

> *CAUTION: Unlike shareholder-employees of C corporations, partners (and LLC members treated as partners) owning more than a 10% interest in capital or profits cannot borrow against their qualified retirement plan accounts [IRC §4975]. This is a disadvantage of partnership taxation compared to C corporation taxation. (S corporation shareholder-employees who own more than 5% of the corporate stock also are prevented from borrowing against their qualified retirement plan accounts.)*

The partnership tax rules are also considered more favorable than the S corporation tax rules. While pass-through taxation principles apply to S corporations, they are subject to strict eligibility standards that often make using an S corporation impractical or impossible. In addition, certain favorable pass-through taxation rules apply to partnerships but not to S corporations.

LLCs file Form 1065 and issue Schedules K-1 to their members, who are treated as partners for tax return purposes. The LLC's taxable income, gains, losses, deductions, and credits are passed through to the members, who then take these items into account in preparing their returns.

The various other Internal Revenue Code provisions applicable to partnerships and partners (for example, IRC §448 regarding use of the cash method and IRC §1402 regarding the calculation of self-employment income) also apply to LLCs and their members.

See Chapter 5 for a more complete discussion of the partnership taxation rules, and see Chapters 6 and 8 for discussions of the C corporation and S corporation tax rules, respectively.

LLC Tax-Related Restrictions Compared to S Corporations

Like partnerships and LLCs treated as partnerships, S corporations are pass-through entities. The "problem" with S corporations is that there are a number of shareholder restrictions. There are also restrictions on the equity capital structure of S corporations. If a corporation does not comply with these restrictions, it cannot qualify as an S corporation, and it will be taxed under the C corporation rules.

The federal income tax rules that must be satisfied for a corporation to be eligible for S status are summarized below.

Shareholder Restrictions

An S corporation can have no more than 75 shareholders, and shareholders can only be individuals (other than nonresident aliens), estates, and certain types of trusts.

The limitation regarding types of shareholders can be a significant problem when estate or business succession planning becomes important. For example, an S corporation owner cannot transfer shares to a family limited partnership or to certain trusts without "busting" the corporation's S election.

In contrast, LLCs are not subject to any restrictions on the number of members or types of entities that can be members. In unusual circumstances, some care must be taken to avoid publicly traded status for LLCs ownership interests. Under IRC §7704, publicly traded partnerships (including LLCs treated as partnerships) are treated as C corporations for federal income tax purposes.

One-Class-of-Stock Rule

S corporations are limited by the one-class-of-stock rule. In other words, for the corporation to qualify for S status it can have only one class of equity ownership.

In contrast, LLCs can issue a variety of equity ownership interests specifically tailored to meet the financial requirements of their members. In general, as long as there are at least two members and one member is allocated at least 1% of all tax items, variations in the financial characteristics of the ownership interests will not jeopardize the LLC's ability to be treated as a partnership. For example, different classes of LLC ownership interests can be designed to have varying rights to cash flow, liquidation proceeds, and allocations of tax items.

Ineligible Corporation Rules

Certain corporations are by definition ineligible for S status. These are:

- Corporations that are not domestic corporations;
- Certain financial institutions;
- Domestic international sales corporations (DISCs) or former DISCs;
- Insurance companies other than certain casualty companies; and
- Certain corporations electing to take the IRC §936 possessions tax credit.

In contrast, state LLC statutes and professional standards may restrict the ability of certain types of businesses (such as law and accounting practices) to operate as LLCs. However, the federal income tax laws themselves impose no such restrictions.

Other Restrictions

Note also that a corporation that previously revoked or terminated its S status (and reverted to C corporation status) must wait five years before it can regain S status with a new election.

Finally, a former C corporation that accumulated earnings and profits during its C corporation years must not earn more than 25% of its gross receipts from passive sources in three consecutive years, or it will lose its S status.

For a more complete discussion of the various S corporation restrictions, see Chapter 8.

LLC Taxation Rules Compared to S Corporation Rules

The federal income tax rules applying to S corporations are sometimes described as nearly identical to the partnership taxation rules. However, there are actually significant differences, most of them in favor of partnerships (including LLCs treated as partnerships).

Basis from Entity-Level Debt

S corporation shareholders obtain basis for loss deduction purposes only to the extent of their basis in stock plus the amount of any loans they make to the corporation [IRC §1366]. This is the case even if a shareholder personally guarantees some or all of the corporation's debt. However, LLC members are treated as partners and they obtain additional basis in their LLC interest for their share of LLC debts [IRC §752].

Because no member is personally liable for LLC debt, it will be allocated for basis purposes among the members pursuant to the IRC §752 regulations covering nonrecourse liabilities. However, unless the LLC's debt is qualified nonrecourse financing related to holding real property, the IRC §465 rules generally will disallow an increase in basis for at-risk limitation purposes.

It is important to recognize that the additional basis from LLC debt can eliminate or minimize current taxable gain when a member contributes low-basis property burdened by debt to the LLC. Under IRC §357(c), taxable gain *always* results when the amount of debt exceeds the basis of the property a shareholder contributes to an S (or a C) corporation.

See section 3.10 of this chapter for more on this issue.

Basis Step-Up When Ownership Interests Are Purchased

Under the partnership tax rules, a purchaser of an LLC ownership interest can step up the tax basis of his or her share of appreciated LLC assets to reflect the purchase price. This benefit is available if the LLC makes an IRC §754 optional basis adjustment election.

After a §754 election, the allocations to the purchasing member of deductions related to LLC assets (for example, depreciation deductions) will be based on the higher purchase price rather than on the LLC's historical tax basis. Also, if the LLC sells the appreciated property, the purchasing member's allocation of taxable gain will be smaller.

No similar basis adjustment provision is available to purchasers of S (or C) corporation shares.

Contributions and Distributions of Property

Generally, under the partnership tax rules LLC members can make tax-free contributions of appreciated property to the LLC at any time throughout the life of the entity [IRC §721]. Also, LLCs generally can make tax-free distributions of appreciated property to members [IRC §731].

However, when appreciated property is contributed to an S (or a C) corporation, nonrecognition treatment is available only when the transferor or transferrors are in control of the corporation immediately after the transaction [IRC §351].

When appreciated corporate property is distributed to S (or C) corporation shareholders, gain is recognized at the corporate level as if the property were sold for fair market value (FMV) [IRC §§311(b), 336(a), 1371(a)].

> **OBSERVATION:** The key point is that the partnership taxation rules often give LLCs and their members great flexibility to transfer appreciated property without having to immediately recognize taxable gains. This is not the case for S (or C) corporations and their shareholders.

Special Tax Allocations

Finally, under the partnership taxation rules special tax allocations of income, gain, loss, deduction, or credit can be made among the members [IRC §704]. In contrast, all S corporation pass-though items must be allocated among the shareholders strictly in proportion to stock ownership [IRC §1366]. The ability to make special tax allocations to meet the needs of LLC members can be a significant advantage of LLC status compared to S corporation status.

See Chapter 5 for examples of the above issues and other comparisons of the taxation of S corporations and partnerships.

Technical Termination Rule Affects LLCs

A unique, and often negative, aspect of partnership taxation is the so-called technical termination rule of IRC §708(b). Under this rule, a partnership (including an LLC treated as a partnership) terminates (dissolves) for federal income tax law purposes whenever 50% or more of the interests in capital and profits are sold within a 12-month period.

A technical termination can occur even when (because the partners or members vote to continue) there is no legal dissolution of the entity.

While technical terminations usually do *not* result in gain or loss to the members or the LLC, they *do* have significant tax accounting implications. For example, the LLC must "start over" with regard to accounting methods and elections. This can cause the loss of favorable depreciation and accounting methods. In addition, the technical termination brings the LLC's tax year to a close, which can result in unfavorable bunching of taxable income if the LLC's tax year end differs from those of its members.

There is no S corporation counterpart to the partnership technical termination rule. In other words, changes in S corporation stock ownership generally have no tax accounting implications for the S corporation or its shareholders (unless the ownership change results in more than 75 shareholders or in a type of shareholder that is prohibited under the S corporation rules).

State and Local Tax Considerations

While generally there are not major federal income tax differences between LLCs and partnerships, the same cannot always be said for state income tax rules.

Most states follow the federal income tax treatment for LLCs, and an LLC classified as a partnership for federal income tax purposes will therefore be classified as a partnership for state tax purposes as well. In this context, most states do not distinguish between LLCs formed in-state ("domestic" LLCs) and those formed in other states ("foreign" LLCs). Also in most states, LLCs treated as partnerships are not subject to income tax at the entity level, but members are taxed on their shares of LLC income.

Some states require LLCs to file information returns showing members' shares of income, and some states require LLCs to pay or withhold taxes on behalf of nonresident members. Some states apparently will allow LLCs to file composite returns on behalf of their nonresident individual members. This relieves those members from any further state income tax filing responsibilities.

However, in some states LLCs *are* subject to entity-level state income taxes. For example, Florida LLCs are taxed as corporations; Texas LLCs are subject to the state's franchise tax, which is actually somewhat similar to an income tax; and in Washington and Michigan, LLCs are subject to state business taxes that apply to all business entities.

The issue of whether LLCs must pay state franchise taxes on their capital varies. Some states tax capital only if the LLC is classified as a corporation for federal income tax purposes, some states tax capital no matter what the situation, and the rules in some states are unclear.

With regard to other state and local business taxes, LLCs are generally treated in the same manner as other types of business entities. For example, LLCs generally are required to collect sales taxes and to pay use taxes on items they purchase in other states. LLCs generally must comply with state and local business organization, registration, and licensing rules and pay applicable fees and taxes. Transfers of real estate to LLCs may be subject to state and local real estate transfer taxes. Some states also charge LLCs annual fees.

> **OBSERVATION:** *State and local taxes are often significant enough that they may impact conclusions on the attractiveness of LLCs as business entities. The issue should be carefully assessed as the choice-of-entity decision is being made.*

For basic information on how LLCs are treated for state income tax purposes, see Appendix 3B.

3.10 FEDERAL INCOME TAX RULES SPECIFICALLY AFFECTING LLCs

The partnership taxation rules (discussed at length in Chapter 5) generally apply to LLCs and LLC members. In other words, the basic rule is simply to follow the partnership taxation rules and substitute *LLC* and *member* for *partnership* and *partner*.

See Chapter 5 for coverage of partnership taxation of contributions of property, distributions of property, effects of debt, tax accounting methods and periods, etc.

The purpose of this section is to cover certain significant aspects of partnership taxation for which it may not be entirely clear how the rules apply to LLCs and their members. Throughout the remaining discussion in this section, it is assumed that the LLC is properly classified as a partnership for federal income tax purposes.

Effect of LLC Debt on "Regular" Basis and At-Risk Basis

Under the partnership taxation rules, LLC members obtain additional basis in their LLC ownership interests for their shares of LLC debt. Each member's allocable share of LLC debt is treated as a cash contribution for basis purposes under IRC §752.

Allocations of Basis from Nonrecourse Debt

In general, no LLC member is personally liable for the LLC's debts. This means the LLC's debts are nonrecourse with respect to the members and therefore are allocated for basis purposes among the members using the IRC §752 regulations covering nonrecourse liabilities.

Unless the liabilities are secured by properties contributed by the members, these rules generally result in allocating the basis in proportion to the members' percentage interests in LLC profits.

If a debt that is secured by contributed property exceeds the basis of the property, an allocation of basis equal to the deemed built-in gain (excess of debt over the property's basis on the contribution date) is made to the contributing member (assuming the "traditional" method described in Regs. §1.752-3 is used). The remaining amount of the debt generally is allocated to all members in proportion to their percentage interests in LLC profits. Thus, for "regular" basis purposes, LLC members will obtain increased basis from their allocations of LLC debt under the §752 regulations.

The initial basis of a member's ownership interest is equal to the amount of cash contributed, plus the basis of property contributed, minus the liabilities assumed by the LLC, plus the increased basis from the member's allocation of LLC debt. If the above total results in a negative number, the contributing member recognizes taxable gain equal to the negative amount, and his or her initial basis is zero. (See IRC §§722, 752, 733, 731, and 705.)

> **Example 3.10(1): Increased Basis from LLC Debt**   Barry and Jimmy each contribute $20,000 of cash to start a 50/50 equipment-leasing LLC. The LLC obtains a $200,000 loan and uses all of it to purchase equipment. (The initial $40,000 cash investment is to be used for start-up and initial operating expenses.)
>
> As 50/50 members, Barry and Jimmy each have initial basis in their LLC ownership interests of $120,000 ($20,000 from the cash contributed plus $100,000 from each member's share of the LLC's debt).
>
> If the same facts applied, but Barry and Jimmy each contributed $20,000 to start the business as a 50/50 *S corporation*, each owner's initial basis for purposes of deducting pass-through losses would be limited to his $20,000 basis in S corporation stock. This would be true even if Barry and Jimmy each personally guaranteed 50% of the corporation's loan.

Member's At-Risk Basis Amount

Unfortunately, unless the LLC debt is qualified nonrecourse financing related to holding real property [as defined by IRC §465(b)(6)], the at-risk rules of IRC §465 will generally prevent an increase in basis for at-risk limitation purposes.

This is because, absent a personal guarantee of LLC debt by a member, no member has any personal liability for the LLC's debts. Because members are not at risk for LLC debts, their §465 at-risk basis amounts are not increased.

Therefore, the at-risk limitation rules will often prevent any LLC member from deducting losses in excess of the basis derived from his or her cash and property contributions to the LLC.

However, as the following Example illustrates, the "regular" basis from LLC debt can still be very beneficial in eliminating or minimizing current taxable gain when a member contributes property with debt in excess of basis.

> **Example 3.10(2): Additional "Regular" Basis from LLC Debt Prevents Gain on Contribution (Even Though At-Risk Basis Not Increased)** Able and Buster form a 50/50 LLC to develop raw land. In exchange for his LLC ownership interest, Able contributes land with tax basis of $40,000 and FMV of $100,000. The land is burdened with a $60,000 liability. Assume the liability is *not* qualified nonrecourse financing. Buster contributes $40,000 cash.
>
> The LLC's operating agreement provides for 50/50 allocations of all items of taxable income, gain, deduction, and loss.
>
> The basis from the $60,000 of debt is allocated between Able and Buster as follows: First, $20,000 is allocated to Able, equal to the amount of deemed built-in gain as of the contribution date (the $20,000 difference between the debt of $60,000 and the tax basis of the property of $40,000).
>
> Second, the $40,000 of remaining basis from the debt can be allocated 50/50 between Able and Buster, in proportion to their profit sharing percentages. Therefore, Able is allocated a total of $40,000 of basis from the debt and Buster is allocated $20,000.
>
> Thus, Able will have an initial basis in his ownership interest of $20,000 ($40,000 basis from the contributed land, plus his $40,000 allocation of basis from LLC debt, less $60,000 debt assumed by the LLC). Able will recognize no gain on his contribution of property with debt in excess of basis.
>
> Buster will have an initial basis of $60,000 ($40,000 from his cash contribution, plus his $20,000 allocation of basis from LLC debt).
>
> Note that if Able had made the same contribution to an S or C corporation, he would have been required to recognize $20,000 of taxable gain (equal to the excess of the $60,000 of debt assumed by the corporation over the $40,000 basis of the contributed property). [See IRC §357(c).]
>
> Because the LLC's debt is *not* qualified nonrecourse financing, Able's initial at-risk basis is zero (the basis of the land reduced, but not below zero, by the liability assumed by the LLC). However, the debt added to Able's "regular" basis prevents the recognition of taxable gain upon his contribution of property with debt in excess of basis.
>
> Buster's initial at-risk basis is limited to his $40,000 cash contribution.

At-Risk Basis from Qualified Nonrecourse Financing

As stated earlier, there is an exception to the general rule that nonguaranteed LLC debt does not add to the members' at-risk basis. If the LLC debt is qualified nonrecourse financing, each member's at-risk basis *is* increased by his or her allocable share of the LLC's qualified nonrecourse financing.

Qualified nonrecourse financing is defined as any loan from a qualified person (or federal, state, or local government) that the taxpayer incurs with respect to holding real property and for which no person is personally liable. The loan cannot be convertible debt. [See IRC §465(b)(6).]

> **Example 3.10(3): Effect of Qualified Nonrecourse Financing** Barry and Jimmy each contribute $20,000 cash to start a 50/50 real estate acquisition and redevelopment LLC. The LLC obtains a $200,000 loan from the bank and purchases a "fixer-upper" retail strip center for $200,000. (The $40,000 of cash is to be used to cover start-up and initial redevelopment expenses.)
>
> Because the loan is owed by the LLC, it is nonrecourse with respect to Barry and Jimmy. Assume the loan also meets the definition of qualified nonrecourse financing.
>
> As 50/50 members, Barry and Jimmy each have initial "regular" basis in their LLC ownership interests of $120,000 ($20,000 from the cash contributed plus $100,000 from each member's share of the LLC's debt) for loss deduction purposes.
>
> Because the LLC's debt is qualified nonrecourse financing, each member also has $120,000 of initial at-risk basis for purposes of the §465 at-risk limitation rules.

Are LLC Members Considered Limited Partners under the Passive Rules?

Under the IRC §469 passive loss rules, the ability of members to currently deduct losses passed through by the LLC may be thwarted if they do not materially participate in the trades or businesses conducted by the LLC. For limited partners, much stricter tests apply in determining if the material participation test is met. [See Temp. Regs. §1.469-5T.]

Clearly, LLC members have a major business advantage in common with limited partners: Neither group is liable for entity-level debts. However, LLC members can actively participate in the management of LLCs, while limited partners generally cannot (as discussed in section 3.06 of this chapter). The simple fact is that limited partners and LLC members are *not* identical in a legal sense.

Thus, until the IRS or the courts provide further guidance, it seems fair to conclude that LLC members need not be *automatically* treated as limited partners for purposes of applying the passive loss rules.

However, it also may be proper to conclude that, as a practical matter, certain nonmanager members of manager-managed LLCs may be functionally the same as limited partners. In such cases, the conservative approach would be to assume they are limited partners for purposes of the passive rules.

Ability of LLCs to Use the Cash Method of Accounting

LLCs treated as partnerships generally are eligible to use the cash method of accounting for federal income tax purposes. However, if a C corporation is an LLC member, there potentially are limitations on the availability of the cash method [IRC §448(a)]. The cash method generally *is* allowed if the LLC is in the farming business or if the C corporation is a personal service corporation. Otherwise, the LLC qualifies to use the cash method only if its average annual gross receipts (for the preceding three taxable years) are $5 million or less. [See IRC §448(b).]

In addition, an LLC will *not* qualify to use the cash method if more than 35% of its losses are allocable to "limited entrepreneurs" [IRC §§448(a)(3) and (d)(3)].

There was some concern that all LLC members might be deemed limited entrepreneurs because of their limited liability. However, the IRS has indicated that members of professional LLCs will *not* be viewed as such as long as they participate in management activities. [See Private Letter Rulings (PLRs) 9321047, 9328005, 9350013, 9412030, 9415005, and 9434027.]

However, if more than 35% of losses are allocable to nonmanagers of manager-managed LLCs, apparently the LLC would be ineligible to use the cash method of accounting.

Exposure of LLC Members to Self-Employment Tax

As stated earlier, one premise of this chapter is that LLCs will qualify to be treated as partnerships for tax purposes. In computing the amount of a partner's self-employment (SE) income, the general rule is the partner includes his or her pass-through share of the partnership's income and loss from trade or business activities in SE income [IRC §1402(a)].

However, *limited* partners include in their SE income only guaranteed payments, as described in IRC §707(c), from the partnership for services actually rendered to the partnership. [See IRC §1402(a)(13).] Such payments are commonly referred to as "partner salaries." Assuming the partnership's trade or business activities generate taxable income, this is a favorable rule, because it minimizes the limited partner's SE income and thus his or her SE tax.

Obviously, the SE tax rules were developed before LLCs treated as partnerships existed. The question became: How do LLC members deal with the issue of SE tax, and specifically when can they escape SE tax on the theory that they should be considered limited partners because they are not personally liable for LLC debts?

In other words, if limited partner status applies to LLC members for SE tax purposes, they can apparently avoid SE tax simply by *not* receiving any section 707(c) payments for services. Obviously, big dollars could be at stake, particularly for professional service LLCs.

In response to this "alarming" situation, Treasury issued not one but two sets of proposed regulations (in 1994 and 1997) on the subject of SE tax for limited partners (LLC members). Both generated controversy by in effect proposing that LLC members be required to pay SE tax on certain LLC pass-through income in addition to any Section 707(c) guaranteed payments for services.

Many commentators interpreted the proposed rules as imposing new taxes on LLC members, without the benefit of any supporting legislation. Congress agreed. Section 935 of the Taxpayer Relief Act of 1997 includes language prohibiting the release of any temporary or final regulations on the subject before July 1, 1998. Treasury now concedes that the proposed regulations have no validity. As this was written, there was no indication that further guidance from Treasury will be forthcoming until Congress delivers a statutory clarification.

Thus, an aggressive interpretation of current law is that LLC members can completely avoid SE tax on their pass-through shares of LLC income by avoiding any Section 707(c) guaranteed payments for services. However, the IRS may take the position that at least some of the cash distributions received by LLC members are in fact "disguised" Section 707(c) guaranteed payments for services.

A less-aggressive approach might be for LLC members to concede that they owe tax on a "reasonable" portion of their cash distributions by voluntarily treating such reasonable amounts as Section 707(c) guaranteed payments for services. The members can then make a strong argument that no further SE tax is owed, because they have taken a very conservative approach to interpreting a very unclear law.

> **Note:** There is no confusion regarding the SE tax for individual owners of single-member LLCs involved in trade or business activities. As explained in section 3.11 of this chapter, the existence of the single-member LLC is ignored for federal tax purposes. Accordingly, the business is treated as a sole proprietorship activity of its owner, with the resulting exposure to the SE tax.

3.11 SINGLE-MEMBER LLCs

All but a few state LLC statutes now permit the formation of single-member LLCs. (As this was written, the holdouts were California, Massachusetts, Tennessee, and the District of Columbia. In addition, several states are deemed by the author to allow single-member LLCs because they are not specifically prohibited under the applicable statute.) Under the former entity classification regulations, the federal income tax status of single-member LLCs was unclear. There was no authoritative guidance on point, and there was a significant risk the IRS would enforce *association taxable as a corporation status*. Therefore, single-member LLCs were seldom advisable.

However, the check-the-box regulations resolved the tax classification issue in a very favorable manner. The regulations allow domestic single-owner LLCs to have their existence disregarded for tax purposes. This treatment is by default.

If the default treatment applies, a single-member LLC owned by an individual will be reflected on the owner's tax return as a Schedule C, E, or F activity. No separate return or additional tax reporting is required. The SE tax will apply to income from trade or business activities.

If a single-member LLC is owned by another legal entity, such as a corporation, a partnership, or another LLC, it will be treated the same as an unincorporated branch or division of the parent entity. Again, no additional tax return or special reporting is required. The LLC's income, deductions, assets, and liabilities will simply be reflected on the parent entity's tax return.

Despite being "invisible" for federal tax purposes, the single-member LLC still shields its owner from liabilities related to the LLC's business. Thus, an individual owner's personal assets would be protected. And when an LLC is owned by another legal entity, the parent entity would be shielded from LLC liabilities (and vice versa), even though the parent and the LLC are regarded as a single taxpayer for federal income tax purposes.

Ultimately, the check-the-box regulations' favorable treatment of single-member LLCs may prove to be the area where the regulations have the greatest impact for small businesses. While single-member LLCs are not currently permitted in a few states, it can be expected that most—if not all—of the holdout states will eventually amend their statutes to allow single-member LLCs.

> **OBSERVATION:** *The single-member LLC has become the ideal vehicle for small single-owner businesses, because it teams liability protection with what amounts to pass-through taxation in its simplest form.*

> **Example 3.11(1): Single-Member LLC Owned by Individual**   Amy is a real estate agent who has been operating as a sole proprietor for years and filing Schedule C. She now wants to set up a liability-limiting entity because she has become very successful and has two clerical employees and a receptionist. If Amy forms a single-member LLC, the new entity will deliver the needed liability protection. However, under the federal income tax rules, nothing has happened. Amy's sole proprietor status continues. She files Schedule C as before and computes her self-employment tax on Schedule SE. No additional federal tax returns or forms are required. In this situation, Amy could also consider setting up a solely owned S corporation, but that would require filing an annual corporate tax return (Form 1120S) and federal payroll tax returns for her salary. Additional state tax filings would probably be required as well. In some cases, however, the federal payroll tax savings can make S corporation status worthwhile (as discussed in Chapter 8).

When a single-member LLC is owned by a corporation, partnership, or another LLC, it's treated for federal tax purposes as an unincorporated branch or division of the parent entity. As a result, the LLC's income, deductions, assets, and liabilities will simply be reflected on the parent's tax return. However, the LLC should still shield its parent from liabilities related to the LLC's business. In turn, the LLC is shielded from the parent's liabilities even though the parent and the LLC are regarded as a single taxpayer for federal purposes.

> **Example 3.11(2): Single-Member LLC Owned by Another Legal Entity** Scanners Are Us is a PC scanner manufacturing business set up as a C corporation. To avoid overexposure to the volatile high-tech sector, the company is now about to branch out into two new lines of business: Staplers Are Us and Hole Punches Are Us. Scanners Are Us will form two wholly owned LLCs to operate the new businesses. This legal structure will "wall off" the assets of each business from liabilities related to the other businesses. For federal income tax purposes, the company can continue to file one Form 1120 for the combined operations. If Scanners Are Us were an S corporation, the same structure could be used, with the combined operations all being reported on the parent's Form 1120S.

Generally, single-member LLCs can be formed easily and inexpensively. All that may be required is filing a form with the appropriate state authority (often, the Secretary of State) and paying the applicable filing fee. With only a single owner, there is generally no need to draft an operating agreement, which is often the most expensive aspect of forming a multi-member LLC.

> **WARNING:** *Before concluding that single-member LLC status is a "no brainer" choice for clients currently operating as sole proprietorships, the tax advisor should examine the state tax implications carefully. For example, although Texas allows single-member LLCs, they are subject to the state's corporate franchise tax, while sole proprietorships are not. In other states (for example, Colorado), single-member LLCs are not subject to any additional entity-level taxes. See also the discussion at the end of section 3.08.*

3.12 CONVERTING EXISTING ENTITIES INTO LLCs

Partnership Conversions

Revenue Ruling 95-37 (1995-1 CB 130) confirms that generally an existing domestic general or limited partnership can be converted into a domestic multi-member LLC classified as a partnership without federal income tax consequences to the converting partnership or partners.

The former partners usually become LLC members without recognizing any gain on the transaction, and the taxable year of the converting partnership does not close. In other words, for federal income tax purposes the new LLC is considered a continuation of the old partnership. (There is no termination under IRC §708.)

These outcomes apparently apply whether the partnership conversion is accomplished by formal liquidation of the partnership and formation of an LLC, or by a merger with a newly formed LLC, or by a purely legal conversion to LLC status. In addition, the tax consequences are the same whether the LLC is formed in the same state as the converting partnership or in a different state. (See Revenue Ruling 95-37 in conjunction with earlier letter rulings, such as PLR 9321047.)

Mechanics of Partnership Conversions

Conversion by liquidation of the old partnership can be accomplished most easily by having the partnership contribute all its assets and liabilities to the newly formed LLC in exchange for LLC ownership interests. This step generally is tax-free, under IRC §721. The LLC interests are then distributed by the old partnership to its partners in liquidation. This step also generally is tax-free, under IRC §731. After the transactions, the former partners hold interests in the new LLC, and the LLC holds all the assets and liabilities of the old partnership.

Alternatively, a liquidation can be accomplished by having the partners contribute their partnership interests to the newly formed LLC in exchange for LLC interests. (Again, this step generally is tax-free, under IRC §721.) The partnership then distributes all assets and liabilities to the LLC in liquidation (generally tax-free under IRC §731). Again, the former partners now hold interests in the new LLC, and the LLC now holds all the assets and liabilities of the old partnership.

State law may permit an existing partnership to merge with the newly formed LLC with the LLC being the surviving entity. When allowed, merger transactions generally are "cleaner" from a legal standpoint than liquidations, because the LLC simply assumes all rights and obligations of the former partnership by operation of law. LLC members who were former partners with personal liability for the debts of the old partnership remain liable for those preexisting debts after the merger with the LLC.

Several state LLC statutes permit the members of a partnership to convert their business entity into an LLC simply by filing articles of organization and complying with certain other filing and paperwork requirements. Like a merger transaction, this is "cleaner" than a transaction involving a liquidation of the old partnership. The assets and liabilities of the old partnership become those of the new LLC by operation of law. As with mergers, LLC members who were former partners with personal liability for the debts of the old partnership remain liable for those preexisting debts after conversion to LLC status.

General Tax Implications of Partnership Conversions

With regard to the tax implications of converting an existing general or limited partnership into an LLC by *any* of the above methods, Revenue

Ruling 95-37 (when read in conjunction with earlier letter rulings, such as PLR 9321047) leads to the following conclusions:

- Former partners do not recognize gain on the conversion unless changes in their percentages of liabilities (under IRC §752) would cause the basis in their interests to fall below zero.
- Former partners obtain the same basis in their new LLC interests as they had in their old partnership interests, unless the conversion results in changes in their shares of liabilities under IRC §752.
- The members' holding periods for the new LLC interests tack onto the holding periods for the old partnership interests.
- The LLC is considered a continuation of the former partnership. As a result, the tax year continues and there is no need for a new taxpayer identification number (TIN). The LLC continues to use the former partnership's tax accounting methods and elections. The LLC's holding periods for its assets include the holding periods of the old partnership.

Example 3.12(1): Conversion of General Partnership into LLC   BC Joint Venture, a general partnership, converts into an LLC by simply filing its articles of organization in the state in which it does business. The name of the entity is now BC Joint Venture, LLC.

The two equal partners in the old partnership, Betty and Charlotte, are now 50/50 members of the new LLC. (Assume their shares of the entity's liabilities under IRC §752 are unchanged from before the conversion.) The only real impact of the conversion is a reduction in each member's exposure to the entity's liabilities.

Per Revenue Ruling 95-37, the federal income tax implications are as follows:

1. None of the players—Betty, Charlotte, the old partnership, or the new LLC—recognizes any gain or loss on the conversion;
2. The members' bases in their new LLC ownership interests are the same as their bases in their old partnership interests, and their holding periods in their LLC ownership interests include the holding periods of their old partnership interests; and
3. The LLC is considered a continuation of the existing taxable entity, so BC Joint Venture, LLC, continues to use the same TIN, tax year, accounting and depreciation methods, tax elections, asset holding periods, etc.

Conversions of S Corporations and C Corporations

Mechanics of Corporate Conversions

Converting an existing S or C corporation into a multi-member LLC can be accomplished in several ways. It is especially likely that certain S corporations will consider converting to LLC status to escape the S corporation limitations on stock ownership and capital structure. (See discussion of these limitations in section 3.09 of this chapter and in Chapter 8.)

The assets of the corporation can be contributed to the newly formed LLC in return for LLC ownership interests that are then distributed to the shareholders in complete liquidation of the corporation.

Alternatively, the corporation can distribute its assets to the shareholders in complete liquidation, and the shareholders can then contribute their undivided interests in the assets to the newly formed LLC in exchange for LLC ownership interests.

Finally, state law may permit the corporation to merge with the newly formed LLC, with the LLC being the surviving entity. The corporation does this by making a tax-free contribution of all assets and liabilities to the LLC in exchange for LLC interests (under IRC §721). The corporation then goes out of existence by distributing the LLC interests to shareholders in complete liquidation.

General Tax Implications of Corporate Conversions

In any of the above cases, there will be corporate-level gain or loss recognition as if the property distributed in complete liquidation were sold by the corporation for FMV [IRC §336(a)]. This means a converting corporation with appreciated assets may recognize significant taxable income or gain as a result of the liquidation transaction—whether the corporation is an S or C corporation. (See the Examples below.)

At the shareholder level, the receipt of the liquidating distribution in exchange for corporate stock is treated as a taxable sale or exchange of the stock for proceeds equal to the FMV of the distributed property [IRC §331(a)]. The shareholder may recognize gain or loss on the transaction— depending on whether the FMV of the distributed property is greater or less than the basis of the corporate stock exchanged.

In the case of a converting S corporation, any corporate-level gain is passed through and increases the shareholders' basis in their stock [IRC §1367(a)]. Therefore, the gain already recognized at the corporate level is not recognized again when the stock is deemed sold in exchange for the liquidating distribution. However, if the S corporation is a former C corporation, the IRC §1374 built-in gains tax may apply to some or all of the corporate-level gain.

In the case of a converting C corporation, the shareholders receive no step-up in basis from any corporate-level gain. As a result, generally there is taxable gain at both the corporate level and the shareholder level upon the liquidation of a C corporation with appreciated assets.

> **OBSERVATION:** *Since converting an S or C corporation to LLC status involves liquidation transactions, the federal income tax cost for corporations with significantly appreciated assets will often be unacceptably high. In such situations, there will often be unfavorable state income tax consequences as well. However, if the corporation does not hold significantly appreciated assets, liquidation and conversion to LLC status can be accomplished without adverse tax consequences.*

CAUTION: Before concluding that an existing S or C corporation can convert to LLC status "painlessly," consider whether goodwill exists. It does not often appear on the balance sheet, but goodwill is the classic example of an appreciated corporate asset. Especially in cases involving professional practices, goodwill with very significant value (and zero tax basis) will exist. The tax impact of such goodwill may preclude conversion.

Example 3.12(2): Conversion of a C Corporation into an LLC Cee Corp decides to convert into an LLC by making liquidating distributions of its property to its two equal shareholders, Fred and Mary. Then Fred and Mary will each contribute their distributed property to the newly formed LLC in exchange for their 50% LLC ownership interests.

Cee Corp owns two assets: undeveloped land with FMV of $2.5 million and tax basis of $1 million, and cash of $750,000. (There is no goodwill.)

Fred and Mary each have basis of $500,000 in their Cee Corp shares, which they have held for a number of years.

Under IRC §336(a), Cee Corp recognizes a $1.5 million corporate-level gain on the liquidating distribution, because the transaction is deemed a taxable sale of the corporate property for its FMV. Assume the corporate-level tax is $510,000 (34% of the taxable gain).

Cee Corp pays the tax and distributes the remaining $240,000 of cash ($120,000 each to Fred and Mary) and the land (equal undivided interests to Fred and Mary).

Fred and Mary each receive liquidating distributions with FMV equal to $1,370,000 (cash of $120,000 plus land worth $1,250,000) in exchange for their Cee Corp stock. These exchanges are treated as sales of their stock under IRC §331(a).

Therefore, Fred and Mary will each recognize taxable long-term capital gains from their stock sales of $870,000 (proceeds of $1,370,000 less basis in their shares of $500,000).

Fred and Mary will then contribute their distributed cash and land (with total basis of $1,370,000 each) in exchange for their 50% LLC ownership interests. Under IRC §721, the contributions are tax-free. Under IRC §722, their initial bases in their LLC interests are $1,370,000 each. Under IRC §723, the LLC's total basis in the contributed assets is $2,740,000 ($240,000 basis in the cash and $2.5 million basis in the land).

Reality Check: In this case, the corporate and shareholder-level taxable gains resulting from conversion to LLC status are a heavy price to pay—probably too heavy in real life. Fred and Mary probably would opt *not* to convert the corporation into an LLC.

Example 3.12(3): Conversion of an S Corporation into an LLC Assume the same facts as in the previous Example, except the corporation is now Ess Corp (which has always been an S corporation), and Fred and Mary each have basis in their shares of $875,000.

Ess Corp will convert into an LLC by making liquidating distributions of its property to Fred and Mary, and they will each then contribute their distributed property to the newly formed LLC in exchange for 50% LLC ownership interests.

As in the previous Example, the corporation owns two assets: undeveloped land with FMV of $2.5 million and tax basis of $1 million, and cash of $750,000.

Under IRC §336(a), Ess Corp recognizes a $1.5 million corporate-level gain on the liquidating distribution, because the transaction is deemed a taxable sale of the corporate property for its FMV.

There is no corporate-level tax, but the gain is passed through to Fred and Mary ($750,000 each). They will pay tax on the gain, but it increases their basis in their shares to $1,625,000 each (preliquidation basis of $875,000 plus the $750,000 increase from the pass-through gain).

Ess Corp then distributes its $750,000 of cash ($375,000 each to Fred and Mary) and the land (equal undivided interests to Fred and Mary).

Fred and Mary each receive liquidating distributions with FMV equal to $1,625,000 (cash of $375,000 plus land worth $1,250,000) in exchange for their Ess Corp stock.

These exchanges are treated as sales of their stock under IRC §331(a). In this case, however, Fred and Mary recognize no additional gains upon their stock sales, because the proceeds match their stock basis.

Fred and Mary will then contribute their distributed cash and land (with total basis of $1,625,000 each) in exchange for their 50% LLC ownership interests. Under IRC §721, the contributions are tax-free. Under IRC §722, their initial bases in their LLC interests are $1,625,000 each. Under IRC §723, the LLC's total basis in the contributed assets is $3,250,000 ($750,000 basis in the cash and $2.5 million basis in the land).

Reality Check: Although there was only a single level of taxation in this case, the conversion of Ess Corp into an LLC still required recognition of significant corporate-level gains, which were then passed through to the shareholders. In a real-life situation similar to the one described above, the owners probably would opt *not* to convert an S corporation into an LLC, because of the magnitude of the gains that would be recognized.

Corporate Conversions into Single-Member LLCs

If state law permits single-member LLCs, the federal income tax implications of converting a C corporation or S corporation will be the same as discussed earlier in this section. The transaction will be treated as a taxable liquidation of the corporation, with the resulting negative tax implications if the corporation holds significantly appreciated assets.

Tax Accounting Implications of Conversions

As stated earlier, converting an existing partnership into a multi-member LLC that will be taxed as a partnership generally is treated as a continuation of the same entity for federal income tax purposes. The new LLC will simply succeed to the old partnership's employer identification number (EIN) and its tax accounting methods, periods, and elections.

In contrast, when a corporate conversion is undertaken, the resulting multi-member LLC will be a new taxable entity treated as a partnership, assuming the partnership classification test discussed earlier is passed. The LLC will need to obtain a new EIN, and it will have the same choices as any new partnership regarding tax accounting methods and elections and permissible taxable years.

When a corporation converts into a single-member LLC, the tax rules for corporate liquidations will apply, and the tax "life" of the corporation will end. In most cases, the individual owner or parent entity will be able to continue to use the accounting methods and elections of the old corporation. However, the ability to use a fiscal year end may be lost.

For example, a C corporation can use any year end for federal income tax purposes, while partnerships and S corporations must generally use calendar year ends. If a calendar-year partnership converts its 100% owned C corporation into a single-member LLC, the tax results from the corporation's business will have to be reported on a calendar year-end basis. Of course, partnerships can elect to use alternative year ends by making IRC §444 elections. Also, in relatively unusual circumstances, partnerships can qualify to use "business purpose" year ends that do not come to a close on December 31.

3.13 COMPARISONS WITH OTHER ENTITY CHOICES

This section has the greatest relevance if the entity selection process has been narrowed down to a choice between a multi-member LLC and one of the types of entities discussed below. If that is not the case, the practitioner should strongly consider using the entity selection software program that comes with this book. The program is designed to help make a choice-of-entity decision that is consistent with the major tax and nontax issues facing the client. If the program leads to the LLC as apparently the best choice, this section can be reviewed to solidify that conclusion.

LLCs Compared to General Partnerships

Clearly, LLCs are superior to general partnerships for limiting owner liability. First, in a partnership all general partners are jointly and severally liable for *all* debts and obligations. By contrast, in an LLC the personal assets of members generally are not exposed to the LLC's debts and obligations.

Second, each general partner generally has the power to act as an agent of the partnership and enter into contracts that are legally binding on the partnership (and therefore on the other partners). In manager-managed LLCs, generally only the managers are able to legally bind the LLC.

However, as discussed in section 3.06 of this chapter, LLCs do *not* protect their members from personal liability in *all* circumstances. For example, members typically are personally liable for their own tortious acts, professional malpractice, or negligence, and for any personally guaranteed LLC debts.

> **NOTE:** *In somewhat unusual cases, the co-owners of a business may be relatively unconcerned about personal liability exposure, because there is little or no debt and because other liability concerns can be managed with insurance. If the co-owners of such a business have a high degree of trust in each other, operating as a general partnership may make sense.*

As discussed in section 3.10 of this chapter, there are relatively few significant federal income tax law differences between general partnerships and LLCs treated as partnerships. However, in a few states, LLCs are treated less favorably than general partnerships for state income tax purposes. (See discussion in section 3.09 of this chapter.)

The key negative factors affecting LLCs are the issues of legal uncertainty and state LLC statute variability. Also, some businesses (such as certain professional practices) may be prohibited under state law and/or professional standards from operating as LLCs. (See discussions of these issues in sections 3.02 and 3.03 of this chapter.)

In summary, compared to general partnerships, LLCs generally are superior if:

- There are liability exposures that cannot be managed at an acceptable cost with insurance;
- The co-owners are concerned about the ability of other co-owners to take actions that are legally binding on them;
- The business or investment activity in question can be operated as an LLC under state law;
- The state income tax consequences of LLC status are acceptable; and
- The co-owners can live with the legal uncertainties associated with LLC status.

LLCs Compared to Limited Partnerships

LLCs possess two significant advantages over limited partnerships for limiting owner liability: First, a limited partnership must have at least one general partner with unlimited exposure to partnership liabilities. As a practical matter, this problem can be addressed by forming a corporate general partner—usually an S corporation owned by the partners. Under this strategy, the amount the general partner can lose is effectively limited to the value of the assets held by the corporation. Of course, setting up and maintaining another entity for this purpose creates administrative burdens that owners may prefer to avoid. (See the discussion of limited partnerships in Chapter 5.)

No LLC member need be exposed to *any* LLC liabilities. In effect, from a liability standpoint all members of an LLC are treated as limited partners.

Second, limited partners can lose their limited liability protection by becoming too actively involved in managing the limited partnership. As a result, limited partnerships are not suitable for activities such as the practice of a profession where all partners are by definition heavily involved in the business. Again, this issue can be addressed by using a corporate general partner, with the corporation owned by the limited partners in proportion to their limited partnership ownership percentages. Again, however, the existence of an additional legal entity creates administrative and tax filing headaches. State limited partnership laws based on the Revised Uniform Limited Partnership Act give some relief by specifying a number of actions that limited partners can take *without* being deemed to participate in management. Nevertheless, the issue is always a significant one for limited partners.

For LLC members, on the other hand, this issue simply is not a concern. They can have any degree of management involvement without risking loss of their limited liability protection.

As discussed in section 3.10 of this chapter, there are relatively few significant federal income tax law differences between limited partnerships and LLCs treated as partnerships. However, in a few states, LLCs are treated less favorably than limited partnerships for state income tax purposes. (See discussion in section 3.09 of this chapter.)

The key negative factors affecting LLCs are the issues of legal uncertainty and state LLC statute variability. Also, some businesses (such as certain professional practices) may be prohibited under state law and/or professional standards from operating as LLCs. (See discussions of these issues in sections 3.02 and 3.03 of this chapter.)

In summary, compared to limited partnerships, LLCs generally are superior if:

- The business or investment activity in question can be operated as an LLC under state law;
- The state income tax consequences of LLC status are acceptable; and
- The co-owners can live with the legal uncertainties associated with LLC status.

LLCs Compared to Limited Liability Partnerships (LLPs)

As discussed in Chapter 4, LLPs are allowed by statute in many states and usually are treated as a special form of general partnership for state law purposes. LLPs are primarily intended to be used by professional practices.

In some states (such as Texas), LLP partners are jointly and severally liable as general partners for the LLP's so-called contract liabilities (accounts payable, leases, etc.). In these states, LLC status generally is preferred to LLP status because of the liability protection issue.

In other states (such as California and New York), LLP partners are *not* personally liable for the LLP's contract liabilities unless the liabilities are expressly guaranteed by the partners. In these states, LLPs are the equal of LLCs in terms of offering the "complete package" of liability protection benefits. However, even in states not offering LLC-like liability protection, LLPs can still make sense in at least three circumstances.

First, LLCs may be unavailable for the practice of certain professions under state law and/or applicable professional standards (such as state bar rules). In contrast, in states with LLP statutes, LLPs generally can be used for professional practices if partnerships can be used. This is because, in fact, an LLP is simply a special type of partnership. (The administrative work needed to adopt or convert to LLP status—for example, to meet state board of accountancy regulations—should be minimal.)

Second, in a few states (such as Texas), LLCs are subject to entity-level state taxes, while LLPs are not. Thus, even when professionals are allowed to practice as LLCs, LLPs can be more attractive for state tax reasons. However, before LLP status is chosen over LLC status, the co-owners should be very comfortable that their exposure to the entity's contract liabilities (the Achilles' heel of LLPs) will be tightly managed.

Third, as discussed in sections 3.02 and 3.08 of this chapter, LLCs are subject to legal uncertainties. If the co-owners are uncomfortable with these issues, they may prefer to operate as an LLP, a more cautious choice.

In summary, compared to LLPs in states not offering LLC-like liability protection to LLP partners, LLCs generally are superior *unless*:

- LLCs are unavailable because of statutory and/or professional standard restrictions; or

- The state tax rules applying to LLCs are unfavorable enough to outweigh the liability-limiting advantage of LLCs over LLPs; or

- The legal uncertainties of LLCs are a decisive negative factor.

LLCs Compared to C Corporations

As discussed in section 3.06 of this chapter, the personal assets of C corporation shareholders and LLC members enjoy similar protections against entity-level liabilities.

The obvious advantage of LLCs is that they can qualify for partnership taxation, avoiding the C corporation pitfall of double taxation (discussed at length in Chapter 6).

The other advantages (and the relatively few disadvantages) of partnership taxation are highlighted in section 3.09 of this chapter and covered at length in Chapter 5.

OBSERVATION: To be treated as a partnership for federal income tax purposes, an LLC must have at least two members. In contrast, C corporations can be formed with only one shareholder. In general, as long as there are at least two LLC members the LLC will be respected as a partnership. In some cases, the two-member rule may appear to be a significant roadblock. However, as discussed in Chapter 5, there are often ways to address this issue—for example, by forming a husband–wife partnership.

The key negative factors affecting LLCs are the issues of legal uncertainty and state LLC statute variability. Also, some businesses (such as certain professional practices) may be prohibited under state law and/or professional standards from operating as LLCs. (See discussions of these issues in sections 3.02 and 3.03 of this chapter.)

Another potentially significant disadvantage of LLCs compared to C corporations is the inability of certain LLC members to borrow against their qualified retirement plan account balances. Unlike shareholder-employees of C corporations, LLC members who are treated as partners and own more than 10% interests in capital or profits cannot borrow against their qualified retirement plan accounts [IRC §4975]. This is a disadvantage of partnership taxation compared to C corporation taxation. (S corporation shareholder-employees who own more than 5% of the corporate stock also are prevented from borrowing against their qualified retirement plan accounts.)

In summary, compared to C corporations, LLCs generally are superior if:

- There are at least two owners (but not so many owners that the ownership interests would be considered publicly traded under IRC §7704—see below);
- The co-owners can accept the fact that they may not be able to borrow against their qualified retirement plan accounts;
- The benefits of partnership taxation are desired;
- The business or investment activity in question can be operated as an LLC under state law;
- The co-owners can live with the legal uncertainties associated with LLC status.

CAUTION: Although LLC statutes place no limits on the number of members, a tax problem arises if ownership interests are so widely held that they are "publicly traded" within the meaning of IRC §7704. If an LLC's ownership interests are publicly traded, the LLC will be treated as a C corporation for federal income tax purposes.

LLCs Compared to S Corporations

As discussed in section 3.06 of this chapter, the personal assets of S corporation shareholders and LLC members enjoy similar protections against entity-level liabilities.

The biggest advantage of LLCs over S corporations is that LLCs qualify for the benefits of pass-through taxation without the numerous restrictions that apply to S corporations. These restrictions are summarized in section 3.09 of this chapter and covered in more depth in Chapter 8.

Because LLCs are treated as partnerships for federal income tax purposes, they qualify for tax advantages beyond pass-though taxation. In general, the partnership taxation rules are significantly more generous and flexible than the provisions applying to S corporations. The differences between partnership taxation and S corporation taxation are highlighted in section 3.09 of this chapter and covered in depth in Chapter 5.

> *OBSERVATION: To be treated as a partnership for federal income tax purposes, an LLC must have at least two members. In contrast, S corporations can be formed with only one shareholder. In general, as long as there are at least two LLC members the LLC will be respected as a partnership. In some cases, the two-member rule appears to be a significant roadblock. However, as discussed in Chapter 5, there are often ways to address this issue—for example, by forming a husband–wife partnership.*

The key negative factors affecting LLCs are the issues of legal uncertainty and state LLC statute variability. Also, some businesses (such as certain professional practices) may be prohibited under state law and/or professional standards from operating as LLCs. (See discussions of these issues in sections 3.02 and 3.03 of this chapter.)

Compared to S corporations, LLCs generally are superior if:

- There are at least two owners;
- The co-owners desire pass-through taxation, but qualifying as an S corporation would be inconvenient, difficult, or impossible; *or*
- The entity could qualify as an S corporation, but the benefits of the partnership taxation rules are significant compared to the S corporation taxation rules; *and*
- The business or investment activity in question can be operated as an LLC under state law and applicable professional standards;
- The co-owners can live with the legal uncertainties associated with LLC status.

Single-Member LLCs Compared to Sole Proprietorships and Corporations

Single-member LLCs are generally the best choice for solely owned businesses when liability protection and pass-through taxation are desired. As explained earlier in this section, the single-member LLC's decisive advantage is maximum simplicity under the federal tax rules.

Because single-member LLCs offer their owners liability protection, they are clearly superior to sole proprietorships.

However, in some cases, S corporation status can offer significant federal payroll tax savings, as explained in Chapter 8. Thus, in limited circumstances, operating as an S corporation may be preferable to single-member LLC status, despite the additional tax filing burdens. Of course, in states not permitting single-member LLCs, the S corporation is the only choice for a solely owned business when both liability protection and pass-through taxation are desired.

As explained in Chapters 6 and 7, C corporation status can be appropriate for a solely owned business when the objective is maximizing business cash flow by minimizing current tax liabilities.

Nevertheless, when single-member LLC status is available under state law, it will be—as mentioned earlier—the best choice for the great majority of solely owned businesses.

3.14 SUMMARY STATEMENT ON WHEN LLCs ARE ATTRACTIVE

LLCs are suitable for many business and investment activities, including, but not limited to, the following:

- Corporate joint ventures (where the corporate co-owners desire both pass-through taxation and limited liability);
- Real estate investment and development activities (because the partnership taxation rules allow investors to obtain basis from entity-level debt and because special tax allocations can be made to investors);
- Oil and gas exploration (where the partnership rules can be used to make special allocations of intangible drilling cost deductions to investors);
- Venture capital investments (where the partnership rules allow pass-through taxation and the creation of "customized" ownership interests with varying rights to cash flow, liquidating distributions, and tax items);
- Business start-ups expected to have tax losses in the initial years (which can be passed through to investors); and
- Professional practices—if allowed under state law and applicable professional standards (where pass-through taxation can be combined with specially tailored ownership interests that reflect each member's contributions to the practice); and
- Estate-planning vehicles (where the older generation can gift LLC ownership interests to younger family members while retaining control by functioning as the managers, and where all taxable income is passed through to the members).

Under some state laws and/or applicable professional standards (such as state bar association rules), LLCs may be prohibited from operating certain professional practices. When permitted, however, LLCs are an excellent choice. In some states, professional LLCs offer better liability protection than limited liability partnerships (LLPs) do, as discussed in

Chapter 4. And the ability to create differing types of LLC ownership interests (for example, to reflect the activity levels of the members) can be attractive to professional groups.

Some states do not permit the use of LLCs in certain lines of business, such as banking, insurance, and farming.

> **CAUTION:** *Although LLC statutes place no limits on the number of members, a tax problem arises if ownership interests are so widely held that they are "publicly traded" within the meaning of IRC §7704. If an LLC's ownership interests are publicly traded, the LLC will be treated as a C corporation for federal income tax purposes.*

Because LLCs allow all members to participate fully in management without risk of losing limited liability protection (which can happen with a limited partnership, as discussed in section 3.06 of this chapter), they are ideal for closely held entrepreneurial businesses.

In summary, LLCs may be the best choice for business and investment ventures if:

- There will be more than one owner;
- Limited liability protection for the co-owners is an important consideration;
- Pass-through taxation is desired;
- The advantages of partnership taxation are significant compared to the alternative of S corporation taxation, or the entity cannot qualify for S corporation status (see discussion in section 3.09 of this chapter);
- The business (or investment) activity can be operated as an LLC under state law and applicable professional standards; and
- The co-owners can tolerate the uncertainties of LLC status.

Appendix 3A: Limited Liability Company Statutes

State	LLC Statutes	Year Legislation Effective	Secretary of State or Equivalent
Alabama	Ala. Code §§10-12-1 to 10-12-61	1993	Secretary of State Corporate Section P.O. Box 5616 Montgomery, AL 36103
Alaska	Title 10, Ch. 50 Alaska Statutes	1995	Division of Banking, Securities and Corporations P.O. Box 110808 Juneau, AK 99811
Arizona	Ariz. Rev. Statutes §§29-601 to 29-857	1992	Arizona Corporation Commission 1200 West Washington Phoenix, AZ 85007
Arkansas	Ark. Code §§4-32-101 to 4-32-1316	1993	Secretary of State 256 State Capitol Fifth and Woodlane Little Rock, AR 72201
California	Cal. Corp. Code §§17000 to 17705	1994	Secretary of State Limited Liability Company Unit P.O. Box 944228 Sacramento, CA 94224
Colorado	Colo. Rev. Stat. §§7-80-101 to 7-80-1101	1990	Secretary of State Department of State 1560 Broadway, Suite 200 Denver, CO 80202
Connecticut	Conn. Gen. Stat. Chapter 613, §§34-100 to 34-242	1993	Secretary of State 30 Trinity Street Hartford, CT 06106
Delaware	Del. Code §§18-101 to 18-1107	1992	Secretary of State Division of Corporations P.O. Box 898 Dover, DE 19903
District of Columbia	1994 District of Columbia Code Title 29, Chapter 13	1994	Superintendent of Corporations 614 H Street NW, Room 407 Washington, DC 20001
Florida	Fla. Stat. §§608.401 to 608.514	1992	Florida Dept. of State Division of Corporations P.O. Box 6327 Tallahassee, FL 32399
Georgia	Ga. Code §§14-11-100 to 14-11-1107	1993	Business Information & Services Suite 315, West Tower 2 Martin Luther King, Jr. Dr. Atlanta, GA 30334

State	LLC Statutes	Year Legislation Effective	Secretary of State or Equivalent
Hawaii	§1 of 1996 Act 92	——	Director, Dept. of Commerce and Consumer Affairs Business Registration Division P.O. Box 40 Honolulu, HI 96810
Idaho	Idaho Code §§53-601 to 53-672	1993	Secretary of State Statehouse Boise, ID 83720
Illinois	Chapter 805 Ill. Comp. Stat. Ann. §§180/1-1 to 180/60-1	1994	Secretary of State Dept. of Business Services/LLC Division Room 359 Michael J. Howlett Building Springfield, IL 62756
Indiana	Ind. Code §§23-18-1 to 23-18-13	1993	Secretary of State Corporations Division 302 West Washington Street Indianapolis, IN 46204
Iowa	Iowa Code Title XII, Subtitle 2, Chapter 490A	1992	Secretary of State Business Services Division Hoover Building Des Moines, IA 50319
Kansas	Kan. Stat. Ann. §§17-7601 to 17-7652	1990	Secretary of State State Capitol, Second Floor 300 Southwest Tenth Avenue Topeka, KS 66612
Kentucky	1994 Ky. Revised Statutes Chapter 275	1994	Secretary of State Capitol Building, Room 154 Frankfort, KY 40601
Louisiana	La. Corp. Laws §§12:1301 to 12:1369	1992	Secretary of State Corporations Division P.O. Box 94125 Baton Rouge, LA 70804
Maine	Maine Revised Statutes Title 31, §§601 to 762	1995	Secretary of State Department of State Statehouse Station #101 Augusta, ME 04333
Maryland	Md. Code Ann. §§4A.101 to 4A.1103	1992	Dept. of Assessments and Taxation 301 W. Preston Street Baltimore, MD 21201
Massachusetts	MGL Chapter 156C	1996	Corporations Division One Asburton Place, Room 1717 Boston, MA 02108
Michigan	Mich. Comp. Laws §21.198(101) to 21.198(1200)	1993	Michigan Dept. of Consumer and Industry Services Corporation Division 6546 Mercantile Way Lansing, MI 48910

State	LLC Statutes	Year Legislation Effective	Secretary of State or Equivalent
Minnesota	Minn. Stat. §§322B.01 to 322B.960	1993	Secretary of State Business Services Division 180 State Office Building 100 Constitution Avenue St. Paul, NM 55155
Mississippi	Mississippi Code Ann. Title 79, Chapter 29	1994	Secretary of State P.O. Box 136 Jackson, MS 39205
Missouri	Mo. Rev. Stat. §§347.010 to 347.187	1993	Secretary of State P.O. Box 778 Jefferson City, MO 65102
Montana	Mont. Code Ann. §§35-8-101 to 35-8-1307	1993	Secretary of State P.O. Box 202801 Helena, MT 59620
Nebraska	Neb. Rev. Stat. §21-2601 to 21.2653	1994	Secretary of State P.O. Box 94608 Lincoln, NE 68509
Nevada	Nev. Rev. Stat. §§86.011 to 86.571	1991	Secretary of State Limited Liability Division Capitol Complex Carson City, NV 89710
New Hampshire	N.H. Rev. Stat. Title XXVIII, Chapter 304-C, Sections 1 to 85	1993	Secretary of State State House, Room 204 107 North Main Street Concord, NH 03301
New Jersey	N.J. Stat. Title 42, Chapter 2B	1994	Department of State Division of Commercial Recording CN 308 Trenton, NJ 08625
New Mexico	N.M. Stat. §§53-19-1 to 53-19-74	1993	State Corporation Commission Corporation Department P.O. Drawer 1269 Santa Fe, NM 87504
New York	New York Consolidated Laws Chapter 34, Sections 101 to 1403	1994	Secretary of State Department of State 162 Washington Avenue Albany, NY 12231
North Carolina	N.C. Gen. Stat., Chapter 57C	1993	Corporations Division Dept. of the Secretary of State 300 North Salisbury Street Raleigh, NC 27603
North Dakota	N.D. Cent. Code Title 10, Chapter 10-32	1993	Secretary of State State Capitol 600 East Boulevard Avenue Bismarck, ND 58505

State	LLC Statutes	Year Legislation Effective	Secretary of State or Equivalent
Ohio	Ohio Revised Code Title XVII, Chapter 1705	1994	Secretary of State 30 East Broad Street 14th Floor Columbus, OH 43266
Oklahoma	Okla. Stat. Title 18, Chapter 32 §§2000 to 2060	1992	Secretary of State 101 State Capitol Building 2300 N. Lincoln Boulevard Oklahoma City, OK 73105
Oregon	Or. Rev. Stat. §§63.001 to 63.990	1993	Secretary of State Corporation Division—Business Registry 255 Capitol Street NE, Ste. 151 Salem, OR 97310
Pennsylvania	Pennsylvania Consolidated Statutes Title 15, §8901 to 8998	1995	Secretary of the Commonwealth Dept. of State, Corporation Bureau P.O. Box 8722 Harrisburg, PA 17105
Rhode Island	R.I. Gen. Laws §§7-16-1 to 7-16-75	1992	Secretary of State 100 N. Main Street Providence, RI 02903
South Carolina	South Carolina Code Title 33, Chapter 44	1996	Secretary of State P.O. Box 11350 Columbia, SC 29211
South Dakota	S.D. Codified Laws Title 47, Chapter 47-34	1993	Secretary of State State Capitol 500 East Capitol Ave. Pierre, SD 57501
Tennessee	Tennessee Code §48-201-101 to 48-248-606	1994	Department of State Corporations Section James K. Polk Building, 18th Floor Nashville, TN 37243
Texas	Tex. Rev. Civ. Stat. Title 32, Chapter 18	1991	Secretary of State Statutory Filings Division Corporations Section P.O. Box 13697 Austin, TX 78711
Utah	Utah Code Title 48, Chapter 2b	1991	Division of Corporations and Commercial Code Box 146705 Salt Lake City, UT 84114
Vermont	Vermont Statutes Ann. Title 11, Chapter 21	1996	Secretary of State Corporations Division 109 State Street Montpelier, VT 05609
Virginia	Virginia Code Title 13.1, Chapter 12	1991	Clerk of the State Corporation Commission Tyler Building 1300 East Main Street Richmond, VA 23209

State	LLC Statutes	Year Legislation Effective	Secretary of State or Equivalent
Washington	Wash. Rev. Code Title 25, Chapter 25.15	1994	Office of the Secretary of State Corporations Division P.O. Box 40234 Olympia, WA 98504
West Virginia	W. Va. Code Chapter 31B, Articles 1–13	1996	Secretary of State Corporations Division, Bldg. 1, Room 139-W 1900 Kanawha Boulevard East Charleston, WV 25305
Wisconsin	Wis. Stat. §§183.0102 to 183.1305	1994	Department of Financial Institutions Corporations Unit P.O. Box 7846 Madison, WI 53707
Wyoming	Wyoming Statutes §17-15-101 to 144	1995	Secretary of State State Capitol Cheyenne, WY 82002

Appendix 3B: State Income Tax Classification of Limited Liability Companies

CAUTION: The information in this appendix applies only to multi-member LLCs, unless single-member LLCs are specifically mentioned. Be aware that the information was compiled before Treasury issued the check the box entity classification regulations explained in section 3.08 of this chapter. As this publication goes to press, most states have indicated that they will continue to follow the federal classification for multi-member LLCs in the "post–check the box era." In these states, multi-member LLCs with more than two of the four corporate characteristics generally will be classified as partnerships for both federal and state tax purposes, unless they elect to be treated as corporations. It appears that many other states will soon officially agree to follow the federal classification of multi-member LLCs (probably most states will also eventually follow the federal classification of single-member LLCs). Nevertheless, the tax advisor should always confirm the current state tax classification of LLCs (for both multi-member and single-member entities) before advising clients. As indicated in this appendix, only Arkansas, California, Florida, and Texas are known to affirmatively *not* follow the federal tax classification of multi-member LLCs as this book goes to press.

State	State Income Tax Classification of LLCs
Alabama	Same as federal, except single-member LLCs taxed as partnerships.
Alaska	Same as federal.
Arizona	Same as federal.
Arkansas	If LLC has two or more members, it will file partnership tax returns. If LLC only has one member, its sole member will report the LLC's income on his personal return. LLCs must also pay a $100 franchise tax.
California	Same as federal. LLCs must also pay an annual $800 privilege tax plus a small annual fee based on income.
Colorado	Same as federal.
Connecticut	Same as federal.
Delaware	Same as federal. $100 fee due with annual report.
District of Columbia	Same as federal. May owe unincorporated business tax.
Florida	An LLC is an "artificial entity" under Florida law so it is subject to the state's corporate franchise tax.

State	State Income Tax Classification of LLCs
Georgia	Same as federal.
Hawaii	Same as federal.
Idaho	Same as federal.
Illinois	Same as federal.
Indiana	Same as federal.
Iowa	Same as federal.
Kansas	Same as federal. Must pay state franchise tax.
Kentucky	Same as federal.
Louisiana	Same as federal.
Maine	Same as federal.
Maryland	Same as federal.
Massachusetts	Same as federal.
Michigan	Not applicable, because state imposes a tax on all businesses, including LLCs.
Minnesota	Same as federal. May owe a "minimum fee."
Mississippi	Same as federal.
Missouri	Same as federal.
Montana	Same as federal.
Nebraska	Same as federal.
Nevada	No state income tax.
New Hampshire	Same as federal. May owe business profits tax.
New Jersey	Same as federal.
New Mexico	No entity return required, but members pay tax at their level.

State	State Income Tax Classification of LLCs
New York	Same as federal. Must pay annual filing fee based on number of members.
North Carolina	Same as federal.
North Dakota	Same as federal.
Ohio	Same as federal.
Oklahoma	Same as federal.
Oregon	Same as federal.
Pennsylvania	Same as federal.
Rhode Island	Same as federal. May owe minimum Business Corporation Tax.
South Carolina	Same as federal.
South Dakota	No state income tax, however must pay $50 annual fee.
Tennessee	Same as federal. May owe tax on interest and dividends.
Texas	No state income tax, but LLCs are subject to corporation franchise tax based on capital or earned surplus.
Utah	Same as federal.
Vermont	Same as federal. Must pay income tax on behalf of nonresident members and may owe annual minimum tax as well.
Virginia	Same as federal.
Washington	No state income tax.
West Virginia	Same as federal. LLCs must pay withholding tax on distributions of income to nonresident members and a franchise tax on capital.
Wisconsin	Same as federal.
Wyoming	No state income tax, however a nominal tax on capital applies.

Appendix 3C-1: Sample Client Letter When Multi-Member LLC Appears to Be Best Entity Choice

Dear [Client name]:

This letter briefly summarizes some of the major considerations that went into your recent decision to form a new business that will be operated as a limited liability company (LLC).

As you know, LLCs are increasingly popular because they combine the best legal and tax characteristics of corporations and partnerships, while avoiding many of the disadvantages.

Specifically, an LLC can offer limited liability protection to all its owners (referred to as "members") along with the advantages of being treated as a partnership for federal income tax purposes.

Summary of General Legal Considerations

LLCs are unincorporated legal entities created under state law. Even though LLCs are *unincorporated* vehicles, the fundamental intent of LLC statutes is to allow the formation of entities that are legally more similar to corporations than to partnerships. Nevertheless, LLCs usually can be treated as partnerships for federal income tax purposes. The critical point to remember is that, legally, LLCs are *not* corporations, nor are they partnerships.

As mentioned earlier, LLC owners are referred to as "members" rather than as shareholders or partners. This is indicative of the fact that LLCs are completely distinct legal creatures that are permitted and governed by the LLC statute in the state of formation.

Because LLC laws are new, there are inevitable legal uncertainties associated with making the choice to operate as an LLC rather than as a partnership or as a C or S corporation. For example, when an LLC operates in several states with LLC statutes (which can vary considerably), it is not always clear which has precedence: the LLC statute in the state of formation or the laws in the state where operations are conducted. Most LLC statutes provide that the LLC laws in the state of formation apply, but this may be limited to the types of businesses permitted to operate as LLCs in the state where the operations are conducted.

With regard to the specific states where you intend to operate the LLC, we have concluded **[This section should also cover any significant state and local tax issues and uncertainties.]**.

As we discussed, even when an LLC operates only in the state of formation, the novelty of LLC statutes means there are inevitably some legal uncertainties that do not exist with more established types of entities. The LLC statutes provide legal frameworks, but these can never anticipate all the questions and issues that arise from real-life events and transactions.

In summary, LLCs have a very short legal track record. There is essentially no LLC case law. As a result, the rights and obligations of LLC members, creditors, and other third parties contracting with LLCs are just not as well understood as would be the case if operations were conducted via limited or general partnerships or corporations.

You have indicated that you and the other parties who will be the members of the proposed LLC have carefully considered the potentially negative issue of legal uncertainty and have concluded that the LLC form of doing business is still the best choice for your venture.

Limited Liability of LLC Members

An LLC is a separate legal entity (apart from its members and managers) that owns its assets and is liable for its debts. Therefore, the personal assets of LLC members and managers generally are beyond the reach of LLC creditors. The limited liability of *all* LLC members and managers is the fundamental *nontax* advantage of LLC status.

The liability-limiting advantages of LLCs are critically important, but they should not be overstated. While the personal assets of LLC members and managers are protected from "general" LLC debts and obligations (often referred to as "contract liabilities"), these persons generally remain *exposed* to LLC liabilities resulting from their own tortious acts and professional errors and omissions. (Tortious *acts* are defined as wrongful acts leading to civil actions, other than those involving breach of contract.)

LLC members and managers may also be personally liable for negligence in supervising other members, managers, or employees.

In short, LLCs generally do *not* offer liability protection to members and managers beyond what corporations are able to offer to their shareholders who are officers, directors, and employees.

The issue of members' and managers' exposure to liabilities related to tortious acts, omissions, and negligence is a matter of state law. If you have specific questions about this issue, we recommend you consult with your attorney.

Guarantees of LLC Debts

Like corporate shareholders, LLC members may be required on occasion to personally guarantee certain of the entity's debts as a condition of obtaining financing or for other reasons.

Members are personally obligated with respect to LLC debts that are specifically guaranteed.

Treatment of LLCs as Partnerships for Tax Purposes

The key *tax* advantage of LLCs is that they can be treated as partnerships for federal income tax purposes.

Conclusion

Only LLCs are able to offer both the legal advantage of limited liability for all owners and the tax advantage of partnership taxation—which combines pass-through treatment with maximum flexibility. This unique combination of legal and tax benefits is the driving force behind the increasing popularity of LLCs.

We appreciate the opportunity to consult with you as you make the important decision of choosing the most advantageous type of entity to operate your new venture. We look forward to working with you in the future as your LLC is formed and enters the operating phase.

Very truly yours,

Appendix 3C-2: Sample "Generic" Client or Contact Letter Regarding Which Types of Businesses and Activities Are Suited for Multi-Member LLCs

Dear [Client or contact name]:

As we briefly discussed, the limited liability company (LLC) is an exciting new option to consider when selecting the type of legal entity to operate a business or investment venture. Only LLCs are able to offer both the legal advantage of limited liability for all owners and the tax advantage of partnership taxation—which combines pass-through treatment with maximum flexibility. This unique combination of legal and tax benefits is the driving force behind the increasing popularity of LLCs.

As you requested, this letter outlines general considerations regarding the types of business and investment activities that may be suitable for a limited liability company (LLC) to conduct.

Specific Types of Businesses and Activities

Generally, state LLC statutes permit LLCs to conduct any lawful business or investment activity except those prohibited by the statutes themselves or those prohibited under the particular LLC's articles of organization.

Under some state laws and/or applicable professional standards (such as state bar association rules), LLCs may be prohibited from operating certain professional practices. Also, some states do not permit the use of LLCs in certain lines of business, such as banking, insurance, and farming.

Business and investment activities where LLCs can make sense include, but are not limited to, the following:

- Corporate joint ventures (where the corporate co-owners desire both pass-through taxation and limited liability);
- Real estate investment and development activities (where the partnership taxation rules allow investors to receive special allocations of tax losses and obtain basis from entity-level debt);
- Oil and gas exploration (where the partnership taxation rules allow special allocations of deductions for intangible drilling costs);
- Venture capital investments (where the partnership rules allow pass-through taxation and the creation of ownership interests with varying rights to cash flow, liquidating distributions, and tax items);
- Business start-ups expected to have tax losses in the initial years (which can be passed through to investors);
- Professional practices—if allowed under state law and applicable professional standards (where pass-through taxation can be com-

bined with specially tailored ownership interests that reflect each member's contributions to the practice); and

- Estate planning vehicles (where the older generation can gift LLC ownership interests to younger family members while retaining control by functioning as the managers and where all taxable income is passed through to the members).

General Factors to Consider

Because LLCs allow all members to participate fully in management without risk of losing limited liability protection (which can happen with a limited partnership), LLCs are often ideally suited for closely held entrepreneurial businesses and closely held investment activities.

To be more specific, LLCs may be the *best* choice in the following circumstances:

- If there will be more than one owner;
- If limited liability protection for the co-owners is an important consideration;
- If the advantages of partnership taxation are significant compared to the alternative of S corporation taxation, or if the entity cannot qualify for S corporation status;
- If the business or investment activity can be operated as an LLC under state law and applicable professional standards; and
- If the co-owners can tolerate the uncertainties of LLC status.

Conclusion

I enjoyed the opportunity to discuss LLCs with you and hope this letter is helpful. If you have questions or would like additional information about LLCs or other choice-of-entity issues, please give me a call.

Very truly yours,

Appendix 3C-3: Sample Client Letter When Single-Member LLC Appears to Be Best Entity Choice

Dear [Client name]:

This letter briefly summarizes some of the major considerations that went into your recent decision to form a new business that will be operated as a single-member (solely owned) limited liability company (LLC).

Single-member LLCs are popular because they combine the best characteristics of S corporations and sole proprietorships, while avoiding many of their disadvantages. Specifically, a single-member LLC offers liability protection to you, the owner, along with the simplicity of being treated as a sole proprietorship for federal tax purposes.

Summary of General Legal Considerations

LLC owners are referred to as "members." Single-member LLCs are unincorporated legal entities created under state law. The fundamental intent of the LLC statute is to allow the formation of a solely owned entity that is legally similar to a corporation. However, the existence of the single-member LLC is ignored for federal tax purposes.

Because our state's LLC law is relatively new, there are inevitable legal uncertainties associated with making the choice to operate as an LLC rather than as a solely-owned C or S corporation.

For example, when an LLC operates in several states with LLC statutes (which can vary considerably), it is not always clear whether the LLC statute in the state of formation or the laws in the state where operations are conducted has precedence. Most LLC statutes provide that the LLC laws in the state of formation apply, but this may be limited to the types of businesses permitted to operate as LLCs in the state where the operations are conducted.

With regard to the specific states where you intend to operate the LLC, we have concluded [use this paragraph to cover state-specific legal issues and uncertainties].

As we discussed, even when an LLC operates only in the state of formation, the novelty of LLC statutes means there are inevitably some legal uncertainties that do not exist with more established types of entities. The LLC statutes provide legal frameworks, but these can never anticipate all the questions and issues that arise from real-life events and transactions.

In summary, LLCs have a very short legal track record. There is essentially no LLC case law. As a result, the rights and obligations of LLC members, creditors, and other third parties contracting with LLCs are just not as well understood as would be the case if your business were conducted via an S or C corporation.

You have indicated that you have carefully considered the potentially negative issue of legal uncertainty and have concluded that the single-member LLC form of doing business is still the best choice for your venture.

Limited Liability for You

A single-member LLC is a separate legal entity (apart from its owner/member). The LLC owns its own assets and is liable for its own debts. Therefore, the personal assets of the owner/member are generally beyond the reach of the LLC's creditors. This protection from business-related liabilities is the principal nontax advantage of single-member LLC status.

However, your personal assets generally remain exposed to LLC liabilities resulting from your own tortious acts and professional errors and omissions. *Tortious acts* are defined as wrongful acts leading to civil actions other than those involving breach of contract (for example, careless operation of an automobile with resulting property damage or injuries to others). You may also be personally liable for negligence in supervising the LLC's employees. In short, single-member LLCS generally do not offer liability protection beyond that offered by corporations to their shareholders.

The issue of liability exposure is a matter of state law. If you have specific questions, we recommend you consult with your attorney.

Guarantees of LLC Debts

As is the case with corporate shareholders, LLC members may be required on occasion to personally guarantee certain entity debts as a condition of obtaining financing or for other reasons. You will be personally obligated with respect to any LLC debts that you specifically guarantee.

Tax Treatment of Your Single-Member LLC

As mentioned earlier, the existence of a single-member LLC is ignored for federal tax purposes. Accordingly, your business activity will be treated as a sole proprietorship in the eyes of the IRS. Each year, you will file Schedules C and SE with your Form 1040. No separate tax returns will be required for your business, nor are required to file any federal payroll tax forms to account for money you withdraw from the business. Transfers of assets between you and the LLC will have no federal tax ramifications. This tax regime is obviously much simpler than would be the case with a solely owned corporation. With a corporation, you would be required to file a separate federal tax return and carefully account for any transfers of cash and assets between you and the corporation.

From a state tax perspective [use this paragraph to cover any state-specific tax issues and uncertainties associated with single-member LLC status].

Conclusion

The single-member LLC form of doing business offers legal liability protection and plus maximum tax simplicity. No other type of solely owned entity combines both of these advantages.

We appreciate the opportunity to consult with you as you make the important decision of choosing the most advantageous type of entity to operate your new venture. We look forward to working with you in the future as your LLC is formed and enters the operating phase.

Very truly yours,

Appendix 3D: Checklist for LLC Articles of Organization

Purpose: Use this checklist in conjunction with the operating agreement checklist (see Appendix 3F) to gather information and draft LLC governing documents (the articles of organization and the operating agreement) that adequately address the members' wishes about how the LLC will be formed and operated. You may conclude that some of the items listed below are more appropriately included in the operating agreement. (See Appendix 3E for sample articles of organization and Appendix 3G for a sample operating agreement.)

> *CAUTION: To be legally valid, articles of incorporation must, at a minimum, comply with the applicable state LLC statute. This checklist is illustrative and is not intended to ensure compliance with any state LLC statute. The statute may require additional information, or it may not require all the information indicated below. Competent legal counsel should be engaged in connection with the drafting of any LLC governing documents.*

_____   1. State the LLC will be organized in.

_____

_____   2. Exact name of the LLC and confirm with the appropriate state official (usually the Secretary of State) that the desired name is available for use.

_____

_____   3. Name, address, phone, and FAX numbers of the LLC's registered agent.

_____

_____

_____

_____   4. Address, phone, and FAX numbers of the LLC's registered office.

_____

_____

_____

_____   5. Duration of the life of the LLC (in years or until a specific date) or the event (such as completion of a specific business task) that will terminate the legal existence of the LLC.

_____

_____

_____ 6. Provisions for how the LLC will be managed—by all members ("member managed") or by designated managers ("manager managed").

_____

_____

_____ 7. Specific business purpose of the LLC or use general language (for example, "to engage in any lawful business permitted under the LLC statute").

_____

_____

_____ 8. Names and addresses of the persons (the "organizers") who will sign the articles of organization.

_____

_____

_____

_____

_____

_____ 9. Date the legal existence of the LLC will begin.

_____

_____ 10. Names and addresses of the initial members of the LLC.

_____

_____

_____

_____

_____

_____ 11. Terms (for example, "unanimous consent of the members") under which new members may be admitted to the LLC or under which existing members may transfer their ownership interests to others.

_____

_____

_____

_____

_____ 12. Events ("dissolution events") that will legally terminate the existence of the LLC. (For example, dissolution events typically include the death, insanity, bankruptcy, retirement, resignation, or expulsion of any member.)

_____

_____ 13. Action required for the members to consent to continue the LLC after a dissolution event occurs (for example, "unanimous consent of the remaining members").

_____

_____

_____ 14. Indication of whether the LLC intends to be taxed as a C corporation or as a partnership. (A multi-member LLC is treated as a partnership for federal income tax purposes by default. However, the LLC could elect to be treated as an association taxable as a corporation. This would rarely be attractive.)

_____

Appendix 3E: Sample LLC Articles of Organization

CAUTION: To be legally valid, articles of incorporation must, at a minimum, comply with the applicable state LLC statute. This sample document is illustrative and is not intended to ensure compliance with any state LLC statute. The statute may require additional information, or it may not require all the information indicated below. Obviously, the LLC's articles of organization have serious legal implications. Competent legal counsel should be engaged in connection with the drafting of any LLC governing documents.

ARTICLE 1

The name of the limited liability company (the "Company") shall be [name of Company], and it shall be organized under the laws of the State of [name of State].

ARTICLE 2

The name, address, phone, and FAX numbers of the Company's registered agent are as follows:

_____

_____

_____

ARTICLE 3

The address, phone, and FAX numbers of the Company's registered office are as follows:

_____

_____

_____

ARTICLE 4

The Company's legal existence will commence at [specify date and time, or "upon date these Articles of Organization are filed by the Secretary of State of [State of formation], or other time permitted under the statute"].

ARTICLE 5

The latest date upon which the Company shall dissolve is [date].

ARTICLE 6

The Company shall vest management in one or more managers, as provided in the Operating Agreement.

ARTICLE 7

The general purpose of the Company is to transact any and all lawful business for which an LLC may be organized under the laws of the State of [State in which LLC is to be organized]. The Company shall have all powers granted to limited liability companies under the laws of the State of [State in which LLC is to be organized].

ARTICLE 8

The names and addresses of the Company's organizers are as follows:

_____

_____

_____

ARTICLE 9

The following events ("dissolution events") will terminate the legal existence of the Company: the death, insanity, bankruptcy, retirement, resignation, or expulsion of any member.

ARTICLE 10

In the event of the occurrence of any one of the dissolution events specified in Article 9, the legal existence of the Company will be terminated, unless there is a majority of interest vote of the remaining members to continue the business and affairs of the Company.

ARTICLE 11

It is the intent of the members that the Company be classified as a partnership for federal income tax purposes.

Appendix 3F: LLC Operating Agreement Checklist

Purpose: Use this checklist in drafting or reviewing an LLC operating agreement. The operating agreement is a written record describing the members' intentions regarding how the LLC will be formed and operated. However, its provisions must also comply with the applicable LLC statute. Some or all of the items listed below may be beyond the scope of the case at hand. By the same token, the client's situation may demand additional language covering matters not listed below. Competent legal counsel should be engaged in connection with the drafting of any LLC governing documents.

_____ 1. Name of LLC, names of initial members, and date of agreement.

_____

_____

_____

_____ 2. Date the LLC intends to commence its legal existence.

_____

_____ 3. Description of LLC's business or investment purpose or activities.

_____

_____

_____ 4. Duration of the LLC.

_____

_____ 5. Description of LLC's principal place of business, and name and address of LLC's registered agent.

_____

_____

_____ 6. Designation of managers (if appropriate), and provisions for removing existing managers and replacing them with new managers.

_____

_____

_____

_____ 7. Required initial capital contributions and provisions for anticipated and unanticipated future contributions of capital (including what happens to members who fail to make their contributions).

_____

_____

_____

_____ 8. Dates of LLC distributions and rights of members to take draws in advance of formal distribution dates.

_____

_____

_____

_____ 9. Descriptions of how distributions are calculated (for example, if certain members are to receive "preferred returns" with respect to their capital accounts).

_____

_____

_____

_____ 10. Provisions for member salaries (treated as IRC §707 guaranteed payments for tax purposes).

_____

_____

_____

_____ 11. Specific authority for LLC to borrow or incur debts.

_____

_____

_____

_____ 12. Specific authority for members to lend to LLC and/or for LLC to lend to members.

_____

_____

_____

_____ 13. Place where LLC's legal and financial records will be kept, and rights of members to demand an accounting from the entity.

_____

_____

_____

_____ 14. Rights of members to obtain access to LLC's books and records.

_____

_____

_____

_____ 15. Any restrictions on authority of managers to act without member approval (for example, a unanimous vote of the members may be required to amend the operating agreement or to engage in certain major transactions, such as a sale of substantially all of the LLC's assets).

_____

_____

_____

_____ 16. Voting provisions for what is a quorum, how members' votes are counted (per capita or based on percentage interest in the LLC), what majority is needed to conclude on certain issues, etc.

_____

_____

_____

_____ 17. Provisions for periodic meetings of the members.

_____

_____

_____

_____ 18. Procedures for admission of new members.

_____

_____

_____

_____ 19. Provisions for voluntary withdrawal, retirement, or expulsion of members (including what rights these members have to payment for their ownership interests, payment terms, and how such interests will be valued).

_____

_____

_____

_____ 20. Provisions for whether the LLC will take the member's share of the LLC's goodwill into account for purposes of Item 19 above, and how such goodwill will be valued.

_____

_____

_____ 21. Provisions for ability of members to sell, assign, or otherwise transfer their ownership interests to third parties (including rights of first refusal for the LLC or other members to purchase such interests, and how valuation of such interests will be determined).

_____

_____

_____

_____ 22. Provisions for buyouts of member's interests upon retirement, disability, insanity, death, etc. (including how such interests will be valued and what the payment terms will be).

_____

_____

_____

_____ 23. Noncompete provisions after member withdrawals.

_____

_____

_____

_____ 24. Provisions for voting to continue the LLC (or not) after the withdrawal, death, etc., of a member causes a legal dissolution of the entity.

_____

_____

_____

_____ 25. Provisions for the members agreeing to terminate the existence of the LLC, and how the LLC will be terminated in other circumstances.

_____

_____

_____

_____ 26. Provisions for how property will be valued if the LLC is terminated and all assets are distributed in liquidation.

_____

_____

_____

_____ 27. Financial accounting and tax provisions for how profits, losses, and liabilities will be shared, how "book" capital accounts will be maintained (including how they will be adjusted when noncash property is contributed or distributed), how tax items will be allocated among the members, how capital accounts will be maintained for tax accounting purposes, when the LLC will make an IRC §754 election, etc.

_____

_____

_____

_____ 28. Arbitration provisions for resolving disputes between members or between the LLC and a member.

_____

_____

_____

_____ 29. A recitation that the members intend to form an entity that will be treated as a partnership for tax purposes as of the specified commencement date and that they intend to share the profits, losses, and obligations arising from the venture.

_____

_____

_____

CAUTION: _Obviously, an operating agreement has serious legal implications. Competent legal counsel should be engaged in connection with drafting any LLC governing documents._

Appendix 3G: Sample LLC Operating Agreement

CAUTION: To be legally valid, an operating agreement must, at a minimum, comply with the applicable state LLC statute. This sample document is illustrative and is not intended to ensure compliance with any state LLC statute. Obviously, the LLC's operating agreement has serious legal implications. Competent legal counsel should engaged in connection with the drafting of any LLC governing documents.

Limited Liability Company Operating Agreement of:

_____

Table of Contents

Article

This Limited Liability Company Operating Agreement of [Company name] is made as of [date] among [list initial parties] and all of the persons who from time to time shall then be parties hereto. In consideration of the mutual acknowledgments and promises set out herein, the parties agree as follows.

ARTICLE 1:
INTENT

1.1 Intent. The initial parties hereto are contemporaneously herewith forming a limited liability company by filing articles of organization of the Company in accordance with the Act. The initial parties desire to set forth herein their agreement concerning the conduct of the business and affairs of the Company and the relative rights, powers, duties, and obligations of the various Members of the Company. The parties intend for this Agreement to be the "operating agreement" of the Company as such term is defined in the Act.

ARTICLE 2:
DEFINITIONS, TERMINOLOGY,
AND REFERENCES

2.1 Definitions. As used in this Agreement, each of the following terms shall have the meaning set forth below opposite such term:

"Act" means the [name of limited liability company act of the state pursuant to which the Company is to be formed], as amended from time to time.

"Affiliate" means, when used with reference to a specified person, (a) any person who directly or indirectly controls, is controlled by, or is under common control with the specified person; (b) any person who is an officer of, partner in, or trustee of (or who serves in a similar capacity with respect to) the specified person or of which the specified person is an officer, partner, or trustee (or with respect to which the specified person serves in a similar capacity); (c) any person who, directly or indirectly, is the beneficial owner of 10 percent or more of any class of equity securities of, or otherwise has a substantial beneficial interest in, the specified person or of which the specified person is directly or indirectly the owner of 10 percent or more of any class of equity securities or in which the specified person has a substantial beneficial interest; and (d) any relative or spouse of the specified person.

"Agreement" means this Limited Liability Company Operating Agreement of _____, including any exhibits or other attachments hereto, as amended and in effect from time to time.

"Articles" means the articles of organization, as amended, filed with respect to the Company with the Secretary of State of the State.

"Assignee" means (a) each person who acquires by a Transfer all or any portion of a Company Interest, which person is not admitted to the Company as a substituted Member pursuant to this Agreement; and (b) each person who becomes an Assignee pursuant to a specific provision of this

Agreement. The term "**Assignees**" means the group composed of each person who is an Assignee.

"**Bank Rate**" means a fluctuating rate adjusted monthly and compounded on a daily basis equal to two percentage points above the prime rate listed on the last business day of each month in the Midwest Edition of the Wall Street Journal.

"**Capital Account**" means, with respect to any Member or Assignee, the Capital Account maintained for such Member or Assignee pursuant to section 4.3 hereof.

"**Code**" means the Internal Revenue Code of 1986, or any federal income tax law enacted in the place of the Internal Revenue Code of 1986.

"**Company**" means the limited liability company formed pursuant to this Agreement.

"**Company Interest**" means, when used with respect to either a Member or an Assignee, such person's interest in the Company's capital, profits, losses, and distributions; such person's rights, if any, in specific Company property; and such person's rights, if any, to participate in Company management.

"**Event of Withdrawal**" has the meaning given such term in the Act.

"**Fiscal Period**" means each taxable year and other fiscal period of the Company at the end of which the Company's books are closed for tax and accounting purposes pursuant to this Agreement.

"**Gross Income**" and "**Gross Deduction**" mean, in respect of a Fiscal Period, items of Company gross income and gain or gross deduction and loss, respectively, for such Fiscal Period for federal income tax purposes determined subject to the adjustments (a), (b), and (c) described in the definition of "**Net Profits**" and "**Net Loss**."

[Although the members responsible for the day-to-day management of the LLC are referred to as Managing Members, under most LLC statutes the members are not managers unless the articles of organization so provide, and this sample is intended for use as a member-managed LLC.] "**Managing Members**" means _____ and _____ and each person who is named as a replacement Managing Member pursuant to section 9.1 or section 13.2 hereof.

"**Member**" means each of the initial parties hereto and each other person who is admitted to the Company as a Member pursuant to this Agreement, until such time as such person shall cease to be a Member as set out in this Agreement. "Members" means a group composed of each person who is a Member (but does not include any Assignee).

"**Member Nonrecourse Debt**" means a nonrecourse liability of the Company in respect of which a Member bears the economic risk of loss, as determined in accordance with Regulations §1.704-2(b)(4).

"**Member's Loan**" means each loan from a Member to the Company made pursuant to Article 5 hereof.

"**Net Profits**" and "**Net Loss**" mean, respectively, for each Fiscal Period, an amount equal to the Company's taxable income or loss, respectively, for federal income tax purposes for such Fiscal Period (determined without inclusion of Gross Income or Gross Deductions specially allocated pursuant to sections 8.3 through 8.5 of this Agreement), determined in accordance with Code §703(a) (for this purpose, all items of income, gain, loss or deduction required to be stated separately pursuant to Code §703(a)(1) shall be included in taxable income or loss), with the following adjustments: (a) any income of the Company that is exempt from federal income tax and not otherwise taken into account in computing Net Profits or Net Loss pursuant hereto shall be included in income; (b) any expenditures of the Company described in Code §705(e)(2)(B) and not otherwise taken into account in computing Net Profits or Net Loss pursuant hereto shall be deducted from income; and (c) income, gain, loss, and deduction of the Company shall be computed (i) as if the Company purchased any property contributed by a Member on the date of such contribution at a price equal to its fair market value at that date, and (ii) as if the Company had sold any property distributed to a Member on the date of such distribution of a price equal to its fair market value on such date.

"**Regulation**" means the Income Tax Regulations promulgated under the Code, as amended, or any successor income tax regulations.

"**State**" means the state of _____ [the state under whose laws the Company is formed].

"**Transfer**" and "**Transferred**" mean both the passage and the act of effecting the passage of a legal or equitable interest in a Company Interest pursuant to a sale, exchange, gift, assignment, foreclosure, garnishment, or other conveyance or disposition and include without limitation the passage of any such interest by judicial order, bequest, intestate succession, or other operation of law. Notwithstanding the foregoing, such terms do not include within their meaning the passage or the act of effecting the passage of a legal or equitable interest in a Company Interest by pledge, grant of a security interest, or other encumbrance.

"**Unit**" means a quantitative measure of the Company Interests of the Members and Assignees used to distinguish their relative quantitative interests in the Company.

2.2 Terminology. Article headings and section headings used in this Agreement have no legal significance. All personal pronouns used in this Agreement, whether used in the masculine, feminine, or neuter gender, shall, as appropriate to the context in which they are used, include all genders, and the singular shall include the plural and vice versa.

2.3 References. All exhibits attached to this Agreement are incorporated herein by this reference.

ARTICLE 3:
FORMATION

3.1 Formation and Term. The Company will be formed upon the filing of the Articles under the Act. The Company shall continue in existence until it is dissolved and its affairs are wound up pursuant to this Agreement, except to the extent that its separate existence is thereafter continued pursuant to the Act.

3.2 Applicable Law. The Company is formed pursuant to the Act.

3.3 Name. The Company's name shall be "_____." The Members may change the Company's name from time to time pursuant to the provisions of section 9.4 hereof.

3.4 Purpose. The Company may engage in [insert statement of specific purpose for which LLC was formed, if desired, or] any lawful business permitted by the Act.

3.5 Registered Agent and Office; Principal Place of Business. The name and address of the registered agent and office of the Company shall be that listed from time to time in the Articles. The Managing Members from time to time may change the Company's registered agent or office and may establish or change the Company's principal place of business.

3.6 Statutory Compliance. The Managing Members, on behalf of the Company, shall cause the Articles to be filed in the appropriate records of the State. The Managing Members, on behalf of the Company, shall execute and file any assumed or fictitious name certificate or certificates required by law to be filed in connection with the formation and continuation of the Company, and shall execute and file such other documents and instruments as may be necessary or appropriate with respect to the formation and continuation of, and conduct of business by, the Company, and to maintain the Company in good standing as a limited liability company under the Act.

ARTICLE 4:
COMPANY CAPITAL

4.1 Capital Contributions.

(a) Each initial Member shall make the capital contribution described on Exhibit A hereto on the date and pursuant to the terms of such exhibit.

In consideration of and in exchange for the Members' agreements to make such capital contributions, each such party hereby receives the number of Units set out opposite its name on Exhibit A and a corresponding percentage of all of the Company Interests of the Company.

(b) The parties generally intend for the Company to borrow any additional funds which are needed by it to carry on its business. However, in the event that the Company is unable to borrow such funds on terms acceptable to the Company, then the Members and Assignees shall make capital contributions to the Company's capital as described in subsection 4.1(c) below. Any advance or payment by a Member of money to the Company which is not made pursuant to this section 4.1 shall be deemed to be a Member's Loan.

(c) If Members holding _____ % of the Units determine that the Company needs funds to carry on its business and that the Company is unable to borrow such funds on terms acceptable to the Company, then the Members and Assignees shall contribute such needed funds to the Company as provided in this section. Within five days after such person's receipt of notice of such a decision that capital contributions are needed, each Member or Assignee shall contribute cash to the Company's capital in an amount equal to such person's proportionate share of the total funds to be contributed to the Company at such time by all Members and Assignees (based on the proportion that such contributor's Units bears to the total number of Units owned at such time by all of the Members and Assignees).

(d) The Members may require additional capital contributions pursuant to this section 4.1 at any time and from time to time without limitation. There shall be no contributions to the Company's capital except as described in this section 4.1.

(e) In the event that all or any part of a Member's Company Interest is Transferred, such Member, all successor Members substituted in such Member's place, and all of such Member's Assignees shall be jointly and severally liable for and shall immediately make when due the additional capital contributions required of such Member (and not previously contributed by such Member) by this Agreement with respect to such Transferred Company Interest.

4.2 Company Capital. Except as specifically provided in this Agreement, no Member or Assignee has any right to demand or receive the return of the contribution made to the Company's capital with respect to such person's Company Interest. No Member or Assignee has any right to demand or receive property other than cash in return for such capital contribution.

4.3 Capital Accounts.

(a) A separate Capital Account shall be maintained for each Member and Assignee. No Member or Assignee is entitled to receive interest on such person's Capital Account balance.

(b) The determination and maintenance of the Capital Accounts shall be made in accordance with §1.704-1(b) of the Regulations.

(c) In the event any Company Interest is Transferred, the transferee shall succeed to the Capital Account of the transferor to the extent it relates to the Transferred Company Interest.

4.4 Evidence of Ownership. No certificate or other separate evidence of ownership shall be issued by the Company with respect to any Company Interest or Units. Rather, this Agreement shall represent and evidence the Company Interest and Units owned by each Member and Assignee.

ARTICLE 5:
MEMBERS' LOANS

5.1 Advances to Company. If the Company shall from time to time have insufficient cash to pay its obligations (including without limitation its obligations to any Member pursuant to a transaction which is intended or deemed to be between the Company and one who is not a Member) as such obligations become due, the Managing Members may determine that, as an alternative to borrowing cash from third parties or otherwise raising cash, each Member (acting in such person's individual capacity) should be called upon to loan cash to the Company in the amount of such Member's pro rata share (based on Units) of an aggregate amount sufficient to fund the payment of such obligations or the performance of such decision. No Member shall be required to make any such loan and the Members may make disproportionate loans. Each such loan shall be a Member's Loan.

5.2 Loan Terms. No Member's Loan shall increase any Member's Company Interest. Each Member's Loan shall bear interest at the Bank Rate from the date of such loan until payment in full, shall be unsecured, may be prepaid without penalty, and shall be evidenced by the Company's demand promissory note. The exercise and performance of the rights and obligations created by each Member's Loan are intended to be and shall be deemed to be transactions between the Company and one who is not a Member.

ARTICLE 6:
COMPANY RECORDS AND
ACCOUNTING MATTERS

6.1 Profit and Loss Determinations.

(a) The Company's books shall be closed and its profits and losses determined at least annually and otherwise as appropriate hereunder. Company profits and losses shall be determined by use of a method of accounting selected by the Managing Members. For purposes of Company accounting and income tax reporting, the Company shall operate on a calendar year.

(b) Except as specifically provided in this Agreement, all decisions as to accounting matters and tax return preparation (including without limitation elections required or permitted to be made by the Company under the Code) shall be made by the Managing Members consistent with the Company's accounting practices.

6.2 Accounting Records. The Company shall maintain or cause to be maintained adequate accounting books and records, and such other books and records as may be necessary or appropriate to the conduct of the Company's business, at the Company's principal place of business, which books and records shall be open at all reasonable times for inspection by any Member or such Member's agent at such Member's expense. The ownership of a Unit as of a particular time shall be determined on the basis of the Company's records.

6.3 Financial Statements. Upon the annual closing of the Company's books hereunder, statements showing the financial condition of the Company and its profits or losses from operations shall be prepared or reviewed by an independent certified public accountant selected by the Managing Members. Copies of such statements shall be furnished to each Member.

6.4 Tax Returns. The Company's tax returns shall be prepared or reviewed by an independent certified public accountant selected by the Managing Members. Each person who owned any Company Interest during a calendar year shall be furnished a copy of such individual tax information as shall be necessary for the preparation of such person's federal and state income and other tax returns with respect to the Company's operations.

6.5 Bank Accounts. The Company shall maintain checking and other accounts at such banks and other financial institutions as the Managing Members shall determine, and all funds received by the Company shall be deposited therein. Withdrawals from such accounts shall be made on such signatures as the Managing Members shall determine.

ARTICLE 7:
COMPANY DISTRIBUTIONS

7.1 Distributions Prior to Liquidation. Distributions of cash and other Company assets prior to liquidation of the Company shall be subject to the discretion of the Managing Members. If and to the extent such distributions are made, distributions to the Members and Assignees shall be based on the relative number of Units owned by them.

7.2 Liquidation Distributions. Subject to the provisions of the Act, upon the dissolution of the Company and the winding up of its affairs, all Company property, if any, shall be distributed, to the extent sufficient:

(a) To the payment of all debts and liabilities of the Company, including debts owed to Members, and to the setting up of such reserves as the

Managing Members may reasonably deem necessary for any contingent liabilities or obligations of the Company; provided, any such reserves shall be paid over to an escrow agent (which may be a Member or an Affiliate of a Member) to be held by such agent or its successor for such period as the Managing Members shall deem advisable for the purpose of applying such reserves to the payment of such liabilities or obligations and at the expiration of such period, the balance of such reserves, if any, shall be distributed as provided in this section 7.2; and

(b) To the Members and Assignees in proportion to and to the extent of their respective positive Capital Account balances as determined after taking into account all Capital Account adjustments for the Company's taxable year during which such liquidation occurs (other than those made pursuant to this requirement).

ARTICLE 8:
ALLOCATION OF PROFITS AND LOSSES

8.1 Allocation of Net Profits. In respect of each Fiscal Period, Net Profits shall be allocated (a) first, to Members with a deficit balance in their Capital Accounts in proportion to, and to the extent of, such deficits and (b) then, to all Members in proportion to the number of Units owned by each of them. In determining whether a Member has a deficit Capital Account for this purpose, such Member's Capital Account shall be (x) increased by that amount that such Member is treated as being obligated to restore pursuant to the next to last sentences of Regulations §§1.704-2(g)(1) and (i)(5) (determined after taking into account thereunder any changes during such Fiscal Period in any minimum gain and in minimum gain attributable to any Member Nonrecourse Debt, as described in section 8.4 of this Agreement) and (y) decreased by the items described in Regulations §§1.704-1(b)(2)(ii)(d)(4), (5), and (6).

8.2 Allocation of Net Loss. In respect of each Fiscal Period, Net Loss shall be allocated to all Members in proportion to the number of Units owned by each of them, provided, however, that Net Loss shall not be allocated to any Member to the extent that such allocation would create or increase a deficit in such Member's Capital Account (adjusted as provided in the second sentence of section 8.1 of this Agreement).

8.3 Qualified Income Offset. In the event that any Member receives any adjustment, allocation, or distribution described in Regulations §1.704-1(b)(2)(ii)(d)(4), (5), or (6) that creates or increases a deficit balance in its Capital Account (adjusted as provided in the second sentence of section 8.1 of this Agreement), then Gross Income shall be specially allocated to such Member in an amount and manner sufficient to eliminate the deficit balance created by such adjustment, allocation or distribution as quickly as possible.

8.4 Minimum Gain. If during any Fiscal Period there is a net decrease in Company minimum gain (as defined by Regulations §§1.704-2(b) and (d)), then each Member shall be allocated Gross Income for such Fiscal Period (and, if necessary, for subsequent Fiscal Periods) in the manner provided in Regulations §§1.704-2(f) and (j). Likewise, if there is a net decrease during any Fiscal Period in the minimum gain attributable to a Member Nonrecourse Debt (as defined in Regulations §1.704-2(i)(3) in respect of partner nonrecourse debt), then any Member with a share of the minimum gain attributable to such debt at the beginning of such Fiscal Period shall be allocated items of Gross Income for such Fiscal Period (and, if necessary, for subsequent Fiscal Periods) in the manner provided in Regulations §1.704-2(i)(4). This section 8.4 is intended to comply with, and shall be interpreted to be consistent with, the minimum gain chargeback requirements of Regulations §1.704-2.

8.5 Federal Taxable Income and Loss.

(a) Except as otherwise provided in section (b) of this section 8.5, taxable income, gain, loss or deduction of the Company (as well as any credits and the basis of property to which such credits apply) as determined for federal income tax purposes shall be allocated in the same manner as the corresponding income, gain, loss or deduction is allocated for purposes of adjusting Capital Accounts under sections 8.1 through 8.4 of this Agreement.

(b) In the event that Company property is subject to §704(c) of the Code or is revalued on the books of the Company in accordance with §1.704-1(b)(2)(iv)(f) of the Regulations, the Members' Capital Accounts shall be adjusted in accordance with §1.704-1(b)(2)(iv)(g) of the Regulations for allocations to them of depreciation, amortization and gain or loss, as computed for book purposes (and not tax purposes) with respect to such property.

ARTICLE 9:
COMPANY MANAGEMENT

9.1 Company Management Generally.

(a) The parties intend to distinguish between the ongoing management of the Company, which generally shall be the responsibility of the Managing Members, and the making of policy decisions for the Company, which shall be done by all of the Members. The provisions of this Article 9 shall be construed accordingly.

(b) The Company shall have two Managing Members, who shall be Members of the Company. The initial Managing Members shall be _____ and _____ . Each Managing Member shall serve until the occurrence of an Event of Withdrawal with respect to such Managing Member, or until such Managing Member's removal. A Managing Member may be removed by the decision of Members pursuant to the procedures set forth in section 9.4 hereof. A Managing Member who has been removed may be replaced pursuant to the procedures set forth in section 9.4 hereof.

(c) The Managing Members shall be responsible for and are granted the right, power, authority, and duty to manage and control the Company's day-to-day business and affairs, and the Managing Members are hereby vested with all rights and powers generally necessary, advisable, or convenient to the discharge of their rights and duties under this Agreement. No Member other than the Managing Members shall have any right or authority to act for or bind the Company, except pursuant to specific action of the Members taken pursuant to section 9.4 hereof.

(d) In furtherance, and not in limitation, of the Managing Members' general power and authority hereunder, but subject to the provisions of sections 9.2 and 9.3 hereof, the Managing Members are granted the right, power, and authority to act for and do from time to time on behalf of the Company and at the Company's expense and risk, all things which the Managing Members deem necessary or appropriate on behalf of the Company, including without limitation the right, power, and authority to:

(i) borrow money for Company purposes (which borrowings may be evidenced by promissory notes, contracts, or otherwise) and, if security is required therefor, mortgage or grant deeds of trust on Company real estate or pledge or otherwise encumber all or any part of the Company's property, and refund, refinance, and extend the maturity of any indebtedness created by such borrowings;

(ii) employ and discharge agents, employees, independent contractors, attorneys, accountants, brokers, and others whose services are reasonably required to assist the Managing Members in the performance of the Managing Members' rights and duties under this Agreement;

(iii) negotiate and enter into contracts, agreements, commitments, and undertakings relating to the acquisition, development, improvement, maintenance, rental, operation, management, or disposition of all or any part of any Company property or relating to any other transaction with respect to the Company's business;

(iv) bring or defend, pay, collect, compromise, arbitrate, resort to legal action, or otherwise adjust claims or demands of or against the Company;

(v) establish from funds constituting income or capital and administer cash reserves in such amounts and for such liabilities (contingent or accrued), contingencies, anticipated expenses, debt service, capital expenditures, and other purposes as the Managing Members shall deem appropriate;

(vi) construct, alter, raze, repair, and replace improvements on any Company real estate;

(vii) make, cancel, or renew any lease or approve of any sublease regarding all or any part of the Company's real estate;

(viii) except as otherwise specifically provided in this Agreement, make or revoke any election available to the Company under any tax law;

(ix) negotiate and enter into insurance contracts which the Managing Members deem necessary for the protection or benefit of the Company or its property;

(x) enforce the Company's rights and perform its obligations under all agreements to which the Company is a party;

(xi) carry out the decisions of the Members made pursuant to this Agreement; and

(xii) execute, acknowledge, swear to, and deliver any instruments, and expend Company funds, necessary or appropriate to effect any of the foregoing.

(e) _____ , or such other Member as shall be designated from time to time by the Managing Members, shall be the "tax matters partner" (as such term is used in the Code) for federal income tax purposes. [Note: Code §6231(a)(7) provides that the tax matters partner must be a general partner. Applicability of this provision to LLCs is unclear at this time.]

9.2 Policy Decisions.

(a) All decisions respecting Company policy (including in particular the policy decisions described in this section 9.2) or decisions which do not relate merely to management of the day-to-day affairs of the Company shall be made by the Members. For purposes of this Agreement, the policy decisions which must be made by the Members shall include, without limitation:

(i) decisions respecting the incurring of debt (not including any Member's Loan) by the Company in an amount greater than $100,000;

(ii) decisions respecting the granting of security interests in the Company's property to secure debts of the Company (not including any Member's Loan) in an amount greater than $100,000;

(iii) decisions respecting the sale or other voluntary disposition of all or substantially all of the assets of the Company;

(iv) decisions respecting the entering into or the material modification of any contract between the Company and a Member or an Affiliate of a Member;

(v) all decisions respecting the entering into or the material modification of any single contract, agreement, commitment, or undertaking which requires a total consideration from the Company of more than $100,000;

(vi) decisions respecting causing the Company to change the nature of its business or respecting any transaction or agreement not apparently for the carrying on of the Company's business in the usual way or the terms of which make it impossible to carry on the ordinary business of the Company; and

(vii) decisions that pursuant to other provisions of this Agreement are to be made by the Members.

(b) The Members may designate any decision to be made respecting the Company's business and affairs to be a policy decision which must be made by the Members.

9.3 Limitations on Managing Members' Powers.

(a) Notwithstanding any other provision of this Agreement, without in each instance receiving the prior decision of the Members pursuant to section 9.4 hereof, the Managing Members shall not have the authority to, and the Managing Members shall not, cause the Company to:

(i) do any act with respect to any decision which this Agreement provides shall be made by the Members, until such decision has been made by the Members pursuant to this Agreement, and then only if such act is consistent with such decision; or

(ii) knowingly and to the extent within the Managing Members' control permit the business or affairs of the Company to be conducted in any manner which would constitute a breach or default of any provision of this Agreement.

9.4 Members' Decisions and Other Actions.

(a) Any Member may submit to the Members pursuant to this section all questions and matters which this Agreement provides are to be done by, consented to, or decided by the Members.

(b) A Members' meeting may be called at any time by any Member. The Member or Members calling such meeting shall give each Member written notice of the time and place of such meeting, which notice must be received by all Members at least five days before the date of such meeting. Any such notice may be waived by the Member entitled thereto signing a written waiver of such notice, either before or after such meeting, and such waiver shall be deemed to be the equivalent of such Member's receipt of timely formal notice of such meeting. A Member's attendance at such meeting in person or by power of attorney granted to another Member shall constitute such Member's waiver of notice thereof unless such Member or such Member's attorney-in-fact shall attend such meeting for the express purpose, stated at the opening of the meeting, of objecting to the transaction of any business at such meeting because the meeting is not properly called. Each Members' meeting shall be held at such reasonably convenient time and place in the State as the Member or Members calling such meeting shall designate in the written notice of such meeting; provided, such meetings shall be held at the Company's principal place of business unless it is not available for such purpose.

(c) The Member or Members who call a meeting shall designate a Member who shall preside thereat and shall keep the minutes thereof, unless the Members shall otherwise decide. Attendance at a Members' meeting, in person or by power of attorney granted to another Member, of Members who own in the aggregate over 51 percent of all Units owned by all of the Members shall constitute a proper quorum. All actions, consents, and decisions made at a Members' meeting by the vote of Members, acting in person or by power of attorney granted to another Member, who own in the aggregate over 51 percent of all Units shall constitute and be a valid and binding act of the Members; provided, if this Agreement shall specifically require the unanimous action, consent, or decision of the Members, then only such unanimous action, consent, or decision shall constitute and be a valid and binding act of the Members. Each Unit owned by a Member shall count as one vote, and each fractional part of a Unit owned by a Member shall count as that fractional part of one vote as such fractional part of such Unit bears to a whole Unit. Each Unit owned jointly by two or more Members or two or more Members and Assignees shall be deemed to be owned in equal shares by the joint owners thereof as disclosed by the Company's records. Any Member may grant a written power of attorney to any other Member (but not an Assignee or any third party) in order to constitute such Member as the grantor's attorney-in-fact for the purpose of representing the grantor at Members' meetings, and at such meetings to cast such votes as the grantor would be entitled to cast if personally present, and the grantor shall be deemed to be present and voting in person at each such meeting at which the grantor's attorney-in-fact is present and voting. Each Member who acquires one or more Units by a Transfer from a Member or Assignee shall not be deemed to own such Units as a Member, and shall not be entitled to vote such Units at a Members' meeting and such Units shall not be otherwise recognized or taken into account in the decision-making process established in section 9.4, unless such Member shall be admitted to the Company as a Member pursuant to this Agreement with respect to such Units.

(d) Any consent or decision which may be made or any action which may be taken at a Members' meeting may be made or taken without a meeting in the manner provided in this subsection 9.4(d). Any Member may circulate among all of the other Members documents describing in sufficient detail any question or matter which such Member wants to be done by, consented to, or decided by the Members. If all of the Members, within a 30-day period of each other, shall date, sign, and return to the circulating Member statements setting out their consent to or approval of a decision with respect to a question or matter described in such documents, such action, consent, or decision shall constitute and be a valid and binding act of the Members. Such statements may be so dated, signed, and returned in two or more counterparts, all of which taken together shall be deemed to be a single document. If all of the Members shall not have so dated, signed, and returned such statements within such 30-day period, the statements shall be of no force and effect, and those Members, if any, who did so date, sign, and return such statements within such 30-day period shall not be bound by such action, consent, or decision.

9.5 Status of Assignees. No Assignee shall participate in the control of the business of the Company, and no Assignee shall have any right or authority to act for or bind the Company. In particular, no Assignee shall have any right or authority to require any information or account of Company transactions or to inspect the Company's books. An Assignee shall only have the right to receive to the extent Transferred the Member's interest in and right to the Company's capital, profits, losses, and distributions as set out in this Agreement.

ARTICLE 10:
MEMBERS' COMPENSATION;
EXPENSE REIMBURSEMENT

10.1 Company Related Expenses.

(a) Each Member and Assignee shall personally bear all taxes, expenses (including without limitation tax audit expenses and attorneys' and accountants fees), and other charges incurred by such person with respect to or as a consequence of such person's acquisition, ownership, or disposition of a Company Interest.

(b) The Company shall bear (and pay or reimburse from Company funds) all Company organization expenses and all expenses of operating the Company's business.

(c) The Managing Members (acting in their individual capacities) may from time to time pay Company obligations from their individual funds, and the Company shall promptly reimburse the Managing Members for all such payments. The payments and reimbursements required by this subsection 10.1(c) are intended to be and shall be deemed to be transactions between the Company and one who is not a Member.

(d) Except as otherwise specifically provided herein, no Member and no Assignee is authorized to pay any Company obligation, and no Member and no Assignee shall be entitled to any reimbursement from the Company for any expenditure made with respect to the Company or its business.

10.2 Contracts with Members and Affiliates. As an alternative to contracting with third parties for the performance of services or for the provision of products to the Company, the Managing Members are authorized:

(a) to contract with any Member (acting in its individual capacity) or any Affiliate of a Member to perform any services or provide any products reasonably required by the Company for the management or operation of the Company; and

(b) to compensate such Member or such Affiliate for any such services or products; provided, such compensation shall not exceed that charged by unrelated third parties for comparable services or products.

All transactions made pursuant to this section 10.2 between the Company and either a Member or an Affiliate of a Member are intended to be and shall be deemed to be transactions between the Company and one who is not a Member.

ARTICLE 11:
MEMBERS' STANDARDS AND
INDEMNIFICATIONS

11.1 Fiduciary Duty. Except to the extent qualified in this Agreement, the Managing Members shall have a fiduciary duty to the Company, including in particular a duty to safeguard the Company's funds and to use such funds only for Company purposes.

11.2 Limitation on Managing Members Liability. The Managing Members shall not be liable, responsible or accountable, in damages or otherwise, to any Member for any act performed by the Managing Members within the scope of the authority conferred on them by this Agreement, except for acts of fraud, gross negligence, or willful misconduct.

11.3 Members' Efforts.

(a) The Managing Members shall devote themselves to the management and operation of the Company's business and affairs to the extent reasonably necessary and appropriate for the efficient carrying on thereof and for the discharge of the Managing Members' duties hereunder. The Members acknowledge that while _____ and _____ are the Managing Members, they will have other business activities which will take the major part of their total efforts.

(b) No Member except the Managing Members shall be required to devote any effort to the management and operation of the Company's business and affairs, except such effort as is reasonably necessary and appropriate for the consideration of questions and matters to be decided by the Members pursuant to this Agreement. This provision shall not absolve any Member from any liability to the Company or to the other Members and Assignees arising as a result of such Member's breach of its fiduciary duties to the Company or to the other Members and Assignees.

11.4 Other Business Ventures. No Member or Assignee or any person affiliated with a Member or Assignee shall be under any duty to present any investment opportunity to the Company or to any other Member or

Assignee, even if such opportunity is of a character which, if so presented, could be taken by the Company or by another Member or Assignee. Each Member and Assignee and their Affiliates may engage in or possess an interest in any other business ventures of every nature and description, independently or with others, and neither the Company nor the other Members or Assignees shall have any right or interest in or to such independent ventures or in or to the capital, profits, losses, or distributions derived therefrom.

11.5 Standards and Indemnifications.

(a) The Company shall indemnify and hold harmless the Managing Members and the Managing Members' Affiliates from and against any liability, loss, or damage (including, without limitation, attorneys' fees and other costs of litigation and appeal) incurred by the indemnitee by reason of any act or omission on behalf of the Company, except for acts of fraud, gross negligence, or willful misconduct, provided that any indemnity provided by this section 11.5 shall be provided out of and to the extent of Company assets only, and no Member shall have any personal liability on account thereof.

(b) Each Member and Assignee shall indemnify and hold harmless the Company and the other Members and Assignees from and against any liability, loss, or damage incurred by the indemnitee by reason of the indemnitor's fraud, gross negligence, or willful misconduct.

ARTICLE 12:
TRANSFERS; WITHDRAWAL

12.1 Binding Effect of Agreement. Any person, whether a substituted Member or an Assignee, who acquires by a Transfer all or any part of a Member's or Assignee's Company Interest shall be subject to and bound by this Agreement as if such person were an original party hereto. No such person shall become a substituted Member except pursuant to section 12.3 or section 12.5 hereof.

12.2 Involuntary Transfer of Company Interest. In the event of any involuntary Transfer of any Company Interest (such as would or might occur on the death, bankruptcy, or divorce of a Member or Assignee): (a) the successor of the Member or Assignee shall not become a Member, but rather shall be a mere Assignee, with respect to such Company Interest; and (b) the transferor shall have no further right, title, or interest to or in the Company, or to or in its property, business, or affairs, with respect to such Company Interest. Prior to the Company's recognition of any claimed rights or interests of a person claiming to be such a successor of a Member or Assignee, the Company may require such acknowledgments of Transfer, indemnifications, ratifications, and other documentation as the Managing Members shall deem prudent.

12.3 Voluntary Transfer of Company Interest.

(a) No Member or Assignee may voluntarily Transfer any of such Member's or Assignee's Company Interest without the prior written consent of Members who own more than one-half of all of the then-outstanding Units not included in the Transfer. Any act in violation of this restriction shall be null and void as against the Company. No Member or Assignee shall have any right, power, or authority to grant unilaterally the right to become a Member to an Assignee of any of such Member's Company Interest.

(b) Upon any Transfer which is made with the consent of the Members pursuant to this section, the transferor shall cease to be a Member with respect to the Company Interest so Transferred. The person who acquired such Company Interest shall be admitted to the Company as a Member with respect to such Company Interest if the consent granted with respect to the Transfer so provided (and otherwise such person shall be a mere Assignee with respect to such interest).

(c) Upon any Transfer or attempted Transfer by a Member or Assignee which is not made with the consent of the Members pursuant to subsection 12.3(a) (i.e., a "Wrongful Transfer"), the transferor, if a Member, shall cease to be a Member and shall become an Assignee with respect to any of the transferor's Company Interest which was not the subject of the Wrongful Transfer or with respect to which the Wrongful Transfer was not effective.

(d) Upon any Wrongful Transfer, the Assignee of any Member's interest which may have been effectively Transferred despite the provisions of this Agreement shall not thereby become a Member, but shall be a mere Assignee with respect to such interest. Prior to the Company's recognition of any claimed rights or interests of a person claiming to be such a successor of a Member or Assignee, the Company may require such acknowledgments of Transfer, indemnifications, ratifications, and other documentation as the Managing Members shall deem prudent.

12.4 Withdrawal by Members.

(a) No Member or Assignee shall have any right to, and no Member or Assignee shall, withdraw (as defined in the Act) from the Company. Any Member who withdraws from the Company in violation of this Agreement shall be liable to the Company for all damages directly or indirectly caused by such withdrawal, and the Company may (without limiting any other remedy it may have in such event) offset such damages against any amounts distributable to such Member upon such withdrawal.

(b) A Member who withdraws from the Company in breach of this Agreement shall be entitled to receive the fair value of his Company Interest, less: the costs of determining such fair value; any portion of such fair value which is attributable to intangibles, such as goodwill; and the damages caused by such withdrawal, which shall include all costs and expenses (including attorneys' fees) of carrying out and enforcing the provisions of this section 12.4.

(c) Payment for the Company Interest of a Member who has withdrawn from the Company in breach of this Agreement may be deferred by the Company to the extent which the Managing Members deem necessary to prevent unreasonable hardship to the Company.

12.5 Assignees Becoming Members. Any Assignee may at any time be admitted to the Company as a Member upon obtaining the written consent to such admission of (a) Members owning more than 50 percent of all then outstanding Company Interest; or (b) all of the Members, if at least one-half of the then outstanding Company Interest are owned by one or more Assignees; such consent may be granted or denied by the Members in their sole and absolute discretion. Except as otherwise expressly provided for herein, no Member or Assignee shall have any right, power, or authority to grant unilaterally the right to become a Member to an Assignee of any interest in any of such Member's Company Interest.

ARTICLE 13:
DISSOLUTION

13.1 Dissolution.

(a) The Company shall be dissolved upon the first to occur of: (i) the written consent of all Members to such dissolution; (ii) the occurrence of any Event of Withdrawal; (iii) the occurrence of any other event which causes the dissolution of the Company under the Act; or (iv) December 31, 2045.

(b) If: (i) the Company is dissolved due solely to the occurrence of an Event of Withdrawal; (ii) the Company has at least one remaining Member following such Event of Withdrawal; and (iii) if within 90 days after the occurrence of such event Members owning more than 50 percent of all then outstanding Units consent in writing to reconstitute and continue the Company despite such Event of Withdrawal, then the Company shall be deemed to be reconstituted by the Members and Assignees, without the necessity of further action or documentation, and shall continue to exist and be governed by this Agreement as if such dissolution had not occurred. If the Event of Withdrawal relates to a Managing Member, a replacement Managing Member may be named pursuant to the procedures set forth in section 9.4 hereof.

13.2 Winding Up. Upon the dissolution of the Company, unless the Company is reconstituted pursuant to the terms hereof, or unless such dissolution is due to the Company not being the surviving entity in a merger or consolidation to which it is a party, the Managing Members shall make full account of the Company's property and liabilities and the Company shall commence to wind up its affairs (which the Managing Members shall control) as promptly as is consistent with obtaining the fair value of its property, and the Company's property may be liquidated in the manner and to the extent and for such consideration as the Managing Members shall determine. The Company's property or the proceeds thereof, after the payment or the establishment of reserves for the payment of all of the Company's liabilities in accordance with the Act, shall be applied or distributed as provided in Article 7.

ARTICLE 14:
ADMINISTRATIVE PROVISIONS

14.1 Company Property. All property, real, personal, or mixed, from time to time owned by the Company shall be held in the Company's name unless the Managing Members shall decide that, for convenience, legal title to any such property shall be held in the name of one or more of the Members; provided, all Company property held in the name of one or more Members shall be equitably and beneficially owned by the Company and such Member or Members shall be the Company's nominee and trustee of the bare legal title to such property for the Company's sole benefit. Each such Member or Members shall fully account to the Company with respect to all transactions and matters regarding such property.

14.2 Notices and Payments.

(a) Any notice, consent, or other communication required or permitted by this Agreement shall be made in writing (unless expressly provided otherwise herein) and shall be deemed to have been received by a party when:

(i) delivered by messenger to such party;

(ii) sent by telecopy to such party at the telecopy number, if any, of such party set forth on Exhibit A hereto;

(iii) on the fifth day after deposit in the United States mail, postage prepaid and certified (return receipt requested), addressed to such party at the address of such party set forth of Exhibit A hereto; or

(iv) on the first day after proper and timely deposit, freight prepaid, with a nationally recognized next-day delivery service providing next-day service to the location of the recipient, addressed to such party at the address of such party set forth on Exhibit A hereto. The addresses and telecopy numbers of the parties are as set forth on Exhibit A hereto, except that each party may change its address or telecopy number (or both) by notice to the other parties.

14.3 Fees and Expenses. Each party shall pay all costs and expenses, including without limitation attorneys' fees and disbursements, that it incurs with respect to the negotiation, execution, delivery, performance, and amendment of this Agreement.

14.4 Miscellaneous. (a) This Agreement shall become effective when it has been signed by each party hereto; thereafter, this Agreement shall be binding upon, inure to the benefit of, and be enforceable by the parties hereto and all other persons who shall be deemed to be parties to this Agreement and their respective heirs, personal representatives, successors, and assigns.

(b) This Agreement shall be governed by the internal laws (and not the laws pertaining to conflicts or choice of law) of the State. To the extent allowed by applicable law, each person who is or becomes a party to or bound by this Agreement hereby agrees for such person and such person's successors in interest that the provisions of this Agreement shall govern in the event of any inconsistency between such provisions and the provisions of the Act, and each such person hereby waives any rights which such person may have under the Act which are inconsistent with the provisions of this Agreement.

(c) In the event any one or more of the provisions contained in this Agreement or any application thereof shall be invalid, illegal, or unenforceable in any respect, the validity, legality, and enforceability of the remaining provisions of this Agreement or any other application thereof shall not in any way be affected or impaired thereby.

(d) The application of any provision of this Agreement may be waived by the party or parties entitled to the benefit thereof; provided, no delay or failure on the part of any party hereto in exercising any rights hereunder, and no partial or single exercise thereof, shall constitute a waiver of any other rights hereunder. This Agreement represents the entire agreement of all of the persons bound hereby and supersedes all prior understandings or agreements, oral or written, among all or any of such persons. This Agreement shall not be amended except by a written agreement made by all of the Members of the Company.

(e) This document, and the page or pages hereof on which the signatures of the parties appear, may be executed in two or more counterparts.

The initial parties hereto have executed this Agreement as of the date first shown above to evidence their intent that it be a binding contract.

Exhibit A to Limited Liability Company
Operating Agreement of

_____

Names and Addresses of Initial Members:	*Date and Amount of Capital Contributions:*	*Number of Units:*

CHAPTER 4 • LIMITED LIABILITY PARTNERSHIPS—FOR PROFESSIONAL PRACTICES

CONTENTS

4.01 INTRODUCTION

Like the multi-member limited liability company (LLC) discussed in Chapter 3, the limited liability partnership (LLP) is relatively new type of entity. LLPs are formed and operated pursuant to state LLP statutes.

State LLP laws were enacted in response to the enormous personal liability problems faced by partners in law and accounting general partnerships. These arose largely from claims of professional malpractice after the numerous thrift and financial institution failures of the 1980s.

It seems unfair to hold a partner of a professional firm personally liable for the professional acts or omissions of another partner in the same firm. The LLP vehicle addresses this concern and has, therefore, become a viable entity choice for professional practices in today's environment.

All 50 states and the District of Columbia have enacted LLP statutes.

> ***CAUTION:*** *Because state LLP statutes vary, the discussion of LLPs in this chapter is by necessity general and may be inconsistent with the provisions of certain LLP statutes. While this chapter conveys useful information, practitioners should address specific client issues only after a detailed examination of the applicable LLP statute. Legal counsel should be engaged to answer all specific questions regarding the liability protection offered by LLPs.*

4.02 WHAT IS AN LLP?

LLPs are formed pursuant to state LLP statutes and generally are treated as a special breed of general partnership under state law. They can be a very attractive form of doing business for professional practices. In many states, the LLP statute simply consists of modifications or amendments to the existing general partnership statute. As a result, LLP statutes can vary considerably. On a favorable note, in 1996 the National Conference of Commissioners on Uniform State Laws adopted a "Uniform LLP Amendment." This amendment is intended as an "update" to the Uniform Partnership Act, which has already been adopted by most states. As more states adopt the amendment, there will be increasing uniformity between LLP statutes. (Note that references in this chapter to Uniform LLP Amendment provisions are only relevant in states that have adopted the Amendment or language consistent with the Amendment.)

In some states (for example, Texas), LLP partners remain personally liable for the general debts and obligations of the LLP—sometimes referred to as contract liabilities—such as bank loans, lease obligations, and vendor accounts payable. LLP partners also remain personally liable for their own tortious acts and their own professional errors, omissions, and negligence. (*Tortious acts* are defined as wrongful acts leading to civil actions, other than those involving breach of contract.) An LLP partner may also be personally liable for the professional errors, omissions, and negligence of others who are under the partner's direct supervision (or who should have been). However, LLP partners generally are *not* liable for the professional errors, omissions, and negligence of the other LLP partners and firm employees.

In other states (such as California and New York), LLP partners are *not* personally liable for the firm's contract liabilities. In these states, LLPs offer LLC-like liability protection.

In all states, LLPs offer much greater liability protection than general partnerships, where partners *are* exposed to liabilities related to the professional errors, omissions, and negligence of others plus the firm's contract liabilities.

But, in those states not offering LLC-like liability protection, LLPs offer less protection than LLCs.

Why an LLP Instead of an LLC?

Why a would professional practice ever choose to operate as an LLP rather than as an LLC, especially in states where LLP partners are liable for contract liabilities? That's a very good question. The most common answer is that some state laws and/or professional standards (such as state board of accountancy rules) preclude certain professionals from using LLCs.

In addition, generally it is much easier to convert an existing professional general partnership into an LLP than into an LLC, for the reasons discussed in section 4.09 of this chapter. Finally, in a few states (for example, Texas), LLCs are subject to entity-level taxes, while LLPs are not. Because of these factors, LLCs may be unavailable, unworkable, or unattractive for certain professional service businesses.

When that is the case, the choice-of-entity options are narrowed down to LLPs, general partnerships, C corporations, and S corporations. LLPs offer much better liability protection than general partnerships.

Assuming the exposure (if any) to contract liabilities of the practice can be managed (which is usually the case), LLPs often are viewed as superior to C corporations because of the double taxation problem of the latter. LLPs also may be viewed as superior to S corporations, because of the restrictive S corporation qualification rules and the many advantages of partnership taxation over S corporation taxation.

LLP Advantages and Disadvantages

Because LLPs are partnerships (both for state law and for federal income tax purposes), they are subject to the partnership legal and tax considerations explained in Chapter 5.

Thus, the major advantage of LLPs is the ability to benefit from pass-through taxation without having to "jump through the hoops" of the S corporation qualification rules (discussed in depth in Chapter 8).

In addition, LLPs can take advantage of the other tax advantages that partnerships enjoy over S corporations (discussed in depth in Chapter 5). For example, LLPs generally can make tax-free distributions of appreciated property and create different types of partnership interests with varying rights to cash flow, liquidation proceeds, and tax allocations. S corporations do not have this flexibility.

LLPs are not as attractive as LLCs in states that do *not* offer LLC-like liability protection to LLP partners.

4.03 BUSINESSES ELIGIBLE (AND SUITABLE) TO OPERATE AS LLPs

Generally, LLPs are best suited for professional practices that want liability protection plus pass-through taxation without having to worry about the S corporation qualification rules.

Such practices usually cannot function as limited partnerships, because all members of the firm are active in managing the practice. Limited partners who are too active in the business can lose their limited partner status and become treated as general partners for legal purposes. If this happened with a professional practice, the partners who intended to be limited partners would then be personally exposed (as general partners) to all of the entity's liabilities, including those arising from the tortious acts, errors, omissions, and negligence of the other partners and firm employees.

4.04 NAME OF THE LLP

By law, the name of an LLP must include specified language to convey the fact that the entity is an LLP rather than a "regular" partnership. The magic words may be "limited liability partnership," "registered limited liability partnership," "LLP," or "RLLP," depending on the particular statute. Usually, the required indication of LLP status must appear at the end of the name—for example: Bishop and Dunne, LLP.

4.05 FORMATION AND OPERATING ISSUES

Legal Formation Process

In most states an LLP is a general partnership that, pursuant to the state LLP statute, has filed an application with the Secretary of State to be treated as an LLP.

In some states, an LLP can also be a limited partnership, in which case it may be referred to as a " limited liability limited partnership" (LLLP).

In most states, existing partnerships can convert to LLP status simply by filing an application that has been executed by a majority in interest of the partners or by one more partners authorized to act on behalf of the partnership.

Generally a filing fee (which may be based on the number of partners) is required as well.

If an LLP does business outside the state of its formation, it is required to register in that other state as a "foreign LLP" and pay a filing fee.

Beyond registering with the state, the steps to establish a newly formed LLP are the same as those for any other partnership. These steps generally include:

- Drafting a partnership agreement (which specifies how the entity will be managed; the legal relationships between the partners; the partners' obligations to make contributions of cash or property; the partners' shares of profits, losses, and distributions; the allocations of tax items; the partners' rights upon withdrawal; etc.);

- Opening a bank account in the LLP's name;

- Transferring title to any contributed assets to be owned by a newly formed LLP;

- Obtaining liability, property, business interruption, and worker's compensation insurance coverage;

- Obtaining federal and state employer ID numbers (also used for income tax purposes);

- Establishing accounting and payroll tax withholding and payment procedures;

- Registering with states and localities for collection of sales taxes and obtaining all required business licenses and permits; and

- Registering to do business as an LLP in foreign states (those other than the state of formation).

From a legal perspective, the "new" LLP is treated as a continuation of the "old" general partnership under the Uniform LLP Amendment and most state laws.

Similarly, a registration document must generally be filed and a fee paid to form a new LLP (as opposed to converting an existing general partnership to LLP status).

There is generally not any requirement to file or even have a formal partnership agreement, although this is strongly recommended.

Under the Uniform LLP Amendment, a partnership "elects" LLP status by filing the appropriate paperwork (discussed above) with the state.

Changes in the Partner Group

Some states may impose additional fees when new partners are added to the LLP.

Although most LLP statutes are silent on the effect of withdrawals of partners (for example, due to retirement, death, or sale of LLP interest), under the Uniform Partnership Act LLPs generally are legally dissolved when these events occur. If the remaining partners vote to continue, for legal purposes a new partnership is considered to come into existence.

For federal income tax purposes, LLPs are deemed to continue in existence after such events unless they result in a change in ownership of 50% or more of the capital and profits interests within a 12-month period. [See IRC §708(b)(1)(B).] See Chapter 5 for additional discussion of IRC §708 "technical terminations."

Operating Outside the State of Formation

LLPs operating beyond the borders of their state of registration are referred to as "foreign LLPs." Generally, a foreign LLP must register as an LLP in other states with LLP statutes.

If a foreign LLP fails to register in a state with an LLP statute or operates in a state *without* an LLP statute, it would likely be considered a general partnership for liability purposes. In other words, all LLP partners would be jointly and severally liable for all LLP debts and obligations, including those arising from the professional errors, omissions, and negligence of LLP partners and employees.

Generally, another advantage of registration is that the foreign LLP gains certainty regarding which state's laws (the home state of the LLP or the foreign state in question) will govern operations in the foreign state. Also, without proper registration, a foreign LLP may be prohibited from bringing lawsuits in that state.

Under the Uniform LLP Amendment, the laws of the state where the partnership filed its election to be an LLP will generally apply to the LLP's operations in foreign states.

> **WARNING:** *The issue of liability protection afforded to LLPs operating in foreign states should be assessed by competent legal counsel before commencing any significant activity in a foreign state.*

Other Formation and Operating Issues

In general, the other formation and operating issues faced by LLPs are the same as those faced by general partnerships. See Chapter 5.

In addition, because LLP statutes limit the liability of LLP partners, state law may require an LLP to carry specified levels of insurance or have a minimum amount of capital to meet possible liability claims. For example, California LLPs must document that they possess "security" of $100,000 per licensed professional (this is most commonly in the form of professional malpractice insurance coverage; it could also be in the form of cash or letters of credit held or obtained by the firm).

4.06 LIABILITY OF LLP PARTNERS

An LLP partner generally is not personally liable for debts and obligations of the LLP arising from the professional errors, omissions, or negligence of the LLP's other partners, employees, representatives, etc., *unless* those persons were supervised (or should have been supervised) by that partner.

In most states, LLP partners *remain* personally liable for their own tortious acts and their own professional errors, omissions, or negligence. As stated, they also may be liable for professional acts or omissions of persons they directly supervise.

Tortious acts are defined as wrongful acts leading to civil actions, other than those involving breach of contract. For example, careless operation of a vehicle resulting in injuries or property damage is a tortious act. The issue of whether an LLP partner could be held personally liable for tortious acts of another partner or firm employee (for example, sexual harassment of a co-worker) may not be entirely clear. This, along with all specific questions regarding liability concerns, should be addressed by competent legal counsel.

In some states, LLP partners are *still* personally liable (jointly and severally, as general partners) for the LLP's contract liabilities. Examples of contract liabilities include bank loans, lease obligations, and vendor accounts payable. Partners also may be liable to LLP creditors for the return of distributions that render the LLP insolvent.

On the other hand, some state LLP statutes provide that LLP partners are *not* personally liable for the LLP's contract liabilities unless they have personally guaranteed those liabilities. In these states, LLPs offer LLC-like liability protection to their partners and are therefore just as attractive as LLCs from a legal perspective.

Even in states offering LLC-like liability protection, LLP partners may still be liable for debts incurred while the firm was a general partnership (before conversion to LLP status).

Under the Uniform LLP Amendment, LLP partners are provided LLC-like liability protection.

4.07 WITHDRAWAL OF PARTNERS AND DISSOLUTIONS OF LLPs

Withdrawal and Disassociation of Partners

Generally, the provisions of the partnership agreement will control the rights of partners when they voluntarily withdraw (which may be referred to as "resignation" or "retirement") from the LLP.

Obviously, a withdrawing partner will want to be paid for his or her partnership interest—usually the sooner the better. From the LLP's perspective, however, it is prudent to impose conditions on payment (such as an installment payment arrangement) if the LLP is not expected to hold sufficient liquid assets to immediately pay withdrawing partners.

Note that the LLP generally is legally dissolved upon the withdrawal of a partner. However, the remaining partners can usually vote to continue the existence of the LLP.

Disassociation of an LLP partner can occur for a number of reasons beyond voluntary withdrawal—for example, from a partner's death (or legal dissolution), insanity, bankruptcy, expulsion, or other events specified in the operating agreement.

Like voluntary withdrawals, these other forms of disassociation ("dissolution events") will also terminate the legal existence of the LLP unless the remaining partners vote to continue.

For federal income tax purposes, LLPs are deemed to continue in existence after dissolution events (even if they result in legal termination of the LLP) *unless* they result in a change in ownership of 50% or more of the capital and profits interests within a 12-month period. [See IRC §708(b)(1)(B) and the discussion in Chapter 5.]

> **RECOMMENDATION:** *The partnership agreement (or a separate buy–sell agreement) should specify the methodology that will be used to value the interests of withdrawing or disassociating partners. In addition, the operating agreement (or buy–sell agreement) should specify payment terms, such as installment payments or payment with noncash property distributions. In other words, payment terms should be structured to ensure that required payments to withdrawing or disassociating partners will not cripple the LLP's ability to continue its business operations.*

> **CAUTION:** *After the withdrawal or disassociation of one or more partners, at least two partners must remain for the LLP to continue to be treated as a partnership for federal income tax purposes.*

Dissolution of the LLP

As discussed above, LLPs are considered to legally dissolve upon the occurrence of certain events, such as the retirement, resignation, expulsion, death, or bankruptcy of a partner. (However, the remaining partners can generally vote to continue the existence of the LLP after such dissolution events.)

Also as discussed above, for federal income tax purposes, LLPs are deemed to continue in existence after dissolution events, unless they result in an IRC §708 "technical termination" because of a change in ownership of 50% or more of the capital and profits interests within a 12-month period.

In addition, the LLP's partnership agreement may call for dissolution as of a fixed date, after a designated number of years of existence, or after certain events (such as the disposition of substantially all of the LLP's assets or upon a unanimous vote by the partners to dissolve).

In other words, LLPs have limited legal life spans that end upon the occurrence of specified events, many of which are in the nature of events affecting the LLP partners rather than the LLP itself. This is not the case for corporations, whose legal lives continue indefinitely regardless of the fates of their shareholders.

If the decision is made to dissolve (or "liquidate") the LLP (because the partners fail to vote to continue or because the business of the LLP is to be wound up), certain formalities must be observed. The LLP must generally file papers with the Secretary of State of the state of formation. In addition, state law may require that public notice be given, to ensure the LLP's creditors and other third parties are aware of the impending dissolution.

After dissolution, the LLP continues to exist long enough to wind up its affairs. Assets are sold, the LLP's creditors are paid off, and any remaining assets are distributed to the partners in liquidation of their partnership interests.

> *RECOMMENDATION: The partnership agreement should provide for the possibility that the LLP may hold illiquid assets (such as real estate or nonpublicly traded securities) that will be distributed to partners upon dissolution. The composition of the LLP's assets may be such that some partners will receive only liquid assets, some will receive only illiquid assets, and some may receive a mixture. The critical issue in such cases is how to value the illiquid assets, so that all partners will receive distributed property with the proper value. The partnership agreement can specify valuation methods to prevent disputes upon dissolution.*

4.08 TAXATION OF LLPs

For federal and state tax purposes, an LLP is treated as a partnership.

Many LLPs will be formed by existing general partnerships registering as LLPs ("conversion" from general partnership to LLP status). This will not change the classification of an existing partnership.

Ability to Use Cash Method

The privilege of using the cash method of accounting for tax purposes is important for professional practices. The IRS has issued several private rulings (for example, see PLRs 9420028 and 9423040) clarifying that LLPs are subject to the same rules as other partnerships regarding use of the cash method. (See Chapter 5 for a discussion of the cash method eligibility rules for partnerships.)

Self-Employment Income of LLP Partners

In computing the amount of a partner's self-employment (SE) income, the general rule is the partner includes in SE income his or her pass-through share of the partnership's income or loss from trade or business activities [IRC §1402(a)].

However, *limited* partners include in their SE income only guaranteed payments, as described in IRC §707(c), from the partnership for services actually rendered to the partnership. [See IRC §1402(a)(13).] Assuming the partnership's trade or business activities generate taxable income, this is a favorable rule, because it minimizes the limited partner's SE income and thus his or her SE tax.

Obviously, the SE tax rules were developed before LLPs existed. How do LLP members deal with the issue of SE tax, and specifically can they escape SE tax on the theory that they should somehow be considered as limited partners for SE tax purposes?

In PLR 9432018, the IRS apparently said "No," by ruling that members of a personal service LLC will not be treated as limited partners under IRC §1402(a)(13). The same result would seem to be appropriate for partners of a professional LLP.

However, see section 3.10 regarding the SE tax issue for LLCs. It would seem that the same considerations apply to LLPs that offer LLC-like liability protection.

4.09 CONVERTING EXISTING ENTITIES INTO LLPs

Partnership Conversions

Revenue Ruling 95-55 (1995-2 CB 313) and Revenue Ruling 95-37 (1995-1 CB 130) confirm that, usually, an existing general or limited partnership can be converted into an LLP without federal income tax consequences to the converting partnership or partners.

Under LLP statutes, conversion is generally accomplished simply by registering the existing partnership as an LLP and paying the required fee.

In Revenue Ruling 95-55, that was exactly what happened when an existing New York professional services general partnership converted into a New York registered limited liability partnership (RLLP). The business of the old general partnership was continued by the newly formed RLLP, and each partner had the same percentage interest in the new RLLP as he or she had in the old partnership. (Under New York law, RLLPs actually are similar to LLCs, because no RLLP partner is personally liable for the partnership's contract liabilities.)

Revenue Ruling 95-55 concludes that, for federal income tax purposes, the new RLLP is considered a continuation of the same taxable entity. In other words, converting the old general partnership into the new RLLP does not cause the existing taxable entity to be terminated under IRC §708. (See the discussion of the §708 termination rules in Chapter 5.)

According to Revenue Ruling 95-37 (dealing with conversions into LLCs) and several private letter rulings (e.g., PLR 9321047), the same results apparently would apply to conversions accomplished by liquidating the old partnership or merging it with the new LLP (or RLLP), with the LLP (or RLLP) being the surviving entity.

Mechanics of Partnership Conversions

As specifically discussed in Revenue Ruling 95-55, state LLP statutes may permit an existing partnership to be converted into an LLP by the partners simply registering the existing entity as an LLP and paying the required fee.

This is far simpler and "cleaner" than transactions involving a liquidation or merger of the old partnership (see below). The assets and liabilities of the old partnership become those of the new LLP by operation of law. LLP partners who were former partners with personal liability for the debts of the old partnership remain liable for those preexisting debts after the entity converts to LLP status.

Conversion of the old partnership via liquidation can be accomplished most easily by having the old partnership contribute all its assets and liabilities to the newly formed LLP in exchange for LLP ownership interests. Generally, this step is tax-free under IRC §721. The LLP interests are then distributed to the partners in liquidation of the old partnership. Generally this step is tax-free under IRC §731. After the transactions, the partners in the old partnership hold partnership interests in the new LLP, and the LLP holds all the assets and liabilities of the old partnership.

Alternatively, a liquidation can be accomplished by having the partners contribute their interests in the old partnership to the newly formed LLP in exchange for LLP interests. (Again, this step generally is tax-free under IRC §721.) The old partnership then distributes all its assets and liabilities to the new LLP in liquidation (generally tax-free under IRC §731). Again, the partners in the old partnership now hold partnership interests in the new LLP, and the LLP now holds all the assets and liabilities of the old partnership.

State law may also permit an existing partnership to merge with a newly formed LLP, with the LLP the surviving entity. Like conversions accomplished by simply registering an existing partnership as an LLP, merger transactions generally are "cleaner" from a legal standpoint than liquidations, because the LLP simply assumes all rights and obligations of the old partnership by operation of law. LLP partners who were partners in the old partnership and had personal liability for the debts of the old partnership remain liable for those preexisting debts after the merger with the LLP.

> **RECOMMENDATION:** *Conversion of a partnership simply by registering the existing entity as an LLP is far less complicated than accomplishing the conversion via a liquidation or merger transaction. If a simple registration procedure is available, it should generally be utilized.*

General Tax Implications of Partnership Conversions

With regard to the tax implications of converting an existing general or limited partnership into an LLP by any of the above methods, Revenue Rulings 95-55 and 95-37 (and several earlier letter rulings) lead to the following conclusions:

- Former partners do not recognize gain on the conversion, unless changes in their percentages of liabilities (under IRC §752) would cause the basis in their interests to fall below zero.

- Former partners obtain the same basis in their new LLP partnership interests as in their old partnership interests, unless the conversion results in changes in their shares of liabilities under IRC §752.

- The partners' holding periods for the new LLP interests tack onto the holding periods for the old partnership interests.

- The LLP is considered a continuation of the former partnership. As a result, the tax year continues and there is no need for a new taxpayer identification number (TIN). The LLP continues to use the former partnership's tax accounting methods and elections. The LLP's holding periods for its assets include the holding periods of the former partnership.

Example 4.09(1): Conversion of General Partnership   Gee Partnership, a professional general partnership, converts into an LLP by registering as such and paying the required fee in the state in which it does business.

The name of the partnership is now Gee Partnership, LLP.

The two equal partners, Bill and Phil, remain 50/50 partners in the LLP. As before the conversion, they are both jointly and severally liable, under the state LLP statute, for all of the partnership's contract liabilities.

The real only impact of the conversion is a reduction in each partner's exposure to future liabilities caused by the other partner's professional errors, omissions, or negligence.

Per Revenue Rulings 95-55 and 95-37, the federal income tax implications are as follows:

1. Neither Bill nor Phil, nor the partnership, recognizes any gain or loss on the conversion.

2. The partners' bases in their partnership interests and their holding periods are unchanged.

3. The LLP is considered a continuation of the existing partnership. Therefore, Gee Partnership, LLP, continues to use the same TIN, tax year, accounting and depreciation methods, tax elections, asset holding periods, etc., as it did before.

Conversions of S and C Corporations

Professional practices currently operated as S corporations may consider conversion to LLP status to escape the S corporation limitations on stock ownership and capital structure. (See discussion of these limitations in Chapter 8.) Professional practices currently operated as C corporations may consider conversion to LLP status to eliminate the ongoing problem of double taxation.

Mechanics of Corporate Conversions

An existing S or C corporation can be converted into an LLP in several ways:

1. The assets of the corporation can be contributed to the newly formed LLP in return for LLP ownership interests that are then distributed to the shareholders in complete liquidation of the corporation.

2. The corporation can distribute its assets to the shareholders in complete liquidation, and the shareholders can then contribute their undivided interests in the assets to the newly formed LLP in exchange for LLP ownership interests.

3. State law may permit the corporation to merge with the newly-formed LLP, with the LLP the surviving entity. To do this, the corporation makes a tax-free contribution of all assets and liabilities to the LLP in exchange for LLP interests (under IRC §721) and then goes out of existence by distributing the LLP interests to shareholders in complete liquidation.

General Tax Implications of Corporate Conversions

In any of the above cases, there will be corporate-level gain or loss recognition as if the property distributed in complete liquidation were sold by the corporation for fair market value (FMV) [IRC §336(a)]. This means a converting corporation—whether an S corporation or a C corporation—with appreciated assets may recognize significant taxable income or gain as a result of the liquidation transaction. (See the Examples below.)

At the shareholder level, the receipt of the liquidating distribution in exchange for corporate stock is treated as a taxable sale or exchange of the stock for proceeds equal to the FMV of the distributed property [IRC §331(a)]. The shareholder may recognize gain or loss on the transaction—depending on whether the FMV of the distributed property is greater or less than the basis of the corporate stock exchanged.

In the case of a converting S corporation, any corporate-level gain is passed through and increases the shareholders' basis in their stock [IRC §1367(a)]. Therefore, the gain already recognized at the corporate level is not recognized again when the stock is deemed sold in exchange for the liquidating distribution. However, if the S corporation is a former C corporation, the IRC §1374 built-in gains tax may apply to some or all of the corporate-level gain.

In the case of a converting C corporation, the shareholders receive no step-up in basis from any corporate-level gain. As a result, there generally is taxable gain at both the corporate level and the shareholder level upon the liquidation of a C corporation with appreciated assets.

> OBSERVATION: *Since converting S or C corporations into LLPs involves liquidation transactions, the federal income tax cost for corporations with signifi-*

cantly appreciated assets will often be unacceptably high (as illustrated by the two Examples below). In such situations, there will often be unfavorable state income tax consequences as well. However, if the corporation does not hold significantly appreciated assets, liquidation and conversion to LLP status may be accomplished without adverse tax consequences.

CAUTION: *Before concluding that an existing S or C corporation can convert to LLP status "painlessly," the practitioner must consider whether goodwill exists. It does not often appear on the balance sheet, but goodwill is the classic example of an appreciated corporate asset. Especially in cases involving professional practices, goodwill with very significant value (and zero tax basis) will often exist. The tax impact of such goodwill may preclude conversion.*

Example 4.09(2): Conversion of C Corporation into LLP PCee Corp, a professional corporation, decides to convert into an LLP by making liquidating distributions of its property to its two equal shareholders, Jean and Janice. Then, Jean and Janice will each contribute their distributed property to the newly formed LLP in exchange for their 50% LLP ownership interests.

PCee Corp uses cash-basis accounting for tax purposes and has three assets: the office building used by the practice (with FMV of $1 million and tax basis of $700,000), unrealized receivables of $100,000 (with zero tax basis), and cash of $200,000. (There is no goodwill.)

Jean and Janice each have basis of $450,000 in their PCee Corp shares, which they have held for a number of years.

Under IRC §336(a), PCee Corp recognizes a $400,000 corporate level gain on the liquidating distribution ($300,000 from the building and $100,000 from the receivables), because the transaction is deemed a taxable sale of the corporate property for its FMV. Assume the corporate-level tax is $136,000 (34% of the taxable gain).

PCee Corp pays the tax and distributes the remaining $64,000 of cash ($32,000 each to Jean and Janice), the receivables ($50,000 to each), and the building (equal undivided interests worth $500,000 to each) in complete liquidation of the corporation.

At the shareholder level, Jean and Janice each receive liquidating distributions with FMV equal to $582,000 (cash of $32,000, plus receivables worth $50,000, plus undivided interests in the building worth $500,000) in exchange for their PCee Corp stock. These exchanges are treated as sales of their stock under IRC §331(a).

Therefore, Jean and Janice will each recognize taxable long-term capital gains of $132,000 from their stock sales (proceeds of $582,000 less basis in their shares of $450,000).

Jean and Janice will then contribute their distributed cash and property (with total basis of $582,000 each) in exchange for their 50% LLP ownership interests. Under IRC §721, the contributions are tax-free.

Under IRC §722, their initial bases in their LLP interests are $582,000 each. Under IRC §723, the LLP's total basis in the contributed assets is $1,164,000 ($64,000 basis in the cash, $100,000 basis in the receivables, and $1 million basis in the building).

Reality Check: In this case, the corporate-level and shareholder-level taxable gains resulting from conversion to LLP status are a heavy price to pay—probably too heavy for the owners to follow through with a conversion in real life. However, conversions of C corporations to LLPs can make very good sense when:

1. Corporations do not hold significantly appreciated assets, and
2. The shareholder-level gains upon liquidation will not be too large.

Example 4.09(3): Conversion of S Corporation into LLP Assume the same facts as in the previous Example, except the corporation is now PEss Corp (which has always been an S corporation), and Jean and Janice each have basis in their shares of $450,000.

PEss Corp will convert into an LLP by making liquidating distributions of its property to Jean and Janice, and each partner will then contribute distributed property to the newly formed LLP in exchange for 50% LLP ownership interests.

As in the previous Example, the corporation owns three assets: a building (with FMV of $1 million and tax basis of $700,000), unrealized receivables of $100,000 (with zero tax basis), and cash of $200,000.

Under IRC §336(a), PEss Corp recognizes a $400,000 corporate-level gain on the liquidating distribution, because the transaction is deemed a taxable sale of the corporate property for its FMV.

There is no corporate-level tax, but the gain is passed through to Jean and Janice ($200,000 each). They will pay tax on their gains, but the gains increase their bases in their shares to $650,000 each (preliquidation basis of $450,000 plus the $200,000 increase from the pass-through gain).

PEss Corp then distributes its cash ($100,000 each to Jean and Janice), the receivables ($50,000 each), and the building (undivided interests worth $500,000 each).

Jean and Janice each receive liquidating distributions with FMV equal to $650,000 (cash of $100,000, plus receivables worth $50,000, plus building worth $500,000) in exchange for their PEss Corp stock.

These exchanges are treated as sales of their stock under IRC §331(a). But in this case, Jean and Janice recognize no additional gains upon their stock sales, because their sales proceeds match their stock basis.

Jean and Janice will then contribute their distributed cash and property (with total basis of $650,000 each) in exchange for their 50% LLP ownership interests. Under IRC §721, the contributions are tax-free.

Under IRC §722, their initial bases in their LLP interests are $650,000 each. Under IRC §723, the LLP's total basis in the contributed assets is $1,300,000 ($200,000 basis in the cash, $100,000 basis in the receivables, and $1 million basis in the building).

Reality Check: Although there was only a single level of taxation in this case, converting PEss Corp into an LLP still required recognition of significant corporate-level gains, which were then passed through to the shareholders. In a real life situation, Jean and Janice might be unwilling to convert PEss Corp into an LLP because of the magnitude of those gains. However, in cases where corporations hold only assets with little or no appreciation, conversion may be *highly* advisable.

Tax Accounting Implications of Conversions

As stated earlier, for federal income tax purposes a conversion of an existing general or limited partnership into an LLP is generally treated as a continuation of the same entity. Accordingly, the new LLP will succeed to the old partnership's employer identification number (EIN) and its tax accounting methods, periods, elections, and asset holding periods. (See Revenue Rulings 95-55 and 95-37.)

In contrast, when a corporate conversion is undertaken, the resulting LLP will be a new taxable entity. The LLP will need to obtain a new EIN, and it will have the same choices as any new partnership regarding tax accounting methods, elections, and permissible taxable years.

4.10 COMPARISONS WITH OTHER ENTITY CHOICES

This section has the greatest relevance if the entity selection process has been narrowed down to a choice between an LLP and one of the other types of entities discussed below. If that is not the case, the practitioner should strongly consider using the entity selection software program that comes with this book. The program is designed to help make a choice-of-entity recommendation that is consistent with the major tax and nontax issues facing the client. If the program leads to the LLP as the apparently best choice, this section can be reviewed to solidify those conclusions.

LLPs Compared to LLCs

In states that do not offer LLC-like liability protection to LLP partners, LLCs are clearly preferable to LLPs, because LLCs protect their members from liability for the entity's contract liabilities (bank loans, accounts payable, etc.). Generally, therefore, the LLC form of doing business should be chosen when it is available.

However, there are three circumstances under which LLPs still make sense:

1. Under state law and/or applicable professional standards (such as state bar rules), LLCs may be unavailable for the practice of certain professions, In contrast, in states with LLP statutes, LLPs generally can be used for professional practices if partnerships can be used. This is because, in fact, an LLP is simply a special type of partnership. (The

administrative work needed to adopt or convert to LLP status—for example, to meet state board of accountancy regulations—should be minimal.)

2. In a few states (such as Texas), LLCs are subject to entity-level state taxes, while LLPs are not. Thus, even when professionals are allowed to practice as LLCs, LLPs may be more attractive for state tax reasons. Before LLP status is chosen over LLC status, however, the co-owners should be very comfortable that their exposure to the entity's contract liabilities (the Achilles' heel of LLPs) will be tightly managed.

3. As discussed in Chapter 3, LLCs are subject to legal uncertainties. If the co-owners are uncomfortable about this issue, they may prefer to operate as an LLP, because it is viewed as the more cautious choice.

In states not offering LLC-like liability protection, LLPs are superior to LLCs only if:

- LLCs are unavailable because of statutory and/or professional standard restrictions; or
- The state tax rules applying to LLCs are unfavorable enough to outweigh the liability-limiting advantage of LLCs over LLPs; or
- The legal uncertainties of LLCs are a decisive negative factor.

In states offering LLC-like liability protection to LLP partners, LLPs are just as attractive as LLCs. In these states, LLPs may be preferred to LLCs because of greater legal certainty, and/or greater ease of conversion for existing general partnerships, and/or better state tax treatment.

LLPs Compared to General Partnerships

With regard to the issue of limiting owner liability, LLPs are clearly superior to general partnerships. This is because the personal assets of LLP partners generally are *not* exposed to liabilities arising from the professional errors, omissions, or negligence of the other partners and firm employees. In contrast, the personal assets of general partners *are* exposed to such liabilities.

As discussed in section 4.06 of this chapter, however, LLPs do *not* protect partners from personal liability for their *own* tortious acts or their *own* professional errors, omissions, or negligence.

> **OBSERVATION:** *In somewhat unusual cases, the co-owners of a professional practice may be relatively unconcerned about personal liability exposure, because there is little or no entity-level debt and other liability concerns can be managed with insurance. In such circumstances, operating as a general partnership instead of as an LLP may still seem to make sense. However, since LLP status (when available) can be attained with so little trouble, it will be surprising if a professional practice chooses to operate as a general partnership instead of as an LLP.*

As discussed in section 4.08 of this chapter, there are few, if any, significant federal income tax law differences between general partnerships and

LLPs. Usually, LLPs and general partnerships will be treated identically for state income tax purposes as well.

In summary, compared to general partnerships, LLPs generally are superior if:

- They are available under state law and applicable professional standards, and
- For existing general partnerships, LLP status can be attained without excessive administrative hassles (usually this will be the case).

LLPs Compared to Limited Partnerships

Usually, LLPs will be of interest only to professional practices, because other businesses generally will find LLC status more attractive.

Typically, all members of a professional firm are active in managing the practice. This usually precludes using a limited partnership, because limited partners who are too active in the business can lose their limited partner status and become treated as general partners for legal purposes.

When this happens in a professional practice, a partner who had intended to be a limited partner becomes personally exposed (as a general partner) to all of the entity's liabilities, including those arising from the professional errors, omissions, and negligence of the other partners and firm employees.

The bottom line is that limited partnerships will seldom be an option for professional practices, because the liability exposures are functionally the same as with a general partnership. As discussed earlier in this section, LLPs are superior to general partnerships in their ability to limit liability. They are superior to limited partnerships for the same reason.

LLPs Compared to C Corporations

In states that do not offer LLC-like liability protection to LLP partners, C corporations obviously offer better protection than LLPs. In states that do offer LLC-like protection, the liability protection benefits of LLPs are similar to those of C corporations.

The obvious advantage of LLPs over C corporations is that LLPs benefit from the partnership pass-through taxation rule, avoiding the C corporation pitfall of double taxation covered in depth in Chapter 6. However, as is also discussed in Chapter 6, it is possible to avoid double taxation by "draining off" all of a professional corporation's taxable income; this is done by making deductible compensation payments to the shareholder-employees and deductible contributions to fringe benefit plans set up for those shareholder-employees. Therefore, professional practices can often sidestep the problem of double taxation—as long as appreciating assets (such as real estate used in the business) are kept out of the C corporation.

The other advantages (and the relatively few disadvantages) of partnership taxation are covered at length in Chapter 5.

> **OBSERVATION:** *Because they are partnerships by definition, LLPs must have at least two co-owners. In contrast, C corporations can be formed with only one shareholder.*

Compared to C corporations, LLPs have the potentially significant disadvantage of usually *not* having unlimited legal lives. The retirement, resignation, expulsion, death, bankruptcy, etc., of an LLP partner generally will cause a legal dissolution of the entity, unless the remaining partners vote to continue. In contrast, C corporations have unlimited legal life spans.

Another potentially significant disadvantage of LLP taxation compared to C corporation taxation is the inability of certain LLP partners to borrow against their qualified retirement plan account balances. Unlike shareholder-employees of C corporations, LLP partners with more than 10% interests in capital or profits are not permitted to borrow against their accounts [IRC §4975]. (S corporation shareholder-employees who own more than 5% of the corporate stock also are prevented from borrowing against their qualified retirement plan accounts.)

In summary, compared to C corporations, LLPs generally are superior if:

- There are at least two co-owners (making a partnership possible in the first place);

- LLP status is available under state law and applicable professional standards;

- The co-owners can live with their exposure (if any) to the entity's contract liabilities in return for the benefits of partnership taxation; and

- The co-owners can accept the fact that they may not be able to borrow against their qualified retirement plan accounts.

LLPs Compared to S Corporations

In states that do not offer LLC-like liability protection to LLP partners, S corporations obviously offer better protection than LLPs. In states that do offer LLC-like protection, the liability protection benefits of LLPs are similar to those of S corporations.

The biggest advantage of LLPs over S corporations is that LLPs qualify for the benefit of pass-through taxation without the numerous restrictions that apply to S corporations. (These restrictions are covered in Chapter 8.)

In addition, LLPs qualify for tax advantages beyond pass-though taxation. In general, the partnership taxation rules are significantly more generous and flexible than the provisions applying to S corporations. (The differences between partnership and S corporation taxation are covered in depth in Chapter 5.)

Overall, comparing LLPs to S corporations usually comes down to weighing:

- The additional liability protection offered by S corporations (if any) against

- The hassles caused by the S corporation restrictions and the advantages of partnership taxation over S corporation taxation.

> **OBSERVATION:** *Because they are partnerships by definition, LLPs must have at least two co-owners. In contrast, S corporations can be formed with only one shareholder. Also, LLPs are not available in all states.*

Compared to S corporations, LLPs have the potentially significant disadvantage of usually *not* having unlimited legal lives. The retirement, resignation, expulsion, death, bankruptcy, etc., of an LLP partner generally will cause a legal dissolution of the entity, unless the remaining partners vote to continue. In contrast, S corporations have unlimited legal life spans.

In summary, compared to S corporations, LLPs generally are superior if:

- There are at least two co-owners (making a partnership possible in the first place);

- LLP status is available under state law and applicable professional standards;

- The co-owners desire pass-through taxation, but qualifying as an S corporation would be inconvenient, difficult, or impossible, *or* the entity could qualify as an S corporation, but the benefits of the partnership taxation rules are significant compared to those of the S corporation taxation rules; and

- The co-owners can live with their exposure to the entity's contract liabilities (if any). This consideration will not be a factor in states that offer LLC-like liability protection to LLP partners.

LLPs Compared to Sole Proprietorships

Generally, comparisons of LLPs to sole proprietorships are not meaningful. Sole proprietorships are by definition owned by a single individual; LLPs must have at least two co-owners, because they are by definition partnership ventures.

However, if a business currently operated as a sole proprietorship can be structured to have at least two owners (such as by forming a husband–wife partnership), the comparisons made earlier in this section can be considered.

4.11 SUMMARY STATEMENT ON WHEN LLPs ARE ATTRACTIVE

LLPs are probably the best entity choice when:

1. Pass-through taxation is desired; and

2. LLC status is unavailable or LLP status offers LLC-like liability protection; and

3. LLP status is permitted under the statute and applicable professional standards; and

4. Qualifying as an S corporation would be inconvenient, difficult, or impossible, *or* the entity could qualify as an S corporation but the benefits of the partnership taxation rules are significant compared to those of the S corporation taxation rules; and

5. Co-owners can live with their exposure (if any) to the entity's contract liabilities. (This is *not* a consideration in states that offer LLC-like liability protection to LLP partners.)

Appendix 4A: Comparison of Professional Practice Entities

Explanation: Use the chart on the following page to quickly compare the entity choices for operating professional practices. Note that C corporations are not included, because professional practice owners are typically unwilling to expose their business to the double taxation problem.

> *CAUTION: The information presented in the following table is general in nature and does not reflect state law differences. To assess specific client issues, state statutory provisions must be reviewed in detail.*

Comparison of Professional Practice Entities

Issue	Multi-Member Limited Liability Company (LLC) (see Ch. 3)	Limited Liability (Partnership (LLP))	Subchapter S Professional Corporation (see Ch. 8)	General Partnership (see Ch. 5)	Sole Proprietorship (see Ch. 9)
Personal Liability of Owners	Limited, except for an individual's own errors	Partners are not liable for professional acts, errors, omissions, malpractice, malfeasance, or negligence of others, unless they supervised or were involved. In some states, LLP partners are liable for contractual obligations.	Limited, except for an individual's own errors	Unlimited	Unlimited
Federal Income Tax Treatment	Partnership taxation	Partnership taxation	Single level of taxation	Partnership taxation	Single level
Permitted Number of Owners	No restriction, but need at least 2 for partnership tax treatment (some states allow single-member LLCs)	Unlimited (need at least 2)	Limited to 75	Unlimited (need at least 2)	One
Permitted Types of Owners	No restrictions	No restrictions	Limited to individuals, estates, certain trusts, and certain tax-exempt entities	No restrictions	Individual
Permitted Classes of Ownership Interests	Multiple classes are permitted	Multiple classes are permitted	Can have only one class of stock	Multiple classes are permitted	N/A
Legal Life of Entity	Generally limited	Limited	May be perpetual	Limited	Limited
Special Allocation of Tax Items	Permitted	Permitted	Not permitted	Permitted	N/A
Management	Entity can be managed either by designated managers or by all members	Generally managed by all partners	Managed by board of directors and officers	Managed by general partners	N/A
Transferability of Interests	Usually limited by articles or operating agreement; may be limited by state law	Generally limited by state law and partnership agreement	Often limited by shareholder agreement; must comply with Subchapter S tax requirements	Generally limited by state law and partnership agreement	N/A
Necessary Documentation	Articles of organization; operating agreement	Usually a partnership agreement and annual registration	Articles of incorporation; bylaws; minutes	Usually a partnership agreement	N/A
Regulation of Issuance and Sale of Ownership Interests	Possibly federal and state securities laws; state LLC laws	Interests in LLPs are probably not securities	Federal and state securities law; state corporation laws	State partnership laws	N/A

Appendix 4B: Sample Client Letter When LLP Appears to Be Best Entity Choice

Dear [Client name]:

This letter briefly summarizes some of the major considerations that went into your recent decision to form a new business that will be operated as a limited liability partnership (LLP). As we discussed, LLPs are a relatively new type of entity that can be particularly useful for the operation of professional practices. LLPs are formed and operated pursuant to the state's LLP statute.

Liability of LLP Partners

Like the partners of a general partnership, the partners of an LLP remain personally liable for the general debts and obligations of the LLP—sometimes referred to as "contract liabilities." Contract liabilities include, but are not limited to, bank loans, lease obligations, vendor accounts payable.

In addition, LLP partners remain personally liable for their own tortious acts and professional errors, omissions, and negligence. (*Tortious acts* are defined as wrongful acts leading to civil actions, other than those involving breach of contract.)

However, LLP partners are generally *not* liable for the professional errors, omissions, and negligence of the other LLP partners and employees.

In other words, LLPs offer much greater liability protection than general partnerships, where partners *are* exposed to liabilities related to the professional errors, omissions, and negligence of others.

But, LLPs offer less protection than LLCs, where members generally are not liable for the entity's contract liabilities (unless they are personally guaranteed). As we discussed, you chose not to operate as an LLC because **[give reason, such as adverse state tax consequences or LLC not allowed by state professional standards]**.

[Insert alternative language if state law grants LLC-like liability protection to LLP partners. See Appendix 3A for appropriate language.]

LLP Advantages

LLPs are partnerships (both for state law and for federal income tax purposes), and they are therefore subject to the legal and tax implications that generally apply to partnerships.

The major advantage of LLPs is the ability to benefit from pass-through taxation without being affected by the various restrictions applying to S corporations (the one-class-of-stock rule, etc.).

In addition, LLPs enjoy the other tax advantages that partnerships have over S corporations. For example, LLPs generally can make tax-free distributions of appreciated property and create different types of ownership interests with varying rights to cash flow, liquidation proceeds, and tax allocations. These things cannot be done under the inflexible tax rules that apply to S corporations.

Conclusion

We appreciate the opportunity to consult with you as you make the important decision of choosing the most advantageous type of entity under which to operate your new venture. We look forward to working with you in the future as your LLP is formed and enters the operating phase.

Very truly yours,

Appendix 4C: List of States Offering LLC-Like Liability Protection to LLP Partners

Explanation: As discussed in section 4.06 of this chapter, some state LLP statutes do not protect the personal assets of LLP partners from exposure to the firm's contract liabilities (accounts payable, lease obligations, etc.). LLP statutes in other states do protect LLP partners from contract liabilities. In these latter states, LLPs offer what might be termed "LLC-like" liability protection to LLP partners. The LLP statutes of the states listed below currently offer LLC-like liability protection to LLP partners.

> **CAUTION:** The list below was believed to be accurate at time of publication. However, state legislatures have been active in amending their LLP statutes to provide LLC-like liability protection. Therefore, additional states may offer LLC-like protection by the time you read this. In addition, be aware that the issue of whether an LLP partner can be held personally liable for tortious acts of another partner or firm employee (for example, sexual harassment of a co-worker) may not be entirely clear. This, along with all specific questions regarding liability concerns, should be addressed by competent legal counsel.

Alabama	Missouri
Arizona	Montana
California	Nebraska
Colorado	New Mexico
Connecticut	New York
Delaware	North Dakota
Georgia	Oklahoma
Hawaii	Oregon
Idaho	South Dakota
Indiana	Vermont
Kansas	Washington State
Massachusetts	Wisconsin
Minnesota	Wyoming

CHAPTER 5 • PARTNERSHIPS—GENERAL, LIMITED, AND FAMILY LIMITED PARTNERSHIPS

CONTENTS

5.01 INTRODUCTION

Some time ago, partnerships (both general and limited) enjoyed great popularity. They combined the advantage of pass-through taxation with maximum flexibility to specially tailor ownership interests to meet the financial and tax needs of various members of the ownership group. Such flexibility is not available with the S corporation form of doing business, which was the other alternative if pass-through taxation was desired. (As discussed in Chapters 3 and 4, LLCs and LLPs are now additional options for those seeking the benefits of pass-through taxation.)

Unfortunately, during the 1980s partnerships (especially limited partnerships) got a bad name. They were used by promoters as the vehicles for a multitude of poorly conceived and tax-motivated schemes, which were often characterized as "tax shelters."

Also, the partnership taxation rules were greatly "complexified" by the release of extremely technical new regulations covering partnership tax allocations, basis from partnership debt, etc. This increased the time needed to prepare partnership Forms 1065 and resulted in complicated Schedules K-1 for investors. To this day, the partnership taxation rules "scare away" some practitioners and clients alike.

But when pass-through taxation is desired for a multi-owner operation and the S corporation eligibility rules present problems (see Chapter 8), the use of a partnership, or an LLC treated as a partnership, will usually meet client objectives.

5.02 WHAT IS A PARTNERSHIP?

A *partnership* is simply a business or investment venture conducted jointly by two or more participants (partners) with the intent to divide the income and profits from the undertaking.

Partnerships with limited business purposes (for example, to develop and sell a specific parcel of real estate) are also commonly termed "joint ventures." The legal aspects of partnerships are governed by state partnership statutes, most of which are in conformity with the Uniform Partnership Act (UPA) and the Revised Uniform Limited Partnership Act (RULPA).

From a legal perspective, the use of a limited partnership and/or liability insurance can often offer the partners virtually the same level of liability protection as enjoyed by corporate shareholders and LLC members.

From a federal income tax perspective, partnerships offer the advantage of freedom from double taxation ("pass-through taxation") without the need to worry about the strict S corporation eligibility rules.

General Partnerships versus Limited Partnerships

Partners in general partnerships are jointly and severally liable (without limitation) for *all* the debts and obligations of the partnership. General partners can also be legally bound (and thus held financially responsible) by actions taken by any of the other general partners who appear to be acting on behalf of the partnership.

The alternative to the general partnership is the limited partnership. The limited partners of a limited partnership usually are not financially at risk with respect to any partnership debts and obligations. In other words, all a limited partner stands to lose in the worst case scenario is his or her investment in the partnership, plus any unfulfilled partnership capital contribution obligations.

However, each limited partnership must have at least one general partner who has the fiduciary duty of managing the partnership for the benefit of all partners and who is liable without limitation for all of the debts and obligations of the partnership.

The important issue of partner liability is covered in more depth in section 5.05 of this chapter.

> **OBSERVATION:** *Outside investors will almost universally find unlimited personal liability unacceptable. Therefore, a limited partnership (or an LLC, as discussed in Chapter 3) will have to be formed if such investors are to be involved in the venture.*

5.03 BUSINESSES ELIGIBLE (AND SUITABLE) TO OPERATE AS PARTNERSHIPS

Generally a partnership can be formed under state law to pursue any lawful business or investment opportunity. The "classic" situation calling for the use of a partnership to operate a proposed venture is one in which:

1. Achieving pass-through taxation is a critical goal, and

2. Some or all of the potential owners are prohibited from being S corporation shareholders, and/or

3. The S corporation single-class-of-stock rule prevents the owners from holding the types of ownership interests they want.

Example 5.03(1): The Classic Partnership Scenario   A group of investors is putting together a real estate development venture. They all agree that the project *must* avoid the C corporation double taxation problem. However, several of the investors are foreign individuals, one is a corporation, and one is a partnership. All of these are prohibited from being S corporation shareholders.

In addition, several of the investors are going to contribute money, while several are primarily contributing their real estate expertise. Those contributing money want ownership interests that give them a "preferred return" from the venture's cash flow; they also want disproportionately large allocations of the tax losses that are expected in the first few years of the operation. These benefits are not possible with an S corporation structure, because all S corporation shares must have identical financial rights and allocations of pass-through tax items.

The only way the investors can achieve their financial goals is with a partnership (or an LLC treated as a partnership for tax purposes). If a partnership is formed, there are no rules regarding prohibited types of owners. And the partnership can tailor partnership interests to give the "money partners" the preferred returns and special tax loss allocations they want.

Types of Activities Best Suited for Partnerships

Business and investment activities for which partnerships make sense include, but are not limited to:

- Corporate joint ventures (where the corporate co-owners desire pass-through taxation);
- Real estate investment and development activities (where the partnership taxation rules allow investors to receive preferred returns, special allocations of tax losses, and additional basis from partnership-level debt);
- Oil and gas exploration (where the partnership taxation rules allow preferred returns and special allocations of deductions from intangible drilling costs);
- Venture capital investments (where the partnership rules allow pass-through taxation and the creation of ownership interests with varying rights to cash flow, liquidating distributions, and tax items);
- Business start-ups expected to have tax losses in the initial years (which can be passed through to the partners);
- Professional practices (where pass-through taxation can be combined with specially tailored ownership interests that reflect each member's contributions to the practice); and
- Family limited partnerships used as estate planning vehicles (where the older generation can gift partnership interests to younger family members while retaining control by functioning as the general partners, and where all taxable income is passed through to the partners—see section 5.10 of this chapter).

CAUTION: Although there are no legal limits on the number of partners of a general or limited partnership, there is a tax problem if partnership interests are so widely held that they are "publicly traded" within the meaning of IRC §7704. If a partnership's interests are publicly traded, the partnership will be treated as a C corporation for federal income tax purposes.

CAUTION: As discussed in section 5.05 of this chapter, there is a risk that limited partners can lose their limited liability protection if they become too involved in the management of the partnership.

Should a Partnership or an LLC Be Used?

As discussed in Chapter 3, the author feels LLCs generally are superior to partnerships. However, LLCs are not always available for the type of business at hand, and some clients may be reluctant to embrace LLCs because of the legal uncertainties surrounding them.

Under some state laws and/or applicable professional standards (such as state bar association rules), LLCs may be prohibited from operating certain professional practices. (See Chapter 4, which covers LLPs, a special type of partnership that can be attractive to professional practices.) Also, some states do not permit the use of LLCs in certain industries, such as farming.

In summary, partnerships may be the best choice for business and investment ventures if:

- There will be more than one owner;
- Pass-through taxation is desired;
- Liability concerns can be addressed with insurance or by forming a limited partnership;
- The advantages of partnership taxation are significant compared to the alternative of S corporation taxation, or the entity cannot qualify for S corporation status (see discussion in Chapter 8);
- Under state law or applicable professional standards the business or investment activity cannot be operated as an LLC; *or*
- The co-owners cannot tolerate the uncertainties of LLC status.

5.04 FUNDAMENTAL FORMATION AND OPERATING ISSUES

Legal Formation Process

State partnership statutes set up legal frameworks covering the partnership form of doing business. In effect, the statutes create rules that apply when issues are not addressed in the partnership agreement (see below). The statutes also define the rights of third parties, such as partnership creditors.

General Partnerships

As stated earlier, a *partnership* is simply a business or investment venture conducted jointly by two or more participants (partners) with the intent to divide the income and profits from the undertaking. A general partnership can exist for legal purposes even though there is no formal partnership agreement or other written document.

In most states, general partnerships are governed by state statutes that conform with the Uniform Partnership Act (UPA). Under the UPA, partners can include individuals (other than minors or insane persons) and virtually any other type of entity, including corporations, trusts, other partnerships, and LLCs.

Limited Partnerships

Under state law, limited partnerships usually are required to file a certificate of limited partnership with the appropriate state or local office, describe the business the partnership intends to conduct, describe the partnership's financial structure, and designate the general and limited partners' names.

To qualify as a limited partnership, the entity must comply with all requirements of the state's limited partnership statute. Failing that, an intended limited partnership is treated as a general partnership for legal purposes, and all partners are treated as general partners.

A limited partnership's name should not include the names of any limited partners and *should* include the words "limited partnership." For example, a partnership might be named Ford Road Development Limited Partnership.

In most states, limited partnerships are governed by state statutes that conform with the Revised Uniform Limited Partnership Act (RULPA).

"Creating" More Than One Owner

The fact that a partnership must by definition have more than one owner is a potential impediment when the business or investment activity under consideration in fact will be controlled by one person. Often, however, the owner can solve this problem by forming a partnership with a related person or a controlled entity. For example, a partnership can be formed with a husband and wife as the two partners. Or the main owner can form a partnership with another relative or individual who the owner trusts. Finally, a partnership can be formed between an individual and a wholly owned corporation or other controlled entity or between two controlled corporations. [See Revenue Ruling 93-4 (1993-1 CB 225).]

A limited partnership apparently can be formed with an individual named as the limited partner and a controlled entity designated as the general partner.

Certificate of Assumed Name

In many states, a partnership must file a certificate identifying the assumed name that will be used and the name and address of one or more of the partners. This may be the case even if the partnership's name reflects the actual names of all the partners.

Limited partnerships may be required to publish their certificates of limited partnership.

The Partnership Agreement

Partnership agreements allow partnerships to, in effect, write their own laws regarding how the affairs of the partnership will be conducted. Although a partnership *can* function without a written partnership agreement, it is certainly not recommended.

At the least, a partnership agreement should specify how the entity will be managed; the legal relationships between the partners; the partners' obligations to make contributions of cash or property; the partners' shares of profits, losses, and distributions; the allocations of tax items; the partners' rights upon withdrawal; etc. See Appendix 5C for a sample partnership agreement checklist.

Other Steps in the Formation Phase

Beyond compliance with the statutory requirements described above and drafting of a partnership agreement, the formation phase tasks are essentially the same as for any business activity. They include:

- Opening a bank account in the partnership's name;
- Transferring title to any contributed assets to be owned by the newly formed partnership;
- Obtaining liability, property, business interruption, and workers' compensation insurance coverage;
- Obtaining federal and state employer ID numbers (also used for income tax purposes);
- Establishing accounting and payroll tax withholding and payment procedures; and
- Registering with states and localities for collection of sales taxes and obtaining all required business licenses and permits.

Partner Contributions in Exchange for Partnership Interests

Partners can contribute virtually anything of value in exchange for a partnership interest. In other words, a contribution can be as amorphous as a promise to provide future services to the partnership or granting the partnership the right to use (but not own) property.

Generally, however, partners will contribute cash or other property (such as real estate, securities, equipment, patent rights) in exchange for their partnership interests. These contributions, often referred to as "capital contributions," should be documented by maintaining partner capital accounts as part of the partnership's books and records.

Partners generally are liable to the partnership (and in effect to the partnership's creditors) for any capital contribution requirements that were agreed to but that remain unsatisfied.

> **RECOMMENDATION:** *The partnership agreement (or amendments thereto) should specify the value of noncash capital contributions for purposes of crediting the contributing partner's capital account.*

Flexibility Compared to S Corporations

Like S corporations, partnerships offer the benefit of pass-through taxation. However, partnerships have the distinct advantage of offering a great deal more flexibility in terms of permitted ownership and capital structures. For example, a partnership can have as partners C corporations, S corporations, other partnerships, foreign individuals, trusts, etc., with no limitation on the number of partners (although publicly traded partnerships are treated as C corporations for federal income tax purposes under IRC §7704). S corporations are limited to 75 shareholders, and these can be only individuals (other than nonresident aliens), estates, and certain types of trusts.

Also, partnership ownership interests can be tailored to meet the specific financial and tax-planning needs of investors in that varying rights can be assigned to current and liquidating distributions, gains from asset sales, special allocations of tax losses and deductions, etc. S corporations, on the other hand, are limited to one class of stock; all S corporation shares must have identical economic rights and rights to tax allocations.

> **RECOMMENDATION:** *The effects of the S corporation ownership and capital structure restrictions should be considered as a potential problem not just at formation of the venture, but throughout its life. For example, if a business is expected to grow rapidly and require capital infusions in the relatively near future, the 75-shareholder rule, the limitations on types of shareholders, and the one-class-of-stock rule will almost certainly hamper efforts to raise additional capital. In such situations, starting off as a limited partnership or an LLC may be advisable.*

Partnership Management

Unless the partnership agreement says otherwise, each partner has an equal right to participate in the management of the venture. However, the partnership agreement may assign specific areas of management authority to specific partners—an administrative partner, a financial matters partner, a managing partner (in charge overall), etc. Each partner has a fiduciary duty to exercise his or her management authority in good faith for the benefit of the other partners and the partnership. Generally, each partner has access to the partnership's books and records.

In a limited partnership, the above management rights are vested in one or more general partners, but the limited partners do not have management rights.

Authority of Partners to Legally Bind the Partnership

Each general partner is considered legally an agent of the partnership. Accordingly, each can transact business on behalf of the partnership and can make contracts that are legally binding on the partnership.

The partnership agreement can restrict a partner's right to bind the partnership. But the restriction may not have any effect on a third party who does not know of the restriction, when it appears the partner is acting within the ordinary scope of the partnership's business.

> **OBSERVATION:** *This ability of any general partner to legally bind the partnership usually is considered a major negative factor. In effect, one partner can saddle all partners with liabilities, such as when that partner agrees to an unfavorable long-term lease of a building. The bottom line is that general partnerships are viable only when the partners have a high degree of trust in each other.*

5.05 LIABILITY OF PARTNERS

Limited Partnerships

The unlimited liability of at least one general partner for all debts and obligations puts the limited partnership at an obvious disadvantage compared to C and S corporations. Corporate stockholders generally are not at risk to lose anything beyond the value of their stock investments.

In the real world, however, many shareholders of closely held corporations are required by lenders to personally guarantee the debts of the corporation. This means that, in many situations, the limited liability advantage of corporations may be more apparent than real.

Using a Corporate General Partner

A relatively simple way to work around the general partner's unlimited liability problem is to form a limited partnership with an S corporation as the sole general partner. Typically, the S corporation is owned by the individuals (and in the same proportions) who will actually manage the limited partnership's business. Most often, the limited partnership interests are owned by outside investors.

The owners of the corporate general partner are protected from personal liability exposure by the liability-limiting powers of the corporation. All those owners stand to lose in a worst case scenario is the value of their stock in the corporate general partner. All the other partners are limited partners to begin with.

Therefore, the net effect of using a corporate general partner is that *all* owners are protected from unlimited personal exposure to the liabilities of the limited partnership. In other words, using a corporate general partner "simulates" the liability-limiting effects of operating as a corporation.

Because the S corporation general partner is itself a pass-through entity, the benefits of pass-through taxation are still available to all owners. The downside of using a corporate general partner is the expense to create an additional legal entity and the ongoing administrative and tax filing burdens caused by the existence of the corporation.

Potential Loss of Liability Protection If Limited Partners Are Too Active

Under state law, a limited partner who takes an active role in the management of a limited partnership runs the risk of losing limited partner status. This makes limited partnerships unsuitable for certain activities, such as the practice of a profession where all partners are by definition heavily involved in the business.

This problem too can often be finessed by using a corporate general partner, with the corporation owned by the limited partners in proportion to their limited partnership ownership percentages. Again, however, the existence of an additional legal entity creates administrative and tax filing burdens.

State limited partnership laws based on the Revised Uniform Limited Partnership Act give some relief, specifying a number of actions that limited partners can take *without* being deemed to participate in management. Nevertheless, the issue is always a potential problem for limited partnerships.

If the inability of limited partners to participate in management is unacceptable, LLCs, C corporations, and S corporations will have to be considered as alternatives. As discussed in Chapters 3, 6, and 8, all of these alternative entity choices have their shortcomings (and their advantages).

General Partnerships

A general partner is jointly and severally liable for all debts and obligations of the partnership, *including* those arising from tortious acts, errors, omissions, and negligence of the other partners and the partnership's employees, representatives, etc. *Tortious acts* are defined as wrongful acts leading to civil actions, other than those involving breach of contract. For example, careless operation of a vehicle resulting in injuries or property damage is a tortious act.

As noted in section 5.04 of this chapter, each general partner also has the authority to legally bind the partnership (and indirectly the other general partners), another potential source of liability exposure for general partners.

General Partnerships Compared to LLPs

In most states, an LLP partner is *not* personally liable for the professional errors, omissions, and negligence of other partners and employees who are not under his or her supervision. In some states, however, LLP partners are still personally liable (jointly and severally, as general partners) for the LLP's contract liabilities. Examples of contract liabilities include bank loans, lease obligations, and vendor accounts payable. (See Chapter 4 for a complete discussion of LLPs.)

Indemnification Rights

Under the Uniform Partnership Act (which has been adopted by almost all the states), the partnership indemnifies the partners of a general partnership for all losses and expenses the partners pay. The right to indemnification means that a partner who is forced to pay off "more than his share" of a partnership liability (because of the joint and several liability concept) is entitled to be reimbursed by the partnership.

In turn, the partnership is entitled to be reimbursed by the other partners who paid "less than their shares," even if the liability of the partnership arose because of tortious acts, errors, omissions, or negligence of a "guilty" partner. In other words, a partner who is "guilty" of a tortious or negligent act, error, or omission may be forced to pay off the resulting liability personally, but can then turn around and demand to be indemnified by the general partnership for the excess of the amount paid over his or her normal share of partnership losses. This in effect forces the other "innocent" partners to share the loss.

> **Example 5.05(1): Professional Malpractice and Negligence**   A general partnership is hit with a $100,000 liability because a claimant wins a judgment for professional malpractice. The malpractice was solely attributable to the acts of a partner with a 10% interest in the partnership.
>
> In attempting to collect the judgment, the claimant generally can move first against the assets of the partnership. If those assets are insufficient, the claimant can then move against the personal assets of the "guilty" partner.
>
> If the partnership has no assets, the "guilty" partner will be forced to personally pay off the $100,000 judgment, but can then exercise his or her right to indemnification and demand a $90,000 reimbursement from the partnership. The other "innocent" partners would then be

required to contribute $90,000 to enable the partnership to indemnify the "guilty" partner.

Example 5.05(2): Tortious Act by a Partner   A 10% partner uses his car on partnership business and becomes involved in an accident that causes injuries that result in a $100,000 judgment. The results will be the same as in the preceding Example.

5.06 WITHDRAWAL OF PARTNERS AND DISSOLUTION OF PARTNERSHIPS

Withdrawal and Disassociation of Partners

Generally, the provisions of the partnership agreement will control the rights of partners when they voluntarily withdraw (which may be referred to as "resignation" or "retirement") from the partnership.

Withdrawing partners will want to be paid for their partnership interests—usually the sooner the better. However, from the partnership's perspective, it is prudent to impose conditions on payment (such as an installment payment arrangement) if the partnership is not expected to hold sufficient liquid assets to immediately pay withdrawing partners.

Note that legally a general partnership is dissolved upon the withdrawal of a partner. However, the remaining partners can generally vote to continue. From a legal perspective, the continuing partnership is viewed as a new entity, because the fundamental relationships between the partners have changed even though the venture is continued.

Likewise, the withdrawal of a general partner from a limited partnership causes a legal dissolution of the entity. Again, the partners can choose to continue the venture, although the continuing partnership is considered a new entity for legal purposes. The withdrawal of a limited partner does *not* cause a legal dissolution of a limited partnership.

Disassociation of a general partner can occur for a number of reasons beyond voluntary withdrawal—for example, from a partner's death (or legal dissolution), insanity, bankruptcy, expulsion, or other events specified in the partnership agreement. Like voluntary withdrawals of general partners, these other forms of disassociation ("dissolution events") will also terminate the legal existence of the partnership.

> **RECOMMENDATION:** *The partnership agreement (or a separate buy–sell agreement) should specify the methodology that will be used to value the interests of withdrawing or disassociating partners. In addition, the operating agreement (or buy–sell agreement) should specify payment terms, such as installment payments or payment with noncash property distributions. In other words, payment terms should be structured to ensure that required payments to withdrawing or disassociating partners will not cripple the partnership's ability to continue its business operations.*

> **RECOMMENDATION:** *When a general partner withdraws or otherwise disassociates from a partnership, his or her authority to legally bind the partnership*

ceases. However, notice should be given to third parties. Otherwise, the partnership may continue to be liable for actions taken by the departed partner. (Third parties generally can rely on the apparent authority of a person to act as an agent of the partnership, even after that person is no longer a partner.)

CAUTION: After the withdrawal or disassociation of one or more partners, at least two partners must remain for the entity to continue to be treated as a partnership for federal income tax purposes.

Disassociation Can Cause "Technical Termination" for Tax Purposes

For federal income tax purposes, a partnerships is deemed to continue in existence after a dissolution event (even if the event results in legal termination of the partnership) *unless* it results in a change in ownership of 50% or more of the capital and profits interests within a 12-month period.

This 50% rule applies to both general and limited partnership interests. In other words, changes in ownership of limited partnership interests (even if there is no change in general partnership interests) can trigger a termination of a limited partnership for tax purposes if they aggregate to 50% or more of the interests in capital and profits.

Similarly, any combination of changes in ownership of limited and general partnership interests can cause a tax termination (often referred to as a "technical termination"). [See IRC §708(b)(1)(B) and the discussion in section 5.08 of this chapter.]

Actual Dissolution (or "Liquidation") of the Partnership

As discussed above, partnerships are considered to legally dissolve upon the occurrence of certain events such as the retirement, resignation, expulsion, death, or bankruptcy of a general partner.

Also as discussed above, for federal income tax purposes partnerships are deemed to continue in existence after dissolution events, unless they result in an IRC §708 technical termination because of a change in ownership of 50% or more of the capital and profits interests within a 12-month period.

In addition, the partnership agreement may call for dissolution as of a fixed date, after a designated number of years of existence, or after certain events (such as the disposition of substantially all of the partnership's assets or upon a unanimous vote by the partners to dissolve).

In other words, partnerships have limited legal life spans that end upon the occurrence of specified events, many of which are in the nature of events affecting the partners rather than the entity itself. This is not the case for corporations, whose legal lives continue indefinitely regardless of the fates of their shareholders.

If the decision is made to *actually* dissolve (or "liquidate") the partnership (because the partners fail to vote to continue or because the business is to be wound up), there may be state law public notice requirements to comply with. The intent of these rules is to ensure that the partnership's creditors and other third parties are made aware of the impending dissolution.

Limited partnerships may be required to file certificates of dissolution in accordance with the state's limited partnership statute.

After dissolution, the partnership continues to exist long enough to wind up (or "terminate") its affairs. Assets are sold, partnership creditors are paid off, and any remaining assets are distributed to the partners in liquidation of their partnership interests.

In a limited partnership, the limited partners are entitled to recover their shares of profits and capital before general partners receive payment for their loans to the partnership and their shares of profits and capital.

> **RECOMMENDATION:** *The partnership agreement should provide for the possibility that the partnership may hold illiquid assets (such as real estate or nonpublicly traded securities) that will be distributed to partners upon dissolution. The composition of the partnership's assets may be such that some partners will receive only liquid assets, some will receive only illiquid assets, and some may receive a mixture. The critical issue in such cases is how to value the illiquid assets, so that all partners will receive distributed property with the proper value. Valuation methods can be specified in the partnership agreement to prevent disputes upon dissolution.*

5.07 CLASSIFICATION AS PARTNERSHIP FOR TAX PURPOSES

Under the check the box entity classification regulations, multiple-owner unincorporated entities—such as state-law limited partnerships—are automatically treated as partnerships for federal income tax purposes. As strange as it sounds, under the former entity classification regulations some limited partnerships ran the risk of being treated as associations taxable as corporations. (See Chapter 3 for a complete explanation of the check the box regulations.)

For federal income tax purposes, state-law general partnerships have always been classified unambiguously as partnerships.

> **CAUTION:** *Although there are no limits on the number of partners in a partnership, a tax problem arises if partnership interests are so widely held that they are "publicly traded" within the meaning of IRC §7704. If the partnership interests are publicly traded, the partnership will be treated as a C corporation for federal income tax purposes. The publicly traded partnership issue is rarely a problem, but it could arise in the context of a large limited partnership.*

5.08 FEDERAL INCOME TAXATION OF PARTNERSHIPS

Partnership Taxation in General

Under the federal tax laws, partnerships and their partners are in many ways treated similarly to S corporations and their shareholders (see Chapter 8). Like S corporations, partnerships are pass-through entities rather than taxpaying entities. Under the principle of pass-through taxation, the income, gains, losses, deductions, and credits of the partnership are passed through to the partners, who take these items into account in their own returns.

In addition, the partner's tax basis in his or her partnership interest is increased by the partner's share of partnership income and gain and decreased by the partner's share of losses and deductions.

Distributions also reduce the partner's tax basis in his or her partnership interest, but not below zero. Cash distributions in excess of the partner's basis result in taxable gain.

The partnership taxation rules are found in IRC §§701–777, which constitute Subchapter K of the Tax Code.

See General Practice Aids 5 and 7 in Chapter 10 for illustrations of how the advantage of pass-through taxation can be extremely significant when substantial positive taxable income is earned over a period of several years.

Pass-Through of Taxable Losses

The ability of partnerships to pass through taxable losses is also advantageous, because such losses are often expected in the early years of a venture. The losses can be passed through to the partners, who can deduct them currently (subject to potential tax law limitation under the basis, at-risk, and passive loss rules).

In contrast, taxable losses incurred by a C corporation remain trapped inside the corporation in the form of a net operating loss (NOL). The NOL is useless until the corporation earns taxable income that can be offset by the NOL.

Character of Partnership Pass-Through Items

The partnership's pass-through tax items retain their character at the partner level, which generally represents an advantage over the C corporation tax rules. For example, each partner's shares of partnership capital gains and losses are passed through and treated as capital gains and losses at the partner level. In contrast, long-term capital gains of C corporations receive no special tax treatment. And capital losses of C corporations can only be carried back three years or forward five years to offset capital gains. [IRC §§1211, 1212] If there are no capital gains within this period, the corporation's capital losses expire without providing any tax benefit.

Partnership tax-exempt income is passed through and retains its tax-exempt character at the partner level, and the income increases the partner's tax basis in his or her interest; accordingly, the tax-exempt income is truly tax-free. In contrast, the tax-exempt income of a C corporation generally will result in a greater shareholder-level tax liability when the stock is eventually sold or liquidated for a value that reflects the tax-exempt income earned by the corporation.

Partnership Taxation Compared to S Corporation Taxation

Although the federal income tax rules for partnerships and partners are similar to those for S corporations and shareholders, there are some significant differences, most of which favor partnerships over S corporations.

Basis from Partnership Debt

As discussed in Chapter 8, an S corporation shareholder has basis for loss deduction purposes only to the extent of the basis of his or her stock plus the amount of any loans from the shareholder to the corporation. In contrast, a partner obtains additional basis in his or her partnership interest for his or her share of partnership debt. The share of partnership debt is treated as a cash contribution for basis purposes. [IRC §752]

The rules regarding how basis from debt is allocated among the partners depend on whether the debt is recourse or nonrecourse. Partnership recourse debt is allocated for basis purposes among the general partners (and any other partner who is personally liable for such debt without right of subrogation against the partnership or other partners). Partnership nonrecourse debt (debt for which no partner is personally liable) can be allocated for basis purposes among all partners, *including* limited partners. The regulations under IRC §752 include rather complicated rules for making the precise allocations among partners of basis from partnership debt.

The advantage of the basis from debt rule is that, potentially, partners can deduct losses in excess of their cash investments in their partnership interests. This can be very advantageous if, as is often the case, relatively large tax losses are expected in the early years of a business.

> **Example 5.08(1): Effect of Recourse Debt on Basis** Steve and Kerry each contribute $40,000 cash to start a 50/50 equipment leasing general partnership. The partnership obtains a $400,000 recourse loan and purchases equipment for that amount.
>
> As 50/50 partners, Steve and Kerry each have initial basis in their partnership interests of $240,000 ($40,000 from the cash contributed plus $200,000 from each partner's share of the partnership's debt) for loss deduction purposes.
>
> If Steve and Kerry each contributed $40,000 to start the business as a 50/50 S corporation, each owner's initial basis for loss deduction

purposes would be limited to his $40,000 basis in S corporation stock. Somewhat surprisingly, this is the case even if Steve and Kerry each personally guarantee $200,000 of the corporation's debt.

At-Risk Basis from Partnership Debt

Partners will generally receive IRC §465 at-risk basis only from debt for which they are personally liable (in other words, recourse debt or nonrecourse debt that is personally guaranteed). In the above Example, Steve and Kerry would each have initial at-risk basis in their partnership interests of $240,000. The same would be true if the debt were nonrecourse, but both partners personally guaranteed 50% of the debt.

If there are no personal guarantees, partners receive §465 at-risk basis from partnership *nonrecourse* debt only if it is qualified nonrecourse financing. Therefore, if the partnership has only nonrecourse debt (or if the partner is a limited partner), the at-risk limitation rules often will prevent the partner from deducting losses in excess of the basis derived from his or her cash and property contributions to the partnership.

However, as the following Example illustrates, the "regular" basis from partnership nonrecourse debt can still be very beneficial in eliminating or minimizing current taxable gain when a partner contributes property with debt in excess of basis.

> **Example 5.08(2): Additional "Regular" Basis from Nonrecourse Debt Prevents Gain on Contribution (Even Though At-Risk Basis Not Increased)** Huck and Chuck form a 50/50 partnership to develop raw land. In exchange for his partnership interest, Huck contributes land with tax basis of $80,000 and FMV of $200,000. The land is burdened with a $120,000 nonrecourse liability. However, assume the liability is *not* qualified nonrecourse financing.
>
> Chuck contributes $80,000 cash (equal to the value of the equity in the land contributed by Huck).
>
> The partnership agreement provides for 50/50 allocations of all items of taxable income, gain, deduction, and loss.
>
> The basis from the $120,000 of debt is allocated between Huck and Chuck as follows:
>
> 1. Huck is allocated $40,000. This amount is equal to the deemed built-in gain as of the contribution date (the $40,000 difference between the debt of $120,000 and the tax basis of the property of $80,000).
>
> 2. The $80,000 of remaining basis from the debt can be allocated 50/50 between Huck and Chuck, in proportion to their profit-sharing percentages.
>
> Therefore, Huck is allocated a total of $80,000 of basis from the debt and Chuck is allocated $40,000.
>
> Huck's initial basis in his partnership interest will be $40,000 ($80,000 basis from the contributed land, plus his $80,000 allocation of basis

from partnership debt, less $120,000 debt assumed by the partnership). He will recognize no gain on his contribution of property with debt in excess of basis.

Chuck will have an initial basis of $120,000 ($80,000 from his cash contribution, plus his $40,000 allocation of basis from partnership debt).

Note that if Huck had made the same contribution to an S or C corporation, he would have been required to recognize $40,000 of taxable gain (equal to the excess of the $120,000 of debt assumed by the corporation over the $80,000 basis of the contributed property). [See IRC §357(c).]

Because the partnership's debt is *not* qualified nonrecourse financing, Huck's initial at-risk basis is zero (the basis of the land reduced, but not below zero, by the liability assumed by the partnership). The debt added to Huck's "regular" basis, however, which prevents the recognition of taxable gain upon his contribution of property with debt in excess of basis.

Chuck's initial at-risk basis is limited to his $80,000 cash contribution.

At-Risk Basis from Partnership Qualified Nonrecourse Financing

As stated earlier, there is an exception to the general rule that nonguaranteed nonrecourse debt does not add to a partner's at-risk basis. If the debt is qualified nonrecourse financing, each partner's at-risk basis *is* increased by his or her allocable share of the debt.

Qualified nonrecourse financing is defined as any loan from a qualified person (or federal, state, or local government) that is incurred by the taxpayer with respect to holding real property and for which no person is personally liable. The loan cannot be convertible debt. [See IRC §465(b)(6).]

Example 5.08(3): Effect of Qualified Nonrecourse Financing   Sarah and Jessica each contribute $40,000 cash to start a 50/50 real estate acquisition and redevelopment general partnership. The partnership obtains a $400,000 nonrecourse loan from the bank and purchases a "fixer-upper" retail strip center for that amount.

Assume the bank loan meets the definition of *qualified nonrecourse financing*.

As 50/50 partners, Sarah and Jessica each have initial "regular" basis in their partnership interests of $240,000 ($40,000 from the cash contributed plus $200,000 from each partner's share of the nonrecourse debt) for loss deduction purposes.

Because the debt is qualified nonrecourse financing, each partner also has $240,000 of initial at-risk basis for purposes of the §465 at-risk limitation rules.

Basis from Debt Can Prevent Gain Recognition

As illustrated by Example 5.08(2) above, a potentially critical advantage of the partnership basis from debt rule is that property encumbered with debt in excess of basis can often be contributed without recognition of taxable gain. This is because for basis purposes the contributing partner usually will be allocated at least some of the debt encumbering the contributed property.

In contrast, if a contribution of property with debt in excess of basis is made to an S corporation (or a C corporation), the contributing taxpayer will *always* be forced to recognize taxable gain equal to the excess. [See IRC §357(c).]

> **OBSERVATION:** *The above issue can be the deciding factor in the choice-of-entity decision process when the potential taxable gains are significant. In such cases, the entity options are general partnerships and limited partnerships (as discussed in this chapter) and LLCs and LLPs (as discussed in Chapters 3 and 4, respectively).*

Basis Adjustments When Partnership Interests Change Hands

A unique, and generally favorable, aspect of partnership taxation is that a purchaser of a partnership interest can "step up" the tax basis of his or her share of appreciated partnership assets to reflect the purchase price. This is possible if the partnership makes or has in effect an IRC §754 optional basis adjustment election. [See IRC §§743(b) and 754.]

If the §754 election applies, the purchasing partner's allocations of deductions related to stepped-up partnership assets (for example, depreciation deductions) will be based on the higher purchase price rather than on the partnership's lower historical tax basis in the property.

Also, if the partnership sells the appreciated property, the purchasing partner's allocation of taxable gain will be smaller because of the stepped-up tax basis in the partner's share of the property. (See Example 5.08(4) below.)

No similar basis adjustment mechanism is available to benefit purchasers of S corporation shares.

Example 5.08(4): Impact of §754 Step-Up

Property Owned by Partnership

Alvin and Buxton have a 50/50 joint venture called AB Partnership. The only asset of AB is a patent that is being amortized over 15 years under IRC §197. Assume the original cost basis of the patent was $300,000 and the cumulative §197 amortization is $80,000. Thus, the adjusted tax basis of the patent is now $220,000. The patent has a current FMV of $500,000.

Buxton sells his 50% partnership interest to Beverly for $250,000, and the partnership makes a §754 election.

Accordingly, Beverly's share of the partnership's basis in the patent is stepped up to $250,000 (from the preelection basis of only $110,000 for Beverly's share) to reflect the purchase price of her partnership interest. Alvin is unaffected by the §754 election. After the step-up, the partnership's total tax basis in the patent is $360,000 ($110,000 allocated to Alvin and $250,000 allocated to Beverly).

Assume the partnership now sells the patent for $500,000 and liquidates by distributing $250,000 of cash each to Alvin and Beverly. For Alvin, the sale generates a taxable gain of $140,000 (his $250,000 share of the proceeds less his $110,000 share of the partnership's basis in the patent). This gain is passed through to Alvin, and it increases his basis in his partnership interest. Under IRC §1245, $40,000 of the passed-through partnership gain is ordinary income recapture (equal to Alvin's 50% share of the $80,000 of §197 amortization deductions). The balance is a §1231 gain.

Alvin also recognizes gain or loss on the liquidation of his partnership interest equal to the difference (if any) between the liquidation proceeds of $250,000 and his basis in his partnership interest.

For Beverly, the sale generates a taxable gain of zero (her $250,000 share of the proceeds less her $250,000 share of the partnership's basis in the patent). Beverly recognizes no further gain or loss on the liquidation of her interest, because the liquidation proceeds of $250,000 and her basis in her partnership interest are equal.

Property Owned by S Corporation

Assume the same facts as above, except that the patent is owned by an S corporation. Beverly buys Buxton's shares for $250,000. There is no mechanism to adjust the "inside basis" of the entity's assets to reflect what Beverly pays for her 50% ownership interest. This causes an "inside/outside basis difference," as explained below.

Again assume the patent is sold for $500,000 and the entity is liquidated by distributing $250,000 of cash each to Alvin and Beverly.

At the corporate level, there is a $280,000 taxable gain ($500,000 proceeds less $220,000 basis in the patent). This gain is allocated 50/50 to Alvin and Beverly, and it increases their basis in their S corporation stock. Under IRC §1245, $80,000 of the passed-through gain is ordinary recapture income (equal to the §197 amortization deductions). Thus, $100,000 of IRC §1231 gain and $40,000 of ordinary gain is passed through to each owner.

Alvin will recognize gain or loss on the liquidation transaction (treated as a taxable sale of his stock) equal to the difference (if any) between the $250,000 liquidation proceeds and his basis in his shares.

Beverly's basis in her shares is $390,000 ($250,000 original purchase price plus $140,000 passed through gain from the patent sale). In Beverly's case, the liquidation transaction generates a capital loss of $140,000 ($250,000 liquidation proceeds less her $390,000 basis in her shares). Thus from the sale of the patent and the subsequent liquidation of the corporation, Beverly recognizes the following:

- A capital loss of $140,000,
- A passed-through §1231 gain of $100,000, and
- An ordinary gain of $40,000.

The total gains and losses balance out arithmetically, but the *characters* of the gains and losses are very unfavorable to Beverly.

Conclusion

The above problem is caused solely by the difference between inside basis (the basis to the corporation of Beverly's share of the assets) and outside basis (Beverly's basis in her shares). Obviously, the tax results are not nearly as desirable with an S corporation as they were when the patent was owned by a partnership, where the inside/outside basis problem could be eliminated with a §754 election.

Note that in addition to resolving the inside/outside basis problem, a §754 election would cause Beverly's §197 amortization deductions to be calculated based on her $250,000 share of the partnership's basis in the patent (if the partnership continued to hold the patent instead of selling it).

As this Example illustrates, the ability to make §754 elections can be a very significant advantage of partnership taxation over S corporation taxation.

> **CAUTION:** *The §754 election must be made by the partnership; it cannot be made unilaterally by a partner who would benefit from such election. Also, once a §754 election is made, it is irrevocable without IRS consent. This can be detrimental if the value of partnership property drops. Downward adjustments in basis would then result from subsequent partnership interest purchases, and this would be unfavorable to the purchasing partners. Therefore, the §754 election should not be made without considering the potential long-range effects on current and future partners.*

Ability to Make Tax-Free Property Contributions and Distributions

Generally, partners can make contributions of appreciated property (FMV in excess of basis) to a partnership at any time without recognizing taxable gain [IRC §721]. Also, partnerships generally can distribute appreciated property to partners at any time without recognizing taxable gain [IRC §731].

> **CAUTION:** *Exceptions to the above general nonrecognition rules may apply when appreciated or depreciated property is contributed and later distributed to another partner, when a partner contributes appreciated property and later receives a property distribution from the partnership, or when marketable securities*

are distributed to a partner. [See IRC §§704(c)(1)(B), 737, and 731(c), respectively.]

In contrast, when appreciated property is contributed to an S corporation (or a C corporation), nonrecognition treatment is available *only* if the transferor or transferrors are in control (holding at least 80% of the voting and nonvoting stock of the corporation) immediately after the transaction [IRC §351].

When appreciated property is distributed in nonliquidating distributions to S corporation (or C corporation) shareholders, taxable gain is recognized at the corporate level as if the property were sold for FMV. [See IRC §§311(b) and 1371(a)(1)].

Of course, S corporation shareholders will be allocated the corporate-level gain and receive a corresponding increase in the basis of their stock. If the FMV of the distributed property exceeds the basis of the recipient shareholder's stock, the shareholder will recognize gain in the amount of the excess [IRC §1368].

If an S corporation is a former C corporation, a distribution of appreciated property may also trigger the corporate-level IRC §1374 built-in gains tax.

C corporation shareholders are treated as receiving taxable dividends equal to the FMV of nonliquidating distributions if the corporation has sufficient earnings and profits [IRC §316].

Similarly, the corporation must recognize taxable income when appreciated assets are distributed to shareholders in complete liquidation. In turn, shareholders must recognize taxable gain to the extent that the FMV of the liquidating distributions exceeds the tax basis of their stock [IRC §§331 and 336]. Therefore, when liquidating distributions are necessary to accomplish a "divorce" between corporate shareholders, there will generally be negative tax consequences. In contrast, a partnership can generally make tax-free liquidating distributions of appreciated assets to accomplish a "divorce" between partners [IRC §731(a)(1) and (b)].

The point is that partnerships and their partners have much greater flexibility to make tax-free contributions and distributions of appreciated property than do corporations and their shareholders. This flexibility generally gives partnerships and partners the freedom to make desired transfers of appreciated property (into and out of the business entity) without paying a price in the form of immediate recognition of taxable gain.

Ability to Make Special Tax Allocations

By the term *special tax allocation* is meant an allocation of an item of taxable income, gain, loss, deduction, or credit among the owners of a business that is disproportionate to the ownership interests. For example, the allocation of 80% of the tax losses to a 25% owner is a special tax allocation.

With partnerships, special tax allocations are possible. This is not the case with S corporations, which must pass through all tax items strictly in proportion to stock ownership.

How Special Allocation Deals Typically Work

Generally, a partnership special tax allocation arrangement works as follows. During the first few years of operation, when tax losses are expected, the losses will be specially allocated to partners who need them. Usually these are the so-called "money partners," who supply the initial capital and are passive investors. The other partners, who typically are active in the operation of the business, are allocated a disproportionately small amount of the losses in the start-up phase.

In later years, the partnership usually is expected to generate taxable income or gains (otherwise, the partnership was a bad idea to start with). These will be specially allocated to the money partners to offset their earlier disproportionate allocations of tax losses. After these allocations of income and gains have "restored" the earlier loss allocations, all partnership tax items are allocated in proportion to the stated ownership percentages, and the special allocation phase of the partnership is over.

Over the long term, the expectation is that all partners will receive cumulative allocations of taxable losses and income in proportion to their stated ownership interests. Thus, the special allocations simply affect the timing of when losses and income are recognized by the partners.

The Substantial Economic Effect Rules

Regulations under IRC §704(b) contain extremely complicated rules to ensure that partnership tax allocations are not made in an abusive manner. These regulations have come to be known as the "substantial economic effect rules." What the regulations really stand for is the simple proposition that partners cannot be allocated tax losses or deductions unless they are also allocated the related economic losses. By the same token, partners cannot be allocated taxable income or gain unless they are also allocated the related economic income.

Essentially, the substantial economic effect rules require that partner capital accounts be maintained and that they reflect the allocations of income, gain, loss, and deduction. (Capital accounts are simply a measure of each partner's equity in the partnership under whatever basis of accounting is used for that purpose.) Upon liquidation of the partnership, the partnership must pay partners (or collect money from partners) according to their respective positive or negative capital account balances.

In other words, a special allocation of taxable losses or income generally must result in a potential cost or benefit to the partner in terms of what the partner would receive if the partnership were liquidated. It is permissible for the partners receiving special allocations of tax losses to receive later, "make-up" allocations of income or gain.

However, if the partnership is unsuccessful, partners who received special allocations of losses will never realize the "make-up" allocations of income or gain. They will then pay for their special loss allocations by receiving less money when the partnership is wound up and all partner capital accounts are liquidated. In many cases, this risk is accepted willingly in return for the advantage of receiving tax benefits in the early years of the deal.

Example 5.08(5): Allocation of Tax Items Is Permissible   The Cellular Concepts Limited Partnership is formed with two general partners, Phil and Bill, and ten limited partners. Phil and Bill will contributed $10,101 each and supply the technical expertise. The limited partners will supply $2 million in start-up capital.

Under the partnership agreement, the partnership will maintain capital accounts. Payments to partners or to the partnership upon liquidation will be based on positive or negative capital account balances, respectively. The capital account balances will be kept using "tax basis" accounting. Each partner's capital account will be charged with taxable losses and deductions and credited with taxable income and gains allocated to that partner.

Taxable losses are expected in the first three years of operations. After that, the partnership is projected to begin generating positive taxable income.

Under the partnership agreement, the limited partners will be allocated 99% of cumulative taxable losses up to $2 million. Cumulative losses in excess of $2 million will be allocated 100% to the general partners. Taxable income will be allocated 99% to the limited partners until the cumulative losses allocated to them have been offset and they have received a cumulative 10% annual return on their invested capital. After that, taxable income will be allocated 50/50 between the limited and general partners.

Essentially, after the limited partners have recovered their capital plus a 10% annual return, the economic arrangement between the general and limited partners is a 50/50 deal.

The tax allocation scheme described above will pass muster under the substantial economic effect rules, because if $2 million in losses are allocated to the limited partners and the partnership is liquidated for no value, the limited partners will receive nothing. (Their capital accounts will be "zeroed out" by the tax losses allocated to them.) The limited partners will have paid for their $2 million of deductions by losing their entire investment.

Alternatively, if the partnership is successful, the limited partners will receive current and liquidating distributions equal to their $2 million investment plus the cumulative amount of taxable income allocated to them.

The intent of the substantial economic effect rules is simply to enforce the concept that allocations of tax losses and income must correspond to allocations of the real economic losses and gains realized by the partnership. The above tax allocation scheme meets this standard, even though special tax allocations are involved.

Example 5.08(6): Allocation of Tax Items Fails to Meet Substantial Economic Effect Standard   Assume the same basic facts as in the preceding Example. However, in this case, the partnership agreement provides that the limited partners will be allocated 99% of all taxable losses throughout the life of the partnership, and the general partners will be allocated 99% of all taxable income throughout the life of the partnership. (Bill and Phil have huge NOLs from their other activities, so they have no problem with this allocation.)

Distributions during the life of the partnership and upon liquidation will go 100% to the limited partners until they have recovered their $2 million investment plus a cumulative 10% annual return. Any distributions in excess of that amount will be allocated 50/50 between the limited and general partners.

As in the previous Example, the economic arrangement between the general and limited partners is a 50/50 deal after the limited partners have recovered their capital plus a 10% annual return.

However, this tax allocation scheme is *not* permissible under the substantial economic effect rules, because the limited partners will be allocated taxable losses that clearly will have no effect on the distributions they are entitled to receive from the partnership. By the same token, the general partners will be allocated taxable income that will have no effect on the dollars they actually reap from the deal.

For example, if the partnership is very successful and ultimately is liquidated for $12 million, Bill and Phil will receive 50% of whatever is left after the limited partners receive their $2 million investment plus their 10% return. However, Bill and Phil will have been allocated 99% of the taxable income generated by the deal. This mismatch between the allocation of the economic gain (50/50) and the allocation of taxable income (99/1) is exactly what the substantial economic effect rules are meant to shut down.

Ability to Shift Taxable Income between Family Members

S corporations have limited utility when it comes to shifting taxable income among family members. For example, only certain types of trusts can be S corporation shareholders, which limits parents' opportunities for to shift S corporation income to their children without outright transfers of corporate stock. Also, all S corporation pass-through tax items must be allocated between the shareholders strictly in proportion to stock ownership.

In contrast, there are no limitations on the types of entities that can be partners in a partnership. For example, parents can set up trusts to hold partnership interests, with their children as trust beneficiaries. Also, as discussed above, partnerships have considerable flexibility to allocate tax items between partners, including partners who are members of the same family. (The allocations must meet the substantial economic effect standard discussed earlier.)

Generally, family partnership tax allocations are intended to shift taxable income from high marginal tax rate partners (typically the parents) to lower marginal tax rate partners (typically the children). To prevent abusive allocations, Congress enacted IRC §704(e) and Treasury issued Regs. §1.704(1)-e, referred to as the "family partnership rules."

The rules are intended to enforce the basic principle that family partnership tax allocations should be related to actual interests in partnership capital and the value of any services performed for the partnership. For example, if capital is a material income-producing factor in the partnership's business (as is the case with a real estate or manufacturing partnership), allocations of taxable income attributable to capital should be in proportion to the partners' interests in partnership capital.

Partnership income earned from the performance of services (for example, in an accounting or law partnership) should be allocated to the family member partners who perform those services.

If a family partnership makes tax allocations that are inconsistent with the above principle, the IRS can reallocate tax items among the partners and even determine that a purported partner is *not* a partner for federal income tax purposes. Although the family partnership rules set up guidelines that must be observed in making tax allocations, it is still possible to achieve family income shifting goals within the boundaries of these rules.

See section 5.10 of this chapter for a discussion of family limited partnerships, which are often used as vehicles to shift taxable income between family members *and* achieve estate tax planning objectives.

Tax Allocations Related to Contributed Property

When appreciated or depreciated property is contributed to a partnership, IRC §704(c) requires that partnership tax allocations take into account the differences between tax basis and FMV. This concept is not applicable to S corporations, which must make all tax allocations (including those related to contributed property) strictly in proportion to stock ownership percentages.

The §704(c) rules most commonly apply when the partnership sells contributed appreciated or depreciated property, but they also apply to allocations of deductions (such as depreciation and amortization) related to contributed property.

Example 5.08(7): Allocation of Taxable Gain on Sale of Contributed Appreciated Property   Danette owns appreciated raw land and William owns appreciated oil and gas properties. They decide to diversify their holdings by forming a 50/50 partnership. Each partner contributes properties of equal value to the new DW Venture Partnership.

Two years later, DW sells one of the raw land parcels for $200,000. The property's tax basis is $50,000. At the time the property was contributed, its FMV was $175,000. Thus, the "built-in gain" on the contribution date was $125,000 (FMV of $175,000 less basis of $50,000).

Under IRC §704(c), the first $125,000 of the $150,000 taxable gain on sale must be allocated 100% to Danette, the partner who contributed the property. The remaining $25,000 of taxable gain can be allocated 50/50 between Danette and William.

Example 5.08(8): Allocation of Depreciation Related to Contributed Appreciated Property   Assume the same facts as in the preceding Example, except Danette contributes a single commercial real estate property with FMV of $2,000,000 and tax basis of $1,500,000.

Under §704(c), William will be allocated depreciation deductions based on his share of the FMV of the property contributed by Danette. Danette will be allocated the balance of the depreciation deductions. Thus, William will be allocated 66 $2/3$% of the depreciation deductions (his $1 million share of the property's FMV divided by total tax basis of $1.5 million), and the remaining 33 $1/3$% will be allocated to Danette [Regs. §1.704-1(c)(2)].

> **OBSERVATION:** *The §704(c) rules can be favorable or unfavorable, depending on the circumstances. In the preceding Example, for instance, if William were in a higher tax bracket than Danette, the 66 $2/3$% of the depreciation allocated to him would be more favorable than the 50/50 allocation that would result if the same property were contributed to an S corporation owned equally by William and Danette. In contrast, if Danette were in the higher tax bracket, the 50/50 allocation that would result from using an S corporation would be more favorable.*

Disadvantage of Partnership "Hot Assets" Rules

The general rule is that the taxable gain from the sale of a partnership interest is capital in nature [IRC §741]. However, if a partnership has so-called hot assets, IRC §751 requires that some or all of the gain be treated as ordinary income.

Hot assets include appreciated inventory and unrealized receivables [IRC §751(a)]. *Appreciated inventory* is defined as inventory with FMV in excess of basis to the partnership *plus* other property that is not a §1231 asset or capital asset with FMV in excess of basis [IRC §751(d)]. Included in the definition of *unrealized receivables* is the ordinary income recapture potential (under IRC §§1245, 1250, 1254, etc.) of partnership property. [See IRC §751(c).]

The §751 hot assets rules are intended to force a selling partner to recognize an amount of ordinary income equivalent to what would be recognized if the partner directly owned and then sold his or her share of each individual partnership asset.

This "look-through" concept does *not* apply to gains recognized upon the sale of S corporation stock, which generally are treated as capital gains. Thus, the hot assets rules are a negative aspect of partnership taxation compared to S corporation taxation.

Disadvantage of Partnership Technical Termination Rule

Another unique, and generally negative, aspect of partnership taxation is the so-called technical termination rule of IRC §708(b). For federal income tax purposes, a partnership is considered to terminate (even though it generally does not for legal purposes) whenever 50% or more of the interests in capital and profits are sold within a 12-month period.

Technical terminations usually do *not* result in the partners or the partnership recognizing any taxable gain or loss by. However, the termination can cause the loss of favorable depreciation and accounting methods.

A technical termination also brings the partnership's tax year to a close, which may result in unfavorable bunching of income if the partnership has a taxable year-end that differs from that of its partners.

The technical termination concept does *not* apply to S corporations, which generally is considered a favorable aspect of S corporation taxation compared to partnership taxation.

Disadvantage of Inability to Manipulate Payroll Taxes

As discussed in Chapter 8, S corporations may have the opportunity to reduce federal payroll taxes by limiting the amount paid in the form of wages to shareholder-employees and increasing the amount treated as nontaxable distributions. Unfortunately, this planning opportunity is not available to partnerships.

Partners are considered self-employed for most federal tax purposes. Partnership income derived from trade or business activities and allocable to general partners generally is subject to self-employment (SE) tax. The SE tax is the equivalent of the FICA tax for self-employed persons.

In addition, all guaranteed payments to partners for services (which are equivalent to salaries for partners) also are subject to SE tax. Thus, the SE tax "snares" all the income (and often more) that would be subject to the FICA tax if the business were conducted as a corporation and the partners treated as employees.

Conclusions Regarding Partnership versus S Corporation Taxation

As illustrated by the above discussion, there are *very* significant differences between the taxation of partnerships and the taxation of S corporations, most (but not all) of them in *favor* of partnerships. This fact is often glossed over with general statements to the effect that the partnership and S corporation tax rules are essentially the same. That is simply not the case.

Ability to Use Cash Method of Accounting

Partnerships generally are eligible to use the cash method of accounting for tax purposes (the same is true for S corporations). In contrast, limitations apply to C corporations (see Chapter 6).

However, if a partnership has a C corporation partner, the partnership can use the cash method only if the partnership has average annual gross receipts of $5 million or less for the three preceding tax years.

Also, a *limited* partnership generally will not be able to use the cash method if it allocates more than 35% of its losses to limited partners [IRC §§448(a)(3) and (d)(3)].

Deductibility of Partner-Level Interest Expense

Under the so-called interest-tracing rules, individual taxpayers must classify their interest expense as trade or business, passive, investment, or personal. [See IRC §163(h) and Temp. Regs. §1.163-8T.] Trade or business interest is fully deductible, while limitations exist on the deductibility of the other types of interest expense.

Generally, interest expense from debt incurred to acquire a partnership interest from another taxpayer or to inject capital into a partnership will be classified as trade or business or passive interest (unless the partnership holds investment assets). The classification as trade or business or passive will depend on whether the partner materially participates in the partnership's activities. [The same treatment applies to S corporations—see IRS Notice 89-35 (1989-1 CB 675).]

Thus, potentially the partner can treat the interest expense as fully deductible trade or business interest. In contrast, interest on debt incurred by an individual to acquire C corporation stock or to inject capital into a C corporation is always treated as investment interest. Deductions for investment interest are limited to the taxpayer's investment income. [See IRC §163(d).]

Tax Treatment of Fringe Benefits for Partners

See Chapter 8 for a discussion of the fringe benefit rules for S corporation shareholder-employees. Virtually the same rules apply to partners.

Compared to partnerships and S corporations, C corporations generally have an advantage in being able to offer tax-advantaged fringe benefits to owner-employees. (See Chapter 6.)

Perhaps the most important fringe benefit disadvantage of partnerships (and S corporations) compared to C corporations is the treatment of accident and health insurance premiums. When the partnership pays these premiums for the benefit of partners and their spouses and dependents, the partnership can deduct the costs as guaranteed payments to the partners [per Revenue Ruling 91-26 (1991-1 CB 184)].

However, the partners must include these amounts in their taxable incomes. Under current law, they can then obtain a partial deduction on their individual returns under IRC §162(l), and any amount not deducted under §162(l) can be deducted as a medical expense under IRC §213 (subject to the 7.5%-of-AGI floor). (Essentially the same tax treatment applies to S corporations and their shareholders.)

Inability to Use Fiscal Year-Ends

Partnerships (and S corporations) are limited in their ability to use tax year-ends that differ from the tax year-ends of their owners. A partnership generally is required to use the same year-end as its principal partners (usually December 31), unless it is willing to make tax deposit payments to the government. (See IRC §§444 and 7519.)

The required tax deposit payments are an approximation of the tax deferral benefit gained from using an alternative year-end. However, the tax deposit computation is based on a 40.6% tax rate applied to the deferred taxable income. As a result, relatively few partnerships will choose to use an alternative year-end.

Inability of Partners to Borrow Against Qualified Retirement Plan Accounts

Partners who own more than a 10% interest in capital or profits cannot borrow against their partnership qualified retirement plan accounts. [IRC §4975] This is in contrast to shareholder-employees of C corporations, who can (within limits) make such borrowings. (S corporation shareholder-employees who own more than 5% of the corporate stock also cannot borrow against their corporate qualified retirement plan accounts.)

5.09 CONVERTING EXISTING ENTITIES INTO PARTNERSHIPS

Partnership-to-Partnership Conversions

Revenue Rulings 84-52 (1984-1 CB 157), 95-37 (1995-1 CB 130), and 95-55 (1995-2 CB 313) confirm that the following partnership-to-partnership conversions can usually be accomplished without federal income tax consequences to the partnership or the partners:

- Conversion of a general partnership into a limited partnership, or vice versa;
- Conversion of an LLP into a general or limited partnership, or vice versa;
- Conversion of an LLC treated as a partnership for tax purposes into a general or limited partnership, or vice versa.

In all of the above cases, the new entity is considered a continuation of the former taxable entity for federal income tax purposes. For example, the conversion of a general partnership into a limited partnership does not cause a termination of the existing taxable entity under IRC §708.

According to Revenue Ruling 95-37 (dealing with conversions of existing partnerships into LLCs) and several private letter rulings (e.g., PLR 9321047), the same results apparently apply to conversions accomplished via legal filings (such as when a general partnership is converted into a limited partnership by the filing of a certificate of limited partnership), conversions accomplished by liquidating the old entity, or conversions accomplished via a merger (with the new entity being the one that legally survives the transaction).

Mechanics of Partnership Conversions

If conversion is via liquidation of the old partnership, this can be accomplished most easily by having the old partnership contribute all its assets and liabilities to the newly formed partnership in exchange for new partnership interests. Generally this step is tax-free under IRC §721. The new partnership interests are then distributed to the partners in liquidation of the old partnership, also generally tax-free under IRC §731. After the transactions, the partners in the old partnership hold partnership interests in the new partnership, and the new partnership holds all the assets and liabilities of the old partnership.

Alternatively, a liquidation can be accomplished by having the partners contribute their interests in the old partnership to the newly formed partnership in exchange for new partnership interests. (Again, this step generally is tax-free under IRC §721.) The old partnership then distributes all its assets and liabilities to the new partnership in liquidation (generally tax-free under IRC §731). The partners in the old partnership now hold partnership interests in the new partnership, and the new partnership now holds all the assets and liabilities of the old partnership.

State law may also permit an existing partnership to merge with a newly formed partnership, with the new partnership being the surviving entity. From a legal standpoint, merger transactions generally are "cleaner" than liquidations, because the new partnership simply assumes all rights and obligations of the old partnership by operation of law. Partners in the new partnership who were partners in the old partnership and had personal liability for the debts of the old partnership remain liable for those preexisting debts after the merger with the new partnership.

General Tax Implications of Partnership Conversions

With regard to the tax implications of converting an existing partnership, LLP, or LLC into another form of partnership by any of the above methods, Revenue Rulings 84-52, 95-37, and 95-55 (and several letter rulings) apparently lead to the following conclusions:

- Partners do not recognize gain on the conversion, unless changes in their percentages of liabilities (under IRC §752) would cause the basis in their interests to fall below zero.

- Partners obtain the same basis in their new partnership interests as in their old partnership interests, unless the conversion results in changes in their shares of liabilities under IRC §752.

- The partners' holding periods for the new partnership interests tack onto the holding periods for the old partnership interests.

- The new partnership is considered a continuation of the former partnership. As a result, the tax year continues and there is no need for a new employer identification number (EIN). The new partnership continues to use the former partnership's tax accounting methods and elections. The new partnership's holding periods for its assets include the holding periods of the former partnership.

- If certain partners recognize taxable gains upon conversion (because of deemed distributions arising from reductions in their shares of partnership debt) *and* the partnership has a §754 election in place, the basis of partnership assets will be adjusted to reflect the gains. [See IRC §734(b).] Otherwise, the conversion will have no effect on the basis of the assets held by the converting partnership.

Example 5.09(1): Conversion of General Partnership   Gee Partnership, a general partnership, converts into a limited partnership by filing a certificate of limited partnership with the state. The name of the "new" limited partnership is Gee Limited Partnership.

One of the partners of the former partnership remains the general partner for the new limited partnership. However, all partners retain their existing profit- and loss-sharing percentages, and they all remain jointly and severally liable for all partnership liabilities existing as of the conversion date. The real only impact of the conversion is a reduction in each limited partner's exposure to future liabilities incurred by the partnership.

Per Revenue Ruling 84-52, the federal income tax implications of the conversion are as follows:

1. Neither the partners nor the partnership recognizes any gain or loss on the conversion;
2. The partners' bases in their partnership interests and their holding periods are unchanged; and
3. The limited partnership is considered a continuation of the existing partnership; therefore Gee Limited Partnership continues to use same EIN, tax year, accounting and depreciation methods, tax elections, asset basis and holding periods, etc.

Conversions of S and C Corporations

Businesses currently operated as S corporations may consider converting to partnership status to escape the S corporation limitations on stock ownership and capital structure. (See discussion of these limitations in Chapter 8.) Businesses currently operated as C corporations may consider converting to partnership status to eliminate the ongoing problem of double taxation.

Mechanics of Corporate Conversions

An existing S or C corporation can be converted into a general or limited partnership in several ways. The assets of the corporation can be contributed to the newly formed partnership in return for partnership interests that are then distributed to the shareholders in complete liquidation of the corporation.

Alternatively, the corporation can distribute its assets to the shareholders in complete liquidation, and the shareholders can then contribute their undivided interests in the assets to the newly formed partnership in exchange for partnership interests.

Finally, state law may permit the corporation to merge with the newly formed partnership, with the partnership being the surviving entity. The corporation does this by making a tax-free contribution of all assets and liabilities to the partnership in exchange for partnership interests (under IRC §721). The corporation then goes out of existence by distributing the partnership interests to shareholders in complete liquidation.

General Tax Implications of Corporate Conversions

In any of the above cases, there will be corporate-level gain or loss recognition as if the property distributed in complete liquidation were sold by the corporation for FMV [IRC §336(a)]. This means a converting corporation with appreciated assets—whether an S corporation or a C corporation—may recognize significant taxable income or gain as a result of the liquidation transaction. (See the Examples below.)

At the shareholder level, the receipt of the liquidating distribution in exchange for corporate stock is treated as a taxable sale or exchange of the stock for proceeds equal to the FMV of the distributed property [IRC §331(a)]. The shareholder may recognize gain or loss on the transaction—depending on whether the FMV of the distributed property is greater or less than the basis of the corporate stock exchanged.

In the case of a converting S corporation, any corporate-level gain is passed through and increases the shareholders' basis in their stock [IRC §1367(a)]. Therefore, the gain already recognized at the corporate level is not recognized again when the stock is deemed sold in exchange for the liquidating distribution. However, if the S corporation is a former C corporation, the IRC §1374 built-in gains tax may apply to some or all of the corporate-level gain.

In a converting C corporation, the shareholders receive no basis step-up from any corporate-level gain. As a result, generally there is taxable gain at both the corporate and the shareholder level upon the liquidation of a C corporation with appreciated assets.

OBSERVATION: Since converting S and C corporations into partnerships involves liquidation transactions, the federal income tax cost for corporations with significantly appreciated assets will often be unacceptably high (as illustrated by the two Examples below), and there will often be unfavorable state income tax consequences as well. However, if the corporation does not hold significantly appreciated assets, liquidation and conversion to partnership status can be accomplished without adverse tax consequences.

CAUTION: Before concluding that an existing S or C corporation can convert to partnership status "painlessly," consider whether goodwill or other valuable intangible assets (such as patents, copyrights, secret processes, customer lists, and workforce in place) exist. These assets typically do not appear on the balance sheet, because they usually have no historical cost basis. However, the potential tax liabilities resulting from such appreciated intangible assets may preclude conversion.

Example 5.09(2): Conversion of C Corporation Cee Corp decides to convert into a limited partnership by making liquidating distributions of its property to its two equal shareholders, Jumbo and Jimbo. Jumbo and Jimbo will each then contribute their distributed property to the newly formed limited partnership in exchange for their equal partnership interests. Jumbo and Jimbo will also form a new S corporation to act as the general partner of the new limited partnership.

Cee Corp uses cash-basis accounting for tax purposes and has three assets: the building used by the business (with FMV of $1 million and tax basis of $700,000), unrealized receivables of $100,000 (with zero tax basis), and cash of $200,000. (There is no goodwill.)

Jumbo and Jimbo each have basis of $400,000 in their Cee Corp shares, which they have held for a number of years.

Under IRC §336(a), Cee Corp recognizes a $450,000 corporate-level gain on the liquidating distribution ($300,000 from the building and $100,000 from the receivables), because the transaction is deemed a taxable sale of the corporate property for its FMV. Assume the corporate-level tax is $136,000 (34% of the taxable gain).

Cee Corp pays the tax and distributes the remaining $64,000 of cash ($32,000 each to Jumbo and Jimbo), the receivables ($50,000 to each), and the building (equal undivided interests worth $500,000 to each) in complete liquidation of the corporation.

At the shareholder level, Jumbo and Jimbo each receive liquidating distributions with FMV equal to $582,000 (cash of $32,000, plus receivables worth $50,000, plus undivided interests in the building worth $500,000) in exchange for their Cee Corp stock. These exchanges are treated as sales of their stock under IRC §331(a).

Therefore, Jumbo and Jimbo will each recognize taxable long-term capital gains from their stock sales of $132,000 (proceeds of $582,000 less basis in their shares of $450,000).

They will then contribute their distributed cash and property (with total basis of $582,000 each) in exchange for their new limited partnership interests. Under IRC §721, the contributions are tax-free.

Under IRC §722, their initial bases in their partnership interests are $582,000 each. Under IRC §723, the limited partnership's total basis in the contributed assets is $1,164,000 ($64,000 basis in the cash, $100,000 basis in the receivables, and $1 million basis in the building).

Note that the results would have been exactly the same if Cee Corp had converted into a general partnership rather than a limited partnership.

Reality Check: In this case, the corporate- and shareholder-level taxable gains resulting from conversion to partnership status are a heavy price to pay—probably too heavy for the owners to follow through with a conversion in real life. However, conversions of C corporations to partnerships can make very good sense when:

1. Corporations do not hold significantly appreciated assets, and

2. The shareholder-level gains upon liquidation will not be too large.

Example 5.09(3): Conversion of S Corporation   Assume the same facts as in the previous Example, except the corporation is now Ess Corp (which has always been an S corporation), and Jumbo and Jimbo each have basis in their shares of $450,000.

Ess Corp will convert into a limited partnership by making liquidating distributions of its property to Jumbo and Jimbo, and they will each then contribute their distributed property to the newly formed limited partnership in exchange for equal partnership interests.

As in the previous Example, the corporation owns three assets: a building (with FMV of $1 million and tax basis of $700,000), unrealized receivables of $100,000 (with zero tax basis), and cash of $200,000.

Under IRC §336(a), Ess Corp recognizes a $400,000 corporate level gain on the liquidating distribution, because the transaction is deemed a taxable sale of the corporate property for its FMV.

There is no corporate-level tax; instead, the gain is passed through to Jumbo and Jimbo ($200,000 each). They will pay tax on their gains, but the gains increase their bases in their shares to $650,000 each (preliquidation basis of $450,000 plus the $200,000 increase from the pass-through gain).

Ess Corp then distributes its cash ($100,000 each to Jumbo and Jimbo), the receivables ($50,000 each), and the building (undivided interests worth $500,000 each). Jumbo and Jimbo each receive liquidating distributions with FMV equal to $650,000 (cash of $100,000, plus receivables worth $50,000, plus building worth $500,000) in exchange for their Ess Corp stock.

These exchanges are treated as sales of their stock under IRC §331(a). But in this case, Jumbo and Jimbo recognize no additional gains upon their stock sales, because their sales proceeds match their stock basis.

Jumbo and Jimbo will then contribute their distributed cash and property (with total basis of $650,000 each) in exchange for their new limited partnership interests. Under IRC §721, the contributions are tax-free.

Under IRC §722, their initial bases in their partnership interests are $650,000 each. Under IRC §723, the limited partnership's total basis in the contributed assets is $1,300,000 ($200,000 basis in the cash, $100,000 basis in the receivables, and $1 million basis in the building).

Again, the tax results would have been exactly the same if Ess Corp converted into a general partnership rather than a limited partnership.

Reality Check: Although there was only a single level of taxation, converting Ess Corp into a partnership still required recognition of significant corporate-level gains, which were then passed through to the shareholders. In a real-life situation, Jumbo and Jimbo might be unwilling to convert Ess Corp into a partnership because of the magnitude of those gains. However, when corporations hold only assets with little or no appreciation, conversion may be feasible.

Tax Accounting Implications of Conversions

As stated earlier, converting an existing partnership into another form of partnership (such as a general partnership into a limited partnership or an LLC into a limited partnership) generally is treated as a continuation of the same entity for federal income tax purposes.

Accordingly, the "new" partnership will simply succeed to the former entity's EIN and its tax accounting methods, periods, elections, and asset holding periods. (See Revenue Rulings 84-52, 95-37, and 95-55.)

In contrast, when a corporate conversion is undertaken, the resulting partnership will be a new taxable entity. The partnership will need to obtain a new EIN, and it will have the same choices as any new partnership regarding tax accounting methods and elections and permissible taxable years.

5.10 FAMILY LIMITED PARTNERSHIPS

Family limited partnerships (FLPs) can be very useful tools for estate tax and business succession planning, and they can offer income tax and asset protection advantages as well. Unfortunately, FLPs have recently come under IRS attack. However, if taxpayers avoid deathbed transactions and show a business purpose for FLP formations, FLPs should continue to be viable tax-saving vehicles, as explained in this section.

What Is a Family Limited Partnership?

An FLP is a limited partnership set up under the applicable state limited partnership statute. The partners are members of the same family. The personal assets of family members who are limited partners are not exposed to partnership's liabilities. An FLP must have at least two partners and at least one general partner.

In most cases, the FLP will be structured to include a parent, or an S corporation or LLC controlled by the parents, as the general partner. The children (sometimes grandchildren as well) will be limited partners.

Upon formation of the FLP, the parents contribute assets in exchange for a general partnership interest (typically 1%) and the initial limited partnership interest (typically 99%). Then, over a period of years, the parents gift away most or all of the limited partnership interest to the children. As time passes, the children own an increasing percentage interest in the FLP. The gifts reduce the value of the parents' taxable estate and also allow the FLP to allocate increasing percentages of the partnership's taxable income to the children, who presumably are in lower tax brackets than the parents.

The parents retain effective control of the FLP's assets by functioning as the general partner. They can continue to make all management and investment decisions and decide when and if cash distributions will be made to the limited partners, when property will be sold, when the entity will be liquidated, etc. The limited partners (the children and possibly grandchildren) will have no say in these matters. Thus, the FLP concept allows tax savings for the family group while also addressing typical parental concerns about losing control when property is given outright to children.

The parents can also enhance their personal cash flow by charging reasonable fees (treated as IRC §707 guaranteed payments) for fulfilling their general partner duties.

While the FLP's general partner (parent) has control, he or she still has a fiduciary duty to the limited partners (the children). Therefore, the general partner's control over cash distributions cannot be exercised irresponsibly. For example, a parent's refusal to allow partnership distributions sufficient for the children to pay their personal taxes on passed-through FLP income could be construed as a failure to meet the fiduciary duties of a general partner.

If a parent individually acts as the general partner, his or her personal assets are exposed without limit to any and all liabilities resulting from FLP operations. However, this problem can be finessed by having the parent form an S corporation or an LLC to function as the general partner. If this is done, the parent stands to lose no more than the investment in the S corporation or LLC.

Funding the FLP

Assets suitable for contribution to an FLP include but are not limited to:

- Commercial and residential rental real estate;
- Real estate leased to the parent's closely held C corporation;
- Intangible assets (such as patents, secret processes, and copyrights) leased to the parent's closely held C corporation;
- Farming and ranching property;

- Mineral and timber property;
- Small business assets or stock;
- Interests in other partnerships; and
- Investment property, including publicly traded securities.

However, S corporation stock should *not* be contributed. The S status of the corporation would be terminated, because partnerships are not permitted to own S corporation stock [IRC §1361(b)(1)(B)].

> **OBSERVATION:** *In the author's opinion, assets that are not business or investment property (such as personal residences) do not belong in an FLP, because the FLP must be engaged in a business, financial operation, or venture to meet the federal income tax definition of a* partnership *in the first place (§7701 and Regs. §301.7701-1 and -2).*

In most cases, contributions to FLPs will be tax-free transactions under IRC §721. But the tax advisor must not forget to consider the so-called disguised sale rules explained in Regs. §1.707-3,-4 ,-5, -8, and -9. Under these rules, certain contribution transactions are turned into deemed taxable sales. However, the disguised sale rules are a problem only when a contribution of property is followed by an FLP distribution (other than from cash flow) to the contributing partner (the parent) or when certain property burdened by debt is contributed.

Estate and Gift Tax Issues

The partnership interest owned at death by a general or limited FLP partner is included in his or her estate for federal estate tax purposes. However, the values of limited partnership interests that were previously gifted to other family members are *not* included in the value of the decedent's estate (unless the gift transaction itself is disputed by the IRS, as may happen with FLPs formed in deathbed situations). This is the case even when the parent has effectively retained control over the FLP's property by acting as its general partner. (See Letter Rulings 9415007 and 9546006.)

The IRS has ruled that transfers of limited partnership interests qualify as gifts of present interests and thus qualify for the $10,000 annual gift tax exclusion. (See Letter Rulings 9415007 and 9546006.)

The IRS has also ruled that the IRC §2701 "antifreeze" provisions do not apply when gifted FLP limited partnership interests have the same distribution rights as the partnership interests retained by the donor. (See Letter Ruling 9415007.)

The antifreeze rules simply do not apply to the creation of general and limited FLP partnership interests when the interests are economically equivalent (i.e., have the same potential to generate current income and benefit from future appreciation) except for the limited liability attribute of the limited partnership interests.

For years there seemed to be little question that gifted FLP limited partnership interests could be discounted to reflect the fact that they are minority ownership interests with limited marketability. In Revenue Ruling 93-12 (1993-1 CB 202) and TAM 9432001, the IRS conceded that minority discounts may be appropriate even when family members own, in the aggregate, 100% of the entity in question. Minority and marketability discounts were seen as clearly appropriate for gifts of FLP interests when the underlying FLP assets, such as a family business or real estate, were illiquid.

However, the IRS has recently ruled in several cases that discounts were unavailable because §2703 applied (see, for example, TAMs 9719006 and 9730004). The facts in these rulings were extreme, and whether the IRS will be able to defend its position in litigation remains to be seen. While the ability to make discounted gifts was clearly a major reason for the popularity of FLPs, they are still viable tax-saving vehicles even without such discounts. In other words, they can still be used to gift away interests in valuable or appreciating assets, thereby reducing the value of the donor's estate and shifting taxable income to the donees without loss of donor control.

Federal Income Tax Issues

The general rule is that taxable income generated by the FLP's business and investment activities can be allocated among the partners according to the partnership agreement [IRC §704(a)]. As the children's percentage interests in the FLP become larger over the years (because of recurring gifts by the parents), the taxable income generated by the FLP gradually shifts away from the parent and toward the children. This usually is the desired outcome, since the parent typically is in a higher marginal tax bracket than the children.

However, the FLP's allocations of taxable income, gains, losses, and deductions must be consistent with the "substantial economic effect" principles discussed in the regulations under IRC §704(b). Special rules, under IRC §704(c), apply when appreciated or depreciated property (FMV different from tax basis) is contributed to a partnership. The §704(c) provisions often come into play when FLPs are funded with property rather than cash. These rules generally force the allocation of precontribution taxable gain or loss to the contributing partner (the parents). However, the allocation of subsequent appreciation is not affected. Finally, the IRC §704(e) family partnership tax allocation rules apply to FLPs. However, the family partnership rules will *not* prevent a parent from successfully shifting taxable income allocable to gifted capital interests to the children who receive such interests.

Example 5.10(1): Appropriate Situation for an FLP Dawn is a 65-year old widow (in excellent health) with three adult children who are all in her good graces. She owns a sole proprietorship direct mail business, worth about $2 million and expected to appreciate substantially in the future. For estate tax reasons, Dawn wants to get at least part of the value of the business out of her estate. But she does not want to relinquish operating control.

Dawn sets up an FLP with a 1% general partner (an S corporation owned 100% by her) and a 99% limited partner (Dawn). Dawn then contributes her business to the newly formed entity. She then takes 45% of her 99% interest and divides that into three equal 15% limited partnership interests, which are then gifted to each of her three children. A professional appraiser is engaged to value the gifted interests, and he decides a 40% minority and marketability discount is appropriate.

By setting up the FLP and gifting away the limited partnership interests, Dawn is able to immediately reduce her estate by $900,000 (45% of $2 million) with gifts that are valued for gift tax purposes at only $510,000 [(60% x $900,000) – $30,000 (for the three $10,000 annual gift tax exemptions)]. The gifts can be completely sheltered with Dawn's $600,000 unified estate and gift tax credit equivalent, so no gift tax is due.

Dawn has also managed to shift 45% of the future taxable income from the business to her children via the FLP limited partnership interests they now own. In the future, Dawn can make additional annual gifts of FLP interests to each of her children and over time reduce or eliminate any estate taxes. Of course, married couples can do even more because they have a $1.2 million estate and gift tax credit equivalent to play with.

Asset Protection Advantages

For asset protection, owning property indirectly via FLP interests can be advantageous. Under the laws of most states, creditors cannot obtain full ownership of an FLP interest unless the FLP permits a transfer of the interest to occur. This means creditors typically cannot vote, demand an accounting, force a liquidating distribution, etc. However, a creditor may be able to obtain a "charging order" against the debtor's FLP interest. A charging order gives the creditor the right to receive any distributions that would otherwise go to the debtor partner. However, if the debtor is a relative of the general partner, the charging order may be relatively worthless, because the general partner can simply prevent the FLP from making any distributions. The debtor will nevertheless be allocated the taxable income from the partnership interest subject to the charging order, so he or she may incur a tax liability without receiving any cash to pay those taxes.

From the parents' perspective, this asset protection feature offers several advantages. First, the parents may benefit from protection against their personal creditors, as explained above. Second, when the parents retains only a limited partnership interest (for example, by using a 100% owned S corporation as the general partner), they are effectively shielded from creditors of the FLP as well. Finally, the FLP may succeed in protecting a spendthrift child's share of FLP assets from that child's personal creditors.

Practical Considerations

Setting up an FLP can be relatively expensive. Professional fees will be incurred to do the following:

- Draft the partnership agreement and form the S corporation or LLC that will function as the general partner;
- Transfer the legal title to the assets contributed to the FLP;
- Obtain appraisals of the values of gifted limited partnership interests;
- Prepare gift tax returns (if necessary) and prepare federal, state, and local partnership returns for the FLP and returns for the entity that will function as the FLP's general partner.

Because of these costs, the value of the assets used to fund the FLP should probably be at least $1 to $2 million.

Conclusions

From a nontax perspective, the most attractive aspects of FLPs are:

- The ability to create limited partnership interests that protect the donor partners' personal assets from creditors and the donee limited partners' shares of FLP assets from their personal creditors; and
- The ability of the parents to give children or other family members interests in property without really surrendering control.

From a tax perspective, FLPs can be used to:

- Minimize estate taxes by transferring ownership of interests in appreciating assets to the next generation; and
- Shift taxable income (via allocations of the partnership's taxable income) to family members (children and/or grandchildren) who are in lower tax brackets than the parent.

Recent IRS rulings cast some doubt on the ability of donors (parents) to claim valuation discounts for gifted FLP interests, but the IRS position on this issue has not yet been vindicated in the courts. In any case, the potential for gift tax valuation discounts is only an added bonus when donors live long enough to make substantial tax-free gifts under the $10,000 annual exclusion. In such cases, the combination of the $600,000 credit equivalent and the $10,000 exclusion can allow parents to remove most or all of their appreciating property from their estates even without the benefit of any valuation discounts.

5.11 PARTNERSHIPS COMPARED TO OTHER ENTITY CHOICES

This section has the greatest relevance if the entity selection process has been narrowed down to a choice between a general or limited partnership and one of the other types of entities discussed below. If that is not the case, the practitioner and client should strongly consider using the entity selection software program that comes with this book. The program is designed to help make a choice-of-entity recommendation that is consistent with the major tax and nontax issues facing the client. If the program leads to the partnership as the apparently best choice, this section can then be reviewed to solidify those conclusions.

General Partnerships Compared to Limited Partnerships

Limited partnerships are clearly superior to general partnerships with regard to the critical issue of limiting owner liability. First, all general partners are jointly and severally liable for *all* debts and obligations of the partnership. In contrast, the personal assets of limited partners generally are not exposed to the limited partnership's debts and obligations. For the most part, limited partners are personally liable for their own tortious acts and for any personally guaranteed limited partnership debts. A limited partner may be entitled to indemnification from the partnership, however, if he or she pays personally guaranteed indebtedness.

Second, each general partner usually has the power to act as an agent of the partnership and enter into contracts that are legally binding on the partnership (and therefore on the other partners). In a limited partnership, there usually is only one general partner, and thus only one person who can legally bind the partnership.

A negative factor for limited partnerships is that they must have at least one general partner with unlimited exposure to partnership liabilities. As a practical matter, this problem can be addressed by forming a corporate general partner—usually an S corporation owned by the partners. With this strategy, the amount the general partner can lose is effectively limited to the value of the assets held by the corporation. However, setting up and maintaining another entity for this purpose creates administrative burdens that owners obviously would prefer to avoid.

Another potentially significant negative factor is that limited partners can lose their limited liability protection by becoming too actively involved in managing the limited partnership. As a result, limited partnerships are not suitable for certain activities, such as the practice of a profession where all partners are by definition heavily involved in the business.

State limited partnership laws based on the Revised Uniform Limited Partnership Act give some relief by specifying a number of actions that limited partners can take *without* being deemed to participate in management. Nevertheless, this issue is always a potential problem for limited partnerships.

Note that in somewhat unusual cases, the co-owners of a business may be relatively unconcerned about personal liability exposure, because there will be little or no debt and other liability concerns can be managed with insurance. If the co-owners of such a business have a high degree of trust in each other, operating as a general partnership may make sense.

In summary, compared to general partnerships, limited partnerships are superior if:

- There are liability exposures that cannot be managed at an acceptable cost with insurance;

- The owners are concerned about the ability of their co-owners to take actions that are legally binding on them; and

- The co-owners who will be limited partners can live with the fact that they cannot become too actively involved in management of the venture without losing their limited liability protection.

General Partnerships Compared to LLCs

As discussed in Chapter 3, LLCs clearly are superior to general partnerships with regard to the critical issue of limiting owner liability. First, all general partners are jointly and severally liable for *all* debts and obligations of the partnership. In contrast, the personal assets of LLC members generally are not exposed to the LLC's debts and obligations.

Second, each general partner usually has the power to act as an agent of the partnership and enter into contracts that are legally binding on the partnership (and therefore on the other partners). In a manager-managed LLC, generally only the manager is able to legally bind the LLC.

As discussed in Chapter 3, LLCs do *not* protect their members from personal liability in all circumstances. For example, members typically are personally liable for their own tortious acts and professional errors and omissions, and for any personally guaranteed LLC debts.

Note that in somewhat unusual cases, the co-owners of a business may be relatively unconcerned about personal liability exposure, because there will be little or no debt and other liability concerns can be managed with insurance. If the co-owners of such a business have a high degree of trust in each other, operating as a general partnership may make sense.

As discussed in Chapter 3, there are relatively few significant federal income tax law differences between general partnerships and LLCs treated as partnerships. In a few states, however, for state income tax purposes LLCs are treated less favorably than general partnerships.

The key negative issues affecting LLCs are legal uncertainty and the variability of LLC statutes from state to state. Also, state law and/or professional standards may prohibit some businesses (such as certain professional practices) from operating as LLCs.

In summary, compared to general partnerships, LLCs generally are superior if:

- There are liability exposures that cannot be managed at an acceptable cost with insurance;

- The owners are concerned about the ability of their co-owners to take actions that are legally binding on them;

- The business or investment activity in question can be operated as an LLC under state law and/or applicable professional standards;

- The state income tax consequences of LLC status are acceptable; and
- The co-owners can live with the legal uncertainties associated with LLC status.

Limited Partnerships Compared to LLCs

With regard to the issue of limiting owner liability, LLCs possess two significant advantages over limited partnerships. First, a limited partnership must have at least one general partner with unlimited exposure to partnership liabilities. As a practical matter, this problem can be addressed by forming a corporate general partner—usually an S corporation owned by the partners. With this strategy, the amount the general partner can lose is effectively limited to the value of the assets held by the corporation. However, setting up and maintaining another entity for this purpose creates administrative burdens that owners obviously would prefer to avoid. In an LLC, on the other hand, *no* member need be exposed to *any* LLC liabilities. In effect, all members of an LLC are treated as limited partners from a liability standpoint.

Second, a limited partner can lose limited liability protection by becoming too actively involved in managing the limited partnership. As a result, limited partnerships are not suitable for certain activities, such as the practice of a profession where all partners are by definition heavily involved in the business. This problem too can often be addressed by setting up a corporate general partner, with the corporation owned by the limited partners in proportion to their limited partnership ownership percentages. Again, however, the existence of an additional legal entity creates administrative and tax filing burdens. Also, state limited partnership laws based on the Revised Uniform Limited Partnership Act give some relief by specifying a number of actions that limited partners can take *without* being deemed to participate in management. Nevertheless, the issue is always lurking in the background for limited partners.

For LLC members, however, this issue is simply not a concern. LLC members can have any degree of management involvement without risking loss of their limited liability protection.

As discussed in Chapter 3, there are relatively few significant federal income tax law differences between limited partnerships and LLCs treated as partnerships. However, in a few states, for state income tax purposes LLCs are treated less favorably than limited partnerships.

The key negative factors affecting LLCs are legal uncertainty and the variability of LLC statutes from state to state. Also, state law and/or professional standards may prohibit some businesses (such as certain professional practices) from operating as LLCs.

In summary, compared to limited partnerships, LLCs generally are superior if:

- The business or investment activity in question can be operated as an LLC under state law;

- The state income tax consequences of LLC status are acceptable; and
- The co-owners can live with the legal uncertainties associated with LLC status.

General Partnerships Compared to LLPs

As discussed in Chapter 4, LLPs are often relatively attractive vehicles for the conduct of professional practices. With regard to limiting owner liability, LLPs clearly are superior to general partnerships because the personal assets of LLP partners generally are *not* exposed to liabilities arising from the professional errors, omissions, or negligence of the other partners and firm employees.

However, LLPs do *not* protect partners from personal liability for their own tortious acts, errors, omissions, or negligence (nor do general partnerships).

> **OBSERVATION:** *In somewhat unusual cases, the co-owners of a professional practice may be relatively unconcerned about personal liability exposure, because there is little or no entity-level debt and other liability concerns can be managed with insurance. In such circumstances, operating as a general partnership instead of as an LLP may still seem to make sense. However, since LLP status (when available) can be attained with so little trouble, it will be surprising if a professional practice chooses to operate as a general partnership instead of as an LLP.*

There are few, if any, significant federal income tax law differences between general partnerships and LLPs. Usually, LLPs and general partnerships will be treated identically for state income tax purposes as well.

In summary, compared to general partnerships, LLPs generally are superior if:

- They are available under state law and applicable professional standards, and
- For existing general partnerships, LLP status can be attained without excessive administrative hassles (usually this will be the case—see Chapter 4).

Limited Partnerships Compared to LLPs

LLPs usually will be of interest only to professional practices.

All members of a professional firm typically are active in managing the practice. This usually precludes using a limited partnership, because limited partners who are too active in the business can lose their limited partner status and become treated as general partners for legal purposes.

When this happens in the context of a professional practice, a partner who intends to be a limited partner becomes personally exposed (as a general partner) to all of the entity's liabilities, including those arising from the tortious acts, errors, omissions, and negligence of the other partners and firm employees.

The bottom line is that limited partnerships will seldom be an option for professional practices, because the liability exposures are functionally the same as for a general partnership. As discussed earlier in this section, LLPs are superior to general partnerships for limiting liability. Therefore, LLPs are superior to limited partnerships for the same reason.

General Partnerships Compared to C Corporations

For limiting liability, C corporations are far superior to general partnerships, because corporate shareholder-employees (and shareholders in general) are not exposed to entity-level liabilities.

The obvious advantage of general partnerships compared to C corporations is that general partnerships benefit from the partnership pass-through taxation rule. This avoids the C corporation pitfall of double taxation, which is covered in depth in Chapter 6. However, as discussed in that chapter, it may be possible to "drain off" all of a corporation's taxable income, by making deductible compensation payments to the shareholder-employees and deductible contributions to fringe benefit plans set up for those shareholder-employees. In this way, the problem of double taxation can sometimes be sidestepped—as long as appreciating assets (such as real estate used in the business) are kept out of the C corporation.

The other advantages (and the relatively few disadvantages) of partnership taxation are covered at length in section 5.08 of this chapter.

> **OBSERVATION:** *General partnerships must have at least two co-owners. In contrast, C corporations can be formed with only one shareholder.*

A potentially significant disadvantage of general partnerships compared to C corporations is that partnerships do *not* have unlimited legal lives. The retirement, resignation, expulsion, death, bankruptcy, etc., of a partner generally will cause the entity to be liquidated, unless the remaining partners vote to continue (with the continuing partnership treated as a new entity for legal purposes). In contrast, C corporations have unlimited legal life spans. Also, general partners usually cannot freely transfer their partnership interests, while C corporation shareholders typically *can* freely transfer their shares.

Another potentially significant disadvantage of general partnerships compared to C corporations is that certain partners cannot borrow against their qualified retirement plan account balances. Unlike shareholder-employees of C corporations, partners with more than 10% interests in capital or profits cannot borrow against their accounts [IRC §4975]. (S corporation shareholder-employees who own more than 5% of the corporate stock also are prevented from borrowing against their qualified retirement plan accounts.)

In summary, compared to C corporations, general partnerships are superior if:

- There are at least two co-owners (making a partnership possible in the first place);
- Taking into account available insurance, the co-owners can live with their exposure to the entity's liabilities in return for the benefits of partnership taxation; and
- The co-owners can accept the fact that they may not be able to borrow against their qualified retirement plan accounts.

Limited Partnerships Compared to C Corporations

The personal assets of C corporation shareholders and limited partners are offered similar protections against entity-level liabilities. As discussed earlier in this chapter, general partners of a limited partnership are exposed to unlimited exposure to all partnership debts and obligations, but this problem can usually be managed by setting up a corporate general partner.

The obvious advantage of limited partnerships is that they can qualify for partnership taxation. This avoids the C corporation pitfall of double taxation, which is discussed at length in Chapter 6. The other advantages (and the relatively few disadvantages) of partnership taxation are discussed in section 5.08 of this chapter.

> **OBSERVATION:** *To be treated as a partnership for federal income tax purposes, an limited partnership must have at least two owners. In contrast, C corporations can be formed with only one shareholder. In some cases, the two-partner rule may appear to be a significant roadblock. However, as discussed earlier in this chapter, there are often ways to address this issue—for example, by forming a husband–wife partnership.*

A potentially significant disadvantage of limited partnerships compared to C corporations is that limited partnerships usually will *not* have unlimited legal lives. Also, general partners typically cannot freely transfer their partnership interests.

Another potentially significant disadvantage of limited partnerships is that certain partners cannot borrow against their qualified retirement plan account balances. Unlike shareholder-employees of C corporations, partners who own more than 10% interests in capital or profits cannot borrow against their accounts [IRC §4975]. (S corporation shareholder-employees who own more than 5% of the corporate stock also are prevented from borrowing against their qualified retirement plan accounts.)

In summary, compared to C corporations, limited partnerships generally are superior if:

- There are at least two co-owners;
- The co-owners can accept the fact that they may not be able to borrow against their qualified retirement plan accounts;
- The benefits of partnership taxation are desired;

- The co-owners who will be limited partners can live with the fact that they cannot become too actively involved in management (at least not directly) of the venture without losing their limited liability protection; and

- The co-owners can live with the fact that the limited partnership will not have an unlimited legal life or free transferability of all ownership interests.

CAUTION: Although a limited partnership places no limits on the number of partners, there is a tax problem if partnership interests are so widely held that they are "publicly traded" within the meaning of IRC §7704. If the partnership interests are publicly traded, the limited partnership will be treated as a C corporation for federal income tax purposes.

General Partnerships Compared to S Corporations

For limiting liability, S corporations are far superior to general partnerships, because corporate shareholder-employees (and shareholders in general) are not exposed to entity-level liabilities. The biggest advantage of general partnerships over S corporations is that general partnerships qualify for the benefit of pass-through taxation without the numerous restrictions that apply to S corporations. (These restrictions are covered in Chapter 8.)

In addition, general partnerships qualify for tax advantages beyond just pass-though taxation. Overall, the partnership taxation rules are significantly more generous and flexible than the provisions applying to S corporations. (The differences between partnership and S corporation taxation are covered in depth in section 5.08 of this chapter.)

Overall, comparing general partnerships to S corporations usually boils down to weighing:

1. The liability protection offered by S corporations against

2. The hassles caused by the S corporation restrictions and the advantages of partnership taxation over S corporation taxation.

A potentially significant disadvantage of general partnerships compared to S corporations is that general partnerships do *not* have unlimited legal lives. The retirement, resignation, expulsion, death, bankruptcy, etc., of a partner generally will cause the entity to be liquidated, unless the remaining partners vote to continue (with the continuing partnership treated as a new entity for legal purposes). In contrast, S corporations have unlimited legal life spans. Also, general partners usually cannot freely transfer their partnership interests, while S corporation shareholders typically *can* freely transfer their shares.

In summary, compared to S corporations, general partnerships are superior if:

- There are at least two co-owners (making a partnership possible in the first place);

- The co-owners desire pass-through taxation, but qualifying as an S corporation would be inconvenient, difficult, or impossible, *or* the entity could qualify as an S corporation, but the benefits of the partnership taxation rules are significant compared to the S corporation taxation rules; and

- After taking insurance into account, the co-owners can live with their exposure to the entity's liabilities.

Limited Partnerships Compared to S Corporations

The personal assets of S corporation shareholders and limited partners are offered similar protections against entity-level liabilities. As discussed earlier in this chapter, general partners of a limited partnership are exposed to unlimited exposure to all partnership debts and obligations, but this problem can usually be managed by setting up a corporate general partner.

The biggest advantage of limited partnerships over S corporations is that limited partnerships can qualify for the benefits of pass-through taxation without the numerous restrictions that apply to S corporations. These restrictions are covered in depth in Chapter 8.

Limited partnerships qualify for tax advantages beyond just pass-though taxation. In general, the partnership taxation rules are significantly more generous and flexible than the provisions applying to S corporations. The differences between partnership and S corporation taxation are addressed in section 5.08 of this chapter.

> **OBSERVATION:** *To be treated as a partnership for federal income tax purposes, a limited partnership must have at least two owners. S corporations, by contrast, can be formed with only one shareholder. In some cases, the two-partner rule may appear to be a significant roadblock. However, as discussed earlier in this chapter, there are often ways to address this issue—for example, by forming a husband–wife partnership.*

A potentially significant disadvantage of limited partnerships compared to S corporations is that limited partnerships do *not* have unlimited legal lives. The retirement, resignation, expulsion, death, bankruptcy, etc., of a general partner will cause the entity to be liquidated, unless the remaining partners vote to continue (with the continuing partnership treated as a new entity for legal purposes). In contrast, S corporations have unlimited legal life spans. Also, general partners of a limited partnership usually cannot freely transfer their partnership interests, while S corporation shareholders typically *can* freely transfer their shares.

In summary, compared to S corporations, limited partnerships generally are superior if:

- There are at least two co-owners;

- The co-owners desire pass-through taxation, but qualifying as an S corporation would be inconvenient, difficult, or impossible; *or*

- The entity could qualify as an S corporation, but the benefits of the partnership taxation rules are significant compared to those of the S corporation taxation rules; *and*

- The co-owners who will be limited partners can live with the fact that they cannot become too actively involved in management (at least not directly) of the venture without losing their limited liability protection; and

- The co-owners can live with the fact that the limited partnership will not have an unlimited legal life or free transferability of all ownership interests.

> **CAUTION:** *Although there are no limits on the number of partners in a limited partnership, there is a tax problem if partnership interests are so widely held that they are "publicly traded" within the meaning of IRC §7704. If the partnership interests are publicly traded, the limited partnership will be treated as a C corporation for federal income tax purposes.*

General and Limited Partnerships Compared to Sole Proprietorships

Comparisons between partnerships and sole proprietorships generally are not meaningful. Sole proprietorships by definition are owned by a single individual. Partnerships by definition must have at least two co-owners.

However, if a business currently operated as a sole proprietorship can be structured to have at least two owners (such as by forming a husband–wife partnership), the comparisons made earlier in this section can then be considered.

5.12 SUMMARY STATEMENT ON WHEN PARTNERSHIPS ARE ATTRACTIVE

General Partnerships

General partnerships are probably the best entity choice when:

1. There are at least two co-owners; and

2. Pass-through taxation is desired; and

3. LLC and LLP status are unavailable; and

4. Liability concerns can be managed with insurance; and

5. Qualifying as an S corporation would be inconvenient, difficult, or

impossible, *or* the entity could qualify as an S corporation but the benefits of the partnership taxation rules are significant compared to those of the S corporation taxation rules; and

6. The co-owners can live with the fact that the general partnership will not have an unlimited legal life or free transferability of ownership interests.

> *OBSERVATION: In most cases, the need to limit owner liability is so significant that only a limited partnership, as opposed to a general partnership, will make sense to clients.*

Limited Partnerships

Limited partnerships are probably the best entity choice when:

1. There are at least two co-owners; and
2. Pass-through taxation is desired; and
3. LLC status is unavailable; and
4. Qualifying as an S corporation would be inconvenient, difficult, or impossible; *or*
5. The entity could qualify as an S corporation but the benefits of the partnership taxation rules are significant compared to those of the S corporation taxation rules; and
6. The co-owners who will be limited partners can live with the fact that they cannot become too actively involved in management (at least not directly) of the venture without losing their limited liability protection; and
7. The co-owners can live with the fact that the limited partnership will not have an unlimited legal life or free transferability of all ownership interests.

Activities Suitable to Be Conducted via Partnerships

Business and investment activities where partnerships make sense include, but are not limited to, the following:

- Corporate joint ventures (where the corporate co-owners desire pass-through taxation);

- Real estate investment and development activities (where the partnership taxation rules allow investors to receive preferred returns, special allocations of tax losses, and additional basis from partnership-level debt);

- Oil and gas exploration (where the partnership taxation rules allow preferred returns and special allocations of deductions from intangible drilling costs);

- Venture capital investments (where the partnership rules allow pass-through taxation and the creation of ownership interests with varying rights to cash flow, liquidating distributions, and tax items);

- Business start-ups expected to have tax losses in the initial years (which can be passed through to the partners);

- Professional practices (where pass-through taxation can be combined with specially tailored ownership interests that reflect each member's contributions to the practice); and

- Estate planning vehicles (where the older generation can gift partnership interests to younger family members while retaining control by functioning as the general partners and where all taxable income is passed through to the partners—see section 5.10 of this chapter).

Appendix 5A: Sample Client Letter When General Partnership Appears to Be Best Entity Choice

Dear [Client name]:

This letter briefly summarizes some of the major considerations that went into your recent decision to form a new business that will be operated as a general partnership.

Liability of General Partners

The partners of a general partnership are personally liable (without limitation) for all debts and obligations of the partnership. The liability of general partners is "joint and several" in nature. This means that any one of the general partners potentially can be forced to make good on all partnership liabilities. That partner may be able to seek reimbursement from the partnership for payments in excess of his or her share of liabilities. But this depends on the ability of the other partners to contribute funds to allow the partnership to make such reimbursement.

Note also that general partners are jointly and severally liable for partnership liabilities related to the tortious acts, errors, omissions, and negligence of the other general partners and the partnership's employees. (*Tortious acts* are defined as wrongful acts leading to civil actions, other than those involving breach of contract.) In addition, general partners are personally liable for their own tortious acts, errors, omissions, and negligence.

As we further discussed, each general partner usually has the power to act as an agent of the partnership and enter into contracts that are legally binding on the partnership (and ultimately on the other partners). For example, a partner can enter into a lease arrangement that is legally binding on the partnership. You may want to consider adding restrictive provisions to your partnership agreement regarding the ability of partners to act as the partnership's agent and thus legally bind the partnership.

Advantages and Disadvantages of General Partnerships

The major advantage of general partnerships is the ability to benefit from pass-through taxation without being affected by the various restrictions applying to S corporations (the one-class-of-stock rule, etc.).

In addition, general partnerships enjoy the other tax advantages that partnerships have over S corporations. For example, general partnerships can make tax-free distributions of appreciated property and create different types of ownership interests with varying rights to cash flow, liquidation proceeds, and tax allocations. These things cannot be done under the inflexible tax rules that apply to S corporations.

As stated earlier, the primary disadvantage of general partnerships is the personal liability of the partners for the liabilities of the entity. You have indicated you clearly understand that general partnerships offer *less* protection to the owners' personal assets than do limited partnerships, limited liability companies (LLCs), C corporations, or S corporations.

Conclusion

We appreciate the opportunity to consult with you as you make the important decision of choosing the most advantageous type of entity under which to operate your new venture. We look forward to working with you in the future as your general partnership is formed and enters the operating phase.

Very truly yours,

Appendix 5B: Sample Client Letter When Limited Partnership Appears to Be Best Entity Choice

Dear [Client name]:

This letter briefly summarizes some of the major considerations that went into your recent decision to form a new business that will be operated as a limited partnership.

Liability of Limited Partners

A limited partnership is a separate legal entity (apart from its limited partners) that owns its assets and is liable for its debts. Therefore, the personal assets of the limited partners are generally beyond the reach of partnership creditors.

Limited partners are, however, still personally responsible for partnership liabilities resulting from their own tortious acts. (*Tortious acts* are defined as wrongful acts leading to civil actions, other than those involving breach of contract.)

In short, limited partnerships generally do *not* offer liability protection beyond what corporations are able to offer to their shareholders who are officers, directors, and employees.

Liability of General Partners

A negative factor for limited partnerships is that they must have at least one general partner with unlimited personal exposure to partnership liabilities. Usually this problem can be addressed by forming a corporate general partner. This is often an S corporation. This strategy means that the amount the general partner can lose is effectively limited to the value of the assets held by the corporation.

Another potentially significant negative factor is that limited partners can lose their limited-liability protection by becoming too actively involved in managing the limited partnership. As a result, limited partnerships are not suitable for activities where all partners are heavily involved in the business. You have indicated that you considered this issue and concluded that it does not cause difficulties with regard to your venture.

Treatment as Partnership for Tax Purposes

The key tax advantage of limited partnerships is that they can be treated as partnerships for federal income tax purposes.

Conclusion

We appreciate the opportunity to consult with you as you make the important decision of choosing the most advantageous type of entity under which to operate your new venture. We look forward to working with you in the future as your limited partnership is formed and enters the operating phase.

Very truly yours,

Appendix 5C: Partnership Agreement Checklist

Purpose: Use this checklist in drafting or reviewing a partnership agreement. The partnership agreement is a written record describing the partners' intentions regarding how the partnership will be formed and operated. You may conclude that some or all of the items listed below are beyond the scope of what is needed in the case at hand. By the same token, the client situation may demand additional language covering matters not listed below.

_____ 1. Name of partnership, names of initial partners, and date of agreement.

    _____

    _____

    _____

    _____

_____ 2. Date partnership intends to commence its legal existence.

    _____

_____ 3. Description of partnership's business or investment purpose or activities.

    _____

    _____

    _____

    _____

_____ 4. Duration of the partnership.

    _____

_____ 5. Description of partnership's principal place of business.

    _____

    _____

_____ 6. Required initial capital contributions, and provisions regarding anticipated and unanticipated future contributions of capital (including what happens to partners who fail to make their contributions).

    _____

    _____

    _____

    _____

_____ 7. Dates of partnership distributions and rights of partners to take draws in advance of formal distribution dates.

_____

_____

_____

_____

_____ 8. Descriptions of how distributions are calculated (for example, if certain partners are to receive "preferred returns" with respect to their capital accounts).

_____

_____

_____

_____

_____ 9. Provisions regarding partner salaries (treated as IRC §707 guaranteed payments for tax purposes).

_____

_____

_____

_____

_____ 10. Specific authority for partnership to borrow or incur debts.

_____

_____

_____

_____

_____ 11. Specific authority for partners to lend to partnership and/or for partnership to lend to partners.

_____

_____

_____

_____

_____ 12. Indemnification provisions (covering rights of partners to recover from partnership if they pay "more than their share" of partnership liabilities, and rights of partnership to demand contributions from those partners who paid "less than their share").

_____

_____

_____

_____

_____ 13. Place where partnership's legal and financial records will be kept, and rights of partners to demand an accounting from the partnership.

_____

_____

_____

_____

_____ 14. Rights of partners to obtain access to partnership's books and records.

_____

_____

_____

_____

_____ 15. Restrictions on any partner's authority to legally bind the partnership.

_____

_____

_____

_____

_____ 16. Assignments of management authority to partners (including any restrictions on management authority).

_____

_____

_____

_____

_____ 17. Voting provisions regarding what is a quorum, how partners' votes are counted (per capita or based on percentage interest in the partnership), what majority is needed to conclude on certain issues, etc.

_____

_____

_____

_____

_____ 18. Provisions regarding period meetings of the partners.

_____

_____

_____

_____

_____ 19. Procedures for admission of new partners.

_____

_____

_____

_____

_____ 20. Provisions for voluntary withdrawal, retirement, or expulsion of partners (including what rights these partners have to payment for their partnership interests, payment terms, and how such interests will be valued).

_____

_____

_____

_____

_____ 21. Provisions regarding whether the partnership will take the partner's share of partnership goodwill into account for purposes of Item 20 above, and how such goodwill will be valued.

_____

_____

_____

_____

_____ 22. Provisions regarding ability of partners to sell, assign, or otherwise transfer their partnership interests to third parties (including rights of first refusal for partnership or other partners to purchase such interests and how valuation of such interests will be determined).

_____

_____

_____

_____

_____ 23. Provisions regarding buyouts of partners' interests upon retirement, disability, insanity, death, etc. (including how such interests will be valued and payment terms).

_____

_____

_____

_____

_____ 24. Noncompete provisions after partner withdrawals.

_____

_____

_____

_____

_____ 25. Provisions regarding continuing (or not continuing) the partnership after the withdrawal, death, etc., of a partner.

_____

_____

_____

_____

_____ 26. Provisions regarding the partners agreeing to terminate the partnership, and how the partnership will be terminated in other circumstances.

_____

_____

_____

_____

_____ 27. Provisions regarding how property will be valued if the partnership is terminated and all assets distributed in liquidation.

_____

_____

_____

_____

_____ 28. Financial accounting and tax provisions regarding how profits, losses, and liabilities will be shared, how "book" capital accounts will be maintained (including how they will be adjusted when noncash property is contributed or distributed), how tax items will be allocated among the partners, how capital accounts will be maintained for tax accounting purposes, when an IRC §754 election will be made by the partnership, etc.

_____

_____

_____

_____

_____ 29. Arbitration provisions for the resolution of disputes between the partners or between the partnership and a partner.

_____

_____

_____

_____

_____ 30. A recitation that the partners intend to form a partnership for legal purposes as of the specified commencement date and that they intend to share the profits, losses, and obligations therefrom.

_____

_____

_____

_____

_____

CAUTION: *Clearly, a partnership agreement has serious legal implications. Competent legal counsel should engaged in connection with the drafting of any partnership agreement.*

CHAPTER 6 • C CORPORATIONS— BACK FROM THE DEAD

CONTENTS

6.01 INTRODUCTION

For a time, most tax advisors agreed that C corporations were unattractive for two principal reasons. First, corporate income is potentially subject to double taxation (once at the corporate level and again at the shareholder level). Second, individual tax rates were lower than those for corporations, meaning that even corporations that intended to retain all taxable income were at a cash-flow disadvantage compared to pass-through entities.

Because of these dual tax disadvantages, pass-through entities (partnerships, S corporations, and, more recently, LLCs and LLPs) were usually recommended as vehicles for conducting business and investment activities. However, the situation has changed as the federal income tax rates for individuals and corporations have changed.

The relevant considerations under current tax law are explained below.

Favorable Corporate Graduated Rate Structure

C corporations are subject to very favorable tax rates on the first $75,000 of annual taxable income. Specifically, there is a 15% rate on the first $50,000 and a 25% rate on the next $25,000. These low rates allow a company to maximize current cash flow by minimizing the cash outlays needed to pay federal income taxes. For a relatively small but growing business, this can be an important benefit.

Although the income retained by the corporation will eventually be taxed twice, that may not be a major concern if the entity expects to continue in existence for many years.

Favorable Rates on Higher Levels of Taxable Income

The Revenue Reconciliation Act of 1993 might have been more appropriately named the "C Corporation Revival Act of 1993." Since the Act, the highest marginal regular tax rate for individuals is now 39.6%, while the highest marginal rate for C corporations is 39% (for taxable income between $100,000 and $335,000). For the vast majority of C corporations, however, the *average* tax rate will be 34% or less.

This means that even at high levels of taxable income, the current tax cost of operating as a C corporation generally is lower than the tax cost of operating the same business in the form of a pass-through entity. (See the examples in section 6.02 of this chapter.)

Ability to Drain Off Taxable Income with Deductible Payments

Even though C corporations generally have the advantage of minimizing *current* taxes, the disadvantage of double taxation can still make them appear unattractive compared to the pass-through entity alternatives. (For templates comparing the "cradle-to-grave" tax consequences of operating as a C corporation versus as a pass-through entity, see General Practice Aids 5 through 8.)

With many closely held businesses, however, the threat of double taxation is relatively easy to defuse by "draining off" all of the corporation's taxable income with deductible payments for the salaries and benefits of the shareholder-employees.

The conclusion to be drawn is that from a tax standpoint, C corporations are definitely a viable alternative to pass-through entities.

The Two Critical Issues

The two most important issues to consider in evaluating C corporations versus the other entity alternatives are:

1. Double taxation, and
2. The ability of the entity to offer liability protection to its owners.

As discussed briefly above, the current individual and corporate tax rate structures have mitigated some of the ill effects of double taxation. And, arguably, corporations still offer owners the greatest certainty of protection from liabilities, as discussed in section 6.03 of this chapter. (See Chapters 3, 4, and 5 for discussions of the liability-limiting aspects of LLCs, LLPs, and limited partnerships, respectively.)

Therefore, the C corporation is once again a potentially attractive entity option in many circumstances. Much of the remainder of this chapter covers in greater detail the federal income tax rules that apply to C corporations and the most significant nontax considerations, including limited liability.

See section 6.04 of this chapter for comparisons of C corporations to the other entity choices and sole proprietorships.

6.02 FEDERAL INCOME TAXATION OF C CORPORATIONS

The two features of the federal income tax rules that most distinguish C corporations are the favorable corporate graduated rates and double taxation. These and other significant tax issues are covered in this section.

Impact of the Graduated Corporate Rate Structure

The current federal income tax rate structure for a C corporation that is *not* a personal service corporation is as follows:

Taxable income over	But not over	Tax rate
$0	$50,000	15%
$50,000	$75,000	25%
$75,000	$100,000	34%
$100,000	$335,000	39%
$335,000	$10,000,000	34%
$10,000,000	$15,000,000	35%
$15,000,000	$18,333,333	38%
$18,333,333		35%

As can be seen, the first $75,000 of taxable income is taxed at significantly lower rates than the same income earned by an individual taxpayer (either directly or via ownership of a pass-through entity). The rate differential is even more pronounced if the income from the activity under consideration would be on top of other taxable income (for example, from salaries and investments) already earned by high-bracket individual taxpayers. In such cases, the income generated by the activity could be taxed at rates as high as 39.6% if a pass-through entity is used—compared to tax rates as low as 15% if the income is earned by a C corporation.

When a high-income individual uses a C corporation to earn incremental taxable income (thereby taking advantage of the graduated corporate tax rates), it is often referred to as "splitting income" with a corporation. See Example 6.02(2) below and see also Appendix 6A.

Note also that if all income is left inside a corporation, there will be no federal payroll taxes. However, if the business is operated as an LLC, a partnership, or a sole proprietorship, owners may be forced to pay significant amounts of self-employment tax. (See section 6.04 of this chapter for additional discussion of this issue.)

Graduated Corporate Rates Can Maximize Current Cash Flow

When a business intends to retain all its earnings for an indefinite period of time in order to finance its growth internally, the corporate tax rates can make C corporations very attractive compared to pass-through entities. A pass-through entity might have to distribute up to 39.6% of the income earned by the business just so that the owners can pay their personal taxes.

Even at taxable income levels above $75,000, the C corporation tax rates are significantly lower than those for individuals. (See Appendix 6A.) As a result, the use of a C corporation can maximize the current cash flow of the business. It must be remembered, however, that the cost of this current benefit is the potential double taxation that may apply in later years.

> **Example 6.02(1): Using a C Corporation to Minimize Current Taxes for a Growth Business** Larry, Harry, and Mary are founding a growth business that can be operated as either a C corporation or a pass-through entity. The business is projected to earn taxable income averaging $2.5 million annually over the next five years. The owners are all high-income individuals in the 39.6% tax bracket.
>
> If this business is operated as a C corporation and projected levels of taxable income are achieved, the annual federal income tax liability will average $850,000 (34% of $2.5 million).
>
> If the business is conducted via a pass-through entity, it will have to make annual cash distributions of $990,000 (39.6% of $2.5 million) to Larry, Harry, and Mary so they can pay the taxes on their shares of the income.
>
> Over a five-year period, operating as a C corporation will allow the business to retain an additional $700,000 of cash, critically needed to finance the receivables and inventory of a growing business.
>
> If Larry, Harry, and Mary plan to cash out their investments by taking the company public in the relatively near future, the issue of double taxation of C corporation income is of little concern to them. In this circumstance, operating as a C corporation is probably the most sensible choice.

> **Example 6.02(2): Minimizing the Overall Tax Bite by Splitting Income with a C Corporation** Steve is acquiring a new business that is expected to generate taxable income of $50,000 per year. He intends to operate the venture for seven years and then sell out, using the proceeds to help finance his retirement.
>
> Steve has large amounts of income from his other interests, so the incremental income from the business will be taxed at 39.6% if a sole proprietorship or pass-through entity is used. However, if Steve forms a C corporation to operate the business, the corporate tax rate on projected taxable income will be only 15%.
>
> For choice-of-entity evaluation purposes, assume the corporation's retained after-tax income adds to the value of its stock dollar for dollar. Further assume that after seven years Steve will pay a 20%

long-term capital gain tax on this increase in the value of the corporation's stock.

This amounts to an effective shareholder-level tax rate of 17% (20% of the 85% of corporate income left after corporate-level taxes). The shareholder-level tax is in addition to the corporate-level tax of 15%.

Therefore, the *combined* shareholder-level and corporate-level tax bite is 32% (17% plus 15%)—sharply lower than the 39.6% rate that would apply with a sole proprietorship or pass-through entity.

In addition, note that when a C corporation is used, the shareholder-level tax (the 17% portion) is deferred until Steve sells his stock. In contrast, the full 39.6% tax bite is due annually if a C corporation is *not* used.

This Example illustrates the benefits of splitting income with a C corporation and thereby taking advantage of the favorable graduated corporate tax rates. The positive effect of splitting income can overwhelm the negative effect of double taxation—if the shareholder's marginal tax rate is high and the corporation's taxable income is relatively low. (See Appendix 6A.)

If Steve's company meets the definition of a *qualified small business corporation* (QSBC), he may be able to exclude 50% of the capital gain on the sale of his shares and/or benefit from a favorable gain rollover rule. See Chapter 7 for coverage of QSBCs.

Finally, if Steve never draws any salary from the corporation, there will be no federal payroll tax liability. If he were a sole proprietor or a general partner in the same business, he might owe significant amounts of self-employment tax even if no funds are withdrawn from the venture. (See section 6.04 of this chapter.)

Eliminating Double Taxation with Deductible Payments

A closely held C corporation that does not need to retain earnings for growth purposes (such as a personal services business) can often defuse the threat of double taxation simply by making deductible payments—for salaries, bonuses, fringe benefits (including retirement plan contributions), etc.—that directly benefit its shareholders. These payments can "drain off" or "zero out" the corporation's taxable income. When no taxable income is retained "inside" the corporation, double taxation is a nonissue.

As noted, the ability to zero out a corporation's taxable income is particularly feasible with service businesses where capital is not a material income-producing factor and where salaries paid to shareholder-employees are clearly justified by the billings they generate for the corporation.

Deductible payments that benefit shareholder-employees are not limited to salary and fringe benefits. Shareholder-employees should also consider "capital structure" planning by capitalizing the corporation, partly with shareholder loans and partly by leasing property (for example, an office building or medical equipment) to the corporation. Such capital structure planning allows the shareholder-employees to drain off even more of the corporation's taxable income with deductible interest and rent payments.

In addition, the principal of shareholder loans can be collected without adverse tax consequences. In contrast, when C corporation shareholders attempt to withdraw equity capital, the withdrawals may be treated as dividends—taxable to the recipients and nondeductible by the corporation.

Disadvantage—Double Taxation in All Its Forms

As indicated throughout this chapter, the fundamental disadvantage of C corporations is double taxation, which appears in a number of different forms, as explained below.

Double Taxation of Corporate Dividends

The most common manifestation of double taxation is the treatment of nonliquidating C corporation distributions to shareholders. The *general* rule is that such distributions to shareholders are treated as dividends to the extent of the corporation's earnings and profits (E&P). If property rather than cash is distributed, the dividend is equal to the lesser of the FMV of the distributed property or E&P. [See IRC §§301(a), 301(c), and 316.]

The entire amount of a dividend is taxed to the recipient noncorporate shareholder as ordinary income, *regardless* of the shareholder's basis in his or her stock. The shareholder treats a distribution in excess of E&P first as a recovery of stock basis and then as gain from sale or exchange of the stock. [See IRC §§301(c)(2) and (3).]

The corporation receives no deduction for dividends, even though they are taxable income to the recipient shareholders.

Double Taxation on Sale of Stock

When a C corporation earns taxable income, the tax basis of the shareholders' stock is not adjusted upward. In contrast, taxable income earned by a pass-through entity *does* increase the basis of ownership interests in the entity.

The result is that income a C corporation earns and retains is taxed again when shares of the corporation's stock are sold. The retained income increases the value of the stock, which creates a bigger capital gain when shares eventually are sold.

To quantify this effect with calculation templates, see General Practice Aids 5 and 6 in Chapter 10.

Double Taxation on Liquidation

In some cases, corporations seemingly can avoid the double taxation issue by simply not making dividend distributions. However, if the corporation holds appreciated property and eventually liquidates (as is often the case with closely held corporations), the double taxation problem becomes a large negative factor once again. The tax rules that apply to liquidations of C corporations are illustrated by the following Example.

> **Example 6.02(3): Liquidation of C Corporation** Cecilia and Delia are equal owners of CD Enterprises, Inc., a C corporation formed to develop former toxic waste sites into retail shopping centers. The real estate held by the corporation has appreciated in value, but after a failed attempt to raise additional capital with an initial public offering, the two shareholders decide to split up so they can pursue independent projects. They want to liquidate the corporation by distributing its two assets: undeveloped land with FMV of $2.5 million and tax basis of $1 million, and cash of $750,000.
>
> Assume Cecilia and Delia each have basis of $500,000 in their CD shares, which they have held for a number of years.
>
> Under IRC §336(a), CD recognizes a $1.5 million corporate-level gain on the liquidating distribution of the land, because the transaction is deemed a taxable sale of the property for its FMV. Assume the corporate-level tax is $510,000 (34% of $1.5 million).
>
> CD pays the tax and distributes the remaining $240,000 of cash ($120,000 each to Cecilia and Delia) and the land (in two parcels with equal value).
>
> Each of the shareholders receives liquidating distributions with FMV equal to $1,370,000 (cash of $120,000 plus land worth $1,250,000) in exchange for their CD stock. These exchanges are treated as sales of their stock under IRC §331(a). Therefore, Cecilia and Delia will each recognize taxable long-term capital gains of $870,000 from their stock sales (proceeds of $1,370,000 less basis in their shares of $500,000).
>
> Assuming a tax rate of 20% on the gains, Cecilia and Delia pay total tax of $348,000. The combined corporate and shareholder-level taxes amount to $858,000 ($510,000 at the corporate level and $348,000 at the shareholder level)—a heavy price to pay considering the corporation had only $1.5 million worth of appreciation in its assets upon liquidation.

> **OBSERVATION:** *The double taxation on liquidation scenario is commonly encountered in "business divorces," such as the one illustrated in the preceding example. In contrast, a multi-member LLC or partnership can generally distribute appreciated assets in liquidation to its "divorcing" owners on a tax-free basis, as explained in Chapter 5.*

For calculation templates quantifying the effect of double taxation in a liquidation scenario, see General Practice Aids 7 and 8 in Chapter 10.

Double Taxation When Corporation Holds Appreciating Assets

As the preceding Example illustrates, the existence of appreciated corporate assets causes double taxation problems even when the corporation can "zero out" all its taxable income from operations with deductible payments to or for the benefit of shareholder-employees.

Typically, the corporation will *not* be able to offset gains from asset sales with deductible compensation payments to shareholder-employees, because the gains clearly are unrelated to the value of services performed by those shareholder-employees.

> **RECOMMENDATION:** *If the business has assets that are expected to appreciate significantly (such as real estate, patents, or copyrights), these assets should be owned by a pass-through entity (which is in turn owned by the C corporation's shareholders). The pass-through entity can then lease the assets to the C corporation. With this arrangement, the C corporation can reduce its taxable income by making deductible rental payments that benefit its shareholders. Any gains upon the eventual sale of appreciated assets will not be subject to double taxation.*

"Unreasonable Compensation"

Attempting to solve the double taxation problem by draining off corporate income with deductible compensation payments to shareholder-employees is a recurring theme. As a result, the IRS frequently raises the "reasonable compensation" issue when it audits C corporations.

If questioned by the IRS, the corporation must be able to show that the purported compensation payments were not disguised dividends. In other words, the compensation amounts must be "reasonable."

In any evaluation of the reasonableness of such payments, compensation for comparable work in comparable businesses is the bench mark. The IRS will recharacterize amounts in excess of reasonable compensation as dividends, and the corporation's compensation deductions will be reduced accordingly.

The Personal Holding Company Tax

As implied by the above discussion of dividends and liquidations, the impact of double taxation can be negated if a C corporation pays no dividends and stays in business forever. However, the Tax Code includes a number of roadblocks to prevent this from occurring. One roadblock is the personal holding company (PHC) tax, which forces closely held C corporations to pay current taxes on undistributed income when that income is earned from investment activities and/or personal services. The intent is to discourage individuals from forming C corporations to earn and indefinitely hold investment income or compensation income and thereby benefit from the favorable graduated corporate tax rates.

The PHC tax, which is 39.6% of such undistributed income, can be avoided by making dividend distributions. The government naturally wants corporations to pay dividends, because they are taxable ordinary income to shareholders and nondeductible by the corporation. Thus, the PHC tax is another symptom of the C corporation double taxation issue. [See IRC §§541–547.]

A corporation will qualify as a PHC if:

- More than 50% of its stock (by value and voting power) is owned by five or fewer individuals during the last half of the tax year, and

- At least 60% of the corporation's adjusted ordinary gross income is from dividends, certain rents, certain royalties, and certain personal service contracts.

The PHC tax will come into play only if income accumulates in the corporation. Corporations use Schedule PH of Form 1120 to report the amount of PHC income and compute the PHC tax.

The Accumulated Earnings Tax

For C corporations that are not PHCs another tax applies, again with the purpose of discouraging unwarranted accumulations of taxable income. This is the accumulated earnings tax (AET).

The AET can be avoided in two ways. First, the AET does *not* apply if the corporation can show it had no motive to avoid tax at the shareholder level. Second, the AET does *not* apply if the retention of earnings is necessary to meet the reasonable needs of the business.

However, if the IRS is successful in proving that the AET applies, the tax is 39.6% of "accumulated taxable income." *Accumulated taxable income* is defined as the corporation's cumulative taxable income with some adjustments, reduced by the amount required to meet the reasonable business needs of the corporation. [See IRC §§531–537.]

The so-called accumulated earnings credit allows corporations to accumulate up to $250,000 without having to meet the reasonable needs test. For PSCs, however, the accumulated earnings credit is limited to $150,000.

Like the PHC tax, the AET can be avoided if "excess" corporate income is distributed in the form of dividends. Also like the PHC tax, the AET is simply another manifestation of double taxation.

Note that the AET is assessed by the IRS upon audit. Unlike the PHC tax (which is based on a similar principle), the AET is not self-assessed by the taxpayer filing a schedule with the annual corporate income tax return to calculate and pay the tax. Therefore, exposure to the AET is a "stealth" tax issue that is a real trap for the unwary corporate taxpayer.

Treatment of Corporate-Level Capital Gains

Gains from capital assets owned over 12 months are taxed at a maximum rate of 20% if earned by pass-through entities owned by individuals or if earned by a sole proprietorship business.

Unfortunately, net capital gains of a C corporation are taxed like all other taxable income, rather than at a preferential rate. In addition, corporate capital gains are subject to double taxation. To the extent they increase the value of the corporate stock, such gains result in additional taxable gain at the shareholder level when the stock is sold. And if the gains are distributed as dividends, they are treated as ordinary income at the shareholder level.

Treatment of Corporate-Level Tax-Exempt Income

While tax-exempt income is not taxed at the corporate level, the income is not truly tax-free because of its effect at the shareholder level. To the extent the corporation's tax-exempt income increases the value of the corporate stock, additional taxable gain is recognized at the shareholder level when the stock is sold. And if the tax-exempt income is distributed as dividends, the result is ordinary income at the shareholder level.

In contrast, tax-exempt income of pass-through entities is passed through to the owners (where it retains its tax-exempt character), and the income increases the tax basis of ownership interests. As a result, there is no further tax impact if the tax-exempt income is distributed later or if the ownership interests are sold.

Potential Mitigating Effect of "Splitting Income"

As illustrated by Example 6.02(2), the ability to "split income" with a C corporation and thereby take advantage of the graduated corporate rates can sometimes counteract the negative effect of double taxation. (See also Appendix 6A.)

Potential Mitigating Effect of QSBC Rules

As discussed in Chapter 7, the ill effects of double taxation are potentially mitigated for C corporations that meet the definition of *qualified small business corporations* (QSBCs). Gains on the sale of QSBC shares may qualify for partial exclusion and a very favorable gain rollover rule.

Potential Mitigating Effect of Dividends-Received Deduction

Qualified dividends received from domestic corporations are partially deductible when received by other C corporations. This tax break is referred to as the dividends-received deduction.

A distributee corporation holding 20% or more of the distributor corporation's stock (in terms of voting power and value) can deduct 80% of dividends received. A distributee corporation holding less than 20% of the distributor corporation's stock can deduct 70% of dividends received. A

100% deduction applies to dividends received from another member of the distributee corporation's affiliated group. Limitations apply with respect to the distributee corporation's taxable income, the holding period in the stock, and debt-financed stock. [See IRC §§243–247.]

Potential Mitigating Effect of Tax-Fee Dispositions of Corporate Stock

When a C corporation is acquired by another corporation in a tax-free reorganization (under IRC §368), the owners of the target corporation can dispose of their shares (in exchange for shares of the acquiring company) and defer the shareholder-level taxable gain until the shares of the acquiring corporation are sold. This can amount to an indefinite tax deferral for the shareholder. At the same time, the shareholder may be able to trade his or her illiquid shares in the closely held target for readily marketable shares in a publicly traded acquiring corporation.

At the corporate level, there is no current tax on appreciated assets held by the target corporation. The tax basis of target assets is carried over after the reorganization transaction.

In contrast, an exchange of ownership interests in a pass-through entity (other than an S corporation) for corporate stock (whether or not it is readily marketable) will *not* be tax-free unless the owners of the target entity end up in control of the acquiring corporation. [See IRC §351.]

Potential Mitigating Effect of Basis Step-Up upon Shareholder's Death

If a shareholder dies while holding C (or S) corporation stock, the basis of the stock is stepped up to FMV as of the date of death [IRC §1014]. The potential shareholder-level tax liability vaporizes when the step-up occurs. However, if the corporation holds appreciated assets, there still eventually will be a corporate-level tax on that appreciation (or a corporate-level gain in the case of an S corporation).

In contrast, if a decedent holds a partnership interest and an IRC §754 election has been made, the "inside basis" of the decedent's share of partnership assets—as well as the "outside basis" of the partnership interest—is stepped up. (See Chapter 5.)

Disadvantage—Tax Losses Cannot Be Passed Through to Owners

Unfortunately, tax losses incurred by a C corporation are not passed through to the shareholders. Instead, a C corporation's net operating losses (NOLs) can be used only to offset corporate taxable income earned in the 2 years preceding the NOL year or in the 20 years following the NOL year. If the taxable income earned in that period is less than the NOL, all or part of the NOL will expire without generating any tax benefit. [See IRC §172.]

In contrast, tax losses incurred by pass-through entities are passed through to their owners, where they generally can be used currently to offset taxable income from other sources (subject to other potential limitations, such as the passive loss and at-risk basis rules).

> **RECOMMENDATION:** *When significant taxable losses are expected (as is often the case in the early years of a new venture), it generally is advisable, if at all possible, to use a pass-through entity.*

Advantage—Ability to Borrow from Qualified Retirement Plans

C corporation shareholder-employees can borrow from their qualified retirement plan accounts under the same rules as apply to other employees. In contrast, partners (including LLC members treated as partners for federal income tax purposes), shareholder-employees of S corporations, and sole proprietors typically will be precluded from such borrowing.

Specifically, partners who own more than 10% interests in capital or profits cannot borrow against their accounts. The same is true for S corporation shareholder-employees who own more than 5% of the corporate stock and for all sole proprietors. (See IRC §4975.)

A prohibited loan transaction can result in a 5% excise tax *and* a 100% penalty tax if the transaction is not rescinded within the prescribed time period. [See IRC §§4975(a) and (b).]

Advantage—More Tax-Advantaged Fringe Benefits for C Corporation Shareholder-Employees

The term *fringe benefits* describes benefits provided to employees in addition to their regular cash salary or wage compensation. Under IRC §61, the value of fringe benefits must be included in the employee's taxable income, unless it is specifically excluded by another provision in the Tax Code. Fringe benefits that are deductible by the employer and that are *not* taxable to the recipient employee (because they are excludable under specific Tax Code provisions) are often called "tax-advantaged" fringe benefits.

C corporations can offer their employees a number of tax-advantaged fringe benefits. In closely held businesses, where the employees are often the owners as well, this can be a significant advantage of C corporations over pass-through entities.

The most common tax-advantaged fringe benefits are described briefly below.

Accident and Health Plans

Accident and health plans provide for payments to covered employees if the employee (or a family member) becomes ill or is injured. The two most common types of accident and health plans are insured major medical benefit plans and insured dental benefit plans. Uninsured (or self-insured) medical expense reimbursement plans are also common.

For employers, the general rule is that a C corporation employer's contributions to such employee accident and health plans are deductible, even if some or all of the employees are also shareholders.

For employees, the general rule is the C corporation employer's contributions are *not* included in the employee's taxable income [IRC §106]. If the employee receives direct payments from the plan, in most cases payments can also be excluded [IRC §§105(b) and (c)].

If the plan is a self-insured medical reimbursement plan, however, it must meet a nondiscrimination test. If it fails the test, highly compensated employees must include certain amounts in taxable income, but other employees will not be affected. [See IRC §105(h) and Regs. §1.105-11.]

> **OBSERVATION:** *Being able to provide tax-advantaged insured accident and health plans to shareholder-employees is a significant plus for C corporations. In general, businesses operated as sole proprietorships and pass-through entities can deduct only a percentage of health insurance premiums for coverage of owners and their families.*

Group Term Life Insurance

If nondiscrimination rules are met, the value of employer-provided group term life insurance coverage of up to $50,000 can be excluded from employees' taxable incomes. [See IRC §79 and Regs. §1.79-1.] If coverage exceeds $50,000, employees must report taxable income in amounts specified by IRS tables [Regs. §1.79-3(d)].

Dependent Care Assistance

A C corporation can deduct the cost of a qualified dependent care assistance plan for employees [IRC §129]. Employees can exclude from taxable income the value of this benefit up to $5,000 per year ($2,500 for married filing separate status) as long as the cost would be considered employment-related.

Unfortunately, this tax-advantaged benefit is unavailable to many closely held businesses because of the requirement that no more than 25% of the cost paid by the employer be for employees who are also more than 5% shareholders. [See IRC §129(d).]

Educational Assistance Programs

A C corporation employer can deduct the cost of a qualified educational assistance program, and employees can exclude from taxable income up to $5,250 of such benefits per year [IRC §127].

Unfortunately, this tax-advantaged benefit is unavailable to many closely held corporations because of the requirement that no more than 5% of the amounts paid by the employer be provided for employees who are also more than 5% shareholders. However, tax-free §127 assistance can be provided to an owner's nondependent child who is age 21 or older and employed by the business, as long as the child is not a 5% owner in his or her own right. (The qualification rules for employee educational assistance benefits are essentially the same for C corporations and pass-through entities.) [See IRC §§127(b) and (c).]

Cafeteria Benefit Plans

So-called cafeteria benefit plans (sometimes called "flexible spending account plans") allow employees to choose between taxable cash compensation and one or more nontaxable fringe benefits such as accident and health insurance—hence the term "cafeteria benefit plan."

The amount the employee contributes to the cafeteria plan is excluded from taxable wages (for both income tax and FICA tax purposes). This allows the employee to pay for the chosen fringe benefits with before-tax dollars rather than after-tax dollars.

Cafeteria plans are subject to complex nondiscrimination rules set forth in IRC §125 and the corresponding regulations.

Unfortunately, many closely held corporations will find cafeteria benefit plans unattractive, because of the requirement that key employees include in their taxable income any benefits received under a cafeteria plan if more than 25% of total plan benefits are received by such key employees. [See IRC §125(b)(2).]

Disadvantage—Treatment of Personal Service Corporations

Personal service corporations (PSCs)—C corporations whose shareholder-employees are principally devoted to rendering personal services—are subject to several unfavorable special rules that do not apply to other C corporations. The intent of the special rules is to level the playing field for sole proprietorships that offer the same personal services.

Probably the three most significant special PSC tax rules are the following.

1. A flat 35% tax rate applies to all PSC taxable income (the advantageous graduated corporate tax rates discussed earlier do *not* apply).

2. The passive loss rules apply to PSCs in essentially the same manner as they apply to individuals. (See below.)

3. PSCs are limited in their ability to use a tax year different from the calendar year. (See below.)

Given these unfavorable rules, why are PSCs utilized at all? Because PSCs provide can at least some of the C corporation tax-advantaged fringe benefits to shareholder-employees (see earlier discussion). And, if the corporation's taxable income can be "zeroed out" with deductible payments for the benefit of shareholder-employees (as is usually the case), the negatives of the 35% flat tax rate and double taxation become nonissues.

Disadvantage—Limitations on Use of Cash Method Accounting

The general rule is that C corporations *cannot* use the cash method of accounting for tax purposes [IRC §448(a)(1)]. This limits the ability of C corporations to time income and deductions for year-end tax-planning reasons. Fortunately, there are several exceptions to the general rule, as described below.

Small Corporation Exception

Relatively small C corporations (those with annual gross receipts of $5 million or less for the prior three tax years) remain eligible to use the cash method. For new corporations in existence less than three years, the $5 million test is performed using the Corporation's shorter period of existence. For prior tax years of less than 12 months, gross receipts are annualized for purposes of meeting the $5 million test. [See IRC §§448(b)(3) and (c).]

Personal Service and Farming Corporation Exceptions

Qualifying PSCs and C corporations in the farming business are also eligible to use the cash method.

> **CAUTION:** *Notwithstanding the above exceptions, businesses for which the production, purchase, or sale of merchandise is an income-producing factor must compute beginning and ending inventories to determine taxable income for the year, and such businesses must use the accrual method of accounting for purchases and sales. [See Regs. §§1.446-1(a)(4)(i) and (c)(2)(i).]*

Disadvantage—Corporate Alternative Minimum Tax

The alternative minimum tax (AMT) is a separate system of taxation that runs parallel to the regular income tax rules. C corporations are subject to the corporate version of the AMT.

The corporation starts with its "regular" taxable income amount and then adds, subtracts, and recomputes various regular tax items of income and deduction. The resulting "alternative minimum taxable income" is taxed at a flat 20% rate to determine the AMT liability. [See IRC §§55–59.] If the AMT liability exceeds the regular tax liability, the corporation owes the AMT amount.

However, the payment of the differential between the AMT and regular tax liabilities is really nothing more than a prepayment of the corporation's regular tax. This is because, in the years it pays AMT, the corporation generates a minimum tax credit (MTC). The MTC is equal to the differential between the AMT and regular tax and is allowed as a credit against the regular tax in years when the corporation owes no AMT. [See IRC §53.]

Some feel that the real negative impact of the AMT rules is the tax compliance burden they create. In effect, C corporations are forced to keep two sets of books and fixed asset records—one for regular tax purposes and another for AMT purposes.

S corporations and partnerships (including LLCs treated as partnerships for federal income tax purposes) are *not* subject to AMT. However, they don't escape AMT compliance problems entirely. Pass-through entities still must make certain AMT computations and adjustments and then supply this information on the Schedules K-1 they furnish their owners. The owners then compute their AMT income amounts and determine if there is any AMT liability at their level.

Corporate AMT Exemption

Fortunately an AMT exemption for smaller C corporations was included in the Taxpayer Relief Act of 1997; it was then modified by the IRS Restructuring and Reform Act of 1998. The exemption eliminates the AMT as a concern for many corporations. Specifically, it applies to any C corporation with average annual receipts of $7.5 million or less for all three-tax-year periods (or portions thereof) preceding the tax year for which the exemption is claimed. Only taxable years beginning after 1993 are taken into account. However, for the first three-year period (or portion thereof) that begins after 1993 and ends before the year the exemption is claimed, average annual gross receipt cannot exceed $5 million.

Of more interest in the context of this book is a special rule for newly formed corporations. They will automatically be exempt from the AMT for their first tax year. They will be exempt for the second year if initial-year receipts are $5 million or less and for the third year if the average annual receipts for the first two years are $7.5 million or less. They will then continue to be exempt for the fourth year and thereafter as long as average annual receipts for the preceding three-year period are no more than $7.5 million. For short taxable years, receipts must be annualized in applying these rules [IRC §55(e)].

Advantage—Flexibility to Use Fiscal Year End

C corporations (other than PSCs) generally can select any tax year end. This allows seasonal businesses to use the most appropriate tax year end, and it can provide some tax-planning opportunities for payments made to shareholders.

In contrast, pass-through entities (including LLCs treated as partnerships for federal income tax purposes) must make tax deposit payments with the IRS for the privilege of using tax years other than the calendar year. [See IRC §§444, 706(b), 1378, and 7519.]

> **Example 6.03(4): Differing Corporate and Shareholder Year Ends**
> Cee Corp is a C corporation with a June 30 year end. On that date, Cee Corp makes rental payments for property leased from its shareholders, all of whom have December 31 year ends.
>
> The corporation gets a current deduction in its return for the year ending June 30. The shareholders, however, report the income in their calendar-year returns, which creates a six-month deferral of income for the shareholders (assuming additional quarterly estimated tax payments are not required for the shareholders).
>
> *CAUTION: See IRC §267 for limitations on the ability of corporations and controlling shareholders to take advantage of timing differences created by differing tax year ends.*

Advantage—Treatment of Passive Losses

The general rule is that C corporations can use passive losses and credits to offset taxable income from nonpassive sources without limitation. However, less favorable rules apply to PSCs and closely held corporations, as explained below.

Personal Service Corporations

PSCs are subject to the same passive loss rules as individuals. In other words, PSCs generally can use passive losses only to offset passive income [IRC §469(a)].

For purposes of the passive loss rules, a *PSC* is defined as a corporation primarily in the business of delivering personal services performed by employee-owners where more than 10% of the stock is owned by such employee-owners. [See IRC §469(j)(2).]

Closely Held Corporations

Closely held corporations are able to use passive losses to offset only "net active income" (income other than portfolio income) and passive income from other sources. [See IRC §469(e)(2).]

For purposes of the passive loss rules, a *closely held corporation* is a corporation with more than 50% of the value of the stock held directly or indirectly by five or fewer individuals at any time during the last half of the corporation's tax year. [See IRC §469(j)(1).]

Conclusions

Fortunately, many closely held C corporations that are not PSCs will be unaffected by the passive loss limitations. These corporations will have net active income in excess of passive losses, and no limitation will apply.

6.03 NONTAX ADVANTAGES OF THE CORPORATE FORM OF DOING BUSINESS

While it is fair to say that the tax laws generally favor pass-through entities over C corporations, nontax issues generally favor C corporations. The significant nontax issues relevant in evaluating the attractiveness of C corporations are discussed in this section, in approximate order of importance.

Limited Liability for the Ownership Group

The principal nontax advantage of operating a business or an investment activity as a corporation (C or S) is limited liability. For legal purposes, the corporation is a viewed as an independent entity separate and apart from its shareholders. This means the corporation's creditors generally cannot look to the personal assets of the shareholders to satisfy corporate debts and obligations. Similarly, creditors of the shareholders cannot look to the assets of the corporation to satisfy the debts and obligations of the shareholders.

Reality Check for Closely Held Businesses

In many circumstances, unfortunately, the advantage of limited liability for shareholders can be more apparent than real. For instance, while the personal assets of shareholders are protected from general corporate debts and obligations (often referred to as "contract" or "commercial" liabilities), shareholders generally remain *exposed* to corporate liabilities resulting from their own tortious acts or professional errors and omissions.

Tortious acts are defined as wrongful acts leading to civil actions, other than those involving breach of contract. An example is negligent driving of an auto resulting in injuries or property damage.

> **Example 6.03(1): Shareholder Liability for Professional Malpractice and Negligence**   Assume a corporation is used to operate a professional practice. Under state law, generally the corporation itself is primarily liable for professional errors, omissions, and negligence of its shareholder-employees and other employees.
>
> However, the shareholders generally are *also* personally liable for damages caused by their own professional errors and omissions and for their own negligence in directly supervising other professionals (who may be fellow shareholder-employees or "regular" employees).

A claimant usually can move first against the assets of the corporation. If those assets are insufficient to satisfy the judgment, the claimant can then move against the personal assets of the "guilty" shareholder-employee.

A key point is that the assets of the corporation (and the value of the stock held by the "innocent" shareholders) can be wiped out by liabilities resulting from the tortious acts, errors, omissions, or negligence of any one of the corporation's shareholder-employees or other employees. However, the corporation at least protects the personal assets of the "innocent" shareholders from exposure to such liabilities.

Example 6.03(2): Tortious Act by a Shareholder-Employee   A shareholder-employee uses his car on company business and becomes involved in a serious accident that causes injuries and property damage. The corporation may be primarily liable for the damages, but the shareholder-employee will also be personally liable for this tortious act.

As explained in the preceding Example, the injured parties generally can attempt to recover first from the corporation's assets (thus reducing or wiping out the stock investments of the "innocent" shareholders). If the corporations's assets are insufficient to satisfy the claims, the claimants can then pursue the "guilty" shareholder-employee's personal assets. However, the corporation shields the personal assets of the "innocent" shareholders.

> **RECOMMENDATION:** *The issue of shareholder exposure to these types of liabilities is a matter of state law. The practitioner should research it carefully and consider involving legal counsel before attempting to answer specific client questions.*

Remember that the assets of the corporation are always fully exposed to liabilities and claims resulting from the corporation's activities. Thus, shareholders are always exposed to the risk that their stock investments may be lost as a result of a catastrophic event or a judgment against the corporation.

In addition, shareholders of small and closely corporations are often required to personally guarantee certain of the entity's debts. Shareholders are personally obligated with respect to corporate debts that they have specifically guaranteed, but shareholders are still protected against liability for other corporate debts and generally are protected against claims related to the tortious acts and the professional errors, omissions, and negligence of others.

Summary of Liability Considerations

Notwithstanding the above caveats, the limited-liability protection offered by corporations is still extremely valuable if the business is exposed to liabilities or potential liabilities that are not covered by insurance. Operating a business or investment activity as a corporation may be advisable if:

1. The formation and operation of the activity will result in incurring significant debts owed to financial institutions, lessors, vendors, and other creditors;

2. The activity will involve the delivery of professional services, with the resulting inherent risk of malpractice claims;

3. The activity will involve employees whose foreseeable actions can create liabilities (for example, employees are expected to use their cars regularly in the activity);

4. The activity will require the hiring of one or more employees (regardless of the nature of the business itself, employees inevitably create exposure to liabilities in any number of ways—for example, one employee may harass another, employees can be injured on the job or premises, discriminatory hiring or firing practices can be alleged, embezzlement and theft can occur, or unauthorized borrowing or spending transactions can occur);

5. The nature of the activity itself is hazardous (for example, potentially dangerous tools are used, heavy equipment is used, toxic substances are handled, or employees must work at heights or in the middle of vehicular traffic);

6. The potential for product liability claims exists (for example, the products demand specialized training to operate or are inherently dangerous); or

7. There is potential exposure to environmental liabilities (as is the case with almost any manufacturing activity and perhaps any activity that involves the ownership of real estate, which may have pollution, asbestos, or lead problems).

It will be a very rare business or investment activity that does *not* expose its owners to potentially substantial liability risks.

Limited Liability Aspects of Corporations Compared to Limited Partnerships and LLCs

For limiting owner exposure to liabilities, C and S corporations offer identical legal protections. An S corporation is simply a corporation that has made a special election for federal income tax purposes. Similarly, there is no legal difference between a "regular" C corporation and a C corporation that meets the definition of a *qualified small business corporation* (QSBC) for federal income tax purposes. (QSBCs and S corporations are discussed at length in Chapters 7 and 8, respectively.) However, C corporations *do* possess two significant advantages over limited partnerships.

First, a limited partnership must have at least one general partner with unlimited exposure to partnership liabilities. Usually this problem can be addressed by forming a corporate general partner (usually an S corporation), which effectively "stops the bleeding" in that the amount the general partner can lose is limited to the value of the assets held by the corporation.

However, setting up and maintaining another entity for this purpose creates an administrative burden. (See the discussion of limited partnerships in Chapter 5.) In a corporation, on the other hand, *no* shareholders or shareholder-employees need be exposed to *any* corporate liabilities (other than those arising from certain of his own actions).

Second, a limited partner can lose limited-liability protection by becoming too actively involved in managing the limited partnership. As a result, limited partnerships are not suitable for certain activities, such as the practice of a profession where all partners are by definition heavily involved in the business. In some cases, this problem can be addressed by setting up a corporate general partner, with the corporation owned by the limited partners in proportion to their limited partnership ownership percentages. Again, however, the existence of an additional legal entity creates administrative and tax filing burdens. State limited partnership laws based on the Revised Uniform Limited Partnership Act also give some relief by specifying a number of actions that limited partners can take *without* being deemed to participate in management. Nevertheless, the issue is always a potential problem for limited partnerships and their partners. For corporate shareholders and shareholder-employees, however, this issue is simply not a concern. They can have any degree of management involvement without risking loss of their limited-liability protection.

As discussed in Chapter 3, LLCs theoretically offer liability protection equivalent to that of corporations. However, the newness of LLCs means there are legal uncertainties associated with their use. In contrast, the legal statuses of corporations, their shareholders, and third parties (such as corporate creditors) are well settled after years of litigation and statutory fine-tuning.

> **OBSERVATION:** *An alternative view espoused by some commentators is that well-established corporate case law effectively provides a recipe on how to defeat owners seeking to claim corporate liability protection benefits. Thus, some view corporations as possibly less effective than LLCs in protecting owners from liabilities. Supporting this viewpoint is the fact that some LLC statutes may explicitly obviate the need for complying with corporate-type formalities such as conducting annual meetings, keeping minutes, and so forth. Failure to observe these corporate formalities can cause shareholders to lose hoped-for liability protection benefits (see the discussion immediately below). Balancing this consideration is the fact that years of case law also provides a recipe on how* not *to lose the advantages of corporate liability protection. In other words, if the corporate rules are scrupulously followed, there is great certainty that the corporation will indeed deliver the liability protection desired by the shareholders. With their virtually nonexistent legal track record, LLCs cannot necessarily promise the same degree of certainty.*

Observing Formalities to Establish Separate-Entity Concept

The legal rights and obligations of corporations, shareholders (including shareholder-employees), and third parties (such as creditors) are a matter of state law. Arguably, corporations offer the greatest certainty when it comes to protecting owners from liabilities related to the business or investment activities conducted by the entity.

However, this protection does not come "for free." Shareholders must be careful to observe certain formalities to ensure that the corporation and the shareholders are recognized as separate legal entities. If the existence of separate legal entities is not clearly established, the corporation may be viewed as the legal "alter ego" of its shareholders, a risk referred to as "piercing the corporate veil."

The result of piercing the corporate veil is that the shareholders are personally exposed to all of the liabilities associated with the business or investment activity. Piercing the corporate veil also may mean the existence of the corporation is ignored for federal income tax purposes.

The formalities that must be observed to establish the separate legal existence of a corporation vary according to state law. Generally, however, there will be requirements to do the following:

- File articles of incorporation, a corporate charter, and corporate by-laws with the appropriate state agency (usually the Secretary of State);
- Designate a board of directors and corporate officers and hold periodic board of directors and shareholder meetings;
- Maintain a corporate bank account;
- Pay for the necessary business licenses; and
- File corporate income and franchise tax returns and pay any necessary franchise taxes.

Flexible Ownership Structure

Compared to S corporations, C corporations offer much greater flexibility to create ownership interests and capital structures that satisfy the varying financial requirements of the ownership group. (As noted in Chapters 3, 4, and 5, respectively, LLCs, LLPs, and partnerships also have such flexibility; but they must have more than one owner, while a C corporation can be formed with a single shareholder.)

Specifically, a C corporation's capital structure can include both common stock and preferred stock. Several classes of common stock can be created with varying voting, dividend, and liquidation rights. Preferred stock also can be issued, in several classes with varying characteristics. For example, one class may pay a high dividend, while a second class may pay a lower dividend but be convertible into common stock. C corporations are also free to issue stock options, convertible debt securities, and straight debt securities. In addition, there are no limitations on the number or type of shareholders of a C corporation.

In contrast, S corporations are permitted to have only one class of stock. It can have no more than 75 shareholders, all of whom must all be individuals (other than nonresident aliens), estates, and certain types of trusts. These limitations (discussed fully in Chapter 8) often make operating as an S corporation difficult or impossible.

Finally, a corporation that has an S election in effect but fails to meet the S corporation requirements at any time during the year will simply be treated as a C corporation for federal income tax purposes.

Free Transferability of Ownership Interests

Free transferability of ownership interests in an organization exists if owners can substitute for themselves new owners without the consent of the other owners or members of the organization. In plain English, the attribute of free transferability exists when owners are free to sell or transfer *all* of their ownership rights.

By "all ownership rights" is meant both the economic rights (such as the right to current and liquidating distributions) *and* the noneconomic components of ownership interests (such as the right to vote or to demand an accounting of the entity's activities).

Clearly, the ability to freely transfer one's interest is a significant advantage to a business owner. But free transferability may not be exist for ownership interests in LLCs, LLPs, or partnerships (see discussion in Chapters 3, 4, and 5, respectively).

In contrast, shares of corporate stock generally can be transferred without restriction (unless transfers are limited by a buy–sell agreement). Note, however, that for many closely held businesses this corporate attribute, like limited liability, may be more apparent than real.

The fact is that there usually is *not* a ready market for shares of closely held corporations. In other words, the only market for such shares may be the other shareholders and/or the corporation itself.

Continuity of Life

The legal existence of a corporation goes on indefinitely unless the corporation is formally dissolved. For example, a corporation will continue its legal life after events such as the death, disability, insanity, bankruptcy, or insolvency of one or more of its shareholders. In contrast, state laws generally provide that the death, bankruptcy, etc., of a general partner, LLP partner, or LLC member will cause a legal dissolution of the entity unless the remaining members vote to continue the enterprise. (See Chapters 3, 4, and 5, respectively.) Therefore, the attribute of continuity of life is an advantage of corporations over partnership, LLPs, and LLCs.

Note that shareholder events *can* threaten a corporation's S status. For example, the death of a shareholder may result in a prohibited type of trust becoming a shareholder, with the resulting involuntary termination of the corporation's S election. (See Chapter 8.)

6.04 C CORPORATIONS COMPARED TO OTHER ENTITY CHOICES

This section has the greatest relevance if the entity selection process has been narrowed to a choice between C corporations and one of the other types of entities discussed below. If that is not the case, the practitioner and client should strongly consider using the entity selection software program that comes with this book. The program is designed to help make a choice-of-entity recommendation that is consistent with the major tax and nontax issues facing the client. If the program leads to the C corporation as the apparently best choice, this section can then be reviewed to solidify that conclusion.

C Corporations Compared to S Corporations

For liability protection for owners and other legal aspects, there no differences between C corporations and S corporations. S corporations are simply corporations that have elected to be treated as such for federal income tax purposes. Thus, the only relevant issues in comparing C corporations to S corporations are those imposed by the federal tax laws. (See Chapter 8 for an in-depth discussion of S corporations.)

In summary, compared to S corporations, C corporations may be more attractive if:

- The S corporation restrictions make operating an S corporation difficult or impossible; or
- The owners plan to transfer ownership of shares to prohibited types of shareholders (such as partnerships or certain trusts) for estate planning or succession planning reasons; or
- The graduated C corporation tax rates counteract the ill effects of double taxation; or
- The C corporation problem of double taxation can be sidestepped by draining off all corporate income in the form of deductible payments to or for the benefit of the owners; or
- The owners cannot accept the fact that they may not be able to borrow against their qualified retirement plan accounts.

C Corporations Compared to LLCs

As discussed in section 6.03 of this chapter and in Chapter 3, the personal assets of both C corporation shareholders and LLC members are offered protections against entity-level liabilities.

The obvious advantage of LLCs over C corporations is that they can qualify for partnership taxation, avoiding the C corporation pitfall of double taxation. The other advantages (and the relatively few disadvantages) of partnership taxation are covered at length in Chapter 5.

> OBSERVATION: To be treated as a partnership for federal income tax purposes, an LLC must have at least two members; C corporations can be formed with only one shareholder. In some cases, the two-member rule may appear to be a significant roadblock. As discussed in Chapter 5, however, this problem can often be solved—for example, by forming a husband–wife LLC.

As noted in Chapter 3, almost all states now allow single-owner LLCs. Like multi-member LLCs treated as partnerships, single-member LLCs are also subject to only one level of taxation and thus have a tax advantage over C corporations.

The key negative issues affecting LLCs are legal uncertainty and the variability of LLC statutes from state to state. Also, some businesses (such as certain professional practices) may be prohibited under state law and/or professional standards from operating as LLCs. (See Chapter 3.)

A potentially significant disadvantage of LLCs compared to C corporations is that LLCs may *not* have unlimited legal lives or free transferability of ownership interests. C corporations generally will possess both of these attributes.

Another potentially significant disadvantage of LLCs compared to C corporations is that certain LLC members cannot borrow against their qualified retirement plan account balances. Unlike shareholder-employees of C corporations, LLC members who are treated as partners and own more than 10% interests in capital or profits are not permitted to borrow against their accounts [IRC §4975]. (S corporation shareholder-employees who own more than 5% of the corporate stock also are prevented from borrowing against their qualified retirement plan accounts.)

Compared to multi-member LLCs, C corporations may be more attractive if:

- There will be only one owner (making partnership taxation unavailable by definition); or
- Being able to borrow against their qualified retirement plan accounts is a critical issue for the owners; or
- The benefits of partnership taxation are not required (because the graduated corporate rates counteract the ill effects of double taxation or because the venture's income can be drained with deductible payments to or for the benefit of the owners); or
- The business or investment activity in question cannot be operated as an LLC under state law and/or applicable professional standards; or
- The co-owners cannot live with the legal uncertainties associated with LLC status and the fact that the LLC may not have an unlimited legal life or free transferability of ownership interests.

> *CAUTION: Although LLC statutes place no limits on the number of members, there is a tax problem if ownership interests are so widely held that they are "publicly traded" within the meaning of IRC §7704. If an LLC's ownership interests are publicly traded, the LLC will be treated as a C corporation for federal income tax purposes.*

If state law and applicable professional standards (if any), allow the business in question to operate as a single-member LLC, this will generally be preferable to operating as a solely owned C corporation. Exceptions would be when: (1) the favorable C corporation tax rates cancel out the ill effects of double taxation or (2) the owner prefers the (arguably) greater legal certainty of C corporation status.

C Corporations Compared to LLPs

In states that do not offer LLC-like liability protection to LLP partners, C corporations offer better protection than LLPs. In states that do offer LLC-like protection, the liability protection benefits of LLPs are similar to those of C corporations.

The obvious advantage of LLPs over C corporations is that LLPs benefit from the partnership pass-through taxation rule, avoiding the C corporation pitfall of double taxation. As discussed in section 6.02 of this chapter, however, it is often possible to "drain off" all of a corporation's taxable income by making deductible compensation payments to the shareholder-employees and deductible contributions to fringe benefit plans set up for those shareholder-employees. In this way, the problem of double taxation can often be sidestepped—as long as appreciating assets (such as real estate used in the business) are kept out of the C corporation.

The other advantages (and the relatively few disadvantages) of partnership taxation are covered at length in Chapter 5. Chapter 4 discusses other aspects of LLPs.

> **OBSERVATION:** *Because they are partnerships by definition, LLPs must have at least two co-owners. In contrast, C corporations can be formed with only one shareholder. (However, see Chapter 5 for ways to deal with the two-owner requirement.)*

A potentially significant disadvantage of LLPs compared to C corporations is that LLPs usually will *not* have unlimited legal lives. Generally, the retirement, resignation, expulsion, death, bankruptcy, etc., of an LLP partner will cause a legal dissolution of the entity, unless the remaining partners vote to continue. In contrast, C corporations have unlimited legal life spans.

Another potentially significant disadvantage of LLPs compared to C corporations is that certain LLP partners cannot borrow against their qualified retirement plan account balances. Unlike shareholder-employees of C corporations, LLP partners with more than 10% interests in capital or profits are not permitted to borrow against their accounts [IRC §4975]. (S corporation shareholder-employees who own more than 5% of the corporate stock also are prevented from borrowing against their qualified retirement plan accounts.)

Compared to LLPs, C corporations may be more attractive if:

- There will be only one owner (making a partnership impossible by definition); or

- LLP status is unavailable under state law and/or applicable professional standards; or

- Taking into account available insurance, the owners place a higher value on liability protection than on the benefits of partnership taxation; or

- The benefits of partnership taxation are not required (because the graduated corporate rates counteract the ill effects of double taxation or because the venture's income can be drained with deductible payments to or for the benefit of the owners); or

- The owners cannot accept the fact that they may not be able to borrow against their qualified retirement plan accounts.

C Corporations Compared to General Partnerships

For limiting liability, C corporations are far superior to general partnerships, because corporate shareholder-employees (and shareholders in general) are not exposed to entity-level liabilities. In contrast, all general partners are jointly and severally liability for all partnership debts and obligations, including those created by tortious acts and professional errors, omissions, and negligence of other partners or employees.

The obvious advantage of general partnerships over C corporations is that general partnerships benefit from the partnership pass-through taxation rule, avoiding the C corporation pitfall of double taxation. However, as discussed in section 6.02 of this chapter, it may be possible to "drain off" all of a corporation's taxable income by making deductible compensation payments to the shareholder-employees and deductible contributions to fringe benefit plans set up for those shareholder-employees. In this way, the problem of double taxation can sometimes be sidestepped—as long as appreciating assets (such as real estate used in the business) are kept out of the C corporation.

The other advantages (and the relatively few disadvantages) of partnership taxation are covered at length in Chapter 5.

> **OBSERVATION:** *General partnerships must have at least two co-owners, while C corporations can be formed with only one shareholder. (However, see Chapter 5 for ways to deal with the two-owner requirement.)*

A potentially significant disadvantage of general partnerships compared to C corporations is that general partnerships do *not* have unlimited legal lives. Generally, the retirement, resignation, expulsion, death, bankruptcy, etc., of a partner will cause the entity to be legally dissolved, unless the remaining partners vote to continue (with the continuing partnership treated as a new entity for legal purposes). In contrast, C corporations have unlimited legal life spans.

Also, general partners usually cannot freely transfer their partnership interests, while C corporation shareholders typically *can* freely transfer their shares (unless they are limited by the constraints of a stock buy–sell agreement).

Another potentially significant disadvantage of general partnerships over C corporations is that certain partners cannot borrow against their qualified retirement plan account balances. Unlike shareholder-employees of C corporations, partners with more than 10% interests in capital or profits are not permitted to borrow against their accounts [IRC §4975]. (S corporation shareholder-employees who own more than 5% of the corporate stock also are prevented from borrowing against their qualified retirement plan accounts.)

In summary, compared to general partnerships, C corporations may be more attractive if:

- There will be only one owner (making a partnership impossible by definition); or
- Taking into account available insurance, the owners place a higher value on limited liability than on the benefits of partnership taxation; or
- The benefits of partnership taxation are not required (because the graduated corporate rates counteract the ill effects of double taxation or because the venture's income can be drained with deductible payments to or for the benefit of the owners); or
- The owners cannot accept the fact that they may not be able to borrow against their qualified retirement plan accounts.

C Corporations Compared to Limited Partnerships

The personal assets of C corporation shareholders and limited partners are offered similar protections against entity-level liabilities. As discussed earlier in this chapter, general partners of a limited partnership have unlimited exposure to all partnership debts and obligations, but this problem usually can be managed by setting up a corporate general partner.

The obvious advantage of limited partnerships is that they can qualify for partnership taxation, avoiding the C corporation pitfall of double taxation.

The other advantages (and the relatively few disadvantages) of partnership taxation are discussed in Chapter 5.

> **OBSERVATION:** *To be treated as a partnership for federal income tax purposes, an limited partnership must have at least two partners; C corporations can be formed with only one shareholder. In some cases, the two-partner rule may appear to be a significant roadblock. However, as discussed in Chapter 5, there are often ways to address this issue—for example, by forming a husband–wife partnership.*

A potentially significant disadvantage of limited partnerships compared to C corporations is that limited partnerships usually will *not* possess the corporate attribute of continuity of life. Also, general partners typically cannot freely transfer their partnership interests.

Another potentially significant disadvantage is that certain partners cannot borrow against their qualified retirement plan account balances. Unlike shareholder-employees of C corporations, partners who own more than 10% interests in capital or profits are not permitted to borrow against their accounts [IRC §4975]. (S corporation shareholder-employees who own more than 5% of the corporate stock also are prevented from borrowing against their qualified retirement plan accounts.)

In summary, compared to limited partnerships, C corporations may be more attractive if:

- There will be only one owner (making a partnership impossible by definition); or
- The owners who would be limited partners cannot live with the fact that they cannot become too actively involved in management of the venture without losing their limited liability protection; or
- The benefits of partnership taxation are not required (because the graduated corporate rates counteract the ill effects of double taxation or because the venture's income can be drained with deductible payments to or for the benefit of the owners); or
- The owners cannot accept the fact that they may not be able to borrow against their qualified retirement plan accounts; or
- The owners cannot live with the fact that a limited partnership would not have an unlimited legal life or free transferability of all ownership interests.

CAUTION: Although there are no limits on the number of partners in a limited partnership, there is a tax problem if partnership interests are so widely held that they are "publicly traded" within the meaning of IRC §7704. If the partnership interests are publicly traded, the limited partnership will be treated as a C corporation for federal income tax purposes.

C Corporations Compared to Sole Proprietorships

Liability Concerns

A sole proprietorship is an unincorporated business that is legally one and the same as the owner. Therefore, the personal assets of the owner are exposed without limitation to any and all liabilities related to the conduct of the sole proprietorship business. This unlimited liability exposure is the most significant difference between sole proprietorships and the other types of entities discussed in this publication (other than general partnerships, which also expose their owners to unlimited personal liability).

The existence of one or more of the following conditions indicates that operating a business through a C corporation (or other liability-limiting entity, such as an S corporation, an LLC, an LLP, or a limited partnership) should be strongly considered:

- The formation and operation of the activity will result in significant debts owed to financial institutions, lessors, vendors, and other creditors;

- The activity will involve the delivery of professional services, with the resulting inherent risk of malpractice claims;

- The activity will involve employees whose foreseeable actions can create liabilities (for example, employees are expected to use their cars regularly in the activity);

- The activity will require the hiring of one or more employees (regardless of the nature of the business itself, employees inevitably create exposure to liabilities in any number of ways—for example, one employee may harass another, employees can be injured on the job or premises, discriminatory hiring or firing practices can be alleged, embezzlement and theft can occur, or unauthorized borrowing or spending transactions can occur);

- The nature of the activity itself is hazardous (for example, potentially dangerous tools are used, heavy equipment is used, toxic substances are handled, or employees must work at heights or in the middle of vehicular traffic),

- The potential for product liability claims exists (for example, the products demand specialized training to operate or are inherently dangerous); and

- There is potential exposure to environmental liabilities (as is the case with almost any manufacturing activity and perhaps any activity that involves the ownership of real estate, which may have pollution, asbestos, or lead problems).

If there is to be only one owner of the activity, the only liability-limiting entities generally available are the C corporation and the S corporation, either of which can be 100% owned by an individual. The other alternatives (limited partnerships, multi-member LLCs, and LLPs) all require at least two owners, unless state law permits single-member LLCs.

As discussed in Chapter 5, it is possible to "arrange" to have more than one owner—if, for example, the multi-member LLC form of doing business appears to be the most attractive choice.

As a practical matter, liability exposure is not always a critical issue. In some businesses, the risks may be inherently negligible, and/or it may be possible to obtain adequate liability insurance at an acceptable cost. Also, the use of a corporation or other liability-limiting entity is not the cure-all that some think.

For example, if the business in question is a professional practice, the use of a corporation (or any other legal entity) generally will do nothing to protect the practitioner's personal assets from liabilities related to his or her *own* professional errors, omissions, and negligence. The same is true for liabilities related to the owner's tortious acts (such as careless driving resulting in injuries or property damage), whether or not they are committed in the course of business.

When it comes to other common business liabilities, such as bank loans, lease obligations, and vendor payables (often referred to as "contract" or "commercial" liabilities), creditors often will require owners to guarantee the debts personally, whether or not a corporation or other legal entity is used to operate the venture.

Administrative Simplicity of Sole Proprietorships

Some simple initial steps may be required to set up a sole proprietorship. For example, under local law it may be necessary to register and pay a fee to obtain a business license. Filings may be required if the business will use an assumed name (a "DBA").

However, no other legal papers or filings are generally required to initiate and operate a sole proprietorship. Thus, professional fees and burdensome paperwork are minimized.

On an ongoing basis, there is no requirement, for example, to:

- Keep corporate minutes;
- Maintain separate bank accounts (although this is recommended);
- Deposit payroll taxes or file payroll tax returns (unless there are employees);
- File corporate federal, state, or local tax returns;
- Pay state worker's compensation insurance (unless there are employees).

Transferring Ownership Interests

Partial ownership interests in corporations, partnerships, and LLCs can be transferred relatively easily. Such transfers are often made to the owner's spouse or children for estate planning, family income tax planning, business succession planning, or other reasons.

In contrast, it is impractical to transfer ownership of interests in the assets of a sole proprietorship. (Unfortunately, there is nothing else that *can* be transferred.) In any case, once there is more than one owner, a sole proprietorship by definition no longer exists.

If there is a foreseeable need to raise additional equity capital, a corporation, partnership, or LLC provides an established vehicle for taking in new owners. In contrast, if the business is run as a sole proprietorship, taking on an additional owner (for whatever reason) will almost certainly require the creation of a new legal entity to own the business.

For these reasons, it is often advisable to set up a business as a corporation, partnership, or LLC on the front end, rather than postpone dealing with apparently inevitable issues.

Lower Corporate Tax Rates versus Double Taxation

The principal tax advantage of using a C corporation instead of a sole proprietorship lies with the lower corporate graduated tax rates (which are not available to PSCs). These lower rates enable the corporation to maximize its current cash flow by minimizing the cash outlays needed to pay federal income taxes. This allows the corporation to finance more of its growth internally. (See section 6.02 of this chapter, and see also Appendix 6A.)

However, for a small to medium-sized business that is not expected to continue indefinitely beyond the life of its principal owner, the current tax savings may be smaller than the eventual cost of double taxation. (See the General Practice Aids in Chapter 10 for calculation templates to estimate the impact of double taxation in both stock sales and corporate liquidations.)

> **OBSERVATION:** *As discussed earlier, double taxation is not a problem if essentially all of the corporation's taxable income can be drained off via deductible payments for owner compensation, fringe benefits, interest (on loans from the owner to the corporation), and rents (for property leased by the owner to the corporation).*

What If Business Is Expected to Throw Off Tax Losses?

If the business will produce taxable losses because it is in the start-up phase or because cash flow exceeds taxable income (due to deductible noncash expenses like depreciation and amortization), the use of a sole proprietorship allows the owner to deduct the losses currently on Form 1040.

In contrast, if a C corporation is used, the tax losses are trapped inside the corporation in the form of a net operating loss (NOL). The NOL will result in future tax benefits if and only if the corporation earns taxable income in future years.

Payroll Tax Advantage for Corporations

Amounts retained by a C corporation are not subject to federal payroll taxes. In contrast, the self-employment (SE) tax applies to 100% of a sole proprietor's business income, as reported on Schedule C. Thus, the federal payroll taxes owed if the owner is an employee of a C corporation may be significantly less than the SE tax owed if the owner is a sole proprietor.

> **Example 6.04(1): Federal Payroll Tax Rules—Sole Proprietorship versus C Corporation** Danette, a sole proprietor, has $100,000 of Schedule C income from her business in 1999. The $100,000 figure is before her $10,000 contribution to her Keogh retirement plan and her $5,000 of medical insurance premiums (which are 60% deductible).
>
> Danette's SE tax is based on SE income of $100,000. She gets no deductions for the Keogh contribution or medical insurance premiums for SE tax purposes. Thus, her 1999 SE tax liability is $11,902.40 (15.3% of $72,600 plus 2.9% of $27,400).
>
> Now assume Danette instead operates her business as a 100%-owned C corporation and pays herself a salary of $55,000, with a contribution of $10,000 to the company pension plan set up for her benefit, and $5,000 paid for medical insurance covering her. (The

remaining $30,000 of corporate income is retained by the corporation to finance its growth.) FICA taxes are due only on Danette's stated salary of $55,000. Thus, the FICA tax liability is only $8,415 (15.3% of $55,000). Compare this amount to the $11,902.40 of SE tax that is due if Danette operates her business as a sole proprietorship.

> **OBSERVATION:** *The federal payroll tax rules provide a significant incentive to incorporate. Partners are in essentially the same position as sole proprietors when it comes to exposure to the SE tax. Thus, corporations are also superior to partnerships with respect to the issue of minimizing federal payroll taxes.*

Ability to Borrow against Qualified Retirement Accounts

Another potentially significant disadvantage of sole proprietorships over C corporations is that the owner cannot borrow against his or her qualified retirement plan account balances. Within limits, C corporation shareholder-employees *can* borrow against their account balances; but sole proprietors, partners and LLC members who own more than 10% interests in capital or profits, and S corporation shareholder-employees who own more than 5% of the corporate stock cannot [IRC §4975].

State Taxes and Other Tax-Related Issues

Just as the federal income tax impact of operating as a C corporation versus as a sole proprietorship should be evaluated, so should the state and local tax impact be considered. In most cases, state and local tax rules will parallel the federal rules with regard to the double taxation issue and the potential to minimize current taxes with lower graduated corporate tax rates.

As discussed in section 6.02 of this chapter, C corporations generally can deliver more tax-advantaged fringe benefits to owners than can sole proprietorships (or S corporations or partnerships, for that matter). For example, C corporations can deduct 100% of the cost of premiums for medical insurance coverage of shareholder-employees and their families, and the premiums are not included in the taxable incomes of the shareholder-employees [IRC §106]. As discussed in Chapter 9, sole proprietors can deduct 100% of family medical insurance premiums only if the spouse is an employee of the proprietorship. Otherwise, only a percentage is deductible.

Summary—C Corporations versus Sole Proprietorships

Compared to sole proprietorships, C corporations are more attractive if:

- The owner places a higher value on limited liability than on the benefits of a single level of taxation and administrative simplicity; or

- The graduated corporate rates counteract the ill effects of double taxation; or
- The problem of double taxation can be sidestepped by draining off all corporate income in the form of deductible payments to or for the benefit of the owner; or
- The owner wants to set up a vehicle for the future transfer of ownership interests to family members or others; or
- The payroll tax savings of operating as a C corporation are significant; or
- The tax benefit of deducting 100% of medical insurance premiums is significant; or
- The owner cannot accept the fact that borrowing against his or her qualified retirement plan account is not permitted.

6.05 SUMMARY STATEMENT ON WHEN C CORPORATIONS ARE ATTRACTIVE

In general, C corporations may be preferred to S corporations, LLCs, partnerships (including LLPs), and sole proprietorships if:

- Limiting owner liability is a critical concern; *and*
- There will be only one owner (making partnership taxation by definition unavailable) and the S corporation restrictions make operating as an S corporation difficult or impossible; *or*
- The activity cannot be operated as a limited partnership because the owners, who would be limited partners, cannot live with the fact that they must avoid management involvement to maintain their limited liability protection; *and*
- The activity cannot be operated as an LLC under state law and/or applicable professional standards; *or*
- The business cannot be operated as an LLC, because the owners cannot live with the legal uncertainties associated with LLC status; *or*
- The benefits of pass-through taxation are not required (because the graduated corporate rates counteract the ill effects of double taxation or because the venture's income can be drained with deductible payments to or for the benefit of the owners); *or*
- The ability of the owners to borrow against their qualified retirement plan accounts is a critical issue.

If state law and applicable professional standards (if any), allow the business in question to operate as a single-member LLC, this will generally be preferable to operating as a solely owned C corporation. Exceptions would be when: (1) the favorable C corporation tax rates cancel out the ill effects of double taxation or (2) the owner prefers the (arguably) greater legal certainty of C corporation status.

Appendix 6A: Analysis of Effective Tax Rates on C Corporation Income

Explanation: In assessing the attractiveness of a C corporation versus a pass-through entity (LLC, LLP, partnership, or S corporation), a critical issue is the effective combined tax rate (at the entity and owner levels) that will apply to income earned from the activity. Obviously, if a pass-through entity is used, there is no entity-level tax, but the owners may be high-income individuals who are subject to marginal tax rates as high as 39.6% (see Table 2 below). In such cases, a single level of taxation at high marginal rates may be more expensive than double taxation of C corporation income, as shown in Table 3.

Table 1: Current Federal Income Tax Rate Schedule for C Corporations

Taxable Income Over	But Not Over	Tax Rate
$0	$50,000	15%
$50,000	$75,000	25%
$75,000	$100,000	34%
$100,000	$335,000	39%
$335,000	$10,000,000	34%
$10,000,000	$15,000,000	35%
$15,000,000	$18,333,333	38%
$18,333,333		35%

As can be seen, the first $75,000 of a C corporation's income is taxed at a significantly lower rate than the same income earned by an individual taxpayer (see Table 2 below). This is especially true if the income from the activity under consideration will be piled on top of other income (from salaries, other investments, etc.) of high-income individuals. In such cases, the incremental taxable income from the activity may be subject to a 39.6% tax rate if a pass-through entity is used. This means a pass-through entity may be forced to distribute 39.6% of its taxable income to its owners so they can pay their personal tax liabilities. For businesses that need to maximize current cash flow to finance growth, this can be a heavy price to pay for the benefit of pass-through taxation.

Table 2: 1999 Individual Federal Income Tax Rates

Income for Joint Filers	Income for Singles	Tax Rate
$0 to $43,050	$0 to $25,750	15%
$43,051 to $104,050	$25,751 to $62,450	28%
$104,051 to $158,550	$62,451 to $130,250	31%
$158,551 to $283,150	$130,251 to $283,150	36%
Over $283,150	Over $283,150	39.6%

Table 3 shows the combined effective tax rate on a C corporation's taxable income assuming the income (net of tax) is retained and adds to the value of the corporate stock dollar for dollar. The stock is assumed to be sold for a long-term capital gain taxed at 20%. The combined effective rate should be compared to the marginal individual rate (which can be as high as 39.6%, as shown in Table 2) that would apply if the income were instead earned by a pass-through entity.

Table 3: 1999 Combined Corporate and Individual Effective Tax Rates

C Corp Average Tax Rate	Individual Rate on LTCGs	Combined Rate
15%*	20%	32.0%
18.33%**	20%	34.7%
34%***	20%	47.2%

*15% average rate applies to taxable income up to $50,000.

**18.33% average rate applies to taxable income of $75,000.

***34% average rate applies to taxable income between $335,000 and $10 million.

OBSERVATION: *If the time value of money is taken into account, the combined rates shown above will be reduced. This is because the capital gain component of the combined rate on C corporation income is deferred until the stock is sold. In contrast, taxes on pass-through income must be paid currently.*

Appendix 6B: Sample Client Letter When C Corporation Appears to Be Best Entity Choice

Dear [Client name]:

This letter briefly summarizes some of the major considerations that went into your recent decision to form a new business that will be operated as a C corporation.

Limited Liability of Shareholders

As we discussed, the principal advantage of C corporation status is that the corporation is treated as a legal entity separate and distinct from its shareholders. Therefore, the corporation owns its own assets and is liable for its own debts. As a result, the personal assets of shareholders (including shareholder-employees) generally are beyond the reach of corporate creditors.

The liability-limiting protections offered by C corporations are substantial, but they should not be overstated. While the personal assets of shareholders are protected from "general" corporate debts and obligations (often referred to as "contract liabilities"), shareholders generally remain *exposed* to corporate liabilities resulting from their own tortious acts and professional errors and omissions. (*Tortious acts* are defined as wrongful acts leading to civil actions, other than those involving breach of contract.)

The issue of shareholders' exposure to liabilities related to tortious acts is a matter of state law. If you have specific questions about this issue, we recommend you consult with your attorney.

Guarantees of Corporate Debts

Shareholders may be required on occasion to personally guarantee certain of the corporation's debts as a condition of obtaining financing or for other reasons.

Shareholders are personally obligated with respect to corporate debts that are specifically guaranteed, but shareholders are still protected against liability for other corporate debts.

Federal Income Tax Treatment of C Corporations

The key disadvantage of C corporations is that they are subject to double taxation. The double taxation issue appears in several different ways, described briefly here.

Double Taxation of Corporate Dividends

The most common manifestation of double taxation is the treatment of C corporation dividend distributions to shareholders. In order for dividends to be available, the corporation must have earnings, and these are taxed at the corporate level. Dividends are also taxed as ordinary income to the recipient shareholders, but the payments are not deductible by the corporation.

Double Taxation on Sale of Stock

When a C corporation earns taxable income, there is no upward adjustment in the tax basis of the shareholders' stock.

The retained income increases the value of the stock, which creates a bigger capital gain when shares are eventually sold. As a result, the retained income is in effect taxed again when shares are sold.

Double Taxation on Liquidation

In some cases, corporations seemingly can avoid the double taxation issue simply by not making dividend distributions. However, if the corporation holds appreciated property and eventually liquidates, the double taxation problem once again becomes a negative factor.

The property to be distributed in liquidation is treated as sold by the corporation for its fair market value (FMV). The corporation must then pay the resulting taxes. When the corporate assets are distributed to the shareholders in liquidation, shareholders recognize taxable gain to the extent the FMV of the liquidating distributions exceeds the tax basis in their shares.

Double Taxation When Corporation Holds Appreciating Assets

If the corporation holds appreciating assets, the resulting gains will be subject to double taxation if the corporation sells them, if the corporation is liquidated, or if the corporate stock is sold.

We strongly recommend that assets that are expected to appreciate significantly (such as real estate, patents, and copyrights) be owned by a pass-through entity (which is in turn owned by the C corporation's shareholders). The pass-through entity can then lease the assets to the C corporation. With this arrangement, the C corporation can reduce its taxable income by making deductible rental payments, which benefit its shareholders. Any gains upon the eventual sale of the appreciated assets owned by the pass-through entity will not be subject to double taxation.

Treatment of Corporate-Level Capital Gains

Long-term capital gains may be taxed at only 20% if earned by pass-through entities owned by individuals or if earned by a sole proprietorship business.

Unfortunately, capital gains of a C corporation are taxed like all other taxable income rather than at a preferential rate. In addition, corporate capital gains are subject to double taxation. To the extent they increase the value of the corporate stock, such gains result in additional taxable gain at the shareholder level when the stock is sold. And if the gains are distributed as dividends, they are treated as ordinary income at the shareholder level.

Treatment of Corporate-Level Tax-Exempt Income

While tax-exempt income is not taxed at the corporate level, the income is not truly tax-free because of the effect at the shareholder level. To the extent the corporation's tax-exempt income increases the value of the corporate stock, additional taxable gain is recognized at the shareholder level when the stock is sold. And if the tax-exempt income is distributed as dividends, the result is ordinary income at the shareholder level.

In contrast, tax-exempt income of pass-through entities is passed through to the owners (where it retains its tax-exempt character), and the income increases the tax basis of ownership interests. As a result, there is no further tax impact if the tax-exempt income is later distributed or if the ownership interests are later sold.

The "Reasonable Compensation" Issue

Corporations often attempt to solve the double taxation problem by "zeroing out" corporate income with deductible compensation payments to shareholder-employees. As a result, the IRS frequently raises the so-called reasonable compensation issue when C corporations are audited.

When challenged by the IRS, the corporation must be able to show that the purported compensation payments were not dividends in disguise. In other words, the compensation amounts must be "reasonable." If they are not, the IRS will reclassify the excessive amounts as dividends and reduce the corporation's compensation deductions accordingly.

The Personal Holding Company Tax

The personal holding company (PHC) tax is intended to force closely held C corporations to pay current taxes on undistributed income when that income is earned from investment activities and/or personal services. The concept is designed to discourage individuals from forming C corporations to retain investment income or compensation income indefinitely and thereby take advantage of the graduated corporate tax rate structure.

If the PHC tax applies, it must be paid at the rate of 39.6% on such retained income. It can be avoided by making dividend distributions. Unfortunately for the corporation and its shareholders, dividends are not deductible by the corporation and they are treated as taxable ordinary income to recipient shareholders. A corporation will meet the definition of a PHC if:

- More than 50% of its stock (by value and voting power) is owned by five or fewer individuals during the last half of the tax year, and

- At least 60% of the corporation's adjusted ordinary gross income is from dividends, certain rents, certain royalties, and certain personal service contracts.

The Accumulated Earnings Tax

For C corporations that are not PHCs, the accumulated earnings tax (AET) exists to discourage unwarranted accumulations of taxable income. The AET does *not* apply if there is no motive to avoid tax at the shareholder level or if the earnings are necessary to meet the reasonable needs of the business.

However, if the AET *does* apply, the tax is 39.6% of the accumulated taxable income. Accumulated taxable income is essentially taxable income with some adjustments, reduced by the amount retained to meet the reasonable business needs of the corporation.

Like the PHC tax, the AET can be avoided by distributing "excess" corporate income in the form of dividends, with the same undesirable consequences for the corporation and its shareholders.

Potential Mitigating Effect of "Splitting Income"

The ability of high-bracket individuals to "split income" with a C corporation and thereby take advantage of the graduated corporate rates (which can be as low as 15%) can sometimes counteract the negative effects of double taxation. See Exhibit 1.

Note also that if all income is left inside a corporation, there will be no federal payroll taxes for the shareholders. However, if the business is operated as an LLC or a general partnership, the owners may owe significant amounts of self-employment (SE) tax on the pass-through income. SE tax is also owed on the income of a single-owner business operated as a sole proprietorship.

Graduated Corporate Tax Rates Can Maximize Current Cash Flow

When a business intends to retain all its earnings indefinitely in order to internally finance its growth, the corporate tax rates can make C corporations very attractive compared to pass-through entities. A pass-through entity might have to distribute up to 39.6% of the taxable income earned by the business to enable the owners to pay their personal taxes.

Even at taxable income levels above $75,000, the tax rates for C corporations are significantly lower than those for individuals. As a result, the use of a C corporation can maximize the current cash flow of the business. It must be remembered, however, that the cost of this current benefit is the double taxation that may apply in later years.

Tax Losses Cannot Be Passed Through to Owners

Unfortunately, tax losses incurred by a C corporation cannot be passed through to the shareholders. Instead, a C corporation's net operating losses (NOLs) can be used only to offset corporate taxable income earned in the 2 years preceding the NOL year or in the 20 years following the NOL year. If the taxable income earned in that period is less than the NOL, all or part of the NOL will expire without generating any tax benefit.

In contrast, tax losses incurred by pass-through entities are passed through to their owners, where they generally can be used currently to offset taxable income from other sources (subject to other potential limitations of tax law, such as the passive loss rules). When significant taxable losses are expected to be incurred (as is often the case in the early years of a new venture), generally it is advisable to use a pass-through entity if at all possible.

Conclusion

As we discussed, you have considered the above advantages and disadvantages and have concluded that a C corporation is the best choice in your circumstances.

We appreciate the opportunity to consult with you as you make the important decision of choosing the most advantageous type of entity under which to operate your new venture. We look forward to working with you in the future as your corporation is formed and enters the operating phase.

Very truly yours,

Exhibit 1: Analysis of Effective Tax Rates on C Corporation Income

Explanation: In assessing the attractiveness of a C corporation versus a pass-through entity (LLC, LLP, partnership, or S corporation), a critical issue is the effective combined tax rate (at the entity and owner levels) that will apply to income earned from the activity. Obviously, if a pass-through entity is used, there is no entity-level tax, but the owners may be high-income individuals who are subject to marginal tax rates as high as 39.6% (see Table 2 below). In such cases, a single level of taxation at high marginal rates may be more expensive than double taxation of C corporation income, as shown in Table 3.

Table 1: Current Federal Income Tax Rate Schedule for C Corporations

Taxable Income Over	But Not Over	Tax Rate
$0	$50,000	15%
$50,000	$75,000	25%
$75,000	$100,000	34%
$100,000	$335,000	39%
$335,000	$10,000,000	34%
$10,000,000	$15,000,000	35%
$15,000,000	$18,333,333	38%
$18,333,333		35%

As can be seen, the first $75,000 of a C corporation's income is taxed at significantly a lower rates than would apply to the same income earned by an individual taxpayer (see Table 2 below). This is especially true if the income from the activity under consideration will be piled on top of other income (from salaries, other investments, etc.) of high-income individuals. In such cases, the incremental taxable income from the activity may be subject to a 39.6% tax rate if a pass-through entity is used. This means a pass-through entity may be forced to distribute 39.6% of its taxable income to its owners so they can pay their personal tax liabilities. For businesses that need to maximize current cash flow to finance growth, this can be a heavy price to pay for the benefit of pass-through taxation.

Table 2: 1999 Individual Federal Income Tax Rates

Income for Joint Filers	Income for Singles	Tax Rate
$0 to $43,050	$0 to $ 25,750	15%
$43,051 to $104,050	$25,751 to $62,450	28%
$104,051 to $158,550	$62,451 to $130,250	31%
$158,551 to $283,150	$130,251 to $283,150	36%
Over $283,150	Over $283,150	39.6%

Table 3 shows the combined effective tax rate on a C corporation's taxable income assuming the income (net of tax) is retained and adds to the value of the corporate stock dollar for dollar. The stock is assumed to be sold for a long-term capital gain taxed at 20%. The combined effective rate should be compared to the marginal individual rate (which can be as high as 39.6%, as shown in Table 2) that would apply if the income were instead earned by a pass-through entity.

Table 3: 1999 Combined Corporate and Individual Effective Tax Rates

C Corp Average Tax Rate	Individual Rate on LTCGs	Combined Rate
15%*	20%	32.0%
18.33%**	20%	34.7%
34%***	20%	47.2%

*15% average rate applies to taxable income up to $50,000.

**18.33% average rate applies to taxable income of $75,000.

***34% average rate applies to taxable income between $335,000 and $10 million.

OBSERVATION: *If the time value of money is taken into account, the combined rates shown above will be reduced. This is because the capital gain component of the combined rate on C corporation income is deferred until the stock is sold. In contrast, taxes on pass-through income must be paid currently.*

CHAPTER 7 • QUALIFIED SMALL BUSINESS CORPORATIONS—C CORPORATIONS WITH TAX ADVANTAGES

CONTENTS

7.01 INTRODUCTION

Qualified small business corporations (QSBCs) are simply C corporations eligible for two special tax breaks under the Internal Revenue Code. They were created as a small business tax incentive by the Revenue Reconciliation Act of 1993. [See IRC §1202.]

Specifically, certain shareholders of QSBC stock may qualify for exclusion of up to 50% of their long-term capital gains from sales of shares (which generally translates into a 14% tax rate on the gains). The gain exclusion is unavailable to shareholders that are C corporations.

The Taxpayer Relief Act of 1997 added a QSBC stock sale gain rollover rule that may actually prove to be more beneficial than the 50% gain exclusion. Under the gain rollover rule, taxable gains can be deferred indefinitely by rolling over QSBC stock sale proceeds into new investments in QSBC stock.

QSBCs are treated as "regular" C corporations for all other legal and federal income tax purposes. As a result, the other advantages and disadvantages of C corporation status apply to QSBCs. (See Chapter 6 for an in-depth discussion of C corporations.)

> *CAUTION: The QSBC qualification rules, contained in IRC §1202, are detailed and relatively complex. They are not described exhaustively in this chapter because it is more efficient to simply read the language of the Code section itself. Practitioners should review §1202 carefully before concluding that a corporation will meet the definition of a QSBC.*

7.02 EFFECTIVE TAX RATES ON QSBC INCOME

The 50% gain exclusion can mitigate the effects of the double taxation of C corporation income. (Double taxation is discussed at length in Chapter 6.) In fact, for corporations that qualify as QSBCs and that intend to retain income to internally finance growth, the combined benefits of the graduated corporate tax rates and the 50% gain exclusion can make operating as a C corporation very attractive.

Effect of Graduated Corporate Rates and QSBC Gain Exclusion

The current federal income tax rate structure for QSBCs is as follows:

Taxable Income Over	But Not Over	Tax Rate
$0	$50,000	15%
$50,000	$75,000	25%
$75,000	$100,000	34%
$100,000	$335,000	39%
$335,000	$10,000,000	34%
$10,000,000	$15,000,000	35%
$15,000,000	$18,333,333	38%
$18,333,333		35%

As can be seen, the first $75,000 of a QSBC's income is taxed at significantly lower rates than would apply to the same income earned by an individual taxpayer (see the table below). This effect is even more pronounced if the income from the activity under consideration will be piled on top of other income (from salaries, other investments, etc.) of high-income individuals.

In such cases, the incremental taxable income from the activity may be subject to a 39.6% tax rate if a pass-through entity is used. This means a pass-through entity may be forced to distribute 39.6% of its taxable income to its owners so they can pay their personal tax liabilities. For businesses that need to maximize current cash flow to finance growth, this is a heavy price to pay for the benefit of pass-through taxation.

The 1999 federal income tax rates for individual taxpayers are as follows:

Income for Joint Filers	Income for Singles	Tax Rate
$0 to $43,050	$0 to $25,750	15%
$43,051 to $104,050	$25,751 to $62,450	28%
$104,051 to $158,550	$62,451 to $130,250	31%
$158,551 to $283,150	$130,251 to $283,150	36%
Over $283,150	Over $283,150	39.6%

The table on page 291 shows the combined effective tax rate on a QSBC's taxable income, assuming the income (net of tax) is retained and adds to the value of the corporate stock dollar for dollar. The stock is assumed to be sold for a long-term capital gain taxed at an effective rate of 14% (after the exclusion of 50% of the gain).

The combined effective rates should be compared to the marginal individual rate (which can be as high as 39.6%, as shown in the above table) that would apply if the income were instead earned by a pass-through entity.

QSBC Average Tax Rate	Individual Rate on Gains	Combined Rate
15%*	14%	26.9.%
18.33%**	14%	29.8%
34%***	14%	43.2%

*15% average rate applies to taxable income up to $50,000.

**18.33% average rate applies to taxable income of $75,000.

***34% average rate applies to taxable income between $335,000 and $10 million.

> **OBSERVATION:** *If the time value of money is taken into account, the combined rates shown above will be reduced. This is because the capital gain component of the combined rate on QSBC income is deferred until the stock is sold. In contrast, taxes on pass-through income must be paid currently.*

Tax Rate on Nonexcluded Portion of Gain

Unfortunately, the Taxpayer Relief Act of 1997's rate reduction for long-term capital gains was not fully extended to QSBC stock sales eligible for the 50% gain exclusion break. Under current law, the maximum rate on the taxable portion of the gain remains at the old-law figure of 28%, to the extent of the amount of excluded gain (generally 50% of the total gain). Any remaining taxable gain qualifies for the 20% maximum rate.

Thus, the effective tax rate on QSBC stock sale gains will generally be 14%, rather than the 10% that one might expect.

AMT Preference on Excluded Gain

In addition, IRC §57(a)(7) defines an AMT preference equal to 42% of the excluded QSBC stock sale gain. As the example immediately below illustrates, the combination of the 42% preference and the 28% tax rate on the nonexcluded portion of QSBC gains can eliminate much of the advantage of the gain exclusion rule.

Example 7.02(1): Using a QSBC Instead of a Pass-Through Entity
Dedrick is acquiring a manufacturing business expected to generate taxable income of $75,000 per year. Dedrick intends to operate the venture for 10 years and then sell out. Because he has large amounts of income from his other interests, Dedrick's incremental income from the new business would be taxed at 39.6% if a sole proprietorship or pass-through entity is used.

If he sets up shop as a C corporation, however, and the entity meets the definition of a QSBC, the corporate-level tax on projected income will be only 18.33%, and he can exclude 50% of the gain when he sells his stock.

Assume the corporation's retained after-tax income adds to the value of its stock dollar for dollar. After 10 years, Dedrick will pay a

14% long-term capital gain tax (after the 50% gain exclusion for QSBC stock) on 85% of the corporation's taxable income.

This amounts to an effective shareholder-level tax rate of 11.43% (14% of 81.67%) on top of the corporate-level tax of 18.33%. The combined shareholder-level and corporate-level tax bite is therefore only 29.76% (11.43% plus 18.33%). This is significantly lower than the 39.6% rate that would apply with a sole proprietorship or pass-through entity.

If the time value of money is taken into account, the combined effective rate for QSBCs is even lower, because the capital gain component is deferred until Dedrick sells his stock. In contrast, the full 39.6% tax bite is due annually if a pass-through entity or sole proprietorship is used.

This Example illustrates the benefits of "splitting income" with a QSBC and thereby taking full advantage of the favorable graduated corporate tax rates and the gain exclusion when the stock is sold.

Finally, if Dedrick never draws any salary from the corporation, there will be no federal payroll tax liability. If he is a sole proprietor or general partner in the same business, however, he may owe significant amounts of self-employment tax even if no funds are withdrawn from the venture.

Variation: Now assume Dedrick is subject to the individual AMT at the 28% rate and that 42% of any excluded gain is added to his AMT tax base. For AMT purposes, the QSBC gain will initially be taxed at 14% (28% of the 50% nonexcluded portion of the gain). However, the preference will generate an additional AMT liability of 5.88% (42% of the 50% gain exclusion amount, taxed at 28%). Therefore, the effective shareholder-level tax rate is actually 19.88%, which is only marginally better than the 20% maximum rate that generally applies to long-term capital gains from stock sales.

7.03 QUALIFIED SMALL BUSINESS STOCK DEFINED

In order to take advantage of the 50% gain exclusion, three hurdles must be cleared:

1. The stock must be qualified small business stock,
2. The shareholder must satisfy certain rules, and
3. The limitation on excludable gain must not be exceeded.

What Is Qualified Small Business Stock?

To meet the definition of *qualified small business stock*, the stock must be issued after August 10, 1993, by a corporation that is a QSBC as of the date of issuance. A QSBC is a domestic C corporation that is *not*:

- A domestic international sales corporation (DISC);
- A corporation that has an IRC §936 election in effect;
- A REIT, REMIC, or regulated investment company (mutual fund); or
- A cooperative.

The following additional restrictions also apply:

- During substantially all of the stockholder's holding period, the corporation generally cannot hold more than 10% of its assets in the form of real property not used in the active conduct of a qualified trade or business (see below for what constitutes a qualified trade or business).

- During substantially all of the stockholder's holding period, the corporation cannot own portfolio stock or securities with value in excess of 10% of its net worth.

- At all times after August 10, 1993, through the date of issuance of the stock in question, the corporation cannot hold cash (including cash from the stock issue) plus other property with aggregate adjusted basis in excess of $50 million. For this purpose, contributed property is considered to have basis of FMV. If the $50 million limit is exceeded, it does not affect a prior issue of qualified stock. The corporation will simply be unable to issue additional qualifying stock.

- During substantially all of the stockholder's holding period, at least 80% (by value) of the corporation's gross assets must be used in the active conduct of qualified trades or businesses, which do *not* include the following:

  —The provision of personal or professional services;

  —The ownership, dealing, or renting of real property;

  —Any farming business;

  —Any business of operating a hotel, motel, restaurant, or similar business;

  —Any banking, insurance, leasing, financing, investing, or similar business; or

  —Any business involving the production or extraction of products for which percentage depletion is available.

What Are the Shareholder Rules?

The gain exclusion is available to shareholders who meet several conditions:

1. The shareholder must *not* be a C corporation.
2. The holding period for the QSBC stock must be more than *five* years.
3. The stock must have been acquired upon its original issue in exchange for:

- Money or other property (other than stock);
- As compensation for services provided to the issuing corporation; or
- In a tax-free transfer or conversion (such as under IRC §351).

For stock owned by a partnership, an S corporation, a common trust fund, or a regulated investment company, the gain exclusion is available at the partner, shareholder, or participant level if:

1. The entity held the stock more than five years, and
2. The partner, shareholder, or participant held an interest in the entity (which did not increase during the time the stock was held) when the entity acquired the stock and at all times thereafter.

> **OBSERVATION:** *Stock issued on August 11, 1993, and held until August 12, 1998, would satisfy both the issuance date and five-year holding period rules. Therefore, August 12, 1998, is the earliest date that a stock sale could qualify for the 50% gain exclusion.*

7.04 LIMITATIONS ON GAIN EXCLUSION UPON SALE OF QSBC STOCK

There *are* limits on the amount of gain eligible for the 50% exclusion [IRC §1202(b)(1)]. In any taxable year, the eligible gain is limited to the *greater* of:

1. 10 times the taxpayer's aggregate adjusted basis in the qualified small business stock that is sold, or
2. $10 million reduced by the amount of eligible gain taken into account in prior taxable years for dispositions of stock issued by the corporation ($5 million for married filing separate status).

If the taxpayer contributed appreciated property for his or her QSBC stock, the property's basis is considered to be the FMV on the contribution date for purposes of computing the gain potentially eligible for exclusion and for applying the 10 times the stock basis limitation rule [IRC §1202(i)(1)].

In effect, the second limitation above is a lifetime limitation: It applies to the *cumulative* gains recognized by the taxpayer from dispositions of stock in a particular QSBC.

There is no carryover of gain amounts in excess of the limitation amount.

Example 7.04(1): Limitations on Gain Eligible for Exclusion   Buster, a married taxpayer filing a joint return, is limited by the $10 million rule for the taxable year in question. Under that limitation, the maximum gain that Buster can exclude in the taxable year is $5 million (50% of the $10 million eligible gain limitation).

However, if the 10 times the basis limitation gives Buster a better answer, he can use that, in which case there is no dollar cap on the amount of gain eligible for the 50% exclusion. Instead, the eligible gain limitation depends on the basis of the stock. See the following Examples.

Example 7.04(2): The $10 Million Rule   Chester is a married individual who files a joint return. If he sells QSBC stock with a basis of $700,000 for a gain of $20 million, the maximum gain eligible for the 50% exclusion is the *greater* of:

- $7 million (10 times the basis of the stock sold), or
- $10 million reduced by eligible gains taken into account in prior taxable years.

Assuming no previous gains, Chester's maximum eligible gain is $10 million (because that is the greater amount). Thus, he can exclude $5 million of gain (50% of the $10 million eligible gain limitation) in computing his taxable income for the year the stock is sold.

Example 7.04(3): "10 Times the Basis" Rule   Dahlia, a married individual filing a joint return, sells QSBC stock with basis of $2 million for a gain of $11 million. In earlier years, Dahlia had taken eligible gains of $4 million into account.
For Dahlia, the maximum gain eligible for exclusion is the *greater* of:

- $20 million (10 times the basis), or
- $6 million ($10 million less the $4 million already "used up" in Dahlia's prior tax years).

Thus, Dahlia's entire $11 million gain is eligible for the 50% exclusion (under the "10 times the basis" limitation), and she can exclude $5.5 million (50% of the actual gain).

> **OBSERVATION:** *As Example 7.04(3) illustrates, there is no limit on the dollar amount of the eligible gain if the "10 times the basis" rule applies. Therefore, when very large gains will be recognized upon the sale of QSBC stock, it may be beneficial to sell additional stock (with additional basis) so the "10 times the basis" rule—rather than the $10 million rule—will apply.*

7.05 GAIN ROLLOVER PRIVILEGE

The Taxpayer Relief Act of 1997 added a new gain rollover provision for QSBC stockholders. The rollover rule applies to stock sales after August 5, 1997, if the selling taxpayer elects rollover treatment [IRC §1045]. As is the case for the gain exclusion benefit, C corporation shareholders are ineligible. Partnerships, S corporations, common trust funds, and regulated investment companies can qualify. However C corporation participants in such pass-through entities are still ineligible (for example, a C corporation partner in a partnership holding QSBC shares or a C corporation shareholder in a regulated investment company).

Under the rollover rule, the amount of gain recognized is limited to the excess of QSBC stock sales proceeds over the amount reinvested to purchase other QSBC shares ("replacement stock") during a 60-day period. (The 60-day period commences on the date of sale.) The amount of gain rolled over into replacement stock reduces the tax basis of those shares.

The QSBC stock that is sold must have been held over six months. In addition, the replacement stock corporation must satisfy the active business requirement (explained earlier in this section) during the first six months after the replacement stock is acquired [IRC §1045(b)(4)(B)].

If the replacement stock still qualifies as QSBC stock when it is sold, the 50% gain exclusion is available, provided the five-year holding period rule is met. The holding period of the stock sold in the earlier rollover transaction is "tacked on" to the actual holding period of the replacement stock in determining the holding period of the replacement stock for purposes of the five-year rule [IRC §1223].

If the replacement stock still qualifies a QSBC stock when it is sold and it has been held over six months, the gain rollover privilege will also be available (repetitive rollovers are allowed).

Revenue Procedure 98-48 (1998-38 IRB) describes how to make the gain rollover election. The election deadline is the due date (including extensions) for filing the tax return for the year the QSBC stock is sold.

> **OBSERVATION:** *The gain rollover privilege allows a QSBC shareholder to "cash out" on a tax-deferred basis. In fact, this can be done repetitively, as long as the shareholder continues to roll over all sales proceeds into new QSBC investments. The shareholder will still be eligible to take advantage of the 50% gain exclusion benefit upon disposing of his or her final stock investment, provided the company in question is still a QSBC and provided the five-year holding period rule has been met.*

Example 7.05(01): Rolling Over QSBC Stock Sale Gains   On January 1, 1996, Rebecca paid $20,000 for 200 shares of newly issued stock in GrowCo, Inc. Assume the GrowCo shares meet the definition of QSBC stock throughout her holding period, which ends on June 1, 1999. At that time, Rebecca sells her shares for $100,000. Within 60 days, she reinvests the entire amount in newly issued shares of FastCo Inc. Assume FastCo meets the active business requirement for at least six months after Rebecca's investment.

Rebecca elects to roll over her entire $80,000 of her GrowCo gain. In doing so, her basis in the new FastCo stock is reduced from $100,000 to $20,000. Her holding period for the FastCo shares is considered to begin on January 1, 1996, because the holding period of her GrowCo shares is tacked on to the actual time she owns the FastCo stock.

As a result, Rebecca will be eligible for the 50% gain exclusion if she sells her FastCo shares for a profit after January 1, 2001 (assuming the shares still meet the definition of QSBC stock at that time).

Alternatively, Rebecca can sell her FastCo shares at any time after meeting the more-than-six-months holding period rule, and again roll over her gain by reinvesting in QSBC replacement stock within 60 days. Her next QSBC investment would still potentially be eligible for the 50% gain exclusion when it is sold.

7.06 QSBCs COMPARED TO OTHER ENTITY CHOICES

The entity selection software program that comes with this book is designed to help the practitioner make a choice-of-entity recommendation that is consistent with the major tax and nontax issues facing the client. If the program points to the QSBC as the apparently best choice, this chapter and Chapter 6 (covering C corporations in general) can be reviewed to solidify that conclusion.

Generally, the advantages and disadvantages of QSBCs are the same as those of "regular" C corporations. These are discussed at length in Chapter 6. However, the C corporation disadvantage of double taxation is mitigated by the 50% gain exclusion rule that potentially applies to sales of QSBC stock.

See sections 6.04 and 6.05 of Chapter 6 for comparisons of C corporations to other entity choices.

Comparing QSBCs to LLPs is not meaningful, because LLPs generally are attractive only for the conduct of professional practices. Such practices cannot use QSBCs, because they are not qualified trades or businesses under the restrictions explained in section 7.03 of this chapter.

The major disadvantages of the QSBC are its restrictions on the size of the business, types of eligible businesses, and types of assets. In addition, stock must be held for more than five years to qualify for the gain exclusion, and C corporation stockholders do not qualify at all. Thus, in some cases the potential benefits of QSBC status simply will not be available.

7.07 SUMMARY STATEMENT ON WHEN QSBCs ARE ATTRACTIVE

The QSBC is, in effect, a special breed of C corporation. Therefore, the QSBC represents an attractive alternative to pass-through entities, single-member LLCs, and sole proprietorships in the same circumstances as would a "regular" C corporation. See section 6.05 of Chapter 6.

Because the QSBC gain exclusion and gain rollover breaks are tentative rather than guaranteed, the author feels they should be viewed as "icing on the cake" when C corporation status is the preferred choice. In other words, potential QSBC tax benefits should not be viewed as reasons to forego pass-through entity status.

Appendix 7A: Analysis of Effective Tax Rates on QSBC Income

Explanation: In assessing the attractiveness of a C corporation that will qualify as a QSBC versus a pass-through entity (LLC, partnership, S corporation, or single-member LLC), a critical issue is the effective combined tax rate (at the entity and owner levels) that will apply to income earned from the activity. Obviously, if a pass-through entity is used, there is no entity-level tax, but the owners may be high-income individuals who are subject to marginal tax rates as high as 39.6% (see Table 2 below). In such cases, a single level of taxation at high marginal rates may be more expensive than double taxation of QSBC income, as shown in Table 3.

Table 1: Current QSBC Federal Income Tax Rate Schedule

Taxable Income Over	But Not Over	Tax Rate
$0	$50,000	15%
$50,000	$75,000	25%
$75,000	$100,000	34%
$100,000	$335,000	39%
$335,000	$10,000,000	34%
$10,000,000	$15,000,000	35%
$15,000,000	$18,333,333	38%
$18,333,333		35%

As can be seen, the first $75,000 of a QSBC's income is taxed at significantly lower rates than would apply to the same income earned by individual taxpayers (see Table 2 below). This is especially true if the income from the activity under consideration will be piled on top of other income (from salaries, other investments, etc.) of high-income individuals. In such cases, the incremental taxable income from the activity may be subject to a 39.6% tax rate if a pass-through entity is used. This means a pass-through entity may be forced to distribute 39.6% of its taxable income to its owners so they can pay their personal tax liabilities. For businesses that need to maximize current cash flow to finance growth, this can be a heavy price to pay for the benefit of pass-through taxation.

Table 2: 1999 Individual Federal Income Tax Rates

Income for Joint Filers	Income for Singles	Tax Rate
$0 to $43,050	$0 to $ 25,750	15%
$43,051 to $104,050	$25,751 to $62,450	28%
$104,051 to $158,550	$62,451 to $130,250	31%
$158,551 to $283,150	$130,251 to $283,150	36%
Over $283,150	Over $283,150	39.6%

Table 3 shows the combined effective tax rate on a QSBC's taxable income assuming the income (net of tax) is retained and adds to the value of the corporate stock dollar for dollar. The stock is assumed to be sold for a long-term capital gain taxed at an effective rate of 10% (after the 50% gain exclusion). The combined effective rate should be compared to the marginal individual rate (which can be as high as 39.6%, as shown in Table 2) that would apply if the income were instead earned by a pass-through entity.

Table 3: 1999 Combined QSBC and Individual Effective Tax Rates

QSBC Average Tax Rate	Individual Rate on LTCGs	Combined Rate
15%*	14%	26.9%
18.33%**	14%	29.8%
34%***	14%	43.2%

*15% average rate applies to taxable income up to $50,000.
**18.33% average rate applies to taxable income of $75,000.
***34% average rate applies to taxable income between $335,000 and $10 million.

OBSERVATION: *If the time value of money is taken into account, the combined rates shown above will be reduced. This is because the capital gain component of the combined rate on QSBC income is deferred until the stock is sold. In contrast, taxes on pass-through income must be paid currently.*

CAUTION: *42% of the excluded QSBC gain is treated as a tax preference item for AMT purposes under IRC §57(a)(8).*

Appendix 7B: Sample Client Letter When QSBC Appears to Be Best Entity Choice

Dear [Client name]:

This letter briefly summarizes some of the major considerations that went into your recent decision to form a new business to be operated as a C corporation. It is expected that the corporation will also meet the definition of a *qualified small business corporation* (QSBC). As a result, shareholders (other than C corporations) will potentially be eligible to exclude up to 50% of their gains upon sales of the corporation's stock or roll over their gains tax-free into new QSBC stock investments.

As we discussed, a number of restrictions must be met for a corporation to qualify for QSBC status, and shareholders must own their stock for more than five years to benefit from the gain exclusion provision (more than six months for the rollover privilege).

Limited Liability of Shareholders

The principal advantage of C corporation status is that the corporation is treated as a legal entity separate and distinct from its shareholders. Therefore, the corporation owns its own assets and is liable for its own debts. As a result, the personal assets of shareholders (including shareholder-employees) generally are beyond the reach of corporate creditors.

The liability-limiting protections offered by C corporations are substantial, but they should not be overstated. While the personal assets of shareholders are protected from "general" corporate debts and obligations (often referred to as "contract liabilities"), shareholders generally remain *exposed* to corporate liabilities resulting from their own tortious acts or professional errors and omissions. (*Tortious acts* are defined as wrongful acts leading to civil actions, other than those involving breach of contract.)

The issue of shareholders' exposure to liabilities related to tortious acts and professional errors and omissions is a matter of state law. If you have specific questions about this issue, we recommend you consult with your attorney.

Guarantees of Corporate Debts

Shareholders may be required on occasion to personally guarantee certain of the corporation's debts as a condition of obtaining financing or for other reasons.

Shareholders are personally obligated with respect to corporate debts that are specifically guaranteed, but shareholders are still protected against liability for other corporate debts.

Federal Income Tax Treatment of C Corporations

The key disadvantage of C corporations (including QSBCs) is that they are subject to double taxation. The double taxation issue can manifest itself in several ways, described briefly here.

Double Taxation of Corporate Dividends

The most common manifestation of double taxation is the treatment of C corporation dividend distributions to shareholders. In order for dividends to be available, the corporation must have earnings, and these are taxed at the corporate level. Dividends are also taxed as ordinary income to the recipient shareholders, but the payments are not deductible by the corporation.

Double Taxation on Sale of Stock

When a C corporation earns taxable income, there is no upward adjustment in the tax basis of the shareholders' stock. The retained income increases the value of the stock, which creates a bigger capital gain when shares are eventually sold. As a result, the retained income is, in effect, taxed again when shares are sold.

Because your corporation is expected to meet the definition of a *qualified small business corporation* (QSBC), the negative impact of double taxation on the sale of stock could be substantially reduced.

Double Taxation on Liquidation

In some cases, corporations seemingly can avoid the double taxation issue simply by not making dividend distributions. However, if the corporation holds appreciated property and eventually liquidates, the double taxation problem once again becomes a negative factor.

The property to be distributed in liquidation is treated as sold by the corporation for its fair market value (FMV). The corporation must then pay the resulting taxes. When the corporate assets are distributed to the shareholders in liquidation, shareholders recognize taxable gain to the extent the FMV of the liquidating distributions exceeds the tax basis in their shares. (The liquidation transaction is treated by shareholders as sales of their stock in exchange for the distributed cash and/or property.)

Because your corporation is expected to meet the definition of a QSBC, the negative impact of double taxation on the deemed sale of stock upon liquidation could be substantially reduced.

Double Taxation When Corporation Holds Appreciating Assets

If the corporation holds appreciating assets, the resulting gains will be subject to double taxation if the corporation sells them, if the corporation is liquidated, or if the corporate stock is sold.

We recommend that assets expected to appreciate significantly (such as real estate, patents, and copyrights) be owned by a pass-through entity (which is in turn owned by the C corporation's shareholders) if possible. The pass-through entity can then lease the assets to the C corporation. With this arrangement, the C corporation can reduce its taxable income by making deductible rental payments, which benefit its shareholders. Any gains upon the eventual sale of the appreciated assets owned by the pass-through entity will not be subject to double taxation.

Treatment of Corporate-Level Capital Gains

Long-term capital gains are taxed at a maximum rate of 20% if earned by pass-through entities owned by individuals or if earned by a sole proprietorship business.

Unfortunately, capital gains of a C corporation are taxed like all other taxable income rather than at a preferential rate. In addition, corporate capital gains are subject to double taxation. To the extent they increase the value of the corporate stock, such gains result in additional taxable gain at the shareholder level when the stock is sold. (With QSBCs, this negative result is mitigated to the extent the gain exclusion or gain rollover rules apply.) And if the gains are distributed as dividends, they are treated as ordinary income at the shareholder level.

Treatment of Corporate-Level Tax-Exempt Income

While tax-exempt income is not taxed at the corporate level, the income is not truly tax-free because of the effect at the shareholder level.

To the extent the corporation's tax-exempt income increases the value of the corporate stock, additional taxable gain is recognized at the shareholder level when the stock is sold. (With QSBCs, this negative result is mitigated to the extent the gain exclusion or gain rollover rules apply.) And if the tax-exempt income is distributed as dividends, the result is ordinary income at the shareholder level.

In contrast, tax-exempt income of pass-through entities is passed through to the owners (where it retains its tax-exempt character), and the income increases the tax basis of ownership interests. As a result, there is no further tax impact if the tax-exempt income is later distributed or if the ownership interests are later sold.

The "Reasonable Compensation" Issue

Corporations often attempt to solve the double taxation problem by "zeroing out" corporate income with deductible compensation payments to shareholder-employees. As a result, the IRS frequently raises the so-called reasonable compensation issue when C corporations are audited.

When challenged by the IRS, the corporation must be able to show that the purported compensation payments were not dividends in disguise. In other words, the compensation amounts must be "reasonable." If they are not, the IRS will reclassify the excessive amounts as dividends and reduce the corporation's compensation deductions accordingly.

The Accumulated Earnings Tax

The accumulated earnings tax (AET) exists to discourage unwarranted accumulations of taxable income. The AET does *not* apply if there is no motive to avoid tax at the shareholder level or if the earnings are necessary to meet the reasonable needs of the business.

However, if the AET *does* apply, the tax is 39.6% of the accumulated taxable income. Accumulated taxable income is essentially taxable income with some adjustments, reduced by the amount retained to meet the reasonable business needs of the corporation.

The AET can be avoided by distributing "excess" corporate income in the form of dividends. However, dividends are nondeductible to the corporation, and they represent taxable ordinary income to recipient shareholders.

Potential Mitigating Effect of "Splitting Income"

The ability of high-bracket individuals to "split income" with a QSBC and thereby take advantage of the graduated corporate rates (which can be as low as 15%) can counteract the negative effects of double taxation. (See Exhibit 1.)

Note also that if all income is left inside a corporation, there will be no federal payroll taxes for the shareholders. However, if the business is operated as an LLC or a general partnership, the owners may owe significant amounts of self-employment (SE) tax on the pass-through income. SE tax is also owed on the income of a single-owner business operated as a sole proprietorship.

Graduated Corporate Tax Rates Can Maximize Current Cash Flow

When a business intends to retain all its earnings indefinitely in order to internally finance its growth, the corporate tax rates can make C corporations very attractive compared to pass-through entities. A pass-through entity might have to distribute up to 39.6% of the taxable income earned by the business to enable the owners can pay their personal taxes.

Even at taxable income levels above $75,000, the tax rates for C corporations are significantly lower than those for individuals. As a result, the use of a C corporation can maximize the current cash flow of the business. It must be remembered, however, that the cost of this current benefit is the double taxation that may apply in later years. However, in the case of QSBCs, the effects of double taxation are lessened to the extent shareholders can exclude part of their stock sale gains or roll over their gains into new QSBC stock investments.

Tax Losses Cannot Be Passed Through to Owners

Unfortunately, tax losses incurred by a C corporation are not passed through to the shareholders. Instead, a C corporation's net operating losses (NOLs) can be used only to offset corporate taxable income earned in the 2 years preceding the NOL year or in the 20 years following the NOL year. If the taxable income earned in that period is less than the NOL, all or part of the NOL will expire without generating any tax benefit.

In contrast, tax losses incurred by pass-through entities are passed through to their owners where they generally can be used currently to offset taxable income from other sources (subject to other potential limitations such as the passive loss rules).

When significant tax losses are expected to be incurred (as is often the case in the early years of a new venture), generally it is advisable to use a pass-through entity rather than a C corporation.

Comparison to Single-Member LLC

If state law and applicable professional standards (if any), allow your business to operate as a single-member LLC, this will generally be preferable to operating as a solely owned QSBC. Exceptions would be when: (1) the favorable C corporation tax rates and special QSBC tax benefits cancel out the ill effects of double taxation or (2) you as the owner prefer the (arguably) greater legal certainty of C corporation status.

Conclusion

As we discussed, you have considered the above advantages and disadvantages and have concluded that a C corporation qualifying as a QSBC is the best choice in your circumstances.

We appreciate the opportunity to consult with you as you make the important decision of choosing the most advantageous type of entity under which to operate your new venture. We look forward to working with you in the future as your corporation is formed and enters the operating phase.

Very truly yours,

Exhibit 1: Analysis of Effective Tax Rates on QSBC Income

Explanation: In assessing the attractiveness of a C corporation that will qualify as a QSBC versus a pass-through entity (LLC, partnership, S corporation, or single-member LLC), a critical issue is the effective combined tax rate (at the entity and owner levels) that will apply to income earned from the activity. Obviously, if a pass-through entity is used, there is no entity-level tax, but the owners may be high-income individuals who are subject to marginal tax rates as high as 39.6% (see Table 2 below). In such cases, a single level of taxation at high marginal rates may be more expensive than double taxation of QSBC income, as shown in Table 3.

Table 1: Current QSBC Federal Income Tax Rate Schedule

Taxable Income Over	But Not Over	Tax Rate
$0	$50,000	15%
$50,000	$75,000	25%
$75,000	$100,000	34%
$100,000	$335,000	39%
$335,000	$10,000,000	34%
$10,000,000	$15,000,000	35%
$15,000,000	$18,333,333	38%
$18,333,333		35%

As can be seen, the first $75,000 of a QSBC's income is taxed at significantly lower rates than would apply to the same income earned by individual taxpayers (see Table 2 below). This is especially true if the income from the activity under consideration will be piled on top of other income (from salaries, other investments, etc.) of high-income individuals. In such cases, the incremental taxable income from the activity may be subject to a 39.6% tax rate if a pass-through entity is used. This means a pass-through entity may be forced to distribute 39.6% of its taxable income to its owners so they can pay their personal tax liabilities. For businesses that need to maximize current cash flow to finance growth, this can be a heavy price to pay for the benefit of pass-through taxation.

Table 2: 1999 Individual Federal Income Tax Rates

Income for Joint Filers	Income for Singles	Tax Rate
$0 to $43,050	$0 to $25,750	15%
$43,051 to $104,050	$25,751 to $62,450	28%
$104,051 to $158,550	$62,451 to $130,250	31%
$158,551 to $283,150	$130,251 to $283,150	36%
Over $283,150	Over $283,150	39.6%

Table 3 shows the combined effective tax rate on a QSBC's taxable income assuming the income (net of tax) is retained and adds to the value of the corporate stock dollar for dollar. The stock is assumed to be sold for a long-term capital gain taxed at an effective rate of 10% (after the 50% gain exclusion). The combined effective rate should be compared to the marginal individual rate (which can be as high as 39.6%, as shown in Table 2) that would apply if the income were instead earned by a pass-through entity.

Table 3: 1999 Combined QSBC and Individual Effective Tax Rates

QSBC Average Tax Rate	Individual Rate on LTCGs	Combined Rate
15%*	14%	26.9%
18.33%**	14%	29.8%
34%***	14%	43.2%

*15% average rate applies to taxable income up to $50,000.

**18.33% average rate applies to taxable income of $75,000.

***34% average rate applies to taxable income between $335,000 and $10 million.

OBSERVATION: *If the time value of money is taken into account, the combined rates shown above will be reduced. This is because the capital gain component of the combined rate on QSBC income is deferred until the stock is sold. In contrast, taxes on pass-through income must be paid currently.*

CAUTION: *42% of the excluded QSBC gain is treated as a tax preference item for AMT purposes.*

CHAPTER 8 • S CORPORATIONS— BIG STRENGTHS AND BIG WEAKNESSES

CONTENTS

8.01 INTRODUCTION

The most important advantage offered by corporations is that they, arguably, provide the greatest certainty in protecting the personal assets of business owners. This is true of both S corporations and C corporations (discussed in Chapter 6).

In other words, for legal purposes there are no differences between S and C corporations. Both are formed under applicable state corporation laws, and the legal relationships among the corporation, its shareholders, and third parties (such as creditors) are identical.

The distinction between the two is that S corporations qualify for and have made the election to be treated as pass-through entities under the federal income tax laws. Thus, when S corporations and C corporations are compared, the focus is solely on the differing rules that apply to each under the Internal Revenue Code (and differing state and local tax rules, when relevant).

While S corporations are free from double taxation, this advantage comes at a relatively heavy price. As discussed in this chapter, the strict S corporation eligibility rules often make qualifying for S status difficult if not impossible. However, the Small Business Job Protection Act of 1996 liberalized the qualification rules to a significant extent.

When pass-through taxation is desired and the S corporation eligibility rules cannot be met (or would cause the owners undue hardship), the alternatives are partnerships (see Chapter 5), LLCs (see Chapter 3), and LLPs (see Chapter 4). In limited circumstances, sole proprietorships also offer a reasonable alternative to S corporations (see section 8.05 of this chapter and Chapter 9).

8.02 FEDERAL INCOME TAX CONSIDERATIONS

S Corporations versus Partnerships

A misconception that should be immediately dispelled is that the federal income tax rules for S corporations and partnerships are virtually identical. This is simply not the case. While both S corporations and partnerships are pass-though entities (and therefore not subject to double taxation), there are *major* differences between them—most of which favor partnerships (including LLCs treated as partnerships for federal income tax purposes).

The most significant differences are:

- Partners can receive additional tax basis (for loss deduction purposes) from entity-level liabilities, while S corporation shareholders can receive additional tax basis only from loans they make to the corporation. (Shareholder guarantees of corporate debt have no effect on shareholder basis.)
- Partners who purchase a partnership interest from another partner can step up the tax basis of their shares of partnership assets by having the partnership make an IRC §754 election. No such benefit is available to S corporation shareholders, and the result can be so-called inside/outside basis problems. See Example 8.02(3) later in this section.
- Partners and partnerships have much greater flexibility to make tax-free transfers of appreciated property than do S corporations and their shareholders.
- Partnerships can make disproportionate allocations of tax losses and other tax items among the partners. In contrast, all S corporation pass-through items must be allocated among the shareholders strictly in proportion to stock ownership.
- S corporations that are former C corporations remain potentially exposed to several corporate-level taxes, as discussed later in this section.
- Under the Internal Revenue Code, S corporations are subject to a number of strict eligibility requirements, as discussed later in this section. Failure to meet these requirements means the corporation will be taxed as a C corporation and therefore be subjected to double taxation. In contrast, partnerships do not have to jump through hoops to be treated as pass-through entities.

See Chapter 5 for a complete discussion of the differences between S corporation taxation and partnership taxation, including the several disadvantageous tax rules that apply to partnerships but not to S corporations.

S Corporation Pass-Through Taxation— The Basics

Except for the specific corporate-level taxes discussed later in this section, S corporations are not tax-paying entities. Instead, the corporation's items of income, gain, deduction, loss, and credit are passed through to the shareholders, who then take those items into account in their own tax returns.

Stock Basis Adjustments

When the corporation's income and losses are passed through to its shareholders, the basis in their stock is adjusted accordingly. Specifically, a shareholder's basis is increased by his or her passed-through share of the corporation's income and gains and decreased by the corresponding share of losses and deductions.

This procedure—which ensures that income is subject to only a single level of taxation, at the owner level–is termed pass-through taxation. (Pass-through taxation also applies to partnerships—see Chapter 5.)

Distributions to Shareholders

Unless the S corporation has earnings and profits (from years when it operated as a C corporation), nonliquidating cash and property distributions to shareholders are *not* treated as dividends. Instead, the distributions reduce the shareholder's basis in his or her shares. Distributions in excess of basis trigger taxable gain to the shareholder. (See IRC §§1361–1379, which constitute the so-called Subchapter S provisions of the Code.)

Multi-Year Impact of Pass-Through Taxation

Avoiding double taxation of corporate income makes a big difference when the corporation earns substantial amounts of taxable income over several years. For calculation templates with which to estimate the multi-year benefits of pass-through taxation, see General Practice Aids 5–8 in Chapter 10.

> *CAUTION: As explained in Chapter 6, the C corporation tax rates on the first $75,000 of taxable income are considerably lower than the individual tax rates that apply if the same income is passed through by an S corporation. Even at higher income levels, the C corporation rates are still lower than the individual rates. If all income is expected to be retained in the business indefinitely (for example, to finance growing receivable and inventory levels), the more favorable C corporation rates can partially or wholly offset the negative effects of double taxation. In such cases, operating as a C corporation may be preferable to S status. This is even more likely to be the case if the corporation meets the definition of a QSBC (see Chapter 7); shareholders may be able to exclude up to 50% of their taxable gains on the sale of QSBC stock, which in some cases may eliminate the negative effects of double taxation completely. QSBC shareholders are also eligible to roll over stock sale gains by reinvesting in new QSBC stock issued by a different company.*

Pass-Through of Taxable Losses

Often, a new business expects substantial tax losses in its first few years of operation. If the business is conducted via a S corporation (or other pass-through entity), the losses can be passed through to the owners, where they can be deducted currently (subject to possible limitations under the basis, at-risk, and passive loss provisions).

In contrast, tax losses incurred by a C corporation remain trapped inside the entity in the form of net operating losses (NOLs). NOLs can be used only to offset taxable income earned in later years by the corporation. If no taxable income is earned, the NOLs expire after 20 years. If this happens, the tax losses never provide *any* tax benefit to the corporation or its shareholders.

> *RECOMMENDATION: When it is anticipated that significant losses will be incurred in the activity, the use of an S corporation (or other pass-through entity) rather than a C corporation should be strongly considered.*

Pass-Through of Capital Losses

If the business is expected to incur significant capital losses, S corporation status is preferred. The losses can be passed through to the owner(s), where they can offset up to $3,000 of ordinary income plus capital gains for the year. Any unused capital losses are carried forward to future years.

In contrast, if a C corporation is used, the capital losses are "trapped" inside the corporation where they can be used only to offset capital gains. Unused capital losses from a year can be carried back three years or carried forward five years. After the fifth year, unused capital loss carryforwards expire.

> *RECOMMENDATION: When it is anticipated that significant tax losses will be incurred in the activity, the use of an S corporation (or other pass-through entity) rather than a C corporation should be strongly considered.*

Pass-Through of Capital Gains

An S corporation's long-term capital gains from capital assets held over 18 months are passed through to shareholders, where they are taxed *once*, at a maximum rate of 20% for individual taxpayers. In contrast, C corporations pay the regular corporate tax rate (usually 34%) on long-term capital gains. If the gains are paid out later as dividends, they constitute ordinary income and may be taxed at rates as high as 39.6%.

In other words, the double taxation of C corporation long-term capital gains amounts to a stiff penalty compared to the results if the gains are earned by an S corporation.

> *RECOMMENDATION: When it is anticipated that significant long-term capital gains will be earned in the activity, the use of an S corporation (or other pass-through entity) rather than a C corporation should be strongly considered.*

Pass-Through of Tax-Exempt Income

An S corporation's tax-exempt income is passed through to shareholders, where it retains its tax-exempt character. The tax-exempt income also increases the basis of the shareholders' stock.

While C corporations pay no corporate-level tax on tax-exempt income, that income is taxed as ordinary income at the shareholder level if it is paid out later as dividends. The result is that what started out as tax-exempt income of a C corporation may end up as dividend income taxed at rates as high as 39.6%.

If the C corporation retains the tax-exempt income, it increases the value of the corporation and results in larger gains when shareholders sell their stock. Ultimately, therefore, a C corporation's tax-exempt income is going to be taxed at the shareholder level one way or the other.

> **RECOMMENDATION:** *When it is anticipated that significant tax-exempt income will be earned in the activity, the use of an S corporation (or other pass-through entity) rather than a C corporation should be strongly considered.*

Election of S Status

S corporation status is elected by filing Form 2553 (Election by a Small Business Corporation). The form can be filed during the preceding tax year for an election to become effective for the following tax year.

For an S election to be effective for the *current* tax year, it must be filed by the fifteenth day of the third month of that year. (In most cases, this translates into a March 15 deadline.)

Newly formed corporations generally will intend for the election of S status to be effective for the initial tax year. The election must be filed by the fifteenth day of the third month after the "activation date" of the corporation. This is the earliest date the corporation has shareholders, acquires assets, or begins conducting business. [See Regs. §1.1362-6(a)(2)(C).]

Other S Corporation Tax Advantages

Compared to C corporations, S corporations have a number of tax advantages beyond those described earlier in this section. Most of these are reflections of the fact that S corporations are not subject to double taxation.

PHC Tax Is Not Applicable

Unlike C corporations, S corporations are not subject to the personal holding company (PHC) tax. (See Chapter 6 for a discussion of this tax.)

Accumulated Earnings Tax Is Not Applicable

Unlike C corporations, S corporations are not subject to the accumulated earnings tax (AET). (See Chapter 6 for a discussion of this tax.)

Reasonable Compensation Issue Is Not Applicable

Because all S corporation taxable income is passed through to shareholders, there is no need to "drain off" the corporation's income by attempting to characterize amounts paid to shareholder-employees as deductible compensation payments. The thorny issue of reasonable compensation does not arise in the context of S corporations. (See Chapter 6 for a discussion of the reasonable compensation issue as it relates to C corporations.)

> *CAUTION: As described below, S corporations may face the issue of attempting to justify unreasonably* low *compensation levels for shareholder-employees. (Low compensation levels minimize federal payroll taxes.)*

Treatment of Shareholder-Level Interest Expense

Often, individuals will take out personal loans to acquire or capitalize a business. Under the so-called interest tracing rules (set forth in Temp. Regs. §1.163-8T), individual taxpayers must classify their interest expense as business, passive, investment, or personal. While business interest is fully deductible, there are limitations on the deductibility of passive and investment interest, and personal interest is 100% nondeductible.

When an individual's interest expense can be traced to debt used to acquire S corporation stock or to inject capital into an S corporation, it generally will be classified as either business or passive interest expense. If the individual materially participates in the corporation's business, the interest will be treated as 100% deductible business interest (this is an "above the line" deduction). If the individual does not materially participate, the interest will be passive and will be treated under the passive activity loss rules. [See IRS Notice 89-35 (1989-1 CB 675).] Note that essentially the same rules apply to partners who borrow money to acquire partnership interests of contribute capital to a partnership.

If the material participation test is met, the shareholder of an S corporation is in a better tax position than he or she would be in a C corporation. Debt that an individual incurs to acquire C corporation stock or to inject capital into a C corporation is treated as investment interest. It can be deducted only to the extent of investment income, and even then it is a "below the line" itemized deduction [IRC §163(d)].

> *RECOMMENDATION: If the business owners are individuals who will incur substantial interest on personal loans used to capitalize the business, the use of an S corporation (or other pass-through entity) rather than a C corporation should be strongly considered.*

Potential Ability to Minimize Federal Payroll Taxes

Like all employers, S corporations must pay federal payroll taxes, which are the employer's half of the FICA tax and the FUTA tax. In turn, S corporation employees (including shareholder-employees) must pay the employee's half of the FICA tax.

For 1999, the combined employer and employee FICA tax rate is 15.3% on the first $72,600 of compensation income and 2.9% on amounts over

$72,600. Clearly, the FICA tax can be substantial when compensation amounts are relatively large. Self-employed individuals face the same rates in the form of the self-employment tax, but they must pay both the employer and employee halves of the tax.

Under the right circumstances, however, S corporations can effectively minimize federal payroll taxes. For this discussion, federal payroll taxes mean FICA and self-employment (SE) taxes collectively.

The taxable income passed through to S corporation shareholders is *not* subject to self-employment (SE) tax at the shareholder level. Cash distributions from S corporations to their shareholder-employees also are *not* subject to SE tax or FICA tax, *unless* the distributions are in fact disguised compensation. (If the IRS successfully asserts that distributions are disguised compensation, the FICA tax would apply to those distributions.)

The effect of the above rules is that S corporations can set compensation levels for shareholder-employees at relatively low levels and thereby minimize federal payroll taxes. To meet their actual compensation needs, the shareholder-employees can be given additional cash in the form of dividends (which generally are received as tax-free offsets against the basis in their stock).

> **REALITY CHECK:** *If compensation amounts are unreasonably low and the corporation is audited, the IRS will attempt to recharacterize all or part of purported S corporation dividend payments as disguised salary. The corporation will then be hit with back FICA taxes, interest, and possibly penalties.*

Example 8.02(1): Federal Payroll Taxes—S Corporation versus Partnership As 50/50 co-owners, Sport and Tessa are forming a new business that can be operated as either an S corporation or a partnership. The business is projected to earn annual taxable income of $200,000, before retirement plan contributions of $10,000 for each owner and $5,000 of medical insurance premiums for each owner.

Results with Partnership

If the business is operated as a partnership, each owner's SE income is $100,000. For SE tax purposes, 100% of the passed-through share of partnership trade or business income is subject to SE tax, and there are no deductions for retirement plan contributions or medical insurance premiums. Thus, each owner's 1999 SE tax liability is $11,902.40 (15.3% of $72,600 plus 2.9% of $27,400).

Results with S Corporation

Now assume the business is operated as an S corporation and that each owner can be paid a reasonable salary of $55,000. The corporation will also make contributions of $10,000 for each owner to the company pension plan, $5,000 will be paid for each owner's medical insurance. Of the remaining $60,000 of income, $30,000 is distributed to each to the two owners as tax-free dividends.

FICA taxes are due only on the stated salaries of $55,000 plus the medical insurance premiums (which are included in wages for FIT and FICA tax purposes per Revenue Ruling 91-26 (1991-1 CB 184). Thus, the FICA tax liability for each owner is only $9,180 (15.3% of $60,000).

Compare this amount to the $11,902.40 of SE tax that is due for each owner if the business is operated as a partnership. Operating as an S corporation saves over $2,700 in federal payroll taxes for each owner.

Family Income Tax Planning Possibilities

The taxable income of an S corporation must be allocated and passed through to shareholders strictly in proportion to stock ownership percentages. In family-owned corporations, this would seem to prevent attempts to shift income from high marginal rate shareholders (typically the parents) to lower marginal rate shareholders (typically the children).

As the following Example illustrates, however, shareholder-employee compensation amounts can be manipulated to achieve family tax-planning goals.

> **Example 8.02(2): Shifting S Corporation Income for Family Tax-Planning Reasons**   Deion owns 50% of the stock of Deion, Inc., an S corporation. Deionette and Deano, his two children own the remaining stock—25% each. Deion has substantial income from sources other than Deion, Inc., and he is in the 39.6% tax bracket in 1999. Neither of his children has other income, and they are both in the 15% bracket.
>
> The company has always paid Deion a salary equal to 50% of the corporation's taxable income before salary expenses. This has averaged about $50,000 per year. In 1999, however, the corporation has such a good year that Deion has decided to simply take a salary of $50,000; his usual 50% would have amounted to $100,000.
>
> Reducing the corporation's deduction for compensation to its shareholder-employee by $50,000 causes the taxable income that is passed through to all shareholders to be increased by the same amount. This increases the taxable income passed through to Deionette and Deano by $12,500 each (25% of $50,000), and in effect shifts $25,000 out of Deion's return (where it would be taxed at 39.6%) and into his children's returns (where it is taxed at only 15%).
>
> **Reality Check:** If Deion's 1999 salary of $50,000 is noticeably low compared to past salary amounts, his qualifications, and the nature and extent of his work, upon audit the IRS may attempt to reallocate some of the business's taxable income from his children back to him under IRC §1366(e). This Code section gives the IRS the power to reallocate income among family members to properly reflect the value of the services they perform and/or their interests in corporate capital. For purposes of this rule, family members include spouses, ancestors, lineal descendants, and trusts created for such persons. In this Example, however, the IRS probably would be unsuccessful, because Deion's 1996 salary is consistent with prior years' compensation.

Cash Method Accounting

As discussed in Chapter 6, some C corporations are not permitted to use the cash method of accounting. In contrast, S corporations generally *are* able to use the cash method, enabling them to time the receipt of income and the payment of expenses at year end for tax-planning purposes.

> **CAUTION:** *S corporations that allocate more than 35% of their tax losses to limited entrepreneurs (shareholders not actively involved in management of the corporation) are prohibited from using the cash method. [See IRC §§448(a)(3) and (d)(3).]*

The Disadvantageous S Corporation Eligibility Rules

The tax advantages of S corporation status depend on meeting a number of eligibility rules under IRC §1361(b). Unfortunately, these rules greatly restrict stock ownership and capital structure possibilities, and therefore can make operating as an S corporation impossible, difficult, or simply unattractive.

If the eligibility rules are not met at any time during the tax year, the S status of the corporation is immediately terminated and the corporation falls under the C corporation taxation rules described in Chapter 6.

> **RECOMMENDATION:** *In evaluating the various business entity options, consideration should be given not only to the owners' immediate needs but to their probable needs in the foreseeable future. If the S corporation eligibility rules appear likely to create problems in the relatively near future, S corporation status probably is not the right choice.*

To qualify for S status, a corporation must:

- Be a domestic corporation;
- Have no more than 75 shareholders;
- Have no shareholders other than individuals who are U.S. citizens or resident aliens, estates, certain types of trusts, or certain tax-exempt entities;
- Have only one class of stock; and
- Not be an ineligible corporation by definition.

The 75-Shareholder Rule

The 75-shareholder limitation must be met on each day of the tax year. A husband and wife (and their estates) are treated as a single shareholder [IRC §1361(b)]. Obviously, the 75-shareholder limitation can hurt the ability of a business to raise capital, since the permitted number of investors is small.

Restrictions on Types of Shareholders

Only individuals (other than nonresident aliens), estates, and certain types of trusts are allowed to be shareholders of an S corporation [IRC §1361(b)(1)-(B)]. This imposes additional limitations on the ability to raise capital, since partnerships, other corporations, and foreign individuals are prevented from acquiring stock of S corporations.

Effective for tax years beginning after 1997, certain tax-exempt charitable organizations and qualified retirement plan trusts can also own S corporation stock. Each such entity counts as one shareholder for purposes of the 75-shareholder limitation.

IRC §1361(c) identifies the trusts permitted to own stock. Included are grantor trusts, qualified Subchapter S trusts (QSSTs), and electing small business trusts (ESBTs). The trust limitations can cause estate-planning and business succession headaches. With C corporations, partnerships, and LLCs, by contrast, ownership interests generally can be transferred to any type of trust without causing income tax problems.

> **RECOMMENDATION:** *When owners have estate-planning or business succession planning objectives, the S corporation shareholder restrictions should be examined carefully to determine if they will present major problems. These restrictions may make operating as an S corporation unattractive; it is better to come to that conclusion* before *the choice-of-entity decision is implemented. (See the discussion of family limited partnerships in Chapter 5.)*

The One-Class-of-Stock Rule

An S corporation can have only one class of stock [IRC §1361(b)(1)(D)]. This means all outstanding shares must have identical rights to distributions and liquidation proceeds under the corporation's governing provisions (the corporate charter, articles of incorporation, bylaws, and applicable state law).

Note that differences in voting rights are *not* considered to create more than one class of stock. Thus, an S corporation can have voting *and* nonvoting shares, as long as both types of stock have identical economic rights. However, convertible debt instruments, restricted stock, stock options, stock warrants, and certain buy–sell agreements can all cause a corporation to violate the one-class-of-stock rule.

S corporations may be hampered in raising capital because they cannot create equity interests with varying characteristics to meet the specific needs of different investors. For example, a partnership can create partnership interests with preferred returns on capital, disproportionate allocations of tax losses, and limited rights to share in gains upon sale of the business or the sale of certain assets. Such flexibility is impossible under the one-class-of-stock rule.

> **RECOMMENDATION:** *In situations where the one-class-of-stock rule eliminates the S corporation as an entity alternative, the use of a C corporation, partnership, or LLC should be considered.*

Corporations That Are Ineligible by Definition

By definition, certain corporations are ineligible for S status [IRC §1361(b)(2)]:

- Financial institutions allowed to deduct bad debts under IRC §585 or §593;

- Domestic international sales corporations (DISCs), or former DISCs;

- Insurance companies, other than certain casualty companies; and

- Certain corporations electing to take the IRC §936 possessions tax credit.

> **CAUTION:** *A former S corporation that has revoked or terminated its S status (thus reverting to C corporation status) must wait five years before reelecting S status, unless the IRS consents to an earlier reelection. [See IRC §1362(g).]*

Before 1996, S corporations were not allowed to own 80% or more of the stock of a subsidiary corporation without losing their S status. However, S corporations are now permitted to own any percentage of stock of C corporation subsidiaries. Each subsidiary must still pay corporate-level taxes, and dividends passed up to the S corporation parent will be still be passed through as taxable ordinary income to the S shareholders. If there are several 80%-or-more-owned C corporation subsidiaries, they can file a consolidated return among themselves, if that is desirable. Of course, the S corporation parent cannot be included in the consolidated return. (If the parent S corporation is a former C corporation, dividends from subsidiaries generally will *not* cause excess passive income problems.)

Now, S corporations can also have one or more wholly owned qualified Subchapter S subsidiaries (QSSSs). QSSSs are domestic corporations meeting the other S corporation qualification rules. For federal income tax purposes, QSSSs will be ignored (i.e., treated as unincorporated branches or divisions of the parent S corporation), and pass-through taxation will apply to the entire organization. In other words, only one Form 1120S will be required, even though the corporate structure actually includes several different legal entities. The bottom line is the QSSS rules allow S corporations to set up one or more corporate subsidiaries for liability protection reasons without the federal income tax complications ordinarily associated with a multiple-corporation structure.

Former C Corporations with Excess Passive Income

An S corporation that is a former C corporation with accumulated earnings and profits remaining from its C corporation years cannot earn more than 25% of gross receipts from passive sources in three consecutive years. If it does, its S status is terminated [IRC §1362(d)(3)].

Other S Corporation Tax Disadvantages

Inability to Adjust Basis of Assets When Stock Is Purchased

If a partnership makes or has in effect an IRC §754 optional basis adjustment election, a purchaser of an interest in that partnership can "step up" the tax basis of his or her share of appreciated partnership assets to reflect the purchase price. No such privilege is available to S corporations and their shareholders. The significance of this disadvantage of S corporations compared to partnerships is explained below.

If the §754 election applies, the purchasing partner's allocations of deductions related to stepped-up partnership assets (for example, depreciation deductions) will be based on the higher purchase price rather than on the partnership's lower historical tax basis in the property. Also, if the partnership sells the appreciated property, the purchasing partner's allocation of taxable gain will be smaller, because of the stepped-up tax basis in his or her share of the property.

> **Example 8.02(3): Impact of Inability to Step Up Tax Basis of Assets When Stock Changes Hands** This Example explains what happens when ownership interests change hands in a business entity that owns appreciated assets. First, the results of operating the business as a partnership will be covered. Then, the results of operating the same business as an S corporation will be compared to the partnership outcome. (Note that the partnership outcome would also apply to an LLC treated as a partnership for federal income tax purposes.)
>
> *Property Owned by Partnership*
>
> CeeDee Partnership is a 50/50 joint venture between Charles and Dennis. The only asset of CeeDee is a patent, which is being amortized over 15 years under IRC §197. The original cost basis of the patent was $300,000, and cumulative §197 amortization is $80,000. Thus, the adjusted tax basis of the patent is now $220,000. The patent has a current FMV of $500,000.
>
> Dennis sells his 50% partnership interest to Danny for $250,000, and the partnership makes a §754 election. Accordingly, Danny's share of the partnership's basis in the patent is stepped up to $250,000 (from the preelection basis of only $110,000 for Dennis's share), to reflect the purchase price of Danny's partnership interest. Charles is unaffected by the §754 election.
>
> After the step-up, the partnership has total tax basis in the patent of $360,000 ($110,000 allocated to Charles and $250,000 allocated to Danny).
>
> Assume the partnership now sells the patent for $500,000 and liquidates by distributing $250,000 of cash each to Charles and Danny.

For Charles, the sale generates a taxable gain of $140,000 (his $250,000 share of the proceeds less his $110,000 share of the partnership's basis in the patent). This gain is passed through to Charles, and increases his basis in his partnership interest. Under IRC §1245, $40,000 of the passed-through partnership gain is ordinary income recapture (equal to Charles's 50% share of the $80,000 of §197 amortization deductions). The balance is a §1231 gain.

Upon the liquidation of his partnership interest, Charles also recognizes gain or loss equal to the difference (if any) between the liquidation proceeds of $250,000 and his basis in his partnership interest.

For Danny, the sale generates a taxable gain of zero (his $250,000 share of the proceeds less his $250,000 share of the partnership's basis in the patent). Also, Danny recognizes no further gain or loss on the liquidation of his interest because the liquidation proceeds of $250,000 and his basis in his partnership interest are equal.

Property Owned by S Corporation

Now assume the exact same facts, except that the patent is owned by an S corporation. Danny buys Dennis's shares for $250,000. There is no mechanism to adjust the "inside basis" of the entity's assets to reflect what Danny pays for his 50% ownership interest. This causes an "inside/outside basis difference," as explained below.

Again assume the patent is sold for $500,000, and the entity is liquidated by distributing $250,000 of cash to each owner. At the corporate level, there is a $280,000 taxable gain ($500,000 proceeds less $220,000 basis in the patent). This gain is allocated 50/50 to Charles and Danny, and it increases their basis in their S corporation stock. Under IRC §1245, $80,000 of the passed-through gain is ordinary recapture income (equal to the §197 amortization deductions). Thus, each owner is passed through $100,000 of IRC §1231 gain and $40,000 of ordinary gain.

Charles will recognize gain or loss on the liquidation transaction (treated as a taxable sale of his stock) equal to the difference (if any) between the liquidation proceeds of $250,000 and his basis in his shares.

Danny's basis in his shares is $390,000 ($250,000 original purchase price plus $140,000 passed through gain from the patent sale). In Danny's case, the liquidation transaction generates a capital loss of $140,000 ($250,000 liquidation proceeds less his $390,000 basis in his shares). Thus, from the sale of the patent and the subsequent liquidation of the corporation, Danny recognizes:

- A capital loss of $140,000,
- A passed-through §1231 gain of $100,000, and
- An ordinary gain of $40,000.

The total gains and losses balance out arithmetically, but the *characters* of the gains and losses are very unfavorable to Danny.

Conclusion

The above problem is caused solely by the difference between inside basis (the basis to the corporation of Danny's share of the assets) and outside basis (Danny's basis in his shares). Obviously, the tax results with an S corporation are not nearly as desirable as those for a partnership, where the inside/outside basis problem could be eliminated with a §754 election.

Note that in addition to resolving the inside/outside basis problem, a §754 election would cause Danny's §197 amortization deductions to be calculated based on his $250,000 share of the partnership's basis in the patent (if the partnership continued to hold the patent instead of selling it).

Clearly, being able to make §754 elections can be a very significant advantage of partnership taxation over S corporation taxation.

Tax Treatment of Employee-Shareholders' Fringe Benefits

The tax rules covering fringe benefits for S corporation employee-shareholders are less favorable than for C corporation employee-shareholders. However, the fringe benefit rules for S corporations and partnerships are essentially equivalent.

For purposes of employee fringe benefits:

1. S corporations are to be treated as partnerships, and

2. Any S corporation shareholder owning directly or indirectly more than 2% of the stock on any day during the tax year (a "2% shareholder") is treated as a partner [IRC §1372].

The following fringe benefits are available on a tax-advantaged basis (deductible by the S corporation and excludable from the income of 2% employee-shareholders):

- Dependent care assistance, under IRC §129;
- Educational assistance programs, under IRC §127;
- Qualified employee discounts, no additional cost services, working condition fringes, on-premises athletic facilities, and *de minimis* fringes, under IRC §132.

Consistent with the logic of Revenue Ruling 91-26 (1991-1 CB 184), which deals specifically with company-paid accident and health insurance premiums, the following fringe benefits provided to 2% employee-shareholders are treated as employee compensation to the recipients (i.e., deductible to the corporation, taxable income to the employee-shareholder):

- Premiums paid for accident and health insurance plans, and
- The cost of up to $50,000 of group term life insurance coverage.

Obviously, the inability to provide tax-advantaged accident and health insurance coverage to 2% employee-shareholders is a significant shortcoming of S corporations (and partnerships) compared to C corporations.

However, company-paid accident and health insurance premiums for 2% employee-shareholders are treated as passed through to those shareholders, per Revenue Ruling 91-26. Therefore, at the employee-shareholder level, deductions for accident and health insurance premiums may be available under IRC §§162(l) and 213. IRC §162(l) allows a percentage deduction, and §213 allows the remaining amount to be deducted, subject to the 7.5%-of-AGI limitation.

Limitations on Tax Year Ends

S corporations generally are required to use the calendar year for tax purposes, unless the corporation makes tax deposit payments to the government [IRC §§444, 7519, and 1378]. The tax deposits are intended to approximate the shareholder-level tax-deferral benefit of using an alternative year end.

However, the required tax deposits are calculated using a 40.6% tax rate applied to an approximation of the deferred taxable income. As a result of this unfavorable computation method, many S corporations find using alternative year ends unattractive.

Qualified Retirement Plan Loans

Employees of S corporations who also own more than 5% of the stock cannot borrow against their qualified retirement plan accounts [IRC §4975]. (Under a similar rule, partners who own more than 10% of a partnership's profits or capital interests also are prevented from such borrowings.) In contrast, C corporation shareholder-employees can borrow against their company-sponsored qualified retirement plan accounts on the same basis as all other employees.

Former C Corporations May Be Exposed to Corporate-Level Taxes

When former C corporations have converted to S status, three corporate-level taxes can apply. These are exceptions to the general rule that S corporations do not have to worry about paying corporate-level taxes.

Built-In Gains Tax

The built-in gains (BIG) tax is a potential threat when a former C corporation owned built-in gain assets (assets with FMV in excess of tax basis) on the date of the S election. The BIG tax rate is 35%, and it applies when a built-in gain asset is sold within 10 years of the effective date of the corporation's S election [IRC §1374].

CAUTION: The BIG tax can also apply to a corporation that has always been an S corporation if it receives transferred basis property with a built-in gain from a C corporation or another S corporation that was itself subject to the BIG tax. [See IRS Announcement 86-128 (1986-51 IRB 22).]

Excess Passive Income Tax

Former C corporations with undistributed accumulated earnings and profits (AE&P) are exposed to a corporate-level tax if they earn too much net passive investment income. Net passive investment income is similar but not identical to portfolio income under the passive loss rules. The tax can apply to years when passive investment income exceeds 25% of gross receipts. The rate is 35% [IRC §1375].

CAUTION: Of greater concern is the rule that an S corporation has its S election terminated if it has AE&P and passive investment income exceeding 25% of gross receipts for three consecutive tax years [IRC §1362(d)(3)].

LIFO Recapture Tax

When a C corporation using LIFO inventory accounting makes an S election, the LIFO reserve (excess of FIFO inventory amount over the LIFO amount) is recaptured. The resulting income is included in the final C corporation tax return. The incremental tax triggered by this LIFO recapture rule can be paid in four equal annual installments [IRC §1363(d)].

8.03 NONTAX ADVANTAGES OF THE CORPORATE FORM OF DOING BUSINESS

While the tax laws tend to favor partnerships and LLCs treated as partnerships over S corporations, nontax issues generally favor S corporations. The significant nontax issues relevant in evaluating the attractiveness of S corporations are discussed in this section, in approximate order of importance.

Limited Liability for the Ownership Group

The principal nontax advantage of operating a business or an investment activity as a corporation (C or S) is limited liability. For legal purposes, the corporation is a viewed as an independent entity, separate and apart from its shareholders.

This means creditors of the corporation generally cannot look to the personal assets of the shareholders to satisfy corporate debts and obligations. Similarly, creditors of the shareholders cannot look to the assets of the corporation to satisfy the debts and obligations of the shareholders.

Reality Check for Closely Held Businesses

Unfortunately, the advantage of limited liability for shareholders can be more apparent than real in many circumstances. For instance, while the personal assets of corporate shareholders are protected from general corporate debts and obligations (often referred to as "contract" or "commercial" liabilities), shareholders generally remain *exposed* to corporate liabilities resulting from their own tortious acts or professional errors and omissions.

Tortious acts are defined as wrongful acts leading to civil actions, other than those involving breach of contract. An example is negligent driving of an auto resulting in injuries or property damage.

Example 8.03(1): Shareholder Liability for Professional Malpractice and Negligence   Assume an S corporation is used to operate a professional practice. Under state law, generally the corporation itself is primarily liable for professional malpractice and negligence on the part of its shareholder-employees and other employees.

However, the shareholders generally are *also* personally liable for damages caused by their own professional errors and omissions and for their own negligence in directly supervising other professionals (who may be fellow shareholder-employees or "regular" employees).

Usually, a claimant can move first against the assets of the corporation. If those assets are insufficient to satisfy the judgment, the claimant can then move against the personal assets of the "guilty" shareholder-employee.

A key point is that the assets of the corporation (and the value of the stock held by the "innocent" shareholders) can be wiped out by liabilities resulting from the tortious acts and professional errors, omissions, or negligence of any one of the corporation's shareholder-employees or other employees. However, the corporation at least protects the *personal* assets of the "innocent" shareholders from exposure to such liabilities.

Example 8.03(2): Tortious Act by a Shareholder-Employee   An S corporation shareholder-employee uses his car on company business and becomes involved in a serious accident that causes injuries and property damage. The corporation may be primarily liable for the damages, but the shareholder-employee will also be personally liable for this tortious act.

As explained in the preceding Example, the injured parties generally can attempt to recover first from the corporation's assets (thus reducing or even wiping out the stock investments of the "innocent" shareholders). The claimants can then pursue the "guilty" shareholder-employee's personal assets, if the corporations's assets are insufficient to satisfy the claims. However, the corporation shields the *personal* assets of the "innocent" shareholders.

RECOMMENDATION: *Shareholder exposure to these types of liabilities is a matter of state law, and the practitioner should research the issue carefully before answering specific client questions.*

Remember that the assets of the S corporation are always fully exposed to liabilities and claims resulting from the corporation's own activities. Thus, shareholders are always exposed to the risk that their stock investments may be lost as a result of a catastrophic event or judgment against the corporation.

Shareholder Guarantees

Shareholders of S corporations often are required to guarantee certain of the entity's debts personally. Shareholders are personally obligated with respect to corporate debts that they have specifically guaranteed, but they are still protected against liability for other corporate debts.

Unfortunately, S corporation shareholders do not receive any additional tax basis for loss deduction purposes when they guarantee the corporation's debts. However, they *do* receive additional basis if they personally take out the necessary loans and then reloan the borrowed funds to the corporation. This is a so-called back-to-back loan arrangement.

Summary of Liability Considerations

Notwithstanding the above caveats, the limited liability protection offered by S corporations is still extremely valuable if the business is exposed to liabilities or potential liabilities that are not covered by insurance. Operating a business or an investment activity as an S corporation may be advisable if:

1. The formation and operation of the activity will result in significant debts owed to financial institutions, lessors, vendors, and other creditors;

2. The activity will involve the delivery of professional services, with the inherent risk of malpractice claims;

3. The activity will involve employees whose foreseeable actions can create liabilities (for example, if employees are expected to use their cars regularly in the activity);

4. The activity will require the hiring of one or more employers (regardless of the nature of the business itself, employees inevitably create exposure to liabilities in any number of ways—for example, one employee may harass another, employees can be injured on the job or premises, discriminatory hiring or firing practices can be alleged, embezzlement and theft can occur, or unauthorized borrowing or spending transactions can occur);

5. The nature of the activity itself is hazardous (for example, potentially dangerous tools are used, heavy equipment is used, toxic substances are handled, or employees must work at heights or in the middle of vehicular traffic);

6. The potential for product liability claims exists (for example, the products demand specialized training to operate or are inherently dangerous); and

7. There is potential exposure to environmental liabilities (as is the case with almost any manufacturing activity and perhaps any activity that involves the ownership of real estate, which may have pollution, asbestos, or lead problems).

It is a very rare business or investment activity that does *not* expose its owners to potentially substantial liability risks.

Limited Liability Aspects of Corporations Compared to Limited Partnerships and LLCs

As stated earlier, S and C corporations offer identical legal protections to their owners. An S corporation is simply a corporation that has made a special tax election for federal income tax purposes.

However, S corporations *do* possess two significant advantages over limited partnerships.

First, a limited partnership must have at least one general partner with unlimited exposure to partnership liabilities. This problem can usually be addressed by forming a corporate general partner (usually an S corporation), which effectively "stops the bleeding" in that the amount the general partner can lose is limited to the value of the assets held by the corporation. However, setting up and maintaining another entity for this purpose creates an administrative burden. (See the discussion of limited partnerships in Chapter 5.) In an S corporation, however, *no* shareholder or shareholder-employee need be exposed to *any* corporate liabilities (other than those arising from certain of his or her own actions).

Second, a limited partner can lose limited liability protection by becoming too actively involved in managing the limited partnership. As a result, limited partnerships are not suitable for certain activities, such as the practice of a profession where all partners are virtually by definition heavily involved in the business. In some cases, this problem can be addressed by setting up a corporate general partner, with the corporation owned by the limited partners in proportion to their limited partnership ownership percentages. Again, however, the existence of an additional legal entity creates administrative and tax filing burdens. State limited partnership laws based on the Revised Uniform Limited Partnership Act give some relief by specifying a number of actions that limited partners can take *without* being deemed to participate in management. Nevertheless, the issue is always a potential problem for limited partnerships and their partners.

This issue is simply not a concern for S corporation shareholders and shareholder-employees. They can have any degree of management involvement without risking loss of their limited liability protection.

As discussed in Chapter 3, LLCs theoretically offer liability protection equivalent to that of S corporations. However, the newness of LLCs means there are legal uncertainties associated with their use. In contrast, the legal status of S corporations, their shareholders, and third parties (such as corporate creditors) is well settled after years of litigation and statutory fine-tuning.

> **OBSERVATION:** *An alternative view espoused by some commentators is that well-established corporate case law effectively provides a recipe on how to defeat owners seeking to claim corporate liability protection benefits. Thus, some view corporations as possibly less effective than LLCs in protecting owners from liabilities. Supporting this viewpoint is the fact that some LLC statutes may explicitly obviate the need for complying with corporate-type formalities such as conducting annual meetings, keeping minutes, and so forth. Failure to observe these corporate formalities can cause shareholders to lose hoped-for liability protection benefits (see the discussion immediately below). Balancing this consideration is the fact that years of case law also provides a recipe on how not to lose the advantages of corporate liability protection. In other words, if the corporate rules are scrupulously followed, there is great certainty that the corporation will indeed deliver the liability protection desired by the shareholders. With their virtually nonexistent legal track record, LLCs cannot necessarily promise the same degree of certainty.*

Observing Formalities to Establish Separate Entity Concept

The legal rights and obligations of S corporations, their shareholders (including shareholder-employees), and third parties (such as creditors) are a matter of state law. Arguably, corporations offer the greatest certainty when it comes to protecting owners from liabilities related to the entity's business or investment activities.

However, this protection does not come "for free." Shareholders must be careful to observe certain formalities to ensure that the corporation and its shareholders are recognized as separate legal entities. If the existence of separate legal entities is not clearly established, the corporation may be viewed as the legal "alter ego" of its shareholders, a risk referred to as "piercing the corporate veil."

The result of piercing the corporate veil is that the shareholders are personally exposed to all of the liabilities associated with the business or investment activity. Piercing the corporate veil may also mean the existence of the corporation is ignored for federal income tax purposes.

The formalities that must be observed to establish the separate legal existence of a corporation vary according to state law. Generally, however, there will be requirements to do the following:

- File articles of incorporation, a corporate charter, and corporate by-laws with the appropriate state agency (usually the Secretary of State);

- Designate a board of directors and corporate officers and hold periodic board of directors and shareholder meetings;

- Maintain a corporate bank account;

- Pay for the necessary business licenses; and

- File corporate income and franchise tax returns and pay any necessary franchise taxes.

Continuity of Life

The legal existence of an S corporation goes on indefinitely unless the corporation is formally dissolved. For example, a corporation will continue its legal life after events such as the death, disability, insanity, bankruptcy, or insolvency of one or more of its shareholders. In contrast, state laws generally provide that the death, bankruptcy, etc., of a general partner, LLP partner, or LLC member will cause a legal dissolution of the entity unless the remaining members vote to continue the enterprise. (See Chapters 3-5.) Therefore, the corporate attribute of continuity of life is an advantage of S corporations over partnership, LLPs, and LLCs.

> *CAUTION: Shareholder events* can *threaten a corporation's S status. For example, the death of a shareholder may result in a prohibited type of trust becoming a shareholder, with the resulting involuntary termination of the corporation's S election. (See section 8.02 of this chapter.)*

Free Transferability of Ownership Interests

Free transferability of ownership interests in an organization exists if owners can substitute for themselves new owners without the consent of the other owners or members of the organization. In plain English, the attribute of free transferability exists when owners are free to sell or transfer *all* of their ownership rights.

"All ownership rights" means both the economic rights (such as the right to current and liquidating distributions) *and* the noneconomic components of ownership interests (such as the right to vote or demand an accounting for the entity's activities).

Clearly, the ability to freely transfer one's interest is a significant advantage to a business owner. But free transferability may not exist for ownership interests in LLCs, LLPs, or partnerships (see discussion in Chapters 3, 4, and 5, respectively).

In contrast, shares of an S corporation's stock generally can be transferred freely (unless transfers are restricted by a buy–sell agreement). Note, however, that this corporate attribute, like limited liability, may be more apparent than real, for two reasons.

First, there usually is *not* a ready market for shares of S corporations, because they are closely held. In other words, the only market for such shares may be the other shareholders and/or the corporation itself.

Second, shares cannot be transferred to prohibited types of shareholders, and transfers that result in violating the 75-shareholder rule will terminate the corporation's S status (see section 8.02 of this chapter).

8.04 S CORPORATIONS COMPARED TO OTHER ENTITY CHOICES

This section has the greatest relevance if the entity selection process has been narrowed to a choice between S corporations and one of the other types of entities discussed below. If that is not the case, the practitioner and client should strongly consider using the entity selection software program that comes with this book. The program is designed to help make a choice-of-entity recommendation that is consistent with the major tax and nontax issues facing the client. If the program leads you to the S corporation as the apparently best choice, this section can then be reviewed to solidify that conclusion.

See section 8.05 of this chapter for a comparison of S corporations and sole proprietorships.

S Corporations Compared to C Corporations

For liability protection for owners and for other legal aspects, there no differences between S corporations and C corporations. S corporations are simply corporations that have elected to be treated as such for federal income tax purposes. Thus, the only relevant issues in comparing S and C corporations are those imposed by the federal tax laws. (See Chapter 6 for an in-depth discussion of C corporations.)

In summary, compared to C corporations, S corporations may be more attractive if:

- The benefits of pass-through taxation are desired; and

- The S corporation eligibility requirements can be met; and

- The restrictions on eligible S shareholders do not cause undue hardship with regard to the owners' future plans to transfer ownership interests to others for estate planning, family tax planning, or business succession planning purposes; and

- The owners can accept the fact that they may not be able to borrow against their qualified retirement plan accounts.

S Corporations Compared to LLCs

Both S corporations and LLCs protect owners' personal assets against entity-level liabilities. (See Chapter 3 for a general discussion of LLCs.) The biggest advantage of LLCs over S corporations is that LLCs can qualify for the benefits of pass-through taxation without the numerous restrictions that apply to S corporations. These restrictions are covered in more depth in section 8.02 of this chapter.

In addition, LLCs are taxed as partnerships, and the partnership taxation rules are significantly more generous and flexible than the provisions applying to S corporations. (The differences between partnership and S corporation taxation are described in Chapter 5.) However, to be treated as a partnership for federal income tax purposes, an LLC must have at least two members. S corporations, by contrast, can be formed with only one shareholder. (As discussed in Chapter 5, there may be ways to "create" more than one owner—for example, by forming a husband–wife LLC.)

The key negative issues affecting LLCs are legal uncertainty and the variability of LLC statutes from state to state. Also, some businesses (such as certain professional practices) may be prohibited under state law and/or professional standards from operating as LLCs.

A potentially significant disadvantage of LLCs is that they may *not* possess the corporate attributes of continuity of life and free transferability of ownership interests. S corporations generally do possess both of these attributes, but must take care to avoid stock transfers that would result in more than 75 shareholders or in ineligible types of shareholders.

In summary, compared to LLCs, S corporations generally are preferred if:

- The S corporation eligibility rules can be met without undue hardship; *and*

- The restrictions on eligible S shareholders do not cause undue hardship with regard to the owners' future plans to transfer ownership interests to others for estate planning, family tax planning, or business succession planning purposes; *and*

- There will be only one owner (making partnership taxation unavailable by definition); *or*

- The activity cannot be operated as an LLC under state law and/or applicable professional standards; *or*

- The business cannot be operated as an LLC because the owners cannot live with the legal uncertainties associated with LLC status; *or*

- The benefits of partnership taxation compared to those of S corporation taxation are not considered significant enough to warrant operating as an LLC.

If state law and applicable professional standards (if any), allow the business in question to operate as a single-member LLC, this will generally be preferable to operating as a solely owned S corporation. Exceptions would be when: (1) S corporation status can be used to minimize federal payroll taxes or (2) the owner prefers the (arguably) greater legal certainty of corporate status.

S Corporations Compared to LLPs

For limiting liability, S corporations are generally superior to LLPs because corporate shareholder-employees (and shareholders in general) are not exposed to entity-level contract liabilities, while LLP partners are in some states. (See Chapter 4 for complete coverage of LLPs.)

The biggest advantage of LLPs over S corporations is that LLPs qualify for the benefit of pass-through taxation without the numerous restrictions that apply to S corporations. In addition, LLPs fall under the partnership taxation rules, which are significantly more generous and flexible than the provisions applying to S corporations.

Overall, comparing S corporations to LLPs usually boils down to weighing:

1. The additional liability protection (if any) offered by S corporations against

2. The hassles caused by the S corporation restrictions and the advantages of partnership taxation over S corporation taxation.

> **OBSERVATION:** *Because they are partnerships by definition, LLPs must have at least two co-owners; S corporations can be formed with only one shareholder.*

A potentially significant disadvantage of LLPs is that usually they will *not* possess the corporate attribute of continuity of life. The retirement, resignation, expulsion, death, bankruptcy, etc., of an LLP partner generally will cause a legal dissolution of the entity, unless the remaining partners vote to continue. In contrast, S corporations have unlimited legal life spans.

LLPs usually will also lack free transferability of ownership interests, while S corporation shareholders generally are free to transfer their stock as they wish (subject to possible restrictions if a buy–sell agreement exists). However, S corporations must take care to avoid stock transfers that would result in more than 75 shareholders or in ineligible types of shareholders.

Compared to LLPs, S corporations generally are preferred if:

- The S corporation eligibility rules can be met without undue hardship; *and*

- The restrictions on eligible S shareholders do not cause undue hardship with regard to the owners' future plans to transfer ownership interests to others for estate planning, family tax planning, or business succession planning purposes; *and*

- There will be only one owner (making partnership taxation unavailable by definition); *or*

- The activity cannot be operated as an LLP under state law and/or applicable professional standards; *and*

- The liability protections offered by LLPs are considered inadequate (after taking into account available insurance); *and*

- The benefits of partnership taxation compared to those of S corporation taxation are not considered significant enough to warrant operating as an LLP.

S Corporations Compared to General Partnerships

For limiting liability, S corporations are far superior to general partnerships, because corporate shareholder-employees (and shareholders in general) are not exposed to entity-level liabilities. (See Chapter 5 for complete coverage of general partnerships.)

The biggest advantage of general partnerships over S corporations is that general partnerships qualify for the benefit of pass-through taxation without the numerous restrictions that apply to S corporations. In addition, general partnerships are able to take advantage of the partnership taxation rules, which are significantly more generous and flexible than the provisions applying to S corporations.

Overall, comparing general partnerships to S corporations usually boils down to weighing:

1. The liability protection offered by S corporations against
2. The hassles caused by the S corporation restrictions and the advantages of partnership taxation over S corporation taxation.

A potentially significant disadvantage of general partnerships is that usually they will *not* possess the corporate attribute of continuity of life. The retirement, resignation, expulsion, death, bankruptcy, etc., of a general partner usually will cause the entity to be liquidated, unless the remaining partners vote to continue (the continuing partnership is treated as a new entity for legal purposes). In contrast, S corporations have unlimited legal life spans.

General partnerships usually also lack free transferability of ownership interests, while S corporation shareholders usually are free to transfer their stock as they wish (subject to possible restrictions if a buy-sell agreement exists). However, S corporations must take care to avoid stock transfers that would result in more than 75 shareholders or ineligible types of shareholders.

In summary, compared to general partnerships, S corporations usually are preferred if:

- Limiting owner liability is an important issue (after taking into account available insurance); *or*
- The benefits of partnership taxation compared to those of S corporation taxation are not considered significant enough to justify the risks of operating as a general partnership; *or*
- There will be only one owner (making partnership taxation unavailable by definition); *and*
- The S corporation eligibility rules can be met without undue hardship; *and*
- The restrictions on eligible S shareholders do not cause undue hardship with regard to the owners' future plans to transfer ownership interests to others for estate planning, family tax planning, or business succession planning purposes.

S Corporations Compared to Limited Partnerships

Protection of personal assets against entity-level liabilities is much the same for S corporation shareholders as it is for limited partners. As discussed in Chapter 5, however, the general partners of a limited partnership have unlimited exposure to all partnership debts and obligations. The good news is that usually the issue can be handled successfully by setting up a corporate general partner.

The biggest advantage of limited partnerships over S corporations is that limited partnerships can qualify for the benefits of pass-through taxation without having to meet and maintain the numerous requirements that apply to S corporations. Limited partnerships also qualify for tax advantages beyond pass-though taxation. In general, the partnership taxation rules are significantly more generous and flexible than the provisions applying to S corporations.

> **OBSERVATION:** *To be treated as a partnership for federal income tax purposes, a limited partnership must have at least two owners; an S corporation can be formed with only one shareholder. If the two-partner rule appears to be a significant roadblock, there may be ways to address this issue—for example, by forming a husband–wife partnership. (See Chapter 5.)*

A potentially significant disadvantage of limited partnerships compared to S corporations is that limited partnerships do *not* have unlimited legal lives. The retirement, resignation, expulsion, death, bankruptcy, etc., of a general partner will cause the entity to be liquidated, unless the remaining partners vote to continue (the continuing partnership is treated as a new entity for legal purposes). In contrast, S corporations have unlimited legal life spans.

Also, general partners of a limited partnership usually cannot freely transfer their partnership interests, while S corporation shareholders typically *can* freely transfer their shares (subject to possible restrictions if a buy-sell agreement exists). However, S corporations must take care to avoid stock transfers that would result in more than 75 shareholders or in ineligible types of shareholders.

In summary, compared to limited partnerships, S corporations generally are preferred if:

- The S corporation eligibility rules can be met without undue hardship; *and*
- The restrictions on eligible S shareholders do not cause undue hardship with regard to the owners' future plans to transfer ownership interests to others for estate planning, family tax planning, or business succession planning purposes; *and*
- There will be only one owner (making partnership taxation unavailable by definition); *or*
- The activity cannot be operated as a limited partnership because the owners who would be limited partners cannot live with the fact that they must avoid management involvement to maintain their limited liability protection; *or*
- The benefits of partnership taxation compared to those of S corporation taxation are not considered significant enough to warrant operating as a limited partnership.

8.05 S CORPORATIONS COMPARED TO SOLE PROPRIETORSHIPS

Because both can accommodate single-owner businesses, S corporations must be compared to sole proprietorships. This section summarizes the key issues in making such comparisons.

Liability Concerns

A sole proprietorship is an unincorporated business that is legally one and the same as the owner. Therefore, the personal assets of the owner are exposed without limitation to any and all liabilities related to the conduct of the sole proprietorship business.

This unlimited liability exposure is the most significant difference between sole proprietorships and the other types of entities discussed in this publication (other than general partnerships, which also expose their owners to unlimited personal liability). See Chapter 9 for a general discussion of sole proprietorships.

If there is to be only one owner of the activity, the available liability-limiting entities are the S corporation, the C corporation, and the single-member LLC (in most states). Limited partnerships and LLPs require at least two owners. As discussed in Chapter 5, it is often possible to "arrange" to have more than one owner if, for example, the multi-member LLC form of doing business appears to be the most attractive choice.

The liability-limiting advantages of S corporations are discussed in section 8.03 of this chapter.

Corporations Are Not Liability Cure-Alls

As a practical matter, liability exposure is not always a critical issue. In some businesses, the risks may be inherently negligible, and/or it may be possible to obtain adequate liability insurance at an acceptable cost.

Also, the use of a corporation or other liability-limiting entity is not the cure-all that some think. For example, if the business in question is a professional practice, the use of a corporation (or any other legal entity) generally can do nothing to protect the practitioner's personal assets from liabilities related to his or her *own* professional errors, omissions, and negligence. The same is true for liabilities related to the owner's tortious acts (such as careless driving resulting in injuries or property damage), whether or not they are committed in the course of business.

When it comes to other common business liabilities, such as bank loans, lease obligations, and vendor payables (often referred to as "contract" or "commercial" liabilities), creditors frequently will require owners to guarantee the debts personally, whether or not a corporation or other legal entity is used to operate the venture.

Administrative Simplicity of Sole Proprietorships

Some simple initial steps may be required to set up a sole proprietorship. For example, under local law it may be necessary to register and pay a fee to obtain a business license. Filings may be required if the business will use an assumed name (a "DBA").

Generally, however, no other legal papers or filings are required to initiate and operate a sole proprietorship. Thus, professional fees and burdensome paperwork are minimized.

On an ongoing basis, there is no requirement, for example, to:

- Keep corporate minutes;
- Maintain separate bank accounts (although this is recommended);
- Deposit payroll taxes or file payroll tax returns (unless there are employees);
- File corporate federal, state, or local tax returns;
- Pay state worker's compensation insurance (unless there are employees).

Transferring Ownership Interests

Partial ownership interests in corporations, partnerships, and LLCs can be transferred relatively easily. Such transfers are often made to the owner's spouse or children for estate planning, family income tax planning, business succession planning, or other reasons.

In contrast, it is impractical to transfer ownership of interests in the assets of a sole proprietorship. (Unfortunately, there is nothing else that *can* be transferred.) In any case, once there is more than one owner, a sole proprietorship by definition no longer exists.

If there is a foreseeable need to raise additional equity capital, a corporation, partnership, or LLC provides an established vehicle for taking in new owners. In contrast, if the business is run as a sole proprietorship, taking on an additional owner (for whatever reason) will almost require the creation of a new legal entity to own the business.

For these reasons, it is often advisable to set up a business as a corporation, partnership, or LLC on the front end, rather than postpone dealing with apparently inevitable issues.

> *CAUTION: It must be remembered that if S corporation stock is transferred to ineligible shareholders, the corporation's S election will be terminated. (Eligible shareholders are discussed in section 8.02 of this chapter.) Also, there can be no more than 75 shareholders. Thus, S corporations do not offer as much flexibility as C corporations, partnerships, LLCs, and LLPs to accommodate contemplated future transfers of ownership interests. Often, however, such transfers can be made without violating the eligibility rules. In such cases, setting up an S corporation on the front end makes sense.*

Tax Considerations

Operating as a sole proprietorship may not lead to significantly different federal income tax results than operating as an S corporation, because the pass-through taxation concept applies to sole proprietorships as well as to S corporations. There are some differences, however, as discussed below.

Deductibility of Health Insurance Premium Costs

If the spouse of a sole proprietor is a bona fide employee of the proprietorship and the proprietorship provides health insurance coverage for employees, the sole proprietor may be able to deduct 100% of the cost of health insurance premiums for coverage of the owner, spouse, and dependents. The employee-spouse can select family coverage, which also covers the owner and the children. The proprietorship can deduct the premium costs under IRC §162. The employee-spouse can exclude the benefit from taxable income under IRC §§105 and 106. (See PLR 9409006.)

If the spouse is not employed by the business, the above maneuver is not available. Instead, the general rule for sole proprietors applies, and only a percentage of the cost of premiums for health insurance covering the proprietor and his or her family are deductible [IRC §162(l)].

The percentage deduction rule also applies to health insurance premiums an S corporation pays to cover more-than-2% shareholder-employees and their families [IRC §162(l)(5); Revenue Ruling 91-26 (1991-1 CB 184)]. Thus, in this area of the tax law, operating as a sole proprietorship can be more advantageous than operating as an S corporation.

Note that partners are also subject to the percentage deduction rule [IRC §162(l)(1); Revenue Ruling 91-26].

Payroll Tax Advantage for S Corporations

Amounts retained by an S corporation are not subject to FICA taxes (unless the corporation is audited and the stated wages are found to be unreasonably low). In contrast, the self-employment (SE) tax applies to 100% of a sole proprietor's business income, as reported on Schedule C.

In addition, the S corporation's contributions to a qualified retirement plan (other than a 401(k) plan) benefiting the shareholder-employee are not subject to FICA taxes, while a sole proprietor's contributions to a Keogh or SEP plan *are* subject to SE tax. Thus, the FICA taxes that are owed if the owner is an employee of an S corporation may be significantly less than the SE tax owed if the owner is a sole proprietor.

Example 8.05(1): Federal Payroll Tax Rules—Sole Proprietorship versus S Corporation   Wilhelmina is a sole proprietor with $100,000 of Schedule C income from her business in 1999. The $100,000 figure is before her $10,000 contribution to her Keogh retirement plan and her $5,000 of medical insurance premiums (which are 60% deductible).

Wilhelmina's SE tax is based on SE income of $100,000. She gets no deductions for the Keogh contribution or medical insurance premiums for SE tax purposes. Thus, Wilhelmina's 1999 SE tax liability is $11,902.40 (15.3% of $72,600 plus 2.9% of $27,400).

Now assume Wilhelmina instead operates her business as a 100%-owned S corporation and pays herself a reasonable salary of $55,000, with a contribution of $10,000 to the company pension plan set up for her benefit, and $5,000 paid for medical insurance covering her and her family. (The remaining $30,000 of S corporation income is distributed to Wilhelmina as a dividend.) FICA taxes are due only on Wilhelmina's stated salary of $55,000 plus the $5,000 of medical insurance premiums (which are included in her wages for FIT and FICA tax purposes per Revenue Ruling 91-26). Thus, the FICA tax liability is only $9,180 (15.3% of $60,000). Compare this amount to the $11,902.40 of SE tax that is due if Wilhelmina operates hers business as a sole proprietorship.

Reality Check: The federal payroll tax rules encourage S corporation shareholder-employees to set low salaries for themselves to minimize FICA taxes. However, if salary amounts are unreasonably low and the corporation is audited, the IRS will attempt to recharacterize all or part of purported S corporation dividend payments as disguised salary. The corporation will then be hit with back FICA taxes, interest, and possibly penalties.

Additional Basis from Debt

One potentially significant tax advantage of sole proprietorship status compared to S corporation status is that a sole proprietor will receive basis from all business-related debt for loss deduction purposes. In contrast, an S corporation shareholder receives basis only to the extent of the basis in his or her stock plus the amount of any loans made to the corporation. In other words, entity-level debt does not add to the basis available to the owner, even if the debt is personally guaranteed. (The same is true if the business is operated as a C corporation.)

Sole Proprietorship Advantage Regarding Wages Paid to Owner's Minor Children

Another advantage of sole proprietorships compared to S (and C) corporations is in the area of federal payroll taxes for employees. A sole proprietorship (or a husband–wife partnership, for that matter) can pay wages to the owner's under-age-18 child without owing any FICA or FUTA taxes. The child also does not owe the employee's half of the FICA tax. [See IRC §§3121(b)(3) and 3306(c)(5).] The sole proprietor is able to deduct the wages and thereby reduce taxable business income for both income tax (which may be at a rate as high as 39.6%) and self-employment tax (which may be at a rate as high as 15.3%) purposes, without paying the FICA and FUTA taxes that would apply to wages paid to other employees. The child's wage income is earned income. As a result, some or all of it generally can be sheltered by the child's standard deduction amount ($4,300 for 1999).

However, if the business is operated as an S (or C) corporation, the wages of the owner's children are subject to federal payroll taxes just like those of any other employee.

> **REALITY CHECK:** *Of course, the wages paid to the child must be reasonable in relation to the work actually performed, so employing underage children works best with teenage children who can be assigned meaningful duties.*

Summary—S Corporations versus Sole Proprietorships

Compared to sole proprietorships, S corporations are the more attractive choice if:

- The issue of limiting owner liability is important (after taking into account available insurance); and/or

- The owner wants to set up a vehicle that allows for the future transfer of ownership interests to family members or others, and this can be done without violating the S corporation eligibility rules; and/or

- The payroll tax savings of operating as an S corporation are significant; and

- The S corporation eligibility rules can be satisfied without undue hardship; and

- It is not critical for the owner to receive additional tax basis from debt incurred by the business.

8.06 SUMMARY STATEMENT ON WHEN S CORPORATIONS ARE ATTRACTIVE

In general, S corporations may be preferred to C corporations, LLCs, LLPs, partnerships, and sole proprietorships when:

- Limiting owner liability is a critical concern; *and*

- Pass-through taxation is desired; *and*

- The S corporation eligibility rules can be met without undue hardship; *and*

- The restrictions on eligible S shareholders do not cause undue hardship with regard to the owners' future plans to transfer ownership interests to others for estate planning, family tax planning, or business succession planning purposes; *and*

- There will be only one owner (making partnership taxation unavailable by definition); *or*

- The activity cannot be operated as an LLC under state law and/or applicable professional standards; *or*

- The business cannot be operated as an LLC because the owners cannot live with the legal uncertainties associated with LLC status; *or*

- The activity cannot be operated as a limited partnership because the owners who would be limited partners cannot live with the fact that they must avoid management involvement to maintain their limited liability protection; *or*

- Either the business cannot be operated as an LLP or the liability protections offered by LLPs are considered inadequate; *or*

- The benefits of partnership taxation compared to those of S corporation taxation are not considered significant enough to warrant setting up a partnership, LLC, or LLP.

If state law and applicable professional standards (if any), allow the business in question to operate as a single-member LLC, this will generally be preferable to operating as a solely owned S corporation. Exceptions would be when: (1) S corporation status can be used to minimize federal payroll taxes or (2) the owner prefers the (arguably) greater legal certainty of corporate status.

Appendix 8A: Sample Client Letter When S Corporation Appears to Be Best Entity Choice

Dear [Client name]:

This letter briefly summarizes some of the major considerations that went into your recent decision to form a new business that will be operated as a S corporation.

Limited Liability of Shareholders

As we discussed, the principal advantage of corporate status is that the corporation is treated as a legal entity separate and distinct from its shareholders. Therefore, the corporation owns its own assets and is liable for its own debts. As a result, the personal assets of shareholders (including shareholder-employees) generally are beyond the reach of corporate creditors.

The liability-limiting protections offered by corporations are substantial, but they should not be overstated. While the personal assets of shareholders are protected from "general" corporate debts and obligations (often referred to as "contract liabilities"), shareholders generally remain *exposed* to corporate liabilities resulting from their own tortious acts or professional errors and omissions. (*Tortious acts* are defined as wrongful acts leading to civil actions, other than those involving breach of contract.)

The issue of shareholders' exposure to liabilities related to tortious acts and professional errors and omissions is a matter of state law. If you have specific questions about this issue, we recommend that you consult with your attorney.

Guarantees of Corporate Debts

Shareholders may be required on occasion to personally guarantee certain of the corporation's debts as a condition of obtaining financing or for other reasons.

Shareholders are personally obligated with respect to corporate debts that are specifically guaranteed, but shareholders are still protected against liability for other corporate debts.

Federal Income Tax Treatment of S Corporations

The key advantage of S corporations is that they are *not* subject to double taxation. S corporations are not tax-paying entities. Instead, the corporation's items of income, gain, deduction, loss, and credit are passed through to the shareholders, who then take those items into account in their own tax returns.

Stock Basis Adjustments

When the corporation's income and losses are passed through to a shareholder, his or her basis in that stock is adjusted accordingly. Specifically, the shareholder's basis is increased by his or her passed-through share of the corporation's income and gains and is decreased by his or her share of losses and deductions. This procedure, which ensures that income is subject to only a single level of taxation—at the owner level—is termed pass-through taxation.

Distributions to Shareholders

Unless the S corporation has earnings and profits (from years when it operated as a C corporation), nonliquidating cash and property distributions to shareholders are *not* treated as dividends. Instead, the distributions reduce the shareholder's basis in his or her shares. Distributions in excess of basis trigger taxable gain to the shareholder.

Multi-Year Impact of Pass-Through Taxation

The avoidance of double taxation of corporate income makes a big (and favorable) difference when a corporation earns substantial amounts of taxable income over a period of several years.

However, it must be remembered that the C corporation tax rates on the first $75,000 of annual income are considerably lower than the individual tax rates that apply if the same income is passed through by an S corporation. Even at higher income levels, the C corporation tax rates are still lower than the individual tax rates. If all income is expected to be retained in the business indefinitely (for example, to finance growing receivable and inventory levels), the more favorable C corporation rates can partially or wholly offset the negative effects of double taxation. In such cases, operating as a C corporation may be preferable to S status.

Pass-Through of Taxable Losses

Often, substantial tax losses are expected in the first few years of operation of a new business. If the business is conducted via a S corporation (or other pass-through entity), the losses can be passed through to the owners, where they can be deducted currently (subject to possible limitations under the basis, at-risk, and passive loss provisions).

In contrast, tax losses incurred by a C corporation remain trapped inside the entity in the form of net operating losses (NOLs). NOLs can be used only to offset taxable income earned in later years by the corporation. If no taxable income is earned, the NOLs expire after 20 years. If this happens, the tax losses never provide *any* tax benefit to the corporation or its shareholders.

Pass-Through of Capital Losses

If the business is expected to incur significant capital losses, S corporation status is preferred. The losses can be passed through to the owner, where they can offset up to $3,000 of ordinary income plus capital gains for the year. Any unused capital losses are carried forward to future years.

In contrast, if a C corporation is used, the capital losses are "trapped" inside the corporation, where they can be used only to offset capital gains. Unused capital losses from a year can be carried back 3 years or carried forward 5 years. After the fifth year, unused capital loss carryforwards in a C corporation expire.

Pass-Through of Capital Gains

An S corporation's long-term capital gains are passed through to shareholders, where they are taxed *once* at a maximum rate of 20% for individual taxpayers (assuming a holding period of more than 12 months). In contrast, C corporations pay the regular corporate tax rate (usually 34%) on long-term capital gains. If the gains are paid out later in the form of dividends, they constitute ordinary income and may be taxed at rates as high as 39.6%.

In other words, the double taxation of C corporation long-term capital gains amounts to a stiff penalty compared to the results if the gains are earned by an S corporation.

Pass-Through of Tax-Exempt Income

An S corporation's tax-exempt income is passed through to shareholders, where it retains its tax-exempt character. The tax-exempt income also increases the basis of the shareholders' stock.

While C corporations pay no corporate-level tax on tax-exempt income, such income is taxed as ordinary income at the shareholder level if it is paid out later in the form of dividends. The result is that what started out as tax-exempt income of a C corporation may end up as dividend income taxed at rates as high as 39.6%.

If the C corporation retains the tax-exempt income, it increases the value of the corporation and results in larger gains when shareholders sell their stock. Thus, a C corporation's tax-exempt income ultimately is going to be taxed at the shareholder level one way or the other.

Election of S Status

The election of S corporation status is made by filing Form 2553 (Election by a Small Business Corporation). The form can be filed during the preceding tax year for an election to become effective for the following tax year.

For an S election to be effective for the *current* tax year, it must be filed by the fifteenth day of the third month of that year. (In most cases, this translates into a March 15 deadline.) Newly formed corporations generally intend for the election of S status to be effective for the initial tax year. The election must be filed by the fifteenth day of the third month after the "activation date" of the corporation. This is the earliest date the corporation has shareholders, acquires assets, or begins conducting business.

We would be pleased to assist you in filing the Form 2553 to implement your corporation's S election.

Special Restrictions on S Corporations

Achieving S corporation status depends on meeting a number of strict eligibility rules. Unfortunately, these rules greatly restrict stock ownership and capital structure possibilities and can therefore make operating as an S corporation much less attractive than it first appears.

If the eligibility rules are not met at any time during the tax year, the S status of the corporation is immediately terminated and the corporation falls under the C corporation taxation rules.

To qualify for S status, a corporation must:

- Be a domestic corporation;
- Have no more than 75 shareholders;
- Have no shareholders other than individuals who are U.S. citizens or resident aliens, estates, or certain types of trusts and tax-exempt entities;
- Have only one class of stock (issuing both voting and nonvoting shares is permitted, but there can be no preferred stock or common stock classes with differing economic characteristics); and
- Not be by definition an ineligible corporation.

You should assess how the above restrictions might affect you and your co-owners in the foreseeable future as well as how they affect you today. For example, these restrictions may hamper your ability to raise capital in the future or to transfer your stock to trusts set up for the benefit of family members.

Ineligible Corporations

The following types of corporations are by definition ineligible for S status:

- Financial institutions allowed to deduct bad debts,
- Domestic international sales corporations (DISCs) or former DISCs,
- Insurance companies other than certain casualty companies, and
- Certain corporations electing to take the possessions tax credit.

Comparison to Partnerships and LLCs

It is a misconception that the federal income tax rules for S corporations are virtually identical to those for partnerships. While both S corporations and partnerships are pass-though entities (and therefore not subject to double taxation), there are *major* differences. Many of these are in favor of partnerships (including LLCs treated as partnerships for federal income tax purposes).

The most significant differences are as follows:

- Partners can receive additional tax basis (for loss deduction purposes) from entity-level liabilities, while S corporation shareholders can receive additional tax basis only from loans they make to the corporation. (Shareholder guarantees of corporate debt have no effect on shareholder basis.)

- Partners who purchase a partnership interest from another partner can step up the tax basis of their shares of partnership assets.

- Partners and partnerships have much greater flexibility than do S corporations and their shareholders to transfer appreciated property tax-free.

- Partnerships can make disproportionate allocations of tax losses and other tax items among the partners. In contrast, all S corporation pass-through items must be allocated among the shareholders strictly in proportion to stock ownership.

There are also several disadvantageous tax rules that apply to partnerships but not S corporations. However, most tax advisors believe that partnership taxation is more favorable, overall, than S corporation taxation.

Comparison to Single-Member LLCs

If state law and applicable professional standards (if any), allow your business to operate as a single-member LLC, this will generally be preferable to operating as a solely owned S corporation. Exceptions would be when: (1) S corporation status can be used to minimize federal payroll taxes or (2) you as the owner prefer the (arguably) greater legal certainty of corporate status.

Conclusion

As we discussed, you have considered the above advantages and disadvantages and have concluded that the S corporation is the best choice in your circumstances.

We appreciate the opportunity to consult with you as you make the important decision of choosing the most advantageous type of entity under which to operate your new venture. We look forward to working with you in the future as your corporation is formed and enters the operating phase.

Very truly yours,

CHAPTER 9 • SOLE PROPRIETORSHIPS

CONTENTS

9.01 INTRODUCTION

A *sole proprietorship* is, by definition, an unincorporated trade or business owned by a single individual. Thus, a sole proprietorship is not a legal entity separate and apart from its owner. If any other person or legal entity (such as a corporation) has an ownership interest in the business, or if there is a written or unwritten agreement to share profits and losses, there exists for federal income tax purposes either a partnership or an unincorporated association taxable as a C corporation. (See Chapters 5 and 6, respectively.) A sole proprietorship *can* have employees, however.

If there is to be only one owner of the business, the alternatives to sole proprietorship status are C corporations (see Chapters 6 and 7), S corporations (see Chapter 8), and single-member LLCs if allowed under state law (see Chapter 3).

Often, a business will start off as a sole proprietorship for administrative convenience. As the business grows, usually it will be "converted" into one of the other types of entities (corporation, partnership, LLC, etc.) covered in other chapters of this publication.

When an existing business is purchased, sole proprietorships will *not* often be the chosen form for doing business after the transaction. This may be because the newly acquired business is substantial enough to be operated through a "liability-limiting entity" (a corporation, limited partnership, LLC, or LLP) and/or because several owners are teaming up to make the acquisition.

Thus, in many cases sole proprietorships need not be considered at all. In the right circumstances, however, sole proprietorships can be attractive.

9.02 LIABILITY OF SOLE PROPRIETORS

As stated earlier, a sole proprietorship is an unincorporated business that is legally one and the same as its owner. Therefore, the personal assets of the owner are exposed without limitation to any and all liabilities related to the conduct of the sole proprietorship business. This unlimited liability exposure is the most significant difference between sole proprietorships and the other types of entities discussed in this publication (other than general partnerships, which also expose their owners to unlimited personal liability).

The existence of one or more of the following conditions indicates that operating a business through a liability-limiting entity, not a sole proprietorship, should be strongly considered:

- The formation and operation of the activity will result in significant debts to financial institutions, lessors, vendors, and other creditors;
- The activity will involve the delivery of professional services, with the resulting inherent risk of malpractice claims;
- The activity will involve employees whose foreseeable actions can create liabilities (for example, employees are expected to use their cars regularly in the activity);
- The activity will require the hiring of one or more employees (regardless of the nature of the business itself, employees inevitably create exposure to liabilities in any number of ways—for example, one employee may harass another, employees can be injured on the job or premises, discriminatory hiring or firing practices can be alleged, embezzlement and theft can occur, and unauthorized borrowing or spending transactions can occur);
- The nature of the activity itself is hazardous (for example, potentially dangerous tools are used, heavy equipment is used, toxic substances are handled, or employees must work at heights or in the middle of vehicular traffic),
- The potential for product liability claims exists (for example, the products demand specialized training to operate or are inherently dangerous); and
- There is potential exposure to environmental liabilities (as is the case with almost any manufacturing activity and perhaps any activity that involves the ownership of real estate, which may have pollution, asbestos, or lead problems).

9.03 NONTAX ADVANTAGES AND DISADVANTAGES OF SOLE PROPRIETORSHIPS

Advantage of Administrative Simplicity

Some simple initial steps may be required to set up a sole proprietorship. For example, under local law it may be necessary to register and pay a fee to obtain a business license. Filings may be required if the business will use an assumed name (a "DBA").

Generally, no other legal papers or filings are required to initiate and operate a sole proprietorship. Thus, professional fees and burdensome paperwork are minimized.

However, the advantage of administrative simplicity should not be overstated. Even sole proprietorships should generally do the following:

- Open a bank account in the name of the business (not required, but recommended);
- Obtain liability, property, business interruption, and worker's compensation insurance coverage (if there are employees);
- Establish adequate accounting procedures;
- Comply with federal and state estimated tax payment rules (estimated federal income tax deposits are due quarterly and are filed with Form 1040-ES);
- Obtain an employer identification number (EIN) if the business will have employees;
- Establish payroll tax withholding and payment procedures if there are employees); and
- Register as required with states and localities for collection of sales taxes, and obtain all required business licenses and permits.

Disadvantage of Unlimited Owner Liability

As discussed in section 9.02 of this chapter, the owner of a sole proprietorship has *unlimited* personal liability for any debts, claims, or other obligations associated with that business. Thus, the owner's personal assets are always at risk and can be lost entirely if large liabilities or claims arise. These can include claims related to tortious acts of others (such as reckless driving of a vehicle by an employee on business).

As a practical matter, such liability may not be cause for undue alarm. In some businesses, the risks may be inherently negligible, and/or it may be possible to obtain adequate liability insurance at an acceptable cost.

Liability-Limiting Entities Are Not Cure-Alls

The use of a liability-limiting entity such as a corporation is *not* the cure-all that some think. This is another reason why sole proprietorship status may not be as risky as it first appears.

For many commonly encountered business liabilities, such as bank loans, lease obligations, and vendor payables (often referred to as "contract" or "commercial" liabilities), creditors will generally require owners to guarantee the debts personally. This will be true whether the vehicle used to operate the venture is a corporation or some other entity. Thus, operating as a sole proprietorship may not actually increase the owner's exposure to these types of liabilities.

Generally, if the business under consideration is a professional practice conducted by the owner personally, using a corporation (or any other legal entity, for that matter) will do nothing to protect the practitioner's personal assets from liabilities related to his or her own professional errors, omissions, and negligence. The same is true for liabilities related to the owner's tortious acts (such as careless driving resulting in injuries or property damage), whether they are committed in the course of business or not.

Thus, in many cases, the only ways to minimize liability exposures are to carry appropriate liability insurance and to operate in a businesslike and professionally competent manner. Setting up a solely owned corporation or single-member LLC may not shelter the owner's personal assets significantly in such situations.

Disadvantage When Transferring Ownership Interests

Partial ownership in corporations, partnerships, and LLCs can be transferred relatively easily, because the ownership interests—rather than direct interests in the business's assets—can be conveyed. Often, the owner makes such transfers to a spouse or children for estate-planning, family income tax planning, business succession planning, and other reasons.

In contrast, it is impractical to transfer ownership of interests in the assets of a sole proprietorship. Unfortunately, there is nothing else that *can* be transferred, because a sole proprietorship does not have any pieces of paper that represent ownership interests in the business.

If there is a foreseeable need to raise additional equity capital, a corporation, partnership, or LLC provides an established vehicle for taking in new owners. The entity simply issues additional shares of stock or additional partnership or LLC interests.

If the business is run as a sole proprietorship, however, taking in an additional owner (for whatever reason) will always require the creation of a new legal entity to own the business. The minute there is more than one owner, there can no longer be a sole proprietorship.

For the reasons discussed above, it often is obvious that a sole proprietorship will be useful for only a relatively short time. It may be advisable to set up the new business as a corporation, partnership, or LLC from the beginning, to facilitate ownership transfers and/or the entrance of additional owners. As discussed in Chapter 5, there may be ways to form partnerships and multi-member LLCs even when, for all intents and purposes, there is only one initial owner.

9.04 TAX CONSIDERATIONS

As noted earlier, when a business is 100% owned by an individual, the alternatives to sole proprietorship status generally are limited to the C corporation and the S corporation. Also, single-member LLCs are now permitted in most but not all states. As discussed in Chapter 3, they are treated as sole proprietorships for federal tax purposes, so there is no federal income tax difference between a sole proprietorship and a single-member LLC. Partnerships, multi-member LLCs, and LLPs all are required by definition to have more than one owner. Thus, when the tax aspects of operating as a sole proprietorship are being evaluated, the relevant items for comparison are the tax rules of C corporations and those of S corporations.

Tax Accounting Methods

A sole proprietor may use different accounting methods for business and personal activities. For example, the accrual method may be used for the business (in preparing Schedule C and related forms and schedules), while the cash method is used for the personal income and expense items appearing elsewhere on the return.

Note, however, that businesses usually prefer the cash method, because it offers much greater flexibility to shift taxable income and deductions between years for tax-planning purposes.

There are no general limitations on the ability of sole proprietorship businesses to use the cash method of accounting for federal income tax purposes. As discussed in Chapters 3–8, LLCs, LLPs, partnerships, and corporations all have at least potential limitations on when the cash method can be used.

However, any business for which the production, purchase, or sale of merchandise is an income-producing factor must compute beginning and ending inventories to determine taxable income for the year, and such businesses must use the accrual method of accounting for purchases and sales [Regs. §§1.446-1(a)(4)(i) and (c)(2)(i)]. The cash method is unavailable in such cases, even for sole proprietorships.

Sole Proprietorship Compared to C Corporation

Lower Corporate Rates versus Double Taxation

As discussed in Chapter 6, the main tax advantage of C corporation status is the favorable corporate graduated rate structure. The lower rates allow the corporation to maximize its current cash flow by minimizing cash outlays for federal income taxes, which allows the corporation to finance more of its growth internally. Note that personal service corporations (PSCs) are *not* permitted to use the graduate corporate rates. Instead, PSCs are taxed at a flat rate of 35%.

As a practical matter, the benefits of the corporate graduated rates are overwhelmed by the negative effects of double taxation if:

1. The business generates substantial taxable income, and
2. The corporation is not expected to continue in existence for a relatively long period of time (thereby postponing the double taxation day of reckoning).

In most cases, single-owner corporations cannot be expected to continue in existence much beyond the life of the shareholder. Therefore, there usually is *not* the ability to postpone indefinitely the double taxation that results upon sale of the stock or liquidation of the corporation. However, if the corporation meets the definition of a QSBC, the ill effects of double taxation may be mitigated. (See Chapters 6 and 7.)

See General Practice Aids 5–8 in Chapter 10 for calculation templates that estimate the tax cost of operating as a C corporation versus as a sole proprietorship.

> **OBSERVATION:** *As discussed in Chapter 6, double taxation is* not *a problem if the corporation's taxable income can be "zeroed out" with deductible payments for owner compensation, fringe benefits, etc.*

Business Throws Off Tax Losses

If the business is expected to incur tax losses (because, for example, it is in the start-up phase), a sole proprietor can deduct the losses currently on Schedule C of Form 1040. In contrast, if a C corporation is used the tax losses are "trapped" inside the corporation in the form of a net operating loss (NOL). The NOL will result in future tax benefits only if the corporation earns taxable income in future years.

Payroll Tax Advantage for C Corporations

Amounts retained by a C corporation are not subject to federal payroll taxes. In contrast, the self-employment (SE) tax applies to 100% of a sole proprietor's business income, as reported on Schedule C. Thus, the federal payroll taxes owed if the owner is an employee of a C corporation may be significantly less than the SE tax owed if the owner is a sole proprietor. See Example 6.04(1) in Chapter 6.

> **OBSERVATION:** *The federal payroll tax rules can provide a significant incentive to incorporate. See later Example 9.04(1) for the payroll tax effects of operating as an S corporation rather than as a C corporation.*

Inability to Borrow against Qualified Retirement Accounts

Another potentially significant disadvantage of sole proprietorships compared to C corporations is the sole proprietor's inability to borrow against his or her qualified retirement plan account balances. Within limits, C corporation shareholder-employees *can* borrow against their account balances. However, sole proprietors cannot, nor can partners, LLC members who own more than 10% interests in capital or profits, or S corporation shareholder-employees who own more than 5% of the corporate stock [IRC §4975].

Fringe Benefits and State Taxes

As discussed in Chapter 6, C corporations generally can deliver more tax-advantaged fringe benefits to owners than can sole proprietorships (or S corporations or partnerships, for that matter). For example, C corporations can deduct 100% of the cost of premiums for medical insurance coverage of shareholder-employees and their families, and the premiums are not included in the taxable incomes of the shareholder-employees [IRC §106]. As discussed later in this section, under current law, sole proprietors will be able to deduct 100% of medical insurance premiums only if the spouse is an employee of the proprietorship. Otherwise, only a percentage is deductible.

The state tax implications of operating as a C corporation versus as a sole proprietorship should be also be considered carefully. Generally, state and local tax rules parallel federal rules by allowing C corporations favorable graduated tax rates but subjecting them to double taxation.

Sole Proprietorship Compared to S Corporation

Operating a solely owned business as a sole proprietorship may lead to federal income tax results that are not significantly different from those of an S corporation. This is because the pass-through taxation concept applies to S corporations. There are some differences, however, as discussed below.

Deductibility of Health Insurance Premium Costs

If the spouse of a sole proprietor is a bona fide employee of the proprietorship and the proprietorship provides health insurance coverage for employees, the sole proprietor may be able to deduct 100% of the cost of health insurance premiums for coverage of self, spouse, and dependents. The employee-spouse can select family coverage, which also covers the owner and the children. The proprietorship can deduct 100% of the premium costs under IRC §162. The employee-spouse can exclude the benefit from taxable income under IRC §§105 and 106. (See PLR 9409006.)

If the spouse is not employed by the business, the above maneuver is unavailable and the general rule for sole proprietors applies; that is, only a percentage of the cost of premiums for health insurance covering the proprietor and his or her family are deductible [IRC §162(l)].

The percentage deduction rule also applies to health insurance premiums paid by an S corporation for coverage of more-than-2% shareholder-employees and their families [IRC §162(l)(5); Revenue Ruling 91-26 (1991-1 CB 184)]. Partners also are subject to the percentage deduction rule [IRC §162(l)(1); Revenue Ruling 91-26].

As discussed earlier in this section, C corporations can fully deduct premiums for medical insurance coverage of shareholder-employees, and the shareholder-employees recognize no taxable income from this benefit [IRC §106].

Payroll Tax Advantage for S Corporations

Amounts retained by an S corporation are not subject to FICA taxes (unless the corporation is audited and the stated wages are found to be unreasonably low). In contrast, the SE tax applies to 100% of a sole proprietor's business income, as reported on Schedule C.

In addition, the S corporation's contributions to a qualified retirement plan (other than a 401(k) plan) benefiting the shareholder-employee are not subject to FICA taxes, while a sole proprietor's contributions to a Keogh or SEP plan *are* subject to SE tax. Thus, the FICA taxes owed if the owner is an employee of an S corporation may be significantly less than the SE tax owed if the owner is a sole proprietor.

> **Example 9.04(1): Federal Payroll Tax Rules—Sole Proprietorship versus S Corporation**   Danette is a sole proprietor with $100,000 of Schedule C income from her business in 1999. The $100,000 figure is before her $10,000 contribution to her Keogh retirement plan and her $5,000 of medical insurance premiums (which are 60% deductible).
>
> Danette's SE tax is based on SE income of $100,000. She gets no deductions for the Keogh contribution or medical insurance premiums for SE tax purposes. Thus, Danette's 1999 SE tax liability is $11,902.40 (15.3% of $72,600 plus 2.9% of $27,400).
>
> Now assume Danette instead operates her business as a 100% owned S corporation and pays herself a reasonable salary of $55,000, with a contribution of $10,000 to the company pension plan set up for her benefit, and $5,000 paid for medical insurance covering her. (The remaining $30,000 of S corporation income is distributed to Danette as a dividend, which is tax-free to the extent of her basis in her stock.) FICA taxes are due only on Danette's stated salary of $55,000 plus the $5,000 of medical insurance premiums (which are included in her wages for FIT and FICA tax purposes per Revenue Ruling 91-26). Thus, the FICA tax liability is only $9,180 (15.3% of $60,000). Compare this amount to the $11,902.40 of SE tax that is due if Danette operates her business as a sole proprietorship.
>
> **Reality Check:** The federal payroll tax rules encourage S corporation shareholder-employees to set low salaries for themselves to minimize FICA taxes. However, if salary amounts are unreasonably low and the corporation is audited, the IRS will attempt to recharacterize all or part of the purported S corporation dividend payments as disguised salary. The corporation will then be hit with back FICA taxes, interest, and possibly penalties. See Example 6.04(01) in Chapter 6 for the payroll tax effects of operating as a C corporation rather than as an S corporation.

Additional Basis from Debt

One tax advantage of sole proprietorship status is that the owner will receive basis from all business-related debt for loss deduction purposes. In contrast, an S corporation shareholder receives basis only to the extent of the basis in his or her stock plus the amount of any loans made to the corporation. In other words, entity-level debt does not add to the basis available to the shareholder, even if the debt is personally guaranteed.

Tax Advantage for Wages Paid to Owner's Minor Children

An advantage of sole proprietorships over both C and S corporations is in the area of federal payroll taxes. A sole proprietorship (or a husband–wife partnership) can pay wages to the owner's under-age-18 children without owing any FICA or FUTA taxes. The child also does not owe the employee's half of the FICA tax. [See IRC §§3121(b)(3) and 3306(c)(5).]

The sole proprietor is able to deduct the wages and thereby reduce taxable business income for both income tax (which may at a rate as high as 39.6%) and self-employment tax (which may be at a rate as high as 15.3%) purposes without paying the FICA and FUTA taxes that would apply to wages paid to other employees. The child's wage income is earned income, so some or all of it generally can be sheltered by the child's standard deduction amount ($4,300 for 1999).

If the business is operated as a C or S corporation, however, the wages of the owner's children are subject to federal payroll taxes just like those of other employees.

> *REALITY CHECK: Of course, the wages paid to the child must be reasonable in relation to the work actually performed, so hiring one's children works best with teenage children who can be assigned meaningful duties.*

Sole Proprietorship Compared to Single-Member LLC

Single-member LLCs are now available in all but a few states. As explained in section 3.11 of Chapter 3, single-member LLCs are ignored for federal tax purposes. Thus, when a single-member LLC owned by an individual is used to conduct a trade or business activity, it is treated as a sole proprietorship for federal income tax purposes. Accordingly, the owner reports the business income and deductions on Schedule C and computes the SE tax on Schedule SE.

Even though the single-member LLC is "invisible" for federal tax purposes, it still exists for state law purposes and thus protects the owner's personal assets from most business-related liabilities.

Because it offers liability protection advantages, the single-member LLC is almost always preferred to sole proprietorship status. The only exceptions would be when single-member LLCs are treated disadvantageously for under state income tax rules or when LLC status is unavailable under state law or professional standards. For example, Texas single-member LLCs must pay the state's corporate franchise tax, while sole proprietors are exempt. By law, some professionals are unable to operate as single-member LLCs, and some states prohibit using LLCs in certain lines of business, such as agriculture or banking.

When single-member LLC status is available, the LLC can generally be formed quickly and inexpensively by filing a registration statement with the appropriate state authority and paying the required fee. After the initial year, ongoing annual fee payments may be required to maintain the LLC's registration.

9.05 SUMMARY STATEMENT ON WHEN SOLE PROPRIETORSHIPS ARE ATTRACTIVE

The sole proprietorship may be the preferred form of doing business if:

1. There is only a single owner and single-member LLCs are not permitted by state law or applicable professional standards, or are subject to unfavorable state tax rules; and
2. Adequate liability insurance is available at an acceptable cost; *or*
3. The major liability exposures are from the owner's practice of a profession (a problem that generally is not "cured" by operating as a liability-limiting entity); and
4. The business is in the early stages, when minimizing administrative expenses and paperwork is a major objective; and
5. At this time the owner does not wish to deal with the issue of how ownership interests (for estate planning, succession planning, or other reasons) will be transferred in the future; and
6. At this time the owner does not wish to deal with the issue of how additional equity capital might be raised in the future; and
7. The business is small enough that operating as a sole proprietorship is still a rational choice in light of *all* the above considerations.

RECOMMENDATION: *As soon as a business begins to generate significant income and wealth for the owner, the use of a liability-limiting entity is highly advisable. Generally, the single-member LLC or S corporation will be the best choice for a single-owner business, because double taxation is avoided. However, in businesses where it is critical to retain the maximum amount of capital to finance growth, the lower graduated tax rates of the C corporation can make it the better choice. (See Chapters 6 and 7 for discussions of C corporations and qualified small business corporations, respectively.)*

CAUTION: *Advising that a business be operated as a sole proprietorship might be viewed as a "risky" recommendation—because of the issue of unlimited personal liability of the owner. The author strongly recommends that practitioners* *also carefully review the other chapters of this publication and use the entity selection software program that comes with this book. The program is designed to help make a choice-of-entity decision consistent with the major legal and tax issues facing the client. If the program leads to the sole proprietorship as apparently the best choice, this chapter can then be reviewed to solidify that conclusion.*

CHAPTER 10 • GENERAL PRACTICE AIDS FOR CHOICE-OF-ENTITY ENGAGEMENTS

CONTENTS

10.01 INTRODUCTION

This chapter includes a number of general practice aids that practitioners may find useful in choice-of-entity engagements. In addition, see the listing below for additional practice aids found in Chapters 3–8. These additional aids are specifically related to the entity alternatives discussed in those chapters.

Note that all of the practice aids in this chapter and most of the practice aids in the other chapters are included in the software that accompanies this book. The software's practice aids can be edited and printed out for use in client engagements.

Practice
Aid No.   *Description*

LLC Practice Aids in Chapter 3

1. Sample Client Letter When Multi-Member LLC Appears to Be Best Entity Choice (Appendix 3C-1)

2. Sample "Generic" Client or Contact Letter Regarding Which Types of Businesses and Activities Are Suited for Multi-Member LLCs (Appendix 3C-2)

3. Sample Client Letter When Single-Member LLC Appears to Be Best Entity Choice (Appendix 3C-3)

4. Checklist for LLC Articles of Organization (Appendix 3D)

5. Sample LLC Articles of Organization (Appendix 3E)

6. LLC Operating Agreement Checklist (Appendix 3F)

7. Sample LLC Operating Agreement (Appendix 3G)

LLP Practice Aid in Chapter 4

1. Sample Client Letter When LLP Appears to Be Best Entity Choice (Appendix 4B)

Partnership Practice Aids in Chapter 5

1. Sample Client Letter When General Partnership Appears to Be Best Entity Choice (Appendix 5A)

2. Sample Client Letter When Limited Partnership Appears to Be Best Entity Choice (Appendix 5B)
3. Partnership Agreement Checklist (Appendix 5C)

C Corporation Practice Aids in Chapter 6

1. Analysis of Effective Tax Rates on C Corporation Income (Appendix 6A, which is essentially the same as General Practice Aid 4 in this chapter)
2. Sample Client Letter When C Corporation Appears to Be Best Entity Choice (Appendix 6B)

QSBC Practice Aids in Chapter 7

1. Analysis of Effective Tax Rates on QSBC Income (Appendix 7A, which is essentially the same as General Practice Aid 4 in this chapter)
2. Sample Client Letter When QSBC Appears to Be Best Entity Choice (Appendix 7B)

S Corporation Practice Aids in Chapter 8

1. Sample Client Letter When S Corporation Appears to Be Best Entity Choice (Appendix 8A)

10.02 GENERAL PRACTICE AIDS

Practice Aid No.	Description
1.	Sample Choice-of-Entity Engagement Letter
2.	Workprogram for Using This Product *with* the Software Interview Feature
3.	Workprogram for Using This Product *without* the Software Interview Feature
4.	Effective Tax Rates on C Corporation and QSBC Income
5.	Filled-Out "Cradle-to-Grave" Tax Calculator Comparing Results for Pass-Through Entity and C Corporation (Assuming Eventual Sale of Ownership Interests)
6.	Blank "Cradle-to-Grave" Tax Calculator Comparing Results for Pass-Through Entity and C Corporation (Assuming Eventual Sale of Ownership Interests)
7.	Filled-Out "Cradle-to-Grave" Tax Calculator Comparing Results for Pass-Through Entity and C Corporation (Assuming Eventual Sale of Assets and Liquidation of Entity)
8.	Blank "Cradle-to-Grave" Tax Calculator Comparing Results for Pass-Through Entity and C Corporation (Assuming Eventual Sale of Assets and Liquidation of Entity)

General Practice Aid 1: Sample Choice-of-Entity Engagement Letter

Dear [Client name]:

This letter is to confirm the terms of our engagement with [Client/Company name] to provide consulting services in connection with selecting the type of legal entity that will be used to operate the new business.

Our engagement is limited to performing the following services:

1. Consulting with you in determining your short-term and long-term goals for the business itself.
2. Assessing the federal and state income tax ramifications of the various entity alternatives.
3. Consulting with you in determining how the legal and tax implications of the various entity alternatives match up with your income tax planning, estate planning, and business succession objectives.
4. [Add additional services as necessary.]

Our fees for the above services will be based on our standard billing rates for the personnel assigned to your engagement. You will also be billed for necessary out-of-pocket expenses. We expect our fees to be no less than $[amount], but they are not expected to exceed $[amount].

We will bill you at the end of each month for fees and expenses incurred to that point. The total of our billings upon completion of the engagement will not exceed the maximum amount stated above, unless additional work has been approved by you, in advance, by amending this engagement letter.

It is understood that payment of our fees and expenses is not in any way contingent on the final outcome of any proposed or actual transaction, such as the consummation of a purchase agreement.

Our invoices are due and payable upon receipt by you.

If this letter correctly sets forth your understanding of the engagement, please sign in the space provided below. Return the original to us, and retain a copy for your records.

We appreciate this opportunity to consult with you on this important business issue.

Very truly yours,

Accepted by: _____ Date: _____

Title: _____

CAUTION: Engagement letters have legal ramifications. The practitioner as well as clients must be prepared to honor their terms. The author recommends that engagement letters be reviewed by legal counsel.

General Practice Aid 2: Workprogram for Using This Product *with* the Software "Interview" Feature

Take the following steps if you choose to take advantage of the "Interview" feature of the software (strongly recommended).

1. Read the Executive Summary in section 1.02 of Chapter 1.

2. Review General Practice Aid 10 and quickly familiarize yourself with the other practice aids available in this chapter. You are now "up to speed" on the general issues.

3. Consider drafting an engagement letter. See General Practice Aid 1. (An electronic version of this document can be accessed by going to the "Practice Aids Menu" screen in the software and selecting "General Practice Aids.")

4. Use the "Interview" feature in the software program to generate a choice-of-entity recommendation. At the end of the interview process, go to the "Engagement Report Options" screen and save your responses to the interview questions by selecting "Save Interview Q&A Report."

5. Before exiting the software program, again go to the "Engagement Report Options" screen. Select "Print Interview Q&A Report." Carefully review the printout and note any answers that you want to reconsider. If you decide you want to answer certain questions differently, go to Step 6 below. If you are satisfied with your answers, skip Step 6 and go directly to Step 7.

6. If you decide that the answers to certain questions were inappropriate or could "go either way," rerun the software with the new answers and see if different choice-of-entity recommendations result.

If you wind up with two or more different recommendations, review the chapters on the recommended types of entities. Then, make a final decision on the *best* entity choice. Now skip Step 7 and go directly to Step 8.

7. If you are satisfied with your answers to the interview questions, review the chapter on the recommended type of entity to validate the software's recommendation. It may also be prudent to review the chapter on what you consider to be the second-best entity choice, just to make sure you are completely satisfied with your conclusion.

8. Reenter the software and go directly to the "Practice Aids Menu" screen. View the "General Practice Aids" and the "Specific Practice Aids" for the recommended type of entity. Then simply edit, save, and print out the appropriate practice aids for transmittal to the client or inclusion in your workpaper file.

9. You have now completed the choice-of-entity recommendation engagement in a logical, systematic, and efficient manner.

General Practice Aid 3: Workprogram for Using This Product *without* the Software "Interview" Feature

Take the following steps if you choose *not* to take advantage of the "Interview" feature of the software. Using the Interview feature is strongly recommended—even if you are highly competent in this area. The Interview process "forces" you to focus on the most critical issues affecting the choice-of-entity decision.

Note: Even if you forego using the Interview feature of the software, make sure you take advantage of the available electronic practice aids. To review these, follow the instructions to go directly to the "Practice Aids Menu" screen.

Initial Steps

1. Read the Executive Summary in section 1.02 of Chapter 1.

2. Review General Practice Aid 10 and quickly familiarize yourself with the other practice aids available in this chapter. You are now "up to speed" on the general issues.

3. Consider drafting an engagement letter. See General Practice Aid 1. (An electronic version of this document can be accessed by going to the "Practice Aids Menu" screen in the software and selecting "General Practice Aids.")

4. Determine if the business or investment activity in question will have more than one owner. (See section 5.04 of Chapter 5 regarding "creating" more than one owner even in situations where there is effectively only a single owner.)

Secondary Steps If Only a Single Owner

1. Your choices are narrowed down to sole proprietorships, C corporations, qualified small business corporations (QSBCs), S corporations, and single-member LLCs. After reviewing Chapter 9, you should quickly be able to either select or reject the sole proprietorship as the best choice of entity. If you reject sole proprietorship status, go to Step 2 below.

    If the sole proprietorship is the best choice, you are done.

    CAUTION: Advising that a business be operated as a sole proprietorship might be viewed as a "risky" recommendation—because of the issue of unlimited personal liability of the owner.

2. In most cases involving single-owner businesses, the single-member LLC or S corporation turns out to be the best choice, because double taxation is avoided. However, read section 6.02 of Chapter 6 for guidance on when C corporations make sense even in light of double

taxation. Also read Chapter 7 to determine if your client could form a corporation that would meet the definition of a QSBC.

> **OBSERVATION:** *Despite the double taxation disadvantage, C corporations make sense for capital intensive and growth businesses, such as manufacturing and high tech ventures. Such businesses typically need to retain all earnings to finance capital expenditures and growing receivable and inventory levels. Operating as a C corporation maximizes cash flow by minimizing current outlays for federal income taxes. If the corporation is a QSBC, the combined corporate-level and owner-level tax rates on corporate income may be comparable to or lower than the tax rate on income earned by a pass-through entity. (See Chapter 7.) C corporations also make sense when corporate income can be "zeroed out" with deductible payments to or for the benefit of the owners. (See section 6.02 of Chapter 6.)*

3. Review General Practice Aids 4, 5, and 7 in this chapter. Consider completing the blank calculation templates shown in General Practice Aids 6 and 8 to quantify the difference in taxes from using an S corporation or single-member LLC versus a C corporation or QSBC. (Electronic versions of these templates can be accessed and filled out by going to the "Practice Aids Menu" screen in the software and selecting "General Practice Aids.")

4. Review Chapters 6 and 7 (on C corporations and QSBCs), Chapter 8 (on S corporations), and section 3.11 of Chapter 3 (on single-member LLCs) and select the best type of corporation given the facts in your client's situation.

> **CAUTION:** *In evaluating S corporations, make sure you consider the impact of the eligibility rules both now and in the reasonably foreseeable future (see section 8.02 of Chapter 8).*

5. Enter the software and go directly to the "Practice Aids Menu" screen. View the "General Practice Aids" and the "Specific Practice Aids" for the recommended type of corporation. Then simply edit, save, and print out the appropriate practice aids for transmittal to the client or inclusion in your workpaper file.

    Note: If you do not have the software, these same practice aids are reproduced in this chapter.

6. You have now completed the choice-of-entity recommendation engagement in a logical, systematic, and efficient manner.

Secondary Steps If More Than One Owner

1. The full range of entity choices (other than sole proprietorships) is available. Your first task is to determine if the C corporation or the qualified small business corporation (QSBC) represents the best choice or if these alternatives can be eliminated.

2. Read section 6.02 of Chapter 6 for guidance on when C corporations make sense even in light of double taxation. Also read Chapter 7 to

determine if your client(s) could form a corporation that would meet the definition of a QSBC.

> **OBSERVATION:** *Despite the double taxation disadvantage, C corporations make sense for capital intensive and growth businesses, such as manufacturing and high tech ventures. Such businesses typically need to retain all earnings to finance capital expenditures and growing receivable and inventory levels. Operating as a C corporation maximizes cash flow by minimizing current outlays for federal income taxes. If the corporation is a QSBC, the combined corporate-level and owner-level tax rates on corporate income may be comparable to or lower than the tax rate on income earned by a pass-through entity. (See Chapter 7.) C corporations also make sense when corporate income can be "zeroed out" with deductible payments to or for the benefit of the owners. (See section 6.02 of Chapter 6.)*

3. Review General Practice Aids 4, 5, and 7 in this chapter. Consider completing the blank calculation templates shown in General Practice Aids 6 and 8 to quantify the difference in taxes from using a pass-through entity versus a C corporation or QSBC. (Electronic versions of these templates can be accessed and filled out by going to the "Practice Aids Menu" screen in the software and selecting "General Practice Aids.")

4. If the C corporation or QSBC is the best choice, go directly to Step 10 below. If these alternatives are rejected, go to Step 5 to consider pass-through entities.

5. In the author's opinion the LLC, when available, is the best pass-through entity choice. Review Chapter 3 and the description of partnership taxation in section 5.08 of Chapter 5. Conclude whether LLC status should be recommended to your client(s). If "Yes," go directly to Step 10 below. If "No," continue to Step 6.

6. In the author's opinion, the limited partnership is the next best pass-through entity choice. Review Chapter 5 and the description of partnership taxation in section 5.08 of Chapter 5. Conclude whether limited partnership status should be recommended to your client(s). If your answer is "Yes," go directly to Step 10 below. If "No," continue to Step 7.

7. At this point, you have rejected LLCs and limited partnerships. In the author's opinion, the S corporation generally is the third-best pass-through entity choice. However, you must be able to conclude that the S corporation eligibility rules can be met without insurmountable difficulty both now and in the foreseeable future. (Review Chapter 8, especially section 8.02.) If the S corporation is the best choice, go directly to Step 10 below. If S corporation status is unavailable or unacceptable, the remaining choices are limited liability partnerships (LLPs) and general partnerships.

> **CAUTION:** *In evaluating S corporations, make sure you consider the impact of the eligibility rules both now and in the reasonably foreseeable future (see section 8.02 of Chapter 8).*

8. If the business in question is a professional practice, consider whether a limited liability partnership (LLP) might be a better choice than an S corporation. Review Chapter 4 and see section 5.08 of Chapter 5 regarding the advantages of partnership taxation over S corporation taxation. In some states, LLPS do *not* offer protection against the firm's "contract liabilities" (vendor payables, lease obligations, etc.). Choosing an LLP over an S corporation in these states means the liability-limiting advantages of the S corporation are outweighed by the disadvantage of the S corporation eligibility rules and the advantages of partnership taxation. If the LLP is the better choice, go directly to Step 10 below. If not, continue to Step 9.

9. You have eliminated all entity choices except general partnerships. Therefore, the general partnership has been selected by default.

   CAUTION: Advising that a business be operated as a general partnership might be viewed as a "risky" recommendation—because of the issue of unlimited personal liability of the partners. (See Chapter 5.)

10. Enter the software and go directly to the "Practice Aids Menu" screen. View the "General Practice Aids" and the "Specific Practice Aids" for the recommended type of entity. Then simply edit, save, and print out the appropriate practice aids for transmittal to the client or inclusion in your workpaper file.

    Note: If you do not have the software, these same practice aids are reproduced in this chapter.

11. You have now completed the choice-of-entity recommendation engagement in a logical, systematic, and efficient manner.

General Practice Aid 4: Effective Tax Rates on C Corporation and QSBC Income

Explanation: In assessing the attractiveness of the C corporation and qualified small business corporation (QSBC) versus a pass-through entity (LLC, LLP, partnership, or S corporation), a critical issue is the effective combined tax rate (at the entity and owner levels) that will apply to taxable income. Obviously, if a pass-through entity is used, there is no entity-level tax, but the owners may be high-income individuals who are subject to marginal tax rates as high as 39.6% (see Table 2 below). In such cases, a single level of taxation at high marginal rates may be more expensive than double taxation of C corporation and QSBC income, as shown in Tables 3 and 4.

Table 1: Current Federal Income Tax Rate Schedule for C Corporations

Taxable Income Over	But Not Over	Tax Rate
$0	$50,000	15%
$50,000	$75,000	25%
$75,000	$100,000	34%
$100,000	$335,000	39%
$335,000	$10,000,000	34%
$10,000,000	$15,000,000	35%
$15,000,000	$18,333,333	38%
$18,333,333		35%

As can be seen, the first $75,000 of a C corporation's income is taxed at significantly lower rates than the same income earned by individual taxpayers (see Table 2 below). This is especially true if the income from the activity under consideration will be piled on top of other income (from salaries, other investments, etc.) of high-income individuals. In such cases, the incremental taxable income from the activity may be subject to a 39.6% tax rate if a pass-through entity is used. This means a pass-through entity may be forced to distribute 39.6% of its taxable income to its owners so they can pay their personal tax liabilities. For businesses that need to maximize current cash flow to finance growth, this can be a heavy price to pay for the benefit of pass-through taxation.

Table 2: 1999 Individual Federal Income Tax Rates

Income for Joint Filers	Income for Singles	Tax Rate
$0 to $43,050	$0 to $25,750	15%
$43,051 to $104,050	$25,751 to $62,450	28%
$104,051 to $158,550	$62,451 to $130,250	31%
$158,551 to $283,150	$130,251 to $283,150	36%
Over $283,150	Over $283,150	39.6%

Table 3 below shows the combined effective tax rate on a C corporation's taxable income assuming the income (net of tax) is retained and adds to the value of the corporate stock dollar for dollar. The stock is assumed to be sold for a long-term capital gain taxed at 20%. The combined effective rate should be compared to the marginal individual rate (which can be as high as 39.6%, as shown in Table 2) that would apply if the income were instead earned by a pass-through entity.

Table 3: 1999 Combined C Corporation and Individual Effective Tax Rates

C Corp Average Tax Rate	Individual Rate on LTCGs	Combined Rate
15%*	20%	32.0%
18.33%**	20%	34.7%
34%***	20%	47.2%

*15% average rate applies to taxable income up to $50,000.

**18.33% average rate applies to taxable income of $75,000.

*** 34% average rate applies to taxable income between $335,000 and $10 million.

> **OBSERVATION:** *If the time value of money is taken into account, the combined rates shown above will be reduced. This is because the capital gain component of the combined rate on C corporation income is deferred until the stock is sold. In contrast, taxes on pass-through income must be paid currently.*

Table 4 below shows the combined effective tax rate on a QSBC's taxable income assuming the income (net of tax) is retained and adds to the value of the corporate stock dollar for dollar. The stock is assumed to be sold for a long-term capital gain taxed at an effective rate of 14% (after the 50% gain exclusion). The combined effective rate should be compared to the marginal individual rate (which can be as high as 39.6%, as shown in Table 2) that would apply if the income were instead earned by a pass-through entity.

Table 4: 1999 Combined QSBC and Individual Effective Tax Rates

QSBC Average Tax Rate	Individual Rate on LTCGs	Combined Rate
15%*	14%	26.9%
18.33%**	14%	29.8%
34%***	14%	43.2%

*15% average rate applies to taxable income up to $50,000.

**18.33% average rate applies to taxable income of $75,000.

*** 34% average rate applies to taxable income between $335,000 and $10 million.

> **OBSERVATION:** *If the time value of money is taken into account, the combined rates shown above will be reduced. This is because the capital gain component of the combined rate on QSBC income is deferred until the stock is sold. In contrast, taxes on pass-through income must be paid currently.*

> **CAUTION:** *42% of the excluded QSBC gain is treated as a tax preference item for AMT purposes.*

Filled-Out "Cradle-to-Grave" Tax Calculator Comparing Results for Pass-Through Entity and C Corporation Assuming Eventual Sale of Ownership Interests

Assumed Tax Rate Inputs

	Year 1 PSE	Year 1 C corp	Year 2 PSE	Year 2 C corp	Totals PSE	Totals C corp	
A. Enter owner's assumed tax rate on PSE income for each year.	39.6%	n/a	39.6%	n/a	n/a	n/a	A.
B. Enter assumed C corporation tax rate on corporate income for each year.	n/a	34%	n/a	34%	n/a	n/a	B.
C. Enter owner's assumed tax rate on C corporation dividend income for each year.	n/a	39.6%	n/a	39.6%	n/a	n/a	C.
D. Enter owner's assumed tax rate on gain from sale of PSE ownership interest (must be same for all years). 20 %	20%	n/a	20%	n/a	n/a	n/a	D.
E. Enter owner's assumed tax rate on gain from sale of C corporation stock (must be same for all years). 20 %	n/a	20%	n/a	20%	n/a	n/a	E.

Calculation of Tax Benefit from PSE Status

	Year 1 PSE	Year 1 C corp	Year 2 PSE	Year 2 C corp	Totals PSE	Totals C corp	
1. Business taxable income (enter amount for year)	$2,000,000	$2,000,000	$3,000,000	$3,000,000	$5,000,000	$5,000,000	1.
2. PSE distribution to pay taxes [for PSE column: (line 1 x line A rate for year); for C corporations column: n/a]	792,000	n/a	1,188,000	n/a	1,980,000	n/a	2.
3. C corporation tax payment [for PSE column: n/a; for C corporation column: (line 1 x line B rate for year)]	n/a	680,000	n/a	1,020,000	n/a	1,700,000	3.
4. Cash distribution to owner (enter amount for year)	200,000	200,000	300,000	300,000	500,000	500,000	4.
5. Assumed increase in value of ownership interest [for PSE column: (line 1 – line 2 – line 4); for C corporation column: (line 1 – line 3 – line 4)]	1,008,000	1,120,000	1,512,000	1,680,000	2,520,000	2,800,000	5.
6. Increase in basis of ownership interest [for PSE column: (line 1 – line 2 – line 4); for C corporation column: zero]	1,008,000	0	1,512,000	0	2,520,000	0	6.
7. Increase in taxable gain inherent in ownership interest [line 5 – line 6]	0	1,120,000	0	1,680,000	0	2,800,000	7.

	Year 1		Year 2		Totals	
	PSE	C corp	PSE	C corp	PSE	C corp
8. Accrued tax liability on increase in taxable gain inherent in ownership interest [for PSE column: (line 7 x line D rate); for C corporation column: (line 7 x line E rate)]	0	224,000	0	336,000	0	560,000
9. After-tax benefit from increase in value of ownership interest (line 5 – line 8)	1,008,000	896,000	1,512,000	1,344,000	2,520,000	2,240,000
10. Shareholder tax on C corporation distribution [for PSE column: n/a; for C corporation column: (line 4 x line C rate for year)]	n/a	79,200	n/a	118,800	n/a	198,000
11. Practitioner adjustments (enter negative numbers in brackets)	—	—	—	—	—	—
12. After-tax benefit to owner from business income (line 4 + line 9 – line 10 + or – line 11)	$1,208,000	$1,016,800	$1,812,000	$1,525,200	$3,020,000	$2,542,000
13. Tax savings from PSE status (difference in line 12 amounts shown for PSE and C corporation columns)		$191,200		$286,800		$478,000

General Practice Aid 5: Filled-Out "Cradle-to-Grave" Tax Calculator Comparing Results for Pass-Through Entity and C Corporation Assuming Eventual Sale of Ownership Interests

Explanation: This calculator is one way of estimating the annual and cumulative tax savings from operating as a pass-through entity (PSE) rather than as a C corporation. The assumption is that the taxable income of the business each year is the same whether it is operated as a PSE or as a C corporation.

If operated as a PSE, the business is assumed to distribute enough cash to its owner to pay the annual tax on the passed-through income. In addition, you can input amounts for annual cash distributions to the owner (above and beyond what is needed to pay personal taxes). If operated as a C corporation, the business each year pays tax on its income at the corporate rates. Again, you can input amounts distributed as dividends to C corporation shareholders.

It is assumed that there is an annual increase in the value of both the PSE and the C corporation ownership interests equal to the taxable income for the year less taxes paid (for the C corporation) and distributions. In the case of the PSE, it is further assumed that the tax basis of the ownership interest increases each year by an amount equal to the taxable income less the distributions for that year.

Each year, taxes are accrued on the assumed incremental taxable gain (assumed increase in value less increase in basis) inherent in the ownership interests. The numbers on line 12 below represent the assumed annual after-tax benefit to the owner from distributions plus the increase in value of the ownership interest.

Now assume the PSE and C corporation ownership interests are sold at the end of the projection period for realized gains equal to the sum of the annual assumed incremental gains. The cumulative after-tax economic benefit to the owner will equal the amounts shown on line 12 in the total columns.

The differences between the PSE and C corporation line 12 amounts (annual and cumulative) are due solely to the tax savings achieved by operating as a PSE rather than as a C corporation. The tax savings amounts are shown on line 13.

See General Practice Aid 6 for a blank version of this form.

General Practice Aid 6: Blank "Cradle-to-Grave" Tax Calculator Comparing Results for Pass-Through Entity and C Corporation Assuming Eventual Sale of Ownership Interests

Explanation: This calculator is one way of estimating the annual and cumulative tax savings from operating as a pass-through entity (PSE) rather than as a C corporation. The assumption is that the taxable income of the business each year is the same whether it is operated as a PSE or as a C corporation.

If operated as a PSE, the business is assumed to distribute enough cash to its owner to pay the annual tax on the passed-through income. In addition, you can input amounts for annual cash distributions to the owner (above and beyond what is needed to pay personal taxes). If operated as a C corporation, the business each year pays tax on its income at the corporate rates. Again, you can input amounts distributed as dividends to C corporation shareholders.

It is assumed that there is an annual increase in the value of both the PSE and the C corporation ownership interests equal to the taxable income for the year less taxes paid (for the C corporation) and distributions. In the case of the PSE, it is further assumed that the tax basis of the ownership interest increases each year by an amount equal to the taxable income less the distributions for that year.

Each year, taxes are accrued on the assumed incremental taxable gain (assumed increase in value less increase in basis) inherent in the ownership interests. The numbers on line 12 below represent the assumed annual after-tax benefit to the owner from distributions plus the increase in value of the ownership interest.

Now assume the PSE and C corporation ownership interests are sold at the end of the projection period for realized gains equal to the sum of the annual assumed incremental gains. The cumulative after-tax economic benefit to the owner will equal the amounts shown on line 12 in the total columns.

The differences between the PSE and C corporation line 12 amounts (annual and cumulative) are due solely to the tax savings achieved by operating as a PSE rather than as a C corporation. The tax savings amounts are shown on line 13.

See General Practice Aid 5 for a filled-out version of this form.

Blank "Cradle-to-Grave" Tax Calculator Comparing Results for Pass-Through Entity and C Corporation Assuming Eventual Sale of Ownership Interests

	Year 1		Year 2		Year 3		Year 4		Year 5		Totals	
	PSE	C corp	PSE	C corp	PSE	C corp	PSE	C corp	PSE	C corp	PSE	C corp
Assumed Tax Rate Inputs												
A. Enter owner's assumed tax rate on PSE income for each year.												
B. Enter assumed C corporation tax rate on corporate income for each year.												
C. Enter owner's assumed tax rate on C corporation dividend income for each year.												
D. Enter owner's assumed tax rate on gain from sale of PSE ownership interest (must be same for all years). ____%												
E. Enter owner's assumed tax rate on gain from sale of C corporation stock (must be same for all years). ____%												
Calculation of Tax Benefit from PSE Status												
1. Business taxable income (enter amount for year)												
2. PSE distribution to pay taxes [for PSE column: (line 1 x line A rate for year); for C corporations column: n/a]												
3. C corporation tax payment [for PSE column: n/a; for C corporation column: (line 1 x line B rate for year)]												
4. Cash distribution to owner (enter amount for year)												
5. Assumed increase in value of ownership interest [for PSE column: (line 1 – line 2 – line 4); for C corporation column: (line 1 – line 3 – line 4)]												
6. Increase in basis of ownership interest [for PSE column: (line 1 – line 2 – line 4); for C corporation column: zero]												
7. Increase in taxable gain inherent in ownership interest [line 5 – line 6]												

	Year 1		Year 2		Year 3		Year 4		Year 5		Totals	
	PSE	C corp	PSE	C corp	PSE	C corp	PSE	C corp	PSE	C corp	PSE	C corp
8. Accrued tax liability on increase in taxable gain inherent in ownership interest [for PSE column: (line 7 x line D rate); for C corporation column: (line 7 x line E rate)]												
9. After-tax benefit from increase in value of ownership interest (line 5 – line 8)												
10. Shareholder tax on C corporation distribution [for PSE column: n/a; for C corporation column: (line 4 x line C rate for year)]												
11. Practitioner adjustments (enter negative numbers in brackets)												
12. After-tax benefit to owner from business income (line 4 + line 9 – line 10 + or – line 11)												
13. Tax savings from PSE status (difference in line 12 amounts shown for PSE and C corporation columns)												

General Practice Aid 7: Filled-Out "Cradle-to-Grave" Tax Calculator Comparing Results for Pass-Through Entity and C Corporation Assuming Eventual Asset Sale and Liquidation of the Entity

Explanation: This calculator is one way of estimating the annual and cumulative tax savings from operating as a pass-through entity (PSE) rather than as a C corporation. The assumption is that the owner will make the same initial investment to acquire his or her ownership interest in the PSE or C corporation and that subsequent taxable income of the business each year is the same whether the business is operated as a PSE or as a C corporation.

If operated as a PSE, the business is assumed to distribute enough cash to its owner to pay the annual tax on the passed-through income. In addition, you can input amounts for annual cash distributions to the owner (above and beyond what is needed to pay personal taxes). If operated as a C corporation, the business each year pays tax on its income at the corporate rates. Again, you can input amounts distributed as dividends to C corporation shareholders.

It is assumed that there is an annual increase in the value and tax basis of the business assets equal to the taxable income for the year less taxes paid (for the C corporation) and distributions. In the case of the PSE, is further assumed that the tax basis of the ownership interest increases each year by an amount equal to the taxable income less the distributions for that year.

In addition, on line 7 for the final year of the projection period, you can enter the amount of assumed gain on sale of all business assets due to appreciation in the value of those assets. (The same gain amount should be input in both the PSE column and the C corporation column.) Note that this gain increases the basis of the PSE ownership interest.

The PSE and the C corporation are then assumed to be liquidated at the end of the final year, with the owners exchanging their ownership interests for the liquidating distributions shown on line 11.

The differences between the PSE and C corporation line 15 after-tax cash to owner amounts (annual and cumulative) are due solely to the tax savings achieved by operating as a PSE rather than as a C corporation. The tax savings amounts are shown on line 16.

See General Practice Aid 8 for a blank version of this form.

Filled-Out "Cradle-to-Grave" Tax Calculator Comparing Results for Pass-Through Entity and C Corporation Assuming Eventual Asset Sale and Liquidation of the Entity

	Year 1		Year 2		Totals	
	PSE	C corp	PSE	C corp	PSE	C corp
Assumed Tax Rate Inputs						
A. Enter owner's assumed tax rate on PSE income for each year.	39.6%	n/a	39.6%	n/a	n/a	n/a
B. Enter assumed C corporation tax rate on corporate income for each year.	n/a	34%	n/a	34%	n/a	n/a
C. Enter owner's assumed tax rate on C corporation dividend income for each year.	n/a	39.6%	n/a	39.6%	n/a	n/a
D. Enter owner's assumed tax rate on PSE pass-through gain from sale of all assets in final year. ___33%___	n/a	n/a	33%	n/a	n/a	n/a
E. Enter assumed C corporation tax rate on corporate gain upon sale of all assets in final year. ___34%___	n/a	n/a	n/a	34%	n/a	n/a
F Enter owner's assumed tax rate on gain from liquidating exchange of C corporation stock in final year. ___20%___	n/a	n/a	n/a	20%	n/a	n/a
Calculation of Tax Benefit from PSE Status						
1. Business taxable income (enter amount for year)	$2,000,000	$2,000,000	$3,000,000	$3,000,000	$5,000,000	$5,000,000
2. PSE distribution to pay taxes [for PSE column: (line 1 x line A rate for year); for C corporations column: n/a]	792,000	n/a	1,188,000	n/a	1,980,000	n/a
3. C corporation tax payment [for PSE column: n/a; for C corporation column: (line 1 x line B rate for year)]	n/a	680,000	n/a	1,020,000	n/a	1,700,000
4. Cash distribution to owner (enter amount for year)	200,000	200,000	300,000	300,000	500,000	500,000
5. Assumed increase in value of assets from operations [for PSE column: (line 1 – line 2 – line 4); for C corporation column: (line 1 – line 3 – line 4)]	1,008,000	1,120,000	1,512,000	1,680,000	2,520,000	2,800,000
6. Increase in basis of ownership interest from operations [for PSE column: (line 1 – line 2 – line 4); for C corporation column: zero]	1,008,000	0	1,512,000	0	2,520,000	0

	Year 1		Year 2		Totals	
	PSE	C corp	PSE	C corp	PSE	C corp
7. Assumed final-year taxable gain when entity sells all business assets (enter amount in column for final year)	n/a	n/a	5,000,000	5,000,000	5,000,000	5,000,000
8. Increase in basis of ownership interest from final-year taxable gain on sale of all business assets [for PSE column: line 7 amount; for C corporation column: zero]	n/a	n/a	5,000,000	0	5,000,000	0
9. PSE owner final-year tax on line 7 amount [for PSE column: (line 7 x line D rate); for C corporation column: n/a]	n/a	n/a	1,650,000	n/a	1,650,000	n/a
10. C corporation final-year tax on line 7 amount [for PSE column: n/a; for C corporation column: (line 7 x line E rate)]	n/a	n/a	n/a	1,700,000	n/a	1,700,000
11. Final-year liquidating distribution to owner [for PSE column: (sum of line 5 amounts for all years, including the final year, + line 7); for C corporation column: (sum of line 5 amounts for all years + line 7 − line 10)]	n/a	n/a	7,520,000	6,100,000	7,520,600	6,100,000
12. Owner taxable gain on line 11 amount [for PSE column: line 11 − sum of line 6 amounts for all years, including the final year, − line 8); for C corporation column: (line 11 − sum of line 6 amounts for all years, including the final year, − line 8)]	n/a	n/a	0	6,100,000	0	6,100,000
13. Owner tax on line 12 amount [for PSE column: zero; for C corporation column: (line 12 x line F rate)]	n/a	n/a	0	1,220,000	0	1,220,000
14. Shareholder tax on C corporation distribution from operations [for PSE column: n/a; for C corporation column: (line 4 x line C rate for year)]	n/a	79,200	n/a	118,800	n/a	198,000
15. After-tax cash to owner from business income, gains, and liquidating distribution [for PSE column: (line 4 − line 9 + line 11); for C corporation column: (line 4 + line 11 − line 13 − line 14)]	$200,000	$120,800	$6,170,000	$5,061,200	$6,370,000	$5,182,000
16. Tax savings from PSE status (difference in line 15 amounts shown for PSE and C corporation columns)	$79,200		$1,108,800		$1,188,000	

General Practice Aid 8: Blank "Cradle-to-Grave" Tax Calculator Comparing Results for Pass-Through Entity and C Corporation Assuming Eventual Asset Sale and Liquidation of the Entity

Explanation: This calculator is one way of estimating the annual and cumulative tax savings from operating as a pass-through entity (PSE) rather than as a C corporation. The assumption is that the owner will make the same initial investment to acquire his or her ownership interest in the PSE or C corporation and that subsequent taxable income of the business each year is the same whether the business is operated as a PSE or as a C corporation.

If operated as a PSE, the business is assumed to distribute enough cash to its owner to pay the annual tax on the passed-through income. In addition, you can input amounts for annual cash distributions to the owner (above and beyond what is needed to pay personal taxes). If operated as a C corporation, the business each year pays tax on its income at the corporate rates. Again, you can input amounts distributed as dividends to C corporation shareholders.

It is assumed that there is an annual increase in the value and tax basis of the business assets equal to the taxable income for the year less taxes paid (for the C corporation) and distributions. In the case of the PSE, is further assumed that the tax basis of the ownership interest increases each year by an amount equal to the taxable income less the distributions for that year.

In addition, on line 7 for the final year of the projection period, you can enter the amount of assumed gain on sale of all business assets due to appreciation in the value of those assets. (The same gain amount should be input in both the PSE column and the C corporation column.) Note that this gain increases the basis of the PSE ownership interest.

The PSE and the C corporation are then assumed to be liquidated at the end of the final year, with the owners exchanging their ownership interests for the liquidating distributions shown on line 11.

The differences between the PSE and C corporation line 15 after-tax cash to owner amounts (annual and cumulative) are due solely to the tax savings achieved by operating as a PSE rather than as a C corporation. The tax savings amounts are shown on line 16.

See General Practice Aid 7 for a filled-in version of this form.

Blank "Cradle-to-Grave" Tax Calculator Comparing Results for Pass-Through Entity and C Corporation Assuming Eventual Asset Sale and Liquidation of the Entity

	Year 1		Year 2		Year 3		Year 4		Year 5		Totals	
	PSE	C corp	PSE	C corp	PSE	C corp	PSE	C corp	PSE	C corp	PSE	C corp
Assumed Tax Rate Inputs												
A. Enter owner's assumed tax rate on PSE income for each year.												
B. Enter assumed C corporation tax rate on corporate income for each year.												
C. Enter owner's assumed tax rate on C corporation dividend income for each year.												
D. Enter owner's assumed tax rate on PSE pass-through gain from sale of all assets in final year. ___ %												
E. Enter assumed C corporation tax rate on corporate gain upon sale of all assets in final year. ___ %												
F. Enter owner's assumed tax rate on gain from liquidating exchange of C corporation stock in final year. ___ %												
Calculation of Tax Benefit from PSE Status												
1. Business taxable income (enter amount for year)												
2. PSE distribution to pay taxes [for PSE column: (line 1 x line A rate for year); for C corporations column: n/a]												
3. C corporation tax payment [for PSE column: n/a; for C corporation column: (line 1 x line B rate for year)]												
4. Cash distribution to owner (enter amount for year)												
5. Assumed increase in value of assets from operations [for PSE column: (line 1 – line 2 – line 4); for C corporation column: (line 1 – line 3 – line 4)]												
6. Increase in basis of ownership interest from operations [for PSE column: (line 1 – line 2 – line 4); for C corporation column: zero]												

	Year 1		Year 2		Year 3		Year 4		Year 5		Totals	
	PSE	C corp	PSE	C corp	PSE	C corp	PSE	C corp	PSE	C corp	PSE	C corp
7.												
8.												
9.												
10.												
11.												
12.												
13.												
14.	—	—	—	—	—	—	—	—	—	—	—	—
15.	=	=	=	=	=	=	=	=	=	=	=	=
16.	=	=	=	=	=	=	=	=	=	=	=	=

7. Assumed final-year taxable gain when entity sells all business assets (enter amount in column for final year)

8. Increase in basis of ownership interest from final-year taxable gain on sale of all business assets [for PSE column: line 7 amount; for C corporation column: zero]

9. PSE owner final-year tax on line 7 amount [for PSE column: (line 7 x line D rate); for C corporation column: n/a]

10. C corporation final-year tax on line 7 amount [for PSE column: n/a; for C corporation column: (line 7 x line E rate)]

11. Final-year liquidating distribution to owner [for PSE column: (sum of line 5 amounts for all years, including the final year, + line 7); for C corporation column: (sum of line 5 amounts for all years + line 7 – line 10)]

12. Owner taxable gain on line 11 amount [for PSE column: line 11 – sum of line 6 amounts for all years, including the final year, – line 8); for C corporation column: (line 11 – sum of line 6 amounts for all years, including the final year, – line 8)]

13. Owner tax on line 12 amount [for PSE column: zero; for C corporation column: (line 12 x line F rate)]

14. Shareholder tax on C corporation distribution from operations [for PSE column: n/a; for C corporation column: (line 4 x line C rate for year)]

15. After-tax cash to owner from business income, gains, and liquidating distribution [for PSE column: (line 4 – line 9 + line 11); for C corporation column: (line 4 + line 11 – line 13 – line 14)]

16. Tax savings from PSE status (difference in line 15 amounts shown for PSE and C corporation columns)

General Practice Aid 9: Sample Client Letter Summarizing Choice-of-Entity Alternatives

Dear [Client name]:

This letter briefly summarizes some of the major considerations that are relevant in selecting the type of legal entity to be used for operating a business.

Limited Liability Companies (LLCs)

LLCs are increasingly popular, because they combine the best legal and tax characteristics of corporations and partnerships, while avoiding many of their disadvantages. Specifically, an LLC can offer limited liability protection to all its owners (referred to as "members") while being classified as a partnership for federal income tax purposes.

Legal Considerations

LLCs are unincorporated legal entities created under state law. Even though LLCs are unincorporated vehicles, the fundamental intent of LLC statutes is to allow the formation of entities that legally are more similar to corporations than partnerships.

Nevertheless, LLCs can be taxed as partnerships. The critical point to remember is that, legally, LLCs are *not* corporations; nor are they partnerships.

While the personal assets of LLC members and managers are protected from "general" LLC debts and obligations (often referred to as "contract liabilities"), these persons generally remain *exposed* to LLC liabilities resulting from their own tortious acts and their own professional errors and omissions. (*Tortious acts* are defined as wrongful acts leading to civil actions, other than those involving breach of contract.)

The issue of members' and managers' exposure to liabilities related to tortious acts and professional errors and omissions is a matter of state law. If you have specific questions, we recommend that you consult with your attorney.

Like corporate shareholders, LLC members may be required on occasion to personally guarantee certain of the entity's debts as a condition of obtaining financing or for other reasons. Members are personally obligated with respect to LLC debts that are specifically guaranteed.

Tax Treatment of LLCs

The key *tax* attribute of LLCs is that they can be treated as partnerships for federal income tax purposes. The tax advantages of partnership status are covered later in this letter in the discussion of general partnerships.

Conclusions on LLCs

Because LLC laws are new, inevitably there are legal uncertainties associated with making the choice to operate as an LLC rather than as a partnership or a C or S corporation. There are also some unanswered questions regarding how certain federal tax law provisions apply to LLCs. These uncertainties are the major disadvantage of LLCs.

However, only LLCs offer both the legal advantage of limited liability for all owners and the tax advantage of partnership taxation—which combines pass-through treatment with maximum flexibility. This unique combination of legal and tax benefits is the driving force behind the growing use of LLCs.

Limited Liability Partnerships (LLPs)

LLPs are a relatively new type of entity that can be particularly useful for the operation of professional practices. LLPs are formed and operated pursuant to state LLP statutes.

Liability of LLP Partners

Like the partners of a general partnership, LLP partners in some states (for example, Texas) remain personally liable for the general debts and obligations (so called "contract liabilities") of the LLP. Contract liabilities include, but are not limited to, bank loans, lease obligations, and vendor accounts payable.

In other states (such as California and New York), LLP partners are not personally liable for the LLP's contract liabilities unless the liabilities are expressly guaranteed by the partners. In other words, these states offer "LLC-like" liability protection to LLP partners.

In all states, LLP partners generally remain personally liable for their own tortious acts and their own professional errors and omissions. However, LLP partners are generally *not* liable for the professional errors and omissions of the other LLP partners and employees.

In other words, LLPs offer much greater liability protection than general partnerships, and in some states they offer LLC-like protection.

LLP Advantages and Disadvantages

LLPs are partnerships (both for state law and for federal income tax purposes), and they are therefore subject to the legal and tax implications that generally apply to partnerships.

Thus, the major advantage of LLPs is the ability to benefit from pass-through taxation without being affected by the various restrictions applying to S corporations (such as the one-class-of-stock rule and the other limitations discussed later in this letter). In addition, LLPs enjoy the other tax advantages that partnerships have over S corporations.

The primary disadvantage of LLPs in some states is the personal liability of the partners for the contract liabilities of the entity. In these states, LLC status is more attractive than LLP status. However, under some state laws and under certain professional standards, the use of LLCs may be prohibited. In such situations, LLPs offer better liability protection than general partnerships and are not burdened with the double taxation problems of C corporations.

In the states that offer LLP partners LLC-like liability protection, LLPs and LLCs are equally attractive.

General Partnerships

The partners of a general partnership are personally liable (without limitation) for all debts and obligations of the partnership. The liability of general partners is "joint and several" in nature. This means that any one of the general partners can be forced to make good on all partnership liabilities. That partner may be able to seek reimbursement from the partnership for payments in excess of his or her share of liabilities. But this depends on the ability of the other partners to contribute funds to allow the partnership to make such reimbursement.

Note also that general partners are jointly and severally liable for partnership liabilities related to tortious acts and professional errors and omissions of the other general partners and the partnership's employees. In addition, general partners are personally liable for their own tortious acts, errors, and omissions.

Finally, each general partner usually has the power to act as an agent of the partnership and enter into contracts that are legally binding on the partnership (and ultimately on the other partners). For example, a partner can enter into a lease arrangement that is legally binding on the partnership. It is critical, therefore, if a general partnership is to be formed, for co-owners to have high levels of trust in each other.

Advantages of Pass-Through Taxation

The major advantage of general partnerships is the ability to benefit from pass-through taxation without being affected by the various restrictions that apply to S corporations.

The major features of pass-through taxation are as follows:

- Partnerships are not tax-paying entities. Instead, the partnership's items of income, gain, deduction, loss, and credit are passed through to the partners, who then take those items into account in their own tax returns.

- Adjustments to basis in ownership interests. When the partnership's income and losses are passed through, the partner's basis in his or her partnership interest is adjusted accordingly. Specifically, that basis is increased by the partner's passed-through share of income and gains and decreased by his or her share of losses and deductions. This procedure ensures that income is subject to only a single level of taxation, at the partner level.

- Cash distributions. Distributions reduce the partner's basis in his or her interest. Only distributions in excess of basis trigger taxable gain to the partner.

Multi-Year Impact of Pass-Through Taxation

The avoidance of double taxation of entity income makes a big (and favorable) difference when an entity earns substantial amounts of taxable income over a period of several years.

However, it must be remembered that the C corporation tax rates on the first $75,000 of annual income are considerably lower than the individual tax rates that apply if the same income is passed through by a partnership (or an S corporation). Even at higher income levels, the C corporation rates are still lower than the individual rates. (See Exhibit 1.) If all income is expected to be retained in the business indefinitely (for example, to finance growing receivable and inventory levels), the more favorable C corporation rates can partially or wholly offset the negative effects of double taxation. In such cases, operating as a C corporation may be preferable to pass-through entity status.

Differences between Partnership and S Corporation Taxation

The above discussion of pass-through taxation applies to partnerships and S corporations equally. (For S corporations, simply substitute *corporation* and *shareholder* for *partnership* and *partner*, respectively.) However, there are also significant *differences* between partnership taxation and S corporation taxation, most of them in favor of partnerships. They include the following:

- Partners can receive additional tax basis (for loss deduction purposes) from entity-level liabilities, while S corporation shareholders can receive additional tax basis only from loans they make to the corporation. (Shareholder guarantees of corporate debt have no effect on shareholder basis.)

- Partners who purchase a partnership interest from another partner can step up the tax basis of their shares of partnership assets.

- Partners and partnerships have much greater flexibility to transfer appreciated property tax-free than do S corporations and their shareholders.

- Partnerships can make disproportionate allocations of tax losses and other tax items among the partners. In contrast, all S corporation pass-through items must be allocated among the shareholders strictly in proportion to stock ownership.

There are also several disadvantageous tax rules that apply to partnerships but not S corporations. However, most tax advisors believe that partnership taxation is more favorable, overall, than S corporation taxation.

Conclusion on General Partnerships

The critical disadvantage of general partnerships is the unlimited personal liability of *all* partners for *all* liabilities of the entity. Thus, general partnerships offer *less* protection to the owners' personal assets than do LLCs, LLPs, limited partnerships, S corporations, or C corporations. This fact must be balanced against the potential benefits of partnership taxation.

Limited Partnerships

A limited partnership is a separate legal entity (apart from its limited partners) that owns its assets and is liable for its debts. Therefore, the personal assets of the limited partners generally are beyond the reach of partnership creditors. This is the nontax selling point of limited partnerships.

Limited partners are, however, still personally responsible for partnership liabilities resulting from their own tortious acts.

The key negative factor associated with limited partnerships is that they must have at least one general partner with unlimited personal exposure to partnership liabilities. Usually this problem can be addressed by forming a corporate general partner. This is often an S corporation. With this strategy, the amount the general partner can lose is effectively limited to the value of the assets held by the corporation.

Another potentially significant negative factor is that limited partners can lose their limited liability protection by becoming too actively involved in managing the limited partnership. As a result, limited partnerships are not suitable for activities where all partners are heavily involved in the business (for example, professional practices).

The key tax advantage of limited partnerships is that they can be treated as partnerships for federal income tax purposes. (See the above discussion of the partnership tax rules.)

S Corporations

Legally, S corporations and C corporations are identical. Corporations offer the greatest certainty in terms of protecting the personal assets of owners from the risks of the business. A corporation is treated as a legal entity separate and distinct from its shareholders. Therefore, the corporation owns its own assets and is liable for its own debts. As a result, the personal assets of shareholders (including shareholder-employees) generally are beyond the reach of corporate creditors.

Shareholders generally remain *exposed* to corporate liabilities resulting from their own tortious acts and their own professional errors and omissions.

Shareholders may be required on occasion to personally guarantee certain of the corporation's debts as a condition of obtaining financing or for other reasons. Shareholders are personally obligated with respect to corporate debts that are specifically guaranteed.

Federal Income Tax Treatment of S Corporations

See the coverage of pass-through taxation and differences between partnerships and S corporations in the above discussion of general partnerships.

Election of S Status

The election of S corporation status is made by filing Form 2553 (Election by a Small Business Corporation). The form can be filed during the preceding tax year for an election to become effective for the following tax year. For an S election to be effective for the *current* tax year, it must be filed by the fifteenth day of the third month of that year.

Newly formed corporations generally intend for the election of S status be effective for the initial tax year. The election must be filed by the fifteenth day of the third month after the "activation date" of the corporation. This is the earliest date the corporation has shareholders, acquires assets, or begins conducting business.

Special Restrictions on S Corporations

To qualify for the benefits of pass-through taxation, S corporations must meet a number of strict eligibility rules. Unfortunately, these rules greatly restrict stock ownership and capital structure possibilities and can therefore make operating as an S corporation much less attractive than it first appears.

If the eligibility rules are not met at any time during the tax year, the S status of the corporation is immediately terminated and the corporation falls under the C corporation taxation rules.

To qualify for S status, a corporation must:

- Be a domestic corporation;
- Have no more than 75 shareholders;
- Have no shareholders other than individuals who are U.S. citizens or resident aliens, estates, or certain types of trusts and tax-exempt entities; and

- Have only one class of stock (issuing voting and nonvoting shares is permitted, but there can be no preferred stock or common stock classes with differing economic characteristics).

These restrictions can hamper attempts to raise capital, and they may frustrate plans to transfer stock for income tax planning, estate planning, and business succession reasons.

Ineligible Corporations

The following types of corporations are ineligible for S status by definition:

- Financial institutions allowed to deduct bad debt reserves;
- Domestic international sales corporations (DISCs) or former DISCs;
- Insurance companies other than certain casualty companies; and
- Certain corporations electing to take the possessions tax credit.

Conclusion on S Corporations

Assessing the attractiveness of S corporations involves balancing the advantages of superior liability protection for owners and pass-through taxation against the negative implications of the restrictive eligibility rules.

Regular Corporations ("C Corporations")

The principal advantage of C corporations is their ability to protect owners from liabilities related to the business. As discussed earlier, the liability-limiting attributes of C and S corporations are identical.

Federal Income Tax Treatment of C Corporations

The key disadvantage of C corporations is that they are subject to double taxation. The double taxation issue appears in several different ways, described briefly here:

- Dividend distributions. If the corporation has accumulated earnings and profits, nonliquidating distributions to shareholders are treated as dividends. These are taxed as ordinary income to the recipient shareholders, but the payments are not deductible by the corporation. In some situations, the corporation may be forced to make dividend distributions to avoid being hit with corporate-level penalty taxes on "excessive" retained earnings.
- Double taxation on sale of stock. When a C corporation earns taxable income, there is no upward adjustment in the tax basis of the shareholders' stock. The retained income increases the value of the stock, which creates a bigger capital gain when shares are eventually sold. As a result, the retained income is in effect taxed again when shares are sold.

- Double taxation on liquidation. If the corporation holds appreciated property and eventually liquidates, the property to be distributed in liquidation is treated as sold by the corporation for its fair market value (FMV). The corporation must then pay the resulting taxes. When the corporate assets (net of corporate-level taxes) are distributed to shareholders in liquidation, shareholders must also recognize taxable gain to the extent the FMV of the liquidating distributions exceeds the tax basis of their shares.

- Double taxation of appreciating assets. If the corporation holds appreciating assets, the resulting gains will be subject to double taxation if the corporation sells them, if the corporation is liquidated, or if the corporate stock is sold.

We strongly recommend that assets expected to appreciate significantly (such as real estate, patents, and copyrights) be owned by a pass-through entity (which is in turn owned by the C corporation's shareholders). The pass-through entity can then lease the assets to the C corporation. With this arrangement, the C corporation can reduce its taxable income by making deductible rental payments, which benefit its shareholders. Any gains upon the eventual sale of the appreciated assets owned by the pass-through entity will not be subject to double taxation.

Other negative aspects of C corporation taxation apply in the following circumstances:

- When the corporation has significant tax losses; and
- When the corporation has significant long-term capital gains, capital losses, or tax-exempt income.

When Are the Corporate Tax Rules Harmless or Even Favorable?

Often, corporations can solve the double taxation problem by "zeroing out" corporate income with deductible payments to or for the benefit of shareholder-employees. Such payments can be for salary, fringe benefits, interest on shareholder loans, and rent for property owned by shareholders. When corporate income can be zeroed out, the issue of double taxation is not applicable.

Even when zeroing out income is not possible, the favorable graduated corporate tax rates can make C corporations attractive compared to pass-through entities. This is the case when businesses earn relatively small amounts and intend to retain all earnings indefinitely in order to internally finance their growth. A pass-through entity might have to distribute up to 39.6% of the taxable income earned by the business to enable the owners to pay their personal taxes, whereas the average tax rate on the first $75,000 of corporate income is only 18.33%.

Even at taxable income levels above $75,000, the tax rates for C corporations are significantly lower than those for individuals. As a result, the use of a C corporation can maximize the current cash flow of the business. It must be remembered, however, that the cost of this current benefit is the double taxation that may apply in later years. (See Exhibit 1.)

CAUTION: Personal service corporations (PSCs) are ineligible for the favorable corporate graduated tax rates. Instead, all PSC income is taxed at a flat 35% rate.

Conclusion on C Corporations

Empirical evidence shows that businesses that need to retain earnings to finance growth most often operate as C corporations. This allows them to maximize current cash flow by minimizing current outlays for taxes.

Generally, businesses that distribute their income to owners should be operated via one of the pass-through entities to avoid double taxation.

Qualified Small Business Corporations (QSBCs)

If a C corporation meets the definition of a QSBC, shareholders (other than C corporations) potentially are eligible to exclude from taxation up to 50% of their gains on sale of the corporation's stock. In addition, shareholders may be able to roll over gains tax-free by reinvesting in new QSBC stock issued by a different company.

A number of rules must be met for a corporation to qualify for QSBC status, and shareholders must own their stock for more than five years to benefit from the gain exclusion provision and for more than six months to take advantage of the gain rollover rule.

See Exhibit 1 for a table showing how the ill effects of double taxation may be largely offset by the gain exclusion.

QSBCs present a real alternative to pass-though entities in cases where corporations will qualify for QSBC status.

(Note that QSBCs are treated the same as "regular" C corporations for all other tax and legal purposes.)

Single-Member LLCs

Single-member LLCs are now available in all but a few states. The unique attribute of single-member LLCs is that they are ignored for federal tax purposes. Thus, when a single-member LLC owned by an individual is used to conduct a trade or business activity, it is treated as a sole proprietorship for federal income tax purposes. Accordingly, the owner reports the business income and deductions on Schedule C and computes the SE tax on Schedule SE. Both Schedules are filed with the owner's Form 1040.

Similarly, when a single-member LLC owned by an individual is used to hold rental real estate, the owner files Schedule E with his or her Form 1040 to report the income and deductions from the rental activity.

Even though the single-member LLC is "invisible" for federal tax purposes, it still exists for state law purposes and thus protects the owner's personal assets from most business-related liabilities.

Generally, the single-member LLC is the preferred choice when pass-through taxation is desired for a single-owner business. The only other pass-through alternative for a single-owner business is the S corporation, which has strict qualification rules, as explained earlier.

Because it offers liability protection advantages, the single-member LLC is almost always preferred to sole proprietorship status. The only exceptions would be when single-member LLCs are treated disadvantageously for under state income tax rules or when LLC status is unavailable under state law or professional standards. For example, Texas single-member LLCs must pay the state's corporate franchise tax, while sole proprietors are exempt. By law, some professionals are unable to operate as single-member LLCs, and some states prohibit using LLCs in certain lines of business, such as agriculture or banking.

When single-member LLC status is available, the LLC can generally be formed quickly and inexpensively by filing a registration statement with the appropriate state authority and paying the required fee. After the initial year, ongoing annual fee payments may be required to maintain the LLC's registration.

Conclusion

We appreciate the opportunity to consult with you as you make the important decision of choosing the most advantageous type of entity under which to operate your new venture. We look forward to working with you in the future as your business is formed and enters the operating phase.

Very truly yours,

Exhibit 1: Effective Tax Rates on C Corporation and QSBC Income

Explanation: In assessing the attractiveness of the C corporations and the qualified small business corporations (QSBCs) versus a pass-through entity (LLC, LLP, partnership, or S corporation), a critical issue is the effective combined tax rate (at the entity and owner levels) that will apply to taxable income. Obviously, if a pass-through entity is used, there is no entity-level tax, but the owners may be high-income individuals who are subject to marginal tax rates as high as 39.6% (see Table 2 below). In such cases, a single level of taxation at high marginal rates may be more expensive than double taxation of C corporation and QSBC income, as shown in Tables 3 and 4.

Table 1: Current QSBC Federal Income Tax Rate Schedule

Taxable Income Over	But Not Over	Tax Rate
$0	$50,000	15%
$50,000	$75,000	25%
$75,000	$100,000	34%
$100,000	$335,000	39%
$335,000	$10,000,000	34%
$10,000,000	$15,000,000	35%
$15,000,000	$18,333,333	38%
$18,333,333		35%

As can be seen, the first $75,000 of a C corporation's income is taxed at significantly lower rates than the same income earned by an individual taxpayer (see Table 2 below). This is especially true if the income from the activity under consideration will be piled on top of other income (from salaries, other investments, etc.) of high-income individuals. In such cases, the incremental taxable income from the activity may be subject to a 39.6% tax rate if a pass-through entity is used. This means a pass-through entity may be forced to distribute 39.6% of its taxable income to its owners so they can pay their personal tax liabilities. For businesses that need to maximize current cash flow to finance growth, this can be a heavy price to pay for the benefit of pass-through taxation.

Table 2: 1999 Individual Federal Income Tax Rates

Income for Joint Filers	Income for Singles	Tax Rate
$0 to $43,050	$0 to $ 25,750	15%
$43,051 to $104,050	$25,751 to $62,450	28%
$104,051 to $158,550	$62,451 to $130,250	31%
$158,551 to $283,150	$130,251 to $283,150	36%
Over $283,150	Over $283,150	39.6%

Table 3 below shows the combined effective tax rate on a C corporation's taxable income assuming the income (net of tax) is retained and adds to the value of the corporate stock dollar for dollar. The stock is assumed to be sold for a long-term capital gain taxed at 20%. The combined effective rate should be compared to the marginal individual rate (which can be as high as 39.6% as shown in Table 2) that would apply if the income were instead earned by a pass-through entity.

Table 3: 1999 Combined C Corporation and Individual Effective Tax Rates

C Corp Average Tax Rate	Individual Rate on LTCGs	Combined Rate
15%*	20%	32.0%
18.33%**	20%	34.7%
34%***	20%	47.2%

* 15% average rate applies to taxable income up to $50,000.
**18.33% average rate applies to taxable income of $75,000.
*** 34% average rate applies to taxable income between $335,000 and $10 million.

OBSERVATION: *If the time value of money is taken into account, the combined rates shown above will be reduced. This is because the capital gain component of the combined rate on C corporation income is deferred until the stock is sold. In contrast, taxes on pass-through income must be paid currently.*

Table 4 below shows the combined effective tax rate on a QSBC's taxable income assuming the income (net of tax) is retained and adds to the value of the corporate stock dollar for dollar. The stock is assumed to be sold for a long-term capital gain taxed at an effective rate of 14% (after the 50% gain exclusion). The combined effective rate should be compared to the marginal individual rate (which can be as high as 39.6%, as shown in Table 2) that would apply if the income were instead earned by a pass-through entity.

Table 4: 1998 Combined QSBC and Individual Effective Tax Rates

QSBC Average Tax Rate	Individual Rate on LTCGs	Combined Rate
15%*	14%	26.9%
18.33%**	14%	29.8%
34%***	14%	43.2%

* 15% average rate applies to taxable income up to $50,000.
**18.33% average rate applies to taxable income of $75,000.
*** 34% average rate applies to taxable income between $335,000 and $10 million.

OBSERVATION: *If the time value of money is taken into account, the combined rates shown above will be reduced. This is because the capital gain component of the combined rate on QSBC income is deferred until the stock is sold. In contrast, taxes on pass-through income must be paid currently.*

CAUTION: *42% of the exc luded QSBC gain is treated as a tax preference item for AMT purposes.*

Side-by-Side Summary of Entity Attributes

Issue	General Partnership (See Chapter 5)	Limited Partnership (See Chapter 5)	C Corporation* (See Chs. 6 and 7)	S Corporation (See Chapter 8)	Multi-Member LLC (See Chapter 3)	LLP (See Chapter 4)
Legal Formalities of Formation	None.	File Certificate of L.P. with Sec. of State.	File Articles of Incorporation with Sec. of State.	File Articles of Incorporation with Sec. of State.	File Articles of Organization with Sec. of State.	File application with Sec. of State.
Liability of Owners	All partners are jointly and severally liable.	General partners are jointly and severally liable. Limited partners liable only to extent of contributions.	Shareholders liable only to extent of contributions.	Shareholders liable only to extent of contributions.	Members liable only to extent of contributions.	Not liable for professional errors and omissions of other partners or employees unless under direct supervision of partner in question. Same as general partnership for other liabilities in some states. In other states, generally no exposure to other liabilities.
Number of Owners	At least two, but no maximum.	At least one general partner and one limited partner, but no maximum.	No limits.	No more than 75.	At least two, but no maximum (almost all states now permit single-member LLCs, which are generally treated as sole proprietorships for federal tax purposes).	At least two, but no maximum.
Types of Owners	No limits.	No limits.	No limits.	Only individuals, estates, certain trusts, and certain tax-exempt entities may be shareholders.	No limits.	No limits.
Tax on Contributions	Generally none.	Generally none.	Generally none if control test satisfied.	Generally none if control test satisfied.	Generally none.	Generally none.
Basis	Carryover basis from property contributed plus basis from share of liabilities.	Carryover basis from property contributed plus basis from share of liabilities.	Carryover basis from property contributed. No basis from debt of entity.	Carryover basis from property contributed. Basis from loans to corporation. No basis from other debt of entity.	Carryover basis from property contributed plus basis from share of liabilities.	Carryover basis from property contributed plus basis from share of liabilities.
Tax on Income	Taxed directly to partners.	Taxed directly to partners	Entity level tax. No tax to owners unless cash or property is distributed.	Taxed directly to shareholders. Some entity taxes on passive income or gains under certain circumstances.	Taxed directly to members.	Taxed directly to partners.

Tax on Distributions	None to extent of basis.	None to extent of basis.	Distributions taxable to shareholders. No deduction to corporation. Appreciation on any in-kind distributions taxable to corporation.	Generally can make distributions to extent of shareholder's basis without tax. Appreciation on any in-kind distributions is taxable at the corporate level.	None to extent of basis.	None to extent of basis.
Management	Each partner has general agency authority.	Each general partner has general agency authority. Limited partners have limited rights to participate in management.	Shareholders elect board of directors. Board of directors elect officers. Officers hold authority to act on behalf of corporation. Formalities on taking corporate action.	Shareholders elect board of directors. Board of directors elect officers. Officers hold authority to act on behalf of corporation. Formalities on taking corporate action.	If member-managed, each member has general agency authority. If manager-managed, only managers have general agency authority.	Depending on state law, each partner has general agency authority.
Ability to Transfer All Ownership Rights	Transferee cannot become partner without approval of other partners.	Transferee cannot become partner without approval of other partners.	Transferee takes all rights of transferor, including rights to participate in management.	Transferee takes all rights or transferor, including rights to participate in management.	Transferee cannot become member without approval of other members.	Transferee cannot become partner without approval of other partners.
Continuity of Life	Legal dissolution on death, disability, etc., of general partner.	Legal dissolution on death, disability, etc, of general partner.	Perpetual existence permitted.	Perpetual existence permitted.	Legal dissolution on death, disability, etc., of a member.	Legal dissolution on death, disability, etc., of partner.
Flexibility in Tax Allocations	Substantial flexibility in permitted allocations.	Substantial flexibility in permitted allocations.	Some flexibility through use of multiple classes of stock but not as flexible as a partnership.	Only permitted to have single class of stock. Severely restricts flexibility in allocations.	Substantial flexibility in permitted allocations.	Substantial flexibility in permitted allocations.
Tax-Advantaged Fringe Benefits for Owners	Generally not available to partners.	Generally not available to partners.	Wider range of fringe benefits available to shareholder-employees.	Generally not available to shareholder-employees.	Generally not available to members.	Generally not available to partners.

*Including QSBC.

General Practice Aid 10: Side-by-Side Summary of Entity Attributes

The table on the following pages summarizes key entity attributes. However, the information presented is general in nature. See Chapters 2–9 for detailed analysis.

General Practice Aid 11: Summaries of When Each Type of Entity Is Attractive

Limited Liability Companies (LLCs)

LLCs are suitable for many business and investment activities, including but not limited to the following:

- Corporate joint ventures (where the corporate co-owners desire both pass-through taxation and limited liability);
- Real estate investment and development activities (because the partnership taxation rules allow investors to obtain basis from entity-level debt, and special tax allocations can be made to investors);
- Oil and gas exploration (where the partnership rules can be used to make special allocations of intangible drilling cost deductions to investors);
- Venture capital investments (where the partnership rules allow pass-through taxation and the creation of "customized" ownership interests with varying rights to cash flow, liquidating distributions, and tax items);
- Business start-ups expected to have tax losses in the initial years (which can be passed through to investors); and
- Professional practices—if allowed under state law and applicable professional standards (where pass-through taxation can be combined with specially tailored ownership interests that reflect each member's contributions to the practice); and
- Estate-planning vehicles (where the older generation can gift LLC ownership interests to younger family members while retaining control by functioning as the managers, and where all taxable income is passed through to the members).

According to a survey in the December 1995 issue of *Journal of Accountancy*, the top 10 types of businesses operated as LLCs were:

- Engineering and management support services (26%);
- Real estate services (19%);
- Construction and general contracting (12%);
- Investment companies (9%);
- Retailers (8%);
- Health services (7%);
- Agriculture (7%);
- Oil and gas extraction (2%);
- Restaurants (2%); and
- Leasing companies (2%).

Side-by-Side Summary of Entity Attributes

Issue	General Partnership (See Chapter 5)	Limited Partnership (See Chapter 5)	C Corporation* (See Chs. 6 and 7)	S Corporation (See Chapter 8)	LLC** (See Chapter 3)	LLP (See Chapter 4)
Legal Formalities of Formation	None.	File Certificate of L.P. with Sec. of State.	File Articles of Incorporation with Sec. of State.	File Articles of Incorporation with Sec. of State.	File Articles of Organization with Sec. of State.	File application with Sec. of State.
Liability of Owners	All partners are jointly and severally liable.	General partners are jointly and severally liable. Limited partners liable only to extent of contributions.	Shareholders liable only to extent of contributions.	Shareholders liable only to extent of contributions.	Members liable only to extent of contributions.	Not liable for professional errors and omissions of other partners of employees unless under direct supervision of partner in question. Same as general partnership for other liabilities in some states.
Number of Owners	At least two, but no maximum.	At least one general partner and one limited partner, but no maximum.	No limits.	No more than 75.	At least two, but no maximum (some states permit single-member LLCs).	At least two, but no maximum.
Types of Owners	No limits.	No limits.	No limits.	Only individuals, certain estates, certain trusts, and certain tax-exempt entities may be shareholders.	No limits.	No limits.
Tax on Contributions	Generally none.	Generally none.	Generally none if control test satisfied.	Generally none if control test satisfied.	Generally none.	Generally none.
Basis	Carryover basis from property contributed plus basis from share of liabilities.	Carryover basis from property contributed plus basis from share of liabilities.	Carryover basis from property contributed. No basis from debt of entity.	Carryover basis from property contributed. Basis from loans to corporation. No basis from other debt of entity.	Carryover basis from property contributed plus basis from share of liabilities.	Carryover basis from property contributed plus basis from share of liabilities.
Tax on Income	Taxed directly to partners.	Taxed directly to partners	Entity level tax. No tax to owners unless income distributed.	Taxed directly to shareholders. Some entity taxes on passive income or gains under certain circumstances.	Taxed directly to members.	Taxed directly to partners.

	(1)	(2)	(3)	(4)	(5)	(6)
Tax on Distributions	None to extent of basis.	None to extent of basis.	Distributions taxable to shareholders. No deduction to corporation. Appreciation on any in-kind distributions taxable to corporation.	Generally can make distributions to extent of shareholder's basis without tax. Appreciation on any in-kind distributions is taxable at the corporate level.	None to extent of basis.	None to extent of basis.
Management	Each partner has general agency authority.	Each general partner has general agency authority. Limited partners have limited rights to participate in management.	Shareholders elect board of directors. Board of directors elect officers. Officers hold authority to act on behalf of corporation. Formalities on taking corporate action.	Shareholders elect board of directors. Board of directors elect officers. Officers hold authority to act on behalf of corporation. Formalities on taking corporate action.	If member-managed, each member has general agency authority. If manager-managed, only managers have general agency authority.	Each partner has general agency authority.
Ability to Transfer All Ownership Rights	Transferee cannot become partner with approval of other partners.	Transferee cannot become partner without approval of other partners.	Transferee takes all rights of transferor, including rights to participate in management.	Transferee takes all rights or transferor, including rights to participate in management.	Transferee cannot become member without approval of other members.	Transferee cannot become partner without approval of other partners.
Continuity of Life	Legal dissolution on death, disability, etc., of general partner.	Legal dissolution on death, disability, etc, of general partner.	Perpetual existence permitted.	Perpetual existence permitted.	Legal dissolution on death, disability, etc., of a member.	Legal dissolution on death, disability, etc., of partner.
Flexibility in Tax Allocations	Substantial flexibility in permitted allocations.	Substantial flexibility in permitted allocations.	Some flexibility through use of multiple classes of stock but not as flexible as a partnership.	Only permitted to have single class of stock. Severely restricts flexibility in allocations.	Substantial flexibility in permitted allocations.	Substantial flexibility in permitted allocations.
Permitted Acquisitions	No restrictions.	No restrictions.	No restrictions.	No restrictions.	No restrictions.	No restrictions.
Tax-Advantaged Fringe Benefits for Owners	Generally not available to partners.	Generally not available to partners.	Wider range of fringe benefits available to shareholder-employees.	Generally not available to share-holder-employees.	Generally not available to members.	Generally not available to partners.

*Including QSBC.
**Assumed classified as a partnership for federal tax purposes.

Under some state laws and/or applicable professional standards (such as state bar association rules), LLCs may be prohibited from operating certain professional practices. However, when permitted, LLCs are an excellent choice. In some states, professional LLCs offer better liability protection than limited-liability partnerships (LLPs), and the ability to create differing types of LLC ownership interests (for example, to reflect the activity levels of the members) can often be attractive to professional groups.

Some states do not permit the use of LLCs in certain lines of business, such as banking, insurance, and farming.

> **RECOMMENDATION:** *Most advisors agree that the LLC is the best entity alternative if pass-through taxation is desired (such as with a service business that has no need to retain significant amounts of earnings within the business entity). However, empirical evidence shows that LLCs are seldom formed to operate capital-intensive and high-growth businesses, such as manufacturing and high-tech ventures. Such businesses typically need to retain all earnings to finance capital expenditures and growing receivable and inventory levels. These businesses are most often operated as C corporations in order to maximize cash flow by minimizing current outlays for federal income taxes.*

Because LLCs allow all members to participate fully in management without risk of losing limited-liability protection (which can happen with a limited partnership), they are ideally suited for closely held entrepreneurial businesses.

In summary, LLCs may be the best choice for business and investment ventures if:

- There will be more than one owner; and

- Limited liability protection for the co-owners is an important consideration; and

- Pass-through taxation is desired; and

- The advantages of partnership taxation are significant compared to the alternative of S corporation taxation, or the entity cannot qualify for S corporation status; and

- The business (or investment) activity can be operated as an LLC under state law and applicable professional standards; and

- The co-owners can tolerate the uncertainties of LLC status.

> **CAUTION:** *Although LLC statutes place no limits under on the number of members, there is a tax problem if ownership interests are so widely held that they are "publicly traded" within the meaning of IRC §7704. If an LLC's ownership interests are publicly traded, the LLC will be treated as a C corporation for federal income tax purposes.*

As a practical matter, the existence of IRC §7704 and the typical limitations on transferability of ownership interests mean that LLCs generally are appropriate only for closely held businesses.

Limited Liability Partnerships (LLPs)

LLPs are probably the best entity choice for professional service ventures if:

- Pass-through taxation is desired; and
- LLC status is unavailable or the state LLP statute offers LLC-like liability protection; and
- LLP status is permitted under state statutes and applicable professional standards; and
- Qualifying as an S corporation would be inconvenient, difficult, or impossible, *or* the entity could qualify as an S corporation but the benefits of the partnership taxation rules are significant compared to those of the S corporation taxation rules; and
- The co-owners can live with their exposure (if any) to the entity's contract liabilities.

> **RECOMMENDATION:** *As implied by the above, LLPs are not as attractive as LLCs in states that do not offer LLC-like liability protection and are generally less attractive than S corporations in those states. However, they are always more attractive than general partnerships. In many cases, professional practices can be operated as C corporations and avoid the double taxation problem by "zeroing out" corporate income with deductible payments to or for the benefit of the owners. When this is possible, C corporations probably are superior to LLPs.*

General Partnerships

General partnerships may be suitable for business and investment activities including, but not limited to, the following:

- Corporate joint ventures (where the corporate co-owners desire both pass-through taxation and limited liability);
- Real estate investment and development activities (because the partnership taxation rules allow partners to obtain basis from entity-level debt and special tax allocations can be made to investors);
- Oil and gas exploration (where the partnership rules can be used to make special allocations of intangible drilling cost deductions to partners);
- Venture capital investments (where the partnership rules allow pass-through taxation and the creation of "customized" ownership interests with varying rights to cash flow, liquidating distributions, and tax items);
- Business start-ups expected to have tax losses in the initial years (which can be passed through to investors); and
- Professional practices (where pass-through taxation can be combined with specially tailored ownership interests that reflect each member's contributions to the practice).

General partnerships are probably the best entity choice when:

- There are at least two co-owners, all of whom have a high degree of trust in each other; and

- Pass-through taxation is desired; and

- LLC and LLP status are unavailable; and

- Liability concerns can be managed with insurance; and

- Qualifying as an S corporation would be inconvenient, difficult, or impossible, *or* the entity could qualify as an S corporation, but the benefits of the partnership taxation rules are significant compared to those of the S corporation taxation rules; and

- The co-owners can live with the fact that the general partnership will not have an unlimited legal life or free transferability of ownership interests.

> **RECOMMENDATION:** *In most cases, the desire to limit owner liability is so significant that only a limited partnership, as opposed to a general partnership, will make sense. In the case of professional practices, operating as an LLC, LLP, or C corporation should be explored. Most advisors agree that general partnerships and sole proprietorships are by far the least attractive entity options.*

Limited Partnerships

Business and investment activities where limited partnerships make sense include, but are not limited to, the following:

- Real estate investment and development activities (where the partnership taxation rules allow investors to receive preferred returns, special allocations of tax losses, and additional basis from partnership-level debt);

- Oil and gas exploration (where the partnership taxation rules allow preferred returns and special allocations of deductions from intangible drilling costs);

- Venture capital investments (where the partnership rules allow pass-through taxation and the creation of ownership interests with varying rights to cash flow, liquidating distributions, and tax items);

- Business start-ups expected to have tax losses in the initial years (which can be passed through to the partners);

- Estate-planning vehicles (where the older generation can gift limited partnership interests to younger family members while retaining control by functioning as the general partners, and where all taxable income is passed through to the partners.

Limited partnerships can be attractive if:

- There are at least two co-owners; and

- Pass-through taxation is desired; and

- LLC status is unavailable; and
- Qualifying as an S corporation would be inconvenient, difficult, or impossible; *or*
- The entity could qualify as an S corporation, but the benefits of the partnership taxation rules are significant compared to those of the S corporation taxation rules; and
- The co-owners who will be limited partners can live with the fact that they cannot become too actively involved in management of the venture without losing their limited-liability protection; and
- The co-owners can live with the fact that the limited partnership will not have an unlimited legal life or free transferability of all ownership interests.

RECOMMENDATION: *Most advisors agree that LLCs, when available, are superior to limited partnerships. However, when pass-through taxation is desired, limited partnerships are often the second best choice.*

C Corporations

In general, C corporations may be preferred to LLCs, LLPs, general and limited partnerships, and sole proprietorships if:

- Limiting owner liability is a critical concern; *and*
- There will be only one owner (making partnership taxation unavailable by definition), and the S corporation restrictions make operating as an S corporation difficult or impossible; *or*
- The activity cannot be operated as a limited partnership, because the owners who would be limited partners cannot live with the fact that they must avoid management involvement to maintain their limited liability protection; *and*
- The activity cannot be operated as an LLC under state law and/or applicable professional standards; *or*
- The business cannot be operated as an LLC, because the owners cannot live with the legal uncertainties associated with LLC status; *or*
- The benefits of pass-through taxation are not required (because the graduated corporate rates counteract the ill effects of double taxation or because the venture's income can be drained with deductible payments to or for the benefit of the owners); *or*
- Being able to borrow against their qualified retirement plan accounts is a critical issue for the owners.

RECOMMENDATION: *C corporations are underrated because of the issue of double taxation. However, the differences between corporate tax rates and individual tax rates mean that pass-through taxation often results in higher current outlays for federal income taxes. Recent empirical evidence shows that C corporations are still being formed to operate capital-intensive and growth businesses, such as manufacturing and high-tech ventures, because such businesses typically need to retain all earnings to finance capital expenditures and growing receivable* *and inventory levels. Operating as a C corporation maximizes cash flow by minimizing current outlays for federal income taxes. And for very successful businesses, the C corporation format lays the best groundwork for going public.*

Qualified Small Business Corporations (QSBCs)

QSBC shareholders (other than C corporations) potentially qualify to exclude from taxation 50% of their gains upon the sale of shares. However, the shares must be held for more than five years, and a number of other restrictions apply. In addition, shareholders who have held their stock over six months will generally qualify for a favorable gain rollover rule.

In general, C corporations that meet the definition of a QSBC may be preferred over LLCs, partnerships, and sole proprietorships if:

- Limiting owner liability is a critical concern; *and*

- The entity will qualify for QSBC status; *and*

- There will be only one owner (making partnership taxation unavailable by definition) and the S corporation restrictions make operating as an S corporation difficult or impossible; *or*

- The activity cannot be operated as a limited partnership, because the owners who would be limited partners cannot live with the fact that they must avoid management involvement to maintain their limited liability protection; *and*

- The activity cannot be operated as an LLC under state law; *or*

- The business cannot be operated as an LLC, because the owners cannot live with the legal uncertainties associated with LLC status; *or*

- The benefits of pass-through taxation are not required (because the graduated corporate rates and QSBC gain exclusion counteract the ill effects of double taxation, or because the venture's income can be drained off with deductible payments to or for the benefit of the owners); *or*

- Being able to borrow against their qualified retirement plan accounts is a critical issue for the owners.

RECOMMENDATION: *See the above comments regarding C corporations. The same apply to QSBCs, except that QSBCs are more attractive than "regular" C corporations because of the 50% gain exclusion and gain rollover tax breaks.*

S Corporations

In general, S corporations may be preferred over C corporations, LLCs, LLPs, partnerships, and sole proprietorships if:

- Limiting owner liability is a critical concern; *and*
- Pass-through taxation is desired; *and*
- The S corporation eligibility rules can be met without undue hardship; *and*
- The restrictions on eligible S shareholders do not cause undue hardship with regard to the owners' future plans to transfer ownership interests to others for estate planning, family tax planning, or business succession planning purposes; *and*
- There will be only one owner (making partnership taxation unavailable by definition); *or*
- The activity cannot be operated as an LLC under state law and/or applicable professional standards; *or*
- The business cannot be operated as an LLC, because the owners cannot live with the legal uncertainties associated with LLC status; *or*
- The activity cannot be operated as a limited partnership, because the owners who would be limited partners cannot live with the fact that they must avoid management involvement to maintain their limited liability protection; *or*
- The business either cannot be operated as an LLP, or the liability protections offered by LLPs are considered inadequate; *or*
- The benefits of partnership taxation compared to those of S corporation taxation are not considered significant enough to warrant setting up a partnership, LLC, or LLP.

> **RECOMMENDATION:** *Most advisors agree that LLCs and limited partnerships are superior to S corporations. However, when there is a single owner and double taxation must be avoided, the S corporation is the only alternative to sole proprietorship status unless single-member LLCs are permitted under state law.*

Sole Proprietorships

The sole proprietorship may be the preferred form of doing business if:

- There is a single owner and single-member LLCs are not permitted by state law; and
- Adequate liability insurance is available at an acceptable cost; *or*
- The major liability exposures are from the owner's practice of a profession (a problem that generally is not "cured" simply by operating as a liability-limiting entity); and
- The business is in the early stages, and minimizing administrative expenses and paperwork is a major objective; and
- At this time, the owner does not wish to deal with the issue of how ownership interests will be transferred in the future (for estate planning, succession planning, or other reasons); and

- At this time, the owner does not wish to deal with the issue of how additional equity capital might be raised in the future; and
- The business is small enough that operating as a sole proprietorship is still a rational choice in light of *all* the above considerations.

> **RECOMMENDATION:** *The primary attraction of sole proprietorships is their administrative simplicity. As soon as a business begins to generate significant income and wealth for the owner, however, the use of a liability-limiting entity is highly advisable. Generally, the S corporation or single-member LLC (if permitted by state law) will prove the best choice for a single-owner business, because double taxation is avoided. However, when it is critical to retain the maximum amount of capital to finance growth, the C corporation's lower graduated tax rates can make it the better choice—particularly if the corporation can meet the definition of a QSBC.*

Single-Member LLCs

Single-member LLCs are now available in all but a few states. Their unique attribute is that they are ignored for federal tax purposes. For example, a single-member LLC owned by an individual and used to conduct a business activity is treated as a sole proprietorship for federal income tax purposes, which means maximum tax simplicity for the owner.

Even though the single-member LLC is "invisible" for federal tax purposes, it still exists for state law purposes and thus protects the owner's personal assets from most business-related liabilities.

Generally, the single-member LLC is the preferred choice when both liability protection and pass-through taxation are required for a single-owner business. The only other entity meeting both of these requirements for a single-owner business is the S corporation, which has strict and often inconvenient qualification rules.

However, operating as a solely owned S corporation may be preferable when (1) S corporation status can be used to minimize federal payroll taxes, or (2) the owner prefers the (arguably) greater legal certainty of incorporation.

Because it offers liability protection advantages, the single-member LLC is almost always preferred to the sole proprietorship. The only exceptions would be when (1) single-member LLCs are treated disadvantageously under state income tax rules or (2) LLC status is unavailable under state law or professional standards.

FINDING LIST

Acts of Congress

IRS Restructuring and Reform
  Act of 1998 250
Revenue Reconciliation Act of
  1993 3, 235, 281

Revised Uniform Limited
  Partnership Act 39, 50, 81,
  169, 173, 177, 209, 211, 255,
  321
Small Business Job Protection
  Act of 1996 3, 303

Taxpayer Relief Act of 1997
  250, 281, 283
Uniform Partnership Act 39,
  143, 169, 173, 178

Internal Revenue Code Sections

53 250
55(e) 250
55–59 AMT 250
57(a)(7) 283
57(a)(8) 291
61 246
79 247
105 331, 349
105(b), (c) 247
105(h) 247
106 247, 269, 331, 349, 350
125 248
125(b)(2) 248
127 247, 316
127(b), (c) 248
129 247, 316
129(d) 247
132 316
162 331, 349
162(l) 196, 317, 331, 349
162(l)(1) 331, 349
162(l)(5) 331, 349
163(d) 196, 308
163(h) 196
172 245
197 186, 187, 188, 314, 315, 316
213 197, 317
243–247 (div-rec'd deduction)
  245
267 251
301(a) 240
301(c) 240
301(c)(2), (3) 240
311(b) 65, 189
316 189, 240
331 189

331(a) 76, 77, 78, 150, 151, 152,
  200, 201, 202, 241
336 189
336(a) 65, 76, 77, 78, 150, 151,
  152, 200, 201, 202, 241
351 65, 189, 245, 286
357(c) 68, 185, 186
368 245
401(a) 56
444 197, 251, 317
448 62
448(a) 70
448(a)(1) 249
448(a)(3) 70, 196, 311
448(b) 70
448(b)(3) 249
465(b)(6) 67, 69, 185
448(c) 249
448(d)(3) 196, 311
465 65, 67, 69, 184, 185
469 69
469(a) 251
469(e)(2) 251
469(j)(1) 251
469(j)(2) 251
488(d)(3) 70
501(c) 56
531–537 AET 243
541–547(pers hold co) 243
585 313
593 313
701–761 (Subchapter K) 61–62,
  182
703(a) 118
703(a)(1) 118
704 65

704(a) 206
704(b) 190, 206
704(c) 124, 193, 194, 206
704(c)(1)(B) 189
704(e) 193, 206
705 67
705(e)(2)(B) 118
706(b) 251
708(b)(1)(B) 53, 143, 145, 180
707 111, 225
707(c) 70, 146
708 53, 73, 143, 145, 147, 180,
  198
708(b) 65, 194
721 65, 74, 76, 77, 78, 148, 150,
  151, 152, 188, 198, 200, 201,
  202, 205
722 68, 77, 78, 151, 152, 202, 203
723 77, 78, 151, 152, 202, 203
731 65, 67, 74, 148, 188, 198
731(a)(1) and (b) 189
731(c) 189
733 67
734(b) 199
737 189
741 194
743(b) 186
751 194
751(a) 194
751(c) 194
751(d) 194
752 64, 67, 68, 75, 149, 183, 199
754 114, 186, 187, 188, 199, 228,
  245, 304, 314, 316
856(c) 56
936 63, 285, 313

Internal Revenue Code Sections *cont.*

1014 245
1202 281
1202(b)(1) 286
1202(i)(1) 286
1211 182
1212 182
1231 187, 194, 315
1245 187, 194, 315
1250 194
1254 194
1361–1379 (Subchapter S) 305
1361(b) (Subchapter S) 305, 311
1361(b)(1)(B) 205, 312
1361(b)(1)(D) 312
1361(b)(2) 313
1361(c) 312
1362(d)(3) 313, 318

1362(g) 313
1363(d) 318
1366 64, 65
1366(e) 310
1367(a) 76, 150, 200
1368 189
1371(a) 65
1371(a)(1) 189
1372 316
1374 76, 150, 189, 200, 317
1375 318
1378 251, 317
1402 62
1402(a) 70, 146
1402(a)(13) 70, 146, 147
2701 205
2703 206

3121(b)(3) 332, 351
3306(c)(5) 332, 351
4975 62, 83, 156, 197, 213, 214,
    246, 259, 260, 262, 264, 269,
    317, 348
4975(a), (b) 246
6231(a)(7) 126
6662 57
7519 197, 251, 317
7701 205
7701(a)(3) 56
7701(i) 56
7704 15, 41, 59, 83, 86, 172, 175,
    181, 215, 217, 259, 264, 401

Internal Revenue Code Regulations

1.79-1 247
1.79-3(d) 247
1.105-11 247
1.163-8T 196, 308
1.446-1(a)(4)(i) 249, 347
1.446-1(c)(2)(i) 249, 347
1.469-5T 69
1.704(1)-e 193
1.704-1(b) 121
1.704-1(b)(2)(ii)(d)(4), (5), (6)
    123
1.704-1(b)(2)(iv)(f) 124

1.704-1(b)(2)(iv)(g) 124
1.704-1(c)(2) 194
1.704-2 124
1.704-2(b) 124
1.704-2(b)(4) 118
1.704-2(d) 124
1.704-2(f) 124
1.704-2(g)(1) 123
1.704-2(i)(3) 124
1.704-2(i)(4) 124
1.704-2(i)(5) 123
1.704-2(j) 124

1.707-3,-4 ,-5, -8, -9 205
1.752-3 68
1.761-2 57
1.1361-1(c) 56
1.1362-6(a)(2)(C) 307
1.7704-1 59
301.7701-1 - 2 205
301.7701-1 - 3 54, 55, 60
301.7701-2(b) 56
301.7701-4 55

IRS Announcements

86-128 (1986-51 IRB 22) 318

Private Letter Rulings and Technical Advice Memoranda

PLR 9321047 70, 74, 75, 147,
    198
PLR 9328005 70
PLR 9350013 70
PLR 9409006 331, 349

PLR 9415005 70
PLR 9415007 205
PLR 9420028 146
PLR 9423040 146
PLR 9432018 147

PLR 9434027 70
PLR 9546006 205
TAM 9432001 206
TAM 9719006 206
TAM 9730004 206

Revenue Rulings and Procedures

Rev Rul 84-52 (1984-1 CB 157)
197, 198, 199, 203
Rev Rul 91-26 (1991-1 CB 184)
196, 310, 316, 331, 332, 349,
350
Rev Rul 93-12 206

Rev Rul 93-4 (1993-1 CB 225)
173
Rev Rul 95-37 (1995-17 IRB 10)
73–75, 147–149, 153, 197–
198

Rev Rul 95-55 (1995-35 IRB 13)
147–149, 153, 197–198, 203
Rev. Proc. 89-12 54
Rev. Proc. 95-10 54

Tax Forms and Schedules

Form 1040 6, 7, 31, 266, 348
Form 1040-ES 345
Form 1065 62, 169
Form 1120 243

Form 1120S 313
Form 2553 16, 307, 337, 338,
387
Form 8832 59

Schedule C 266, 331, 347, 348,
350
Schedule K-1 62, 169, 250
Schedule PH 243

TOPICAL INDEX

qualified retirement accounts, borrowing against, **267**

state and local taxes, **267**

taxation, **265–267**

transfer of ownership interests, **265**

splitting income, mitigating effect of, **244, 274**

state and local taxes, **267**

taxation

    generally, **18–19, 235–252**

    accident and health plans, **246–247**

    accumulated earnings tax, **243, 274**

    alternative minimum tax, **249–250**

    appreciation of assets, double taxation, **242, 272**

    cafeteria benefit plans/flexible spending accounts, **248**

    capital gains, **243–244, 272–273**

    cash flow, maximization through graduated rate structure, **238–239**

    cash method, use of, **249**

    closely held corporations, passive losses and credits, **251–252**

    death of shareholder, mitigating effect of basis step-up upon, **245**

    dependent care assistance, **247**

    dividends, double taxation of, **240, 271–272**

    double taxation, **236, 240–244**

    draining off taxable income with deductible payments, **236, 239–240**

    educational assistance programs, **247–248**

    farming corporations, use of cash method, **249**

    fiscal year-ends, **250–251**

    fringe benefits, **246–248**

    graduated rate structure, **235–239, 269–270, 274, 276–277**

    group term life insurance, **247**

    letter to client, sample, **271–277**

    liquidation, double taxation on, **241, 272**

    losses, inability to pass through to owners, **245–246, 275**

    passive losses and credits, **251–252**

    personal holding company tax, **242–243, 273–274**

    personal service corporations, **248–249, 251**

    qualified dividends received, mitigating effect of, **244–245**

    qualified retirement plans, borrowing from, **246**

    qualified small business corporation rules, mitigating effect of, **244**

    reasonableness of compensation, double taxation, **242, 273**

    sale of stock, double taxation on, **240, 272**

    small corporations, use of cash method, **249**

    sole proprietorships, compared, **265–267**

    splitting income, mitigating effect of, **244, 274**

    tax-exempt income, **244, 273**

    tax-free dispositions of corporate stock, mitigating effect of, **245**

    tortious acts, limitation of liability, **29–30, 252–253**

    transfer of ownership interests, **257, 265**

D

Death

    corporations, death of shareholder, **245**

    limited liability companies, members, **53**

    limited liability partnerships, **143, 145**

    partnerships, **179–180**

Debts, sources of liability exposure, **28**

Dependent care assistance, corporations, **247**

Disassociation. *See* Withdrawal and disassociation

Dissolution

    limited liability companies, **53–54, 133–134**

    limited liability partnerships, **145–146**

    limited partnerships, **181**

    partnerships, **180–181**

Distributions. *See* Contributions and distributions

limited liability partnerships, **142, 143**

partnerships, **174**

sole proprietorships, **345**

Insurance companies

check-the-box regulations, per se corporations, **55**

S corporation status, eligibility for, **17, 313, 338**

J

Japanese Kabushiki Kaisha, check-the-box regulations, **56**

Joint stock associations, check-the-box regulations, **55**

Joint stock companies, check-the-box regulations, **55**

Joint ventures

limited liability companies, **8, 40, 85, 100, 397**

partnerships, **13, 171, 218, 401**

L

Liability insurance

limited liability companies, formation of, **45**

limited liability partnerships, **142**

partnerships, **174**

sole proprietorships, **345**

Licenses and permits

limited liability companies, formation of, **45**

limited liability partnerships, **142**

partnerships, **174**

sole proprietorships, **345**

LIFO recapture tax, S corporations, **318**

Limitation of liability. *See also* Corporations; Limited liability companies; Limited liability partnerships; Limited partnerships; Partnerships; S corporations; Tortious conduct

generally, **25–32**

qualified small business corporations, **292**

sole proprietorships, **343–346**

sources of liability exposure, **27–28**

Limited liability companies

generally, **3, 6–10, 33–136**

articles of organization, **42–43, 105–109**

authority to bind company, **47**

bankruptcy of member, **53**

"bulletproof" provisions, **44–45, 60**

cash method of accounting, **70**

C corporations, compared, **82–83, 85, 254–255**

check-the-box regulations. Classification as partnership for tax purposes, below

classification as partnership for tax purposes

generally, **54–60**

"bulletproof" state statutes, **44–45, 60**

check-the-box regulations, generally, **55–60**

eligibility for check-the-box rules, **56**

foreign eligible entities, **57, 58**

multiple owner entities, **56–57**

per se corporations, **55–56**

pitfalls and planning opportunities, **59–60**

sample client letters, **99, 103**

separate tax entity, determination of existence of, **55**

state law conformity with check-the-box rules, **60**

transition rules, **57–58**

contributions and distributions, **45, 64, 119–121**

conversions

generally, **73–79**

corporations, conversion of, **75–78**

partnerships, conversion of, **73–75**

single-member limited liability company, conversion of corporation into, **78**

tax implications, **74–79**

creditors, rights of, **48**

death of member, **53**

definition, **37–38**

dissolution of company, **53–54, 133–134**

Sole proprietorships, *cont.*
    accounting methods, **347**
    C corporation, compared, **347–351**
    children, wages paid to owner's, **351**
    corporate rates vs. double taxation, **347–348**
    debt, additional basis from, **351**
    fringe benefits, **349**
    health insurance premiums, deductibility of, **349–350**
    losses, treatment of, **348**
    payroll taxes, **348, 350**
    qualified retirement accounts, borrowing against, **348**
    S corporation, compared, **349–351**
    single-member limited liability companies, compared, **351–352**
    state and local taxes, **349**
    transfer of ownership interests, **346**
Special tax allocations
    limited liability companies, **64**
    partnerships, **189–192**
Start-ups
    limited liability companies, **8, 41, 85, 100, 397**
    limited partnerships, **15, 402**
    partnerships, **13, 171, 219, 401**

T

Taxation. *See* Accumulated earnings tax; Alternative minimum tax; Corporations; Limited liability companies; Limited liability partnerships; Partnerships; Payroll taxes; Personal holding company tax; Sales taxes; S corporations; Sole proprietorships; Special tax allocations

    family limited partnerships, **205–207**
    qualified small business corporations, **281 et seq., 293–298, 366–367**
    state taxation, **22–23**
Technical termination
    limited liability companies, **65**
    limited liability partnerships, **145**
    partnerships, **180, 194–195**
Tortious conduct
    corporations, **29–30, 252–253**
    limited liability companies, **31, 51–52**
    limited liability partnerships, **31–32, 144**
    limited partnerships, **30**
    partnerships, **177**

V

Venture capital investments
    limited liability companies, **8, 41, 85, 100, 397**
    limited partnerships, **15, 402**
    partnerships, **13, 171, 219, 401**

W

Withdrawal and disassociation
    limited liability companies, members, **44, 52–53, 132–133**
    limited liability partnerships, **143, 144–145**
    partnerships, **179–180**
Workers' compensation insurance
    limited liability companies, formation of, **45**
    limited liability partnerships, **142**
    partnerships, **174**
    sole proprietorships, **345**